The City That Lost Control...

The true story of how greed, deception, politics, and a battle over green energy shattered a community

Edward J. Bielarski Jr

Table of Contents

To my wife Melinda, whose love and sacrifice made me the man that I am today. It wasn't easy being married to a Wartime Consigliere, but she accomplished it with skill and grace. Through it all she shaped me as a husband and a father.

To my dad, for all the days he spent helping me in whatever endeavor I had planned. I'll always cherish our days spent working together, particularly our time relaxing after a long day of chores. Time would stop as I'd offer him details of my special journey. I'll never forget the twinkle in his eyes that reflected the pride in his heart.

Author's Note

The foundation of my story rests upon thousands of hours of daily engagement with the Gainesville City Commission, city employees, and the community, as well as my review of tens of thousands of pages of primary source documentation. The specific events and dialogue come from these sources and include, but are not limited to, contemporaneous records such as e-mails, texts, letters, memoranda, speeches, city newsletters, internet news services, period newspaper stories and editorials, transcripts and minutes of meetings, presentations, investigative and informational reports, city and utility accounting records, draft and execute contracts, the city charter and ordinances, procurement documents, interviews conducted by third party investigative sources, photographs, depositions and other legal testimony, social media statements, the utility's historical documents, and personal interviews, logs and diaries. The result is a full and unrelenting account of real-life events.

Prologue

Catching a glimpse of the Gainesville City limits' sign, I reflexively muttered, "There's no turning back now."

Spoken a decibel too loudly, the words moved my wife, Melinda, to open one eye as she peered my way. After a long and restless night, her stare seemed to say, "Really?" I mouthed an "I'm sorry" before turning away to take a deep breath of the town's air, absorbing our new surroundings from my unforgiving perch—the bench seat of the 26-foot, late-model U-Haul Truck filled with the first installment of our prized possessions. I smiled as our sixteen-hour road trip from Pennsylvania was coming to an end.

We coasted into the small, southern college town, whose expansive tree canopies, quaint neighborhoods, and a culture of southern gentility surround the economic engine and social conscience of the community—the fifth largest university in the country, the University of Florida, or just UF.

The town's below the Mason-Dixon Line way of life, infused with a generous helping of professors, students, and aging hippies, made it the Berkeley of the South—an idyllic setting for free thought and expression. That freedom gained a foothold in the music and arts scene, as Gainesville was home to rock legends like Tom Petty, Stephen Stills, Don Felder, and others. An activist, political culture that "won't back down" soon followed. Gainesville was a little blue island in the vast red ideological sea of Florida politics and enormously proud of it.

Over the past two decades, politics in Gainesville had evolved into a more pronounced free-wheeling, altruistic battle over cutting-edge social causes and with little or no thought as to how to pay for them. Those details were best left to grants and other monies from the federal treasury, as well as those of greater means. The political class of Gainesville had better things to do than balancing the municipal checkbook.

Caught in the middle of the battle was the municipally owned utility, Gainesville Regional Utilities, or GRU, as people knew it. UF supported the community, while GRU was the economic engine of local government, led by an elected seven-member commission.

Starting in the early 2000s, GRU, unlike almost any other utility in the country, stretched beyond basic utility services and transformed into the city's funding mechanism for social causes and experiments in city planning and development, including being at the forefront of climate change action. The utility was repeatedly drawn into ill-advised, onerous, and game-changing decisions, weakening its financial underpinnings one deal after another—all at the hands of its governing board—the city has elected seven-member commission.

In 2009, the utility's financial affairs took a quantum leap backward when the commission approved a contract of epic proportions. That contract, known as a power purchase agreement (PPA), obligated GRU to pay over $2.2 billion over its thirty-year term in exchange for the construction of the largest commercial biomass power plant of its day—a 102-megawatt state-of-the-art facility.

In 2013, the biomass plant began commercial operations, whereupon the reality of its stifling payments under the PPA began. The stage was set for a chain reaction of events for which the commission was woefully unprepared. Overnight, GRU morphed from one of the low-cost utilities in Florida into one of the most expensive. The fiscal consequences of social engineering and experimentation with customers' money had finally come home to roost.

In need of a solution, the commission launched a nationwide search for someone, anyone, who could step into the general manager role—to extract the city from the disastrous PPA and somehow right the GRU ship. That person was me.

I brought the truck to a leisurely crawl as we passed by GRU's administrative building. Reaching the entrance to GRU's hundred-year-old Kelly Power Plant, I could see an imposing iron gate emblazoned with a phrase written in bold, gold letters. Stopping to peer out my window, I read the words: "A utility owned by the people it serves." I mumbled to Melinda that it was as good a glittering generality as I had ever heard. She yawned and told me to just keep driving.

We were woefully unaware of the battle that would be fought over these words. Our incognito entry into the city obscured the high drama that awaited us. We were entering a new world of 1960s-style activism, political machines and all set on a collision course with destiny. The implications of which would be felt far beyond Gainesville—at the Florida State Capital, the Governor's mansion, Wall Street, and investors' homes all around the globe. We were in for the roller-coaster ride of a lifetime. Hang on as I chronicle my epic tale.

Ω

Trial of a Wartime Consigliere

For countless Americans, December 7 is remembered as "a date which will live in infamy"—words spoken by President Roosevelt soon after the Japanese attack on US forces in Pearl Harbor in 1941. On the seventy-six-year anniversary of that attack, December 7, 2017, I spun into Gainesville's City Hall parking lot, racing on a path to avoid my own day of infamy—being publicly ousted as the general manager of the city's utility by the elected seven-member commission.

I wasn't sure if I had driven my car from home or simply aimed it as emotions swept over me. Those emotions were aroused even further as I obsessively kept my laptop live streaming the meeting from its precarious perch on the dashboard of my car. The stress of the moment was growing as I felt tingling in my hands, sweat dripping from my brow, and a gnawing sensation in the pit of my stomach. I jammed the car into park, leaped out of my seat, and threw the door shut behind me.

As I hustled towards city hall, I caught a glimpse of my reflection in the glass entrance doors. I saw a picture of how others would see me. With no time to spare, I had abandoned my business attire and thrown on my twice-worn jeans, a rumpled long-sleeved shirt, and seen-better-days sandals. It was tonight's style—my new disheveled look. Now, not only did I feel out of place, I looked out of place. Whether out of place or not, I rushed to place myself in front of the commissioners. I scurried by the security desk, passing through one of the security doors as I entered the city hall chamber.

The metallic rattling of the door's panic bar echoed through the room to signal my entrance. All heads turned towards me. My eyes locked onto the seven faces on the dais. Under the bright theater-style lights, the commissioners could not hide their emotions. Their faces visibly bore the weight of the matter in question. We all knew this night would be a trial with no formal charges, just grievances expressed by certain elected officials. To my chagrin, out of a seven-member commission, it would take only four votes to remove me from my job.

Like a squirrel looking for his hidden nuts, I searched for a seat close to the lectern in the event I was granted the opportunity to speak to my bosses. Once seated, I fidgeted in the chamber's upholstered chair, solidly bolted to its foundation, unlike me. *Okay, I made it. Now's the hard part. Try to settle down.* Of course, I couldn't settle down after forgetting to turn off my laptop as it simulcasted the meeting. I fumbled around long enough to shut it down while everyone looked my way.

I glanced up to where I normally would have been seated on the dais. Even in my spirited emotional state, I grasped the physical juxtaposition. Tonight, my seat was filled by my Chief Business Officer, Lewis Walton, who looked down at me with a gaze of disbelief and sadness.

It was Walton who had triggered my trip to city hall, first with a text, later with a call, as the meeting had entered the commissioner comment phase—the last item on the night's agenda when any commissioner is permitted to express what they may have on their mind. With panic in his voice, Walton had whispered on the phone to me, "Ed, you gotta get down to the meeting." Gone was his smooth Bama accent when he finished with, "I think they're fixin' to fire you."

I could see in Walton's eyes that he felt my pain. He knew that earlier in the day, my wife of almost thirty years, Melinda, had begun her chemotherapy treatment, following up on her complex surgery to remove a cancerous tumor from her pancreas. Knowing that Melinda would need every ounce of my support as she forged her own special journey of survival, Walton offered to take my spot on the dais for the night. He, too, was getting more than he had bargained for. I nervously shook my head from side to side with the recollection of my mother once telling me that no good deed goes unpunished.

Just eighteen months earlier, this same elected body had selected me as the general manager of the city's utility, Gainesville Regional Utilities (GRU). Gazing at the dais, I recognized that every commissioner who had previously voted to hire me was no longer there to support me. With my job hanging on their whims, I wondered if my time as the GM was up.

After settling into my seat, Mayor Lauren Poe acknowledged my arrival with a curt, "I'm glad you're here." The intensity of his stare left me feeling uncomfortable, unwelcome, and uncertain of his claim. I knew that before being elected mayor, Poe had served as a commissioner and was among the minority of those who hadn't chosen me as the new general manager. During my time on the job, he also unnecessarily criticized my performance as well. The thought of Poe presiding over my trial made me feel like a cat on a hot tin roof.

I scanned the room for friendly faces. With each one I saw, I acknowledged their presence with a subtle nod of my head. A few loyal employees drifted my way, hugged me, and whispered words of encouragement. A frequent public attendee, Armando Grundy-Gomes, leaned over and declared, "This is just wrong."

As I lowered my head, I caught sight of the lectern, located prominently in the center of the chamber. It had been the spot where I had stood on those evenings over the past eighteen months when I attempted to get the utility out from under one of the most onerous power purchase contracts in America. This was where I spoke truth to power.

***

In the early 2000s, GRU had decided to develop and construct a new power plant, but rather than build more fossil-fuel generation, they decided on constructing a biomass plant—a so-called carbon-neutral option. Unwilling and unable to finance and construct it alone, the utility entered a contract, or what people in the power industry refer to as a power purchase agreement (PPA), with a rather crafty and renowned businessman, Jim Gordon. Through his web of companies and various enterprises, Gordon had built an energy franchise upon the mantle of green, renewable power.

Gordon's franchise proved to be a perfect fit for Gainesville's youthful university culture. In 2009, the City of Gainesville approved a PPA with a company controlled by Gordon, Gainesville Renewable Energy Center (GREC). That PPA would come to be known as the GREC PPA.

I imagined Gordon striding into Gainesville like the legendary Pied Piper of Hamelin, who, as legend tells us, played his magic flute to lure the rats away in exchange for being paid 1,000 Dutch Guilders. In Gordon's case, he offered the community an opportunity to rid its infestation of fossil-fuel power through the magic of net-zero carbon emissions from a biomass-fired power plant in exchange for being paid handsomely in US Dollars. While the residents of Hamelin reneged on their promise to pay the Pied Piper, GRU and the city did not.

The actual cost of the GREC PPA became public in 2013 when the power plant began its commercial operations. It obligated GRU to pay approximately seventy-four million dollars a year, whether the plant produced power or not. Blindsided by the reality of the arrangement, residents of Gainesville were enraged. They questioned how and why the commission had promoted the magic of net-zero carbon emissions while ignoring the reality of its unbearable costs that threatened the overall finances of their 120-year-old utility.

According to the legend, the Pied Piper retaliated against the town for refusing to pay by leading the children away to drown. In Gainesville's case, the utility's customers were drowning under the weight of their onerous bills. Public opinion dramatically shifted. Residents of the community

4

overwhelmingly agreed—these were consequences the city could no longer endure.

While Gordon was shipping truckloads of money out of town, I had hauled a truckload of belongings into town. My wife and I were committed. As I strived to unravel the GREC PPA, I knew there would be no magic, just demanding work. Restoring a sense of normalcy to the utility would require me to go through Gordon—a man of substantial power and influence.

***

My trial led off when Commissioner Adrian Hayes-Santos delivered his opening remarks, "This is not an easy discussion and one I didn't want to have, but I feel it's a conversation we need to have. I have lost confidence in our GRU manager the last few weeks, and while I thank him for his service to the city, I think it is time for us to move in a different direction. I believe we should bring our city together as one organization—stop moving apart. For our city to succeed, we need to have one clear vision for the city all across departments, all areas, including our charter officers, and I believe it is time to replace our GRU general manager. I want your thoughts and feelings before I make the motion, and there are other issues I don't want to go into. If I have to I will, but I just know what's happened over the past few weeks, what happened with e-mails, and I think we all know things that transpired—and I think we need to move into a different direction for us to succeed in the organization."

Hayes-Santos was a young, promising, progressive-leaning politician who had won his seat on the dais behind a host of promises, including bringing the city together under one leadership authority. Those pledges, along with his good looks and boyish charms, had brought him an avid following. Make no mistake, Hayes-Santos was a man on a mission.

In Hayes-Santos' brief time in office, he had perceived my disagreements with the new interim City Manager, Anthony Lyons, as dangerous and seemingly unforgivable. To make matters worse, our clashes had been reported on by the city's paper of record, the *Gainesville Sun,* with the vigor of a scandal magazine. Tonight, Hayes-Santos referenced these disagreements as Exhibit A in his proof of my defiance of the commission. "I think that many times we keep shooting ourselves in the foot over and over, and over, and over again. It seems like every week we have a negative story coming out. It's like we're doing it to ourselves."

The commissioner wasn't wrong about the frequency of the stories, nor my frustration with the governing body. It's what Hayes-Santos failed to say that was so wrong. In calling for my replacement without any mention of the real elephant in the room, Hayes-Santos was absolving Lyons of any complicity himself.

The pachyderm had been hiding since October 11, when a high-level investigative report was issued. At the heart of the investigation, conducted by the city's Equal Opportunity Director Torrey Alston and City Auditor Carlos Holt, was that, in multiple instances, Lyons had skirted city policy. While any contract over $50,000 required commission approval, the investigation found Lyons failed to refer an $85,000 search firm contract to the commission. Furthermore, under Lyons' watch, "personnel policies weren't followed by human resources during the assistant city manager search by not giving internal candidates an opportunity to interview for the post."

While not the most egregious of offenses, nothing of the sort could be claimed against me. Instead, I was on trial, not Lyons.

***

I had first locked horns with Lyons during an emergency management meeting in response to Hurricane Irma. As the city was marshaling resources to ensure public health as well as the continued delivery of essential services, Lyons announced to the attendees on the call that all allocations of diesel fuel oil would be facilitated through the city's fleet management department. Taken aback, I immediately told the group that Lyons must not be aware of GRU's standard protocol to make plans with fuel suppliers to guarantee the proper fueling of emergency generators at our

Murphree Water Plant, the gas tanks of our fleet of vehicles, along with all the portable generators at over a hundred wastewater lift stations.

Unexpectedly challenged, Lyons immediately shot back that it was a public safety issue. There would be no negotiation. I was stunned at Lyons' response. His actions placed GRU's ability to pump water out of its deep wells at heightened risk, along with placing almost 50,000 water customers at equal risk of losing drinking water, which utilities refer to as potable water. Without the fuel to run portable generators providing emergency power to our lift stations, the utility was also exposed to having raw sewage being released throughout the communities. Lyons, seemingly, needed to show me who was really in charge.

Rather than working through pre-established emergency channels, GRU was forced to regroup and reach out to other suppliers, all while in a statewide emergency. Thanks to the quick and responsive work of my team, GRU was able to reach an arrangement with a local fuel supplier, Almond Oil, to keep our tanks filled during the emergency. After the crisis had passed, the local media virtually ignored the work of GRU staff. There was also no mention of Lyons' breach of protocol. Instead, my actions were portrayed as an overreaction in a risk management game of chicken.

This watery snafu was followed by another intra-organizational disagreement concerning a city-wide implementation of pay increases. It started when HR Director, Eugenia Allen, issued an e-mail that spelled out a major policy change through which salary increases for managers and supervisors would be distributed. The new policy capped salary increases to $1,590 throughout the city, no matter what wage the employee was earning or what professional level that employee held. I saw the directive as a clear violation of the city's existing HR policies which left individual employee increases to each charter officer's discretion. Poe contended that the policy was appropriately modified during a General Policy Committee meeting. I disagreed.

While there were those city employees who derided the $1,590 cap on salary increases by calling it the "1590 plan," the Gainesville Sun *simply reduced the complex issue to a territorial squabble between city officials. Gaining access to my e-mails through a public record's request, the paper used my words as proof of my inflexibility. "I can't and won't* *simply cap the merit increases you may deserve based on an unauthorized memo from the HR Director. If you sense a tone of frustration, you are not incorrect. Let me say that this is not what I envisioned when I told my folks that this is the start of a new era at GRU."*

To his tactical credit, Lyons had fostered a beneficial relationship with city power brokers, particularly the commissioners. Years previously, he had been the director of the city's Community Redevelopment Authority (CRA) but had left for greener pastures and the mountains of Utah. By his own accounts, his wife's desire to return hastened his second act in the city. After a two-year absence, Lyons was welcomed back with open arms.

Under former Mayor Ed Braddy's tenure, Lyons had been appointed leader of a newly formed Blue-Ribbon Committee with the lofty goal of making Gainesville more competitive. Shortly after finishing the Blue-Ribbon Committee's work, which resulted in something called the "Big Idea," Lyons was selected to replace long-tenured City Manager Russ Blackburn. Over the past year, while my thoughts were being consumed on mitigating the fallout from the GREC PPA, Lyons was methodically stacking up a foundation of support from the commission, brick by brick.

As if these incidents weren't enough, I suspect the final straw was when Justin Locke resigned after his successful stint as GRU's Chief Financial Officer. When Locke informed me of his decision to leave, he confided that it was primarily for personal reasons. Locke and his wife had moved from Texas to take the job in Gainesville, leaving their two boys back home. Almost two years into his new job, Locke and his wife missed them terribly. While it was time to go home, Locke also made it clear he wasn't happy with receiving a raise of $1,590 after all that he had done for the utility.

The Gainesville Sun sensationalized Locke's resignation with the headline "High-ranking GRU official resigns over pay." Their reporter quoted my text message to the commission that Locke was "not happy" with the $1,590 salary increase. Hayes-Santos fumed that I had purposely used Locke's resignation to shine a bright light on what I perceived as inherently unfair issues in the 1590 plan. Poe chimed in on the unfolding political drama and opined, "GRU's upper management team is already very well compensated." I was disturbed that the de facto chairperson of the utility's board of directors displayed such apparent resentment over *rewarding employees for their superior work, particularly towards my management team.*

***

The memory of Poe's resentment was just one of several incidents between us that heightened my concern with his icy stare this night. As part of my performance review from the previous year, Poe had been the only commissioner that said that I had not "exceeded job expectations." Most disturbing, he said that I had the same "individual decision-making and lack of transparency that led to the resignation of the previous general manager." As I peered up at him, I wondered what he was thinking now.

My musings ended when the mayor recognized Commissioner Helen Warren as the next speaker. "My comment has been basically that he was hired to perform a duty and with recognition that there were some things that were going to be shaken up, but I feel like there's a mood in this community that it's all or nothing support for," she lamented. "Same with the football team. If you can't win the game, you fire the coach and you go hire and get another coach, and I don't think that's appropriate. I don't think this is the time to put the general manager at the door and say, you've got to go."

Warren finished by saying, "I'm really interested in seeing that this ship can go on a sailing cruise for a long-term, and to change leadership because of one letter, while I understand there's more than one letter, that those people are saying that they're not happy with his leadership and, again, unless we can really have a good measure of that, I just can't support getting rid of a charter officer this easily." Warren was another one of the commissioners who had not voted for me back in 2015. Tonight, her unexpected support allowed me to take my first deep breath.

Commissioner Harvey Budd entered the fray to say, "I pretty much agree with you (Warren) wholeheartedly."

9

"I came onboard just approximately the same time he did, and I can tell you what a great job he's done so far," he elaborated. "But one of his problems, and it's like everybody has faults, is he reacts—he's very defensive and he has certain things he reacts to because he's a leader who wants to run his organization like you would a corporation."

Agreeing once again with Warren's analogy, Budd said, "I do not wish to change ships." I took another deep breath. That's two votes in the good guy's column.

When Melinda and I first arrived in Gainesville, Harvey Budd was one of the first people to welcome us to the community. He took us under his wing, so to speak. I laughed thinking about him helping us get around town - telling us about the best roads and side streets to travel to avoid traffic, as though he was letting us in on a secret. He also warned me to remain like Switzerland—always remaining neutral in all things political in the city. It was good advice.

Budd and his wife, Ilene, were successful businesspeople. Harvey was a CPA with a host of business enterprises, while Ilene was the daughter of a prominent retailer in town, who set up her own Gator-oriented retail shop in town. They were one of Gainesville's original power couples. The jury was still out, as was mine, on which one of them was more powerful.

Buoyed by the support of Warren and Budd, I looked up towards the right side of the dais, where Commissioner Harvey Ward had been given clearance to take off by the mayor. I immediately recognized his discomfort—every so often, he'd be hesitant as our eyes met. He reluctantly admitted, "It's extremely difficult to sit here and talk about somebody's employment."

Nobody's forcing you, I thought.

Ward was another commissioner who had not yet been elected when the previous commission appointed me as the general manager. While he expressed concerns about my ability to make the transition from being a dealmaker to a day-to-day leader, I hoped he was just testing the political waters. He

10

declared, "Mr. Bielarski is doing a good job," followed by, "I think we have a fundamental difference in how we see the organizations to some degree." There was little doubt in my mind that Ward was struggling with balancing his duties and his feelings. His indecisiveness worried me. He could be my second no-vote.

The sum of the night's emotional burden made me slouch further into my seat. Walton's call had started the night with fear and apprehension. My spirit devolved during my trip to city hall as I listened to the commissioners' objections. Fear morphed into anger as I listened to the inarticulate way in which most of the commissioners spoke. It was all too difficult to hear. I reminded myself that there are but a few people who can fully express their authentic emotions, feelings, or reasoning. Regardless if it's in someone's DNA or nurtured ability, my experience has taught me to fully appreciate what someone is trying to say, not just what they actually say. I should listen to their words in context with their actions, body language, and the situation.

I've always had a knack for such understanding, but after thirty years of marriage to Melinda, I've had a little help in refining those skills. My lovely, artistic wife, Melinda, sees the world as a tapestry of colors, emotions, and thoughts. She speaks in the same manner. As our children were growing up, I told them that listening to their mom was like admiring an impressionistic painting; "Your mom talks like Monet painted. Appreciate her overall vision, not a single word or phrase."

My growing antagonism was interrupted with a faint buzz on my cell phone. Pulling it out of my pants pocket a moment too late, I read the message that it was Melinda calling. She was checking in.

In total disdain, I thought, *how dare you all take me away from my wife tonight?* It was painful to envision her home alone to cope with the effects of the day's treatment. I looked over at Grundy-Gomes and remembered his comment spoken a brief time before—*this is just wrong.* Emotionally, I shifted from the fast lane of work to the slow lane of my family life. I cringed as I recalled Melinda patiently allowing the nurse to prepare her for the IV earlier in the day. I couldn't help but notice that out in the world, Melinda looked frail and vulnerable. As she sat quietly, I stared at the IV drip delivering the drugs that mercilessly crept into her body. I reached out to squeeze her hand as she looked up and smiled. I couldn't forget how cold her hands felt. She had been so brave, so strong, and here I was, worried about whether I'd have a job. I felt embarrassed for my selfishness.

I texted Melinda that I had yet to speak to the commission. There was a little more controversy than I had expected. I assured her not to worry. It would all work out. She responded with a smiley-faced emoji.

The sight of the emoji instantly disarmed me. It reminded me of the supportive texts she had sent me during our past year's ordeal. The emoji brought a tear to my eye as emotions welled up inside of me. The feelings I had held inside of me for so long were clamoring to escape. I am sure that others around me thought my tears were driven by the thought of losing my job. It wasn't the case. My worlds were simply colliding.

Ω

Worlds colliding

Six months previously, after months of being consumed by events in my new job, I talked to Dad about planning a visit to Gainesville as soon as he could. We missed each other's company. Since my dad hated to fly, not unlike his son, I bought him train tickets, with his own sleeper compartment, with his arrival scheduled for early July. It was settled.

On the day of his arrival, I drove to Jacksonville to pick him up. As I waited in the parking lot sipping on a coffee, listening to my car radio, I heard the song "My Old Man" by the Zac Brown Band. Never hearing the song before, it was as though the lyrics spoke directly to me. They touched me while at the same time haunted me:

He was a giant, and I was a kid. I was always trying to do everything he did. I can still remember every lesson he taught me. Growing up, learning how to be like my old man.

He was a lion. We were our father's pride. But I was defiant when he made me walk the line. He knew how to lift me up and when to let me fall. Looking back, he always had a plan, my old man.

My old man feels the callous on his hands. And dusty overalls, my old man. Now I finally understand, I have a lot to learn from my old man.

My old man, I know one day we'll meet again. As he's looking down, my old man. I hope he's proud of who I am. I'm trying to fill the boots of my old man. My old man.

13

The song lyrics captured the essence of my relationship with my dad. Its raw emotions led me down a dark path—I sensed that I would soon lose him. Almost simultaneous with that thought, my Chief Change Officer, M Smith, called me to discuss a rather mundane issue. I confided in her how the song had heightened my fears of losing my dad. M was born with an empathetic soul, which made her the perfect Chief Change Officer for the utility. It also made her the perfect voice for me to hear. She shared her positive energy with me. Despite that energy, while it may seem to be presumptuous, I felt as though a divine message had been sent to me telling me to be prepared for my dad's death.

My dad and I had a way of communicating with each other that didn't demand a great deal of talking. While living up north, we would spend hours on our property, stacking wood piles, building sheds, cutting grass, and fixing anything that had broken since his last visit. I suspect he was disappointed when everything was in working order—there was nothing to fix. You see, my dad was my father, but he was also my pal.

Dad only spent a week with us before heading home. Not long after he arrived back home, I received a frantic phone call from his faithful neighbors. They had called an ambulance to take Dad to the hospital. I scrambled to adjust my schedule so I could rush to his bedside.

Upon my arrival, I walked into his hospital room to find him breathing heavily. I had never seen him look frailer. The doctors took me aside to tell me that my father's heart was failing him. He had fluid in his lungs, and he was unable to walk. I stayed the week with him, sleeping in his room, as he grew stronger with the help of potent medications.

It was a process that would repeat itself several times over the summer and fall of 2017. On my business trips to New York City, I would arrange extra time to drive into Baltimore to see him. It broke my heart to see the loss of his physical freedom, now restricted by his need for oxygen. Lost was the time when my dad would walk through the community greeting his neighbors and friends with his signature greeting of "Yoo-hoo." The greeting reminded me of a whistle, that embodied his playfulness. Everyone knew Mr. Ed, the Yoo-hoo man, who was dubbed the unofficial mayor of their community.

On Monday, October 16, 2017, I was in New York, delivering presentations to bond investors. At the same time, Melinda was being admitted for tests and further observation at North Florida Hospital. She had a history of gallbladder ailments, and the doctors suspected the need to remove the failing organ. Knowing the importance of my presentations, combined with my competing desire to be with her in times of need, Melinda maintained radio silence on the news of her admission.

While I was away, Melinda would end her texts with those smiley-faced emojis.

Still unaware of Melinda's hospital admission, I left New York one day later, on October 17, to visit my dad. Unaware of it at the time, my visit would serve as the last time I would see my dad. The last time to be enveloped in his bear hugs, hear his warm, supportive voice, or look at his kind, time-worn face.

Before embarking on my long journey home, I checked in with Melinda, who finally fessed up about her health, telling me that she was in the hospital. Continuing to shield the degree of her sickness, she only disclosed there was the possibility of having her gallbladder removed. She wished me a safe journey and asked me to come to the hospital no matter how late. She missed me.

On the thirteen-hour drive back home, the events of the past week, my father's mortality, and the uncertainty of Melinda's illness spun like tops in my brain. Reaching the hospital around midnight, I parked in the barren lot, dashed to the elevator as I hurried to be by my wife's side. It had been a long day. In moments, that day would grow even longer.

When I reached her room, Melinda looked tired but oddly happy. It offered me a sense of relief, despite how much thinner she looked. She peered into my soul with her big blue eyes and told me to sit down as she said, "I need to tell you something." *Oh boy, this can't be good.* Melinda held my hands and slowly recounted, "The doctors told me I have pancreatic cancer. Don't worry, I'll be all right."

I know Melinda continued to tell me about her experience, but I couldn't get past the words—pancreatic cancer. Shivers ran down my spine and a sinking sensation came over me. Hearing the words pancreatic cancer in a sentence suggesting everything would somehow be all right was unimaginable. I couldn't intellectually process how Melinda seemed so certain of her strength to beat this horrible disease. I broke down and cried, I wept, I hugged her, and I didn't want to let her go, ever.

The hospital staff allowed me to stay with Melinda throughout the night. Lying in a reclining chair next to her bed, we held hands until she fell asleep. I don't remember sleeping that night. I do remember searching the words pancreatic cancer on the internet throughout that night. As I read each article, I'd sneak an occasional glance toward her, wondering how long I'd have her in my life. Faced with the rough road ahead, I vowed to stay by her side as she underwent a battery of tests to see if her tumor was operable.

Not wanting to miss a doctor's visit, I worked from Melinda's hospital room. Nurses and orderlies would come and go as she was carted off for one test after another. After worry-filled days, early one morning, her surgeon, Dr. Brian Pickens, slipped into the room with a smile on his face— Melinda would be one of only 10% of pancreatic cancer patients able to undergo surgery to remove the pancreatic tumor in what he deemed life-saving surgery. While happily reinvigorated, I also learned that Melinda's five-year survival rate was less than 10%.

Despite this miraculous turn of events, I couldn't forget that my dad was still alone, languishing in a hospital bed in a rehabilitation facility way too many miles away from us. It was abundantly clear that I would not be able to be with him any time soon.

On Thursday night, October 19, I spoke to my dad for the last time. Picking up the new smartphone we bought him while in town, I was relieved that his beefy, gnarly, arthritic fingers had been able to navigate the keypad. I told him that Melinda had been diagnosed with pancreatic cancer and she'd need a life-saving operation. The phone fell silent. I told him that I was sorry, but Melinda needed me now. I would see him as soon as I could. His last words to me were, "I understand. Tell her I understand. I love you both." I was sure that he knew his time was growing near.

I couldn't shake the concern I had for my father and the fear over my wife's upcoming surgery. I couldn't quell the imagery that a divine force had taken control of the steering wheel of my life, as though I was a helpless passenger in a car barreling out of control. That divine force came for my dad when two days later, just after 11 PM on Sunday, October 22, he passed away. My father, my buddy, my hero, was gone.

When Melinda went into surgery on October 25, I left the work of the past sixteen months behind. I wasn't surprised that it wasn't really that hard to do. I had already lost Dad. I was going to make damn sure I'd be there for the woman I loved. As Melinda was carted into the operating theater, her nurse took me aside. Talking ever so gently, the nurse told me that the surgeon would know after an hour into the surgery whether he could finish the life-saving aspect of the procedure. She asked for my cell phone number so she could call me. I panicked. *Had I not heard this before?* The nurse proceeded to tell me that the surgeon would decide at that point whether to perform a palliative restoration or the full procedure. *No, I hadn't heard this before.* I had an hour to wonder whether my wife had months to live or could be given an opportunity to live cancer-free. I drifted into the waiting room in a mental fog.

17

In a world that I no longer understood, I sat alone in the waiting room, absurdly working on a eulogy for my dad, who would be laid to rest the next day. Everything else was taken care of. My oldest cousin Bill DiMichele would stand in my place and deliver the words on my behalf. The funeral home would play "My Old Man" and "Hallelujah" during the funeral. As sad as I was at not being able to attend Dad's funeral, I reminisced over what a blessed life he had lived. I was proud of how he had taught me to be a man. When I finished the eulogy, I strolled outside to pull myself away from the coldness of the waiting room. The warmth of the sun against my skin made me feel whole again. I had never been a religious man, however, in this moment, I prayed for Melinda's deliverance from this deadly disease. I felt Dad's presence looking over us both. I asked God to place Melinda's ills upon my shoulders. "Save her, dear Lord," I prayed.

It was then that I received a call from the nurse. Trembling as I answered the call, the nurse told me, "The surgeon is moving forward with the operation."

Not clear as to what I was being told, I asked, "The palliative one or the life-saving operation?"

The nurse answered, "Lifesaving."

I cried, "Thank you, oh thank you." I fell to my knees and cried tears of joy and salvation.

The lyrics of Zac Brown's song rumbled in my head. Indeed, that one day my dad and I met again. I felt his love and strength as if he were hugging me once more. He wasn't gone. He had stepped aside from earthly existence to take his place as our guardian angel. I looked towards the heavens and greeted him once more, "Yoo-hoo, Dad, yoo-hoo."

With renewed strength, I returned to the waiting room, where I counted every minute as the minutes turned into hours. Other families came and went. Friends and colleagues took turns comforting me. After seven hours of waiting, my name was called, and I was escorted into a private room to hear from Dr. Pickens. He came into the room with the broadest of smiles and told me, "She did great. It was the cleanest Whipple surgery I have ever had. I got all of it."

I went numb as I synthesized his words. I thanked him, I hugged him. I think he knew at that moment he was the earthly embodiment of my dad.

Ω

The Verdict

Back in the city hall chambers, my recollections of the past year were interrupted by Ward's voice. "I like Ed Bielarski," he said.

"I want good things to happen for Ed Bielarski."

Seemingly remorseful for the tone of the night, Ward said, "It's horrible the idea we're talking about it with all of the things he's gone through."

When Ward finished, the mayor promptly allowed Hayes-Santos to lead off another round of comments. "I agree with many things that Commissioner Ward said and to just some of the points that Commissioner Warren and Commissioner Budd, this is not something I'm doing willy-nilly." Hayes-Santos seemed desperate to have the other commissioners understand that they needed to take him seriously.

Hayes-Santos went on a rant, "The citizens of the community elected us. We share that vision, and our charter officers to take that vision and go with it. This is not something that I take lightly, on the spur of the moment, or because of one e-mail. I think that was just the building on top of building, on top of the building, on top of the building of where these— I don't think the actions—that was like the last peg. I don't think the actions are the actions of a charter officer. That e-mail did pit our commission against employees and in that e-mail, he said he was not going to follow the commission's directions. Those are two things that a charter officer cannot do. You cannot cross those things even once."

For a moment, Hayes-Santos softened his message, "I think there's another reason we should move in that direction. I think really the larger one, those are all kind of—and Ed Bielarski is a great person. I really do like him as a person, but it's not about who he is as a person."

Done with his verbal pat on the back, Hayes-Santos returned to his complaint. "It's a broader sense of our whole city and our whole organization," Hayes-Santos explained. "For me, I'm not looking at that," he continued sanctimoniously, "I have to look at what is best for our whole city and also my vision for where we go."

"We are one organization and I truly feel it's a heart, and we need to move in this direction. In talking to Mr. Bielarski, he thinks there are two. There are very big separations, and I think that's too big a hill for me—if he does believe there's two organizations, whether he should have the separation, it's something I don't believe, and I think too big an obstacle to be overcome."

Hayes-Santos had delivered his primary accusation—I saw GRU as a separate organization from the rest of the City of Gainesville. Unfortunately for the young commissioner, I was correct. GRU *was* a separate organization under the city charter. He simply didn't like it.

In response to the charges, young Commissioner David Arreola swiftly and bluntly told Hayes-Santos, "This is beyond, beyond anything that I'm prepared to vote for because of my experience working with Mr. Bielarski and all that we've been able to accomplish." I quietly shook my fist in approval, knowing I had my third supportive vote.

Commissioner Charles Gaston brought his microphone closer as he unveiled the slippery elephant that had been hiding in the room—the October 11th investigative report on Lyons. Goston saw the comparison between my treatment tonight and that of Lyons as the hypocrisy of the highest order. Goston would not and did not stand for such treatment. He scolded the commissioners. "I hate to, you know, be the one to bring this back to everybody's memory, but a couple of weeks ago, I was in the same seat that Hayes-Santos is in and I very clearly demonstrated that when you get a report that's 1,000 pages long, and you didn't think that was grounds to look into, and it was looked at like I was a pariah and I had stabbed the city manager in the heart in front of everybody, but the mayor said, and these are his words, everybody has different styles of which they conduct their business and I thought about that and said you're right. You do have people who have different managerial styles."

As opposed to Hayes-Santos, Goston was placing the proper context to the interactions between Lyons and myself. He concluded his skillful admonishment of the commission by declaring, "I wouldn't support getting rid of Mr. Bielarski under any circumstances." Continued with his signature rhetorical roll, he talked directly about my interactions with Lyons, "Now that e-mail that Mr. Bielarski and the city manager were exchanging, you know, that was between them." He explained, "They didn't ask one time for any help from a commissioner. They didn't say y'all come and referee this thing. They never said that."

I grinned when Goston said, "Those are two grown men, fully grown, who are supposed to be professionals, but I understand the duress Mr. Bielarski was going through at the time." I saw it as a throwback phrase from another era.

As a Black man, Goston had grown up against the odds in Gainesville. He had to fight the indignities of segregation and sins of racism at their worst during the 1960s and 1970s. You had to be a full-grown man to survive the brutality of the Jim Crow South. Goston was showing his appreciation for my work at breaking down the "good-ole boy" network at the utility. He was spending well-earned political capital on me to deliver my fourth supportive vote.

22

With all the commissioners having an opportunity to weigh in on their thoughts, the mayor opened the floodgates for any remaining thoughts before he'd deliver any further opinion on the matter.

Budd took a second bite at the apple by proclaiming, "He gets an A+ in my book." He went on in his homespun way. "Yes, everybody has wrinkles. I have a lot of wrinkles. I have a short fuse. I've learned to control my temper. Anyone who is emotionally involved will tell you that because they are so emotionally involved, they have a short fuse."

Hesitantly, Ward took to the microphone to offer another tepid response. "I'm not sure where else to go with that, but here we are in a very difficult, uncomfortable position for everybody and it's not the best time. It's never going to be a good time. It's never going to be a good time, personally." When he finished, all eyes in the chamber turned toward the mayor.

Poe took a moment before looking down on me to make a statement that I will never forget. "I believe that Mr. Bielarski was brought in here for a very specific purpose. I know because I was a part of the commission when the interviews and the hiring was made that it was the will of the majority of the commission to bring somebody in that I will refer to as a Wartime Consigliere," he said.

Did the mayor just invoke the famous phrase from The Godfather? Was the mayor my Michael Corleone?

Poe completed his analogy by stating, "We had a difficult situation and the commission at the time was looking for somebody who was a fighter, who had some experience going up against the sort of big guy and winning and Mr. Bielarski did at that time and still fits that profile."

When he was finished, the mayor asked if I'd like to speak about the allegations. From the moment I arose and proceeded to the lectern, I couldn't get Poe's comment about being a Wartime Consigliere from rattling around in my head. Here was my moment and I was distracted by being a Wartime

23

Consigliere. The more I fought the thought, the more it embedded in my psyche. It was like quicksand.

For a brief time, I pondered the implications of Tom Hagen being declared "out" by mob boss Michael Corleone while I was still "in." Did Poe recognize the irony that the fictional character was being dismissed because he didn't have a wartime mentality, while I was rebuked because I did? *Oh, what the hell. Let's just embrace this whole thing.*

Standing tall at the lectern, I brought the microphone closer to me. Placing my hands on either side of the platform, I looked squarely into the mayor's eyes, recognizing this was the time I had been waiting for. I addressed the allegations straight on and with an added slice of humor. "Thank you, mayor and commissioners. I'm Ed Bielarski, still, I think, the general manager of GRU. Commissioner Santos, I appreciate your passion. I think you're absolutely trying to do the right thing for the community, and I apologize if I, you know, I brought you to the point that you feel you have to bring this to the total commission." I proceeded to look at the mayor and say, "I hope I can be the person that can bridge that (the issues) because as you were talking, Mayor, one of the things that I was thinking about was, yeah, I am a fighter, and I came on down to do the right thing for GRU and the city."

As I spoke, I was buoyed by the expressions on four commissioner's faces—those necessary four. Warren, Budd, Goston, and Arreola held their heads up high and maintained eye contact with me.

On the other hand, the mayor glared lifelessly in my direction, stiff in his mannerisms. Poe, Ward, and Hayes-Santos all looked away from my glances. This night had made me think of them in a unique way—they were the three musketeers of Gainesville. Their motto was "All for one city and one city for all." As if to say, the hell with the city charter, its governing document. Don't get in our way. I took a deep breath as I felt the moment of danger passing.

When I finished speaking to the commissioners, I took a seat once more. I was at peace. I could always lose my job, but no one could take my soul. Looking up, I was surprised when the mayor told the commissioners that the floor was still open for any that wished to make their closing remarks. If he had any hope that minds would be swayed, that hope was soon dashed.

Goston declared, "I won't hold you up. I know everybody is ready to go, but the first thing I want to say to you, Mr. Bielarski, is thank you. Thank you very much." Noticing the Mayor's Wartime Consigliere comment, Goston pointed out, "I admire you because you are a fighter because I wouldn't want you standing next to me if you weren't and I'm serious. That's all I am. Trust me. I love you if you want to do it right, but I'll fight you if you want to do it wrong. I'll fight you in the end, okay."

I bowed my head in respect for the fight Goston displayed. He had placed the final nail in the coffin of this surreal trial. A trial that ended with the commission unable to cobble together a motion that would place my possible termination on the floor for a vote. Even after his strongly worded allegations, the trial's prosecutor, Hayes-Santos, wasn't so bold as to make a motion to fire me. A night that had started out with such apprehension ended on an optimistic note, at least for me.

I wasn't so naïve to forget that despite having the momentary majority support of the commission, one future false move could turn a yes vote into a *no you must go* vote. The commission was a court that allowed double jeopardy.

After Poe slammed down the gavel ending the meeting, I caught Hayes-Santos' eye as he walked off the dais. The fire had left his eyes. I seized the opportunity to address my prime accuser. In hot pursuit, as he walked briskly to the commission offices, I asked him if we could talk now. Looking surprised, hesitantly, he said, "Sure." After settling into an unused conference room behind the city hall chambers, Hayes-Santos looked at me and nervously said, "I want you to know this wasn't personal." I took the longest deep breath of the night and tried not to laugh aloud. I couldn't believe the commissioner had set me up for another scene from *The Godfather. It was Mario Puzo's night. Get out the popcorn!* I envisioned Tom Hagen telling Sonny Corleone, "Even the shooting of your father was business, not personal, Sonny. You should know that by now."

In a final burst of emotional fortitude, I told the commissioner that I understood. I knew that he had a job to do for his constituents, and I appreciated his passion for doing so. I hoped that he knew I did as well. In closing, I said, "Rest assured, I will work hard for the city." We both stood up and shook each other's hands, knowing full well that the fight wasn't over.

As I ambled out of city hall, I reflected on yet another classic and complicated scene from *The Godfather.* The scene begins with a low-level mob hitman, Peter Clemenza, leaving his home to carry out a brutal mission. Despite his life as a professional killer, the scene portrays a normal man in a normal home life. While Clemenza leaves, his wife yells out, "Don't forget the cannoli." Clemenza mutters to himself, "Yeah, yeah, yeah, yeah," as he slides into his car seat and drives off to work. After exacting the ultimate revenge on the Godfather's betrayer, he surveys the crime scene. Clemenza calmly tells his partner Rocco to "Leave the gun" as a message to all that would think about betraying the Corleone family. After remembering his wife's request, Clemenza says, "Take the cannoli." As instructed, Rocco reaches into the car across the bloody body to retrieve the prized Italian dessert.

December 7th was my "take the cannoli" moment. As never before, I recognized that I toiled in a wicked, sometimes divisive world—a world in which political theater could provide cover for the arbitrary firing of a successful general manager. The trio's betrayal of all that I had done would remain in the city's public archives as a formal record of their grievous miscalculation—just like leaving the gun at the murder scene would remain in the minds of all that ever tried to betray the Godfather again.

I realized that those political forces that wished me gone were destroying the utility as much as anything else. I swore then and there that I would not "go gentle into that good night."

Ω

A Sunshine State of Mind

There was a real possibility that one of the most defining moments in my life would never have happened. The reason: the political maelstrom that arose like a Florida summer afternoon thunderstorm on that December 7th evening was, exactly, the turmoil Melinda had feared when she expressed reservations about my pursuit of such a highly visible public position.

Melinda had grown up in a family that shied away from the public spotlight. Her parents had built careers around being civil servants. Her father was a scientist for the Department of Defense, while her mother worked as a guidance counselor in a magnet school in Baltimore City. They were intensely, painfully private people. Falling all too close to her family tree, Melinda inherently grasped the dangers of being thrust onto the center stage of GRU's very public battle.

Unlike my wife, I come from a line of extroverted people. Some of them were just plain showoffs. One of my cousins was Frank Bielarski, who promoted stock car races in Pensacola, Florida, and other southern speedways. His son, Charles, known as Buddy, grew up in the industry and became a legend in the NASCAR circuit as both a driver and a builder.

As Mississippi racing historian, Jack Brown, tells it, when Buddy would thrust his race car (legendary number

in Pennsylvania, where we had found comfort in being surrounded by our kids and grandkids.

***

In early April, my family gathered around the dining room table in our Pennsylvania home as we patiently listened to the commissioners express their views on the remaining candidates for the GRU general manager opportunity. It was reminiscent of a scene from a bygone era of past generations huddled around the radio while a wartime president spoke to a nation in a series of fireside chats. In this era, my family watched and listened, not to the radio, but to my computer laptop, streaming the audio/video feed from the events in Gainesville, Florida.

Like the intermittent radio signals from those days gone by, the internet signal was weak, as a commissioner or two would freeze in the middle of their comments. Invariably, they'd return moments later in the middle of another thought or position. It was as though the applets were struggling to gather enough energy to climb the half mile up the driveway to our gathering. As the applets struggled to make their journey, I couldn't help but ponder on my future dealings with Gordon.

Further north in Nantucket Sound, Massachusetts, Jim Gordon's long-awaited, controversial offshore wind project, named Cape Wind, had been inching along since it was first announced in the summer of 2001, only months ahead of 9-11. In his second decade of battle as the President of Cape Wind, Gordon must have begun to consider the possibilities of failure. I wonder if a naughty limerick had come to his mind, "Fuck it, Nantucket." Knowing Jim Gordon, probably not. Gordon was a fighter, who didn't have the word, quit, in his vocabulary.

Gordon's involvement with the project was recounted in the book of the same name, Cape Wind. The authors profile a young Gordon through his experiences while spending summers at the West End Camp in Maine. At thirteen, his camp nickname became "Cool Hand Luke" because no matter how grueling the punishment, Gordon seemed simply biologically incapable of calling it quits."

In another story, Gordon is participating in a game of tetherball, in which he is "outmatched in age, weight, and height." Rather than appreciate the "fun of the game," Gordon would not "accept an inevitable loss." Now, almost fifty years later, Gordon was stuck in a quest with Cape Wind, which was reminiscent of his tetherball game—it was a quest, as the authors wrote, "He couldn't win, but he was unwilling to lose."

***

While I was aware of Gainesville's hyperactive political climate, I remained undaunted about the opportunity. I was captivated by leading a utility serving a community known as the Berkeley of the South. GRU was one of the top five municipal utilities in Florida, serving almost 100,000 electric customers, another 70,000 water and wastewater customers, and over 30,000 natural gas customers and has a long and proud history.

That history began in 1905 when the city lured the newly formed University of Florida into town with the promise of free water from its pumping facilities at Bouleware Springs. Later in 1912, the city established its own public power system in response to a billing dispute with Gainesville Gas and Electric Company (GGE).

The dispute was over a whopping $7.30 and escalated when GGE shut off the city's street lights for non-payment. True to hometown hero Tom Petty's song lyrics, the community didn't back down. The fiercely independent community vowed never to be left to the mercy of others for their power or water needs. *Note to self: Always remember GRU's roots.*

At the time I was courting GRU, I was serving as the Chief Operating Officer and Chief Financial Officer of a municipal water/wastewater utility called the Lehigh County Authority (Authority). Located just outside of

Allentown, Pennsylvania, I joined the Authority after two decades of experience in the rough and tumble world of independent power producers. I quickly found that my power industry experience easily translated into the world of water and wastewater service.

While I was the heir apparent to long-time CEO Aurel Arndt, the path forward was lined with land mines, the least of which was Arndt himself. His management style was out of phase with my approach, as well as most modern-day accomplished leaders. Arndt represented what I thought of as old Allentown—the lack of inspired thought and action that left the public wanting more while receiving less.

Arndt's status quo thinking reminded me of the lyrics from Billy Joel's classic song "Allentown." In it, Joel accurately portrayed the failure of the area's old-school thinking with, "Well, we're waiting here in Allentown for Pennsylvania we never found."

Arndt had spent his career admirably, keeping utility rates low. Not so admirable was accomplishing it through limiting spending on items that mattered the most. He had deferred expenditures on maintenance and infrastructure projects that would have improved safety and reliability. He fought against needed employee wage increases and additional staffing. As a result of Arndt's actions, I foresaw the Authority facing a day of reckoning in the not-too-distant future.

Anyone following in Arndt's shoes as the Authority's CEO would be confronted with escalating rate pressure as they'd be forced to repair and rehabilitate the Authority's deficient, aging systems. It was the classic, pay me now or pay me later conundrum. Regrettably, "Pay me later" was rounding the bend. Worse yet, after thirty-five-plus years with the Authority, Arndt envisioned the utility as his baby, his legacy. He wasn't open to other opinions, suggestions, or alternate management styles. He simply knew best. In his relentless pursuit of low utility rates, Arndt had turned the Authority into a ticking maintenance time bomb, ready to explode on someone else's watch.

Fortunately for me, even under Arndt's leadership, I was able to bring needed change to the Authority. Unfortunately for me, for all the success I had brought the Authority, I was still not being financially rewarded. The vision of continuing to struggle under Arndt's leadership style was so unacceptable and so unfulfilling I set my sights on other opportunities. There were select areas of the country where Melinda and I decided we could go, Florida being one of them.

Rather than playing a game of hot potato with the Authority, I jumped at the general manager opportunity at GRU. Melinda and I travelled to Gainesville, where we stayed in a top-floor suite in the downtown Hampton Inn which offered a splendid view of the city's remarkably small but efficient downtown.

The Hippodrome Theater sits at the core of downtown, spawned from its early life as a US Post Office and US District Court Building. Lying proudly behind its two-story Corinthian columns and dressed in neoclassical style, the Hipp, as it is called, is home to live theater built to provide an intimate experience. Local movers and shakers can be seen during its popular weekend performances.

Surrounding the Hipp is a combination of great local eateries, like DragonFly Sushi, Mojo's Hogtown Bar-B-Que, and nightclubs and bars. Not seedy, dark, and foreboding places one might find along an interstate, but young, trendy, hipster places for college kids to go. Off the southeastern side of the downtown stands the 3-story, brick, and mortar GRU headquarters lying adjacent to its first power plant, the John R. Kelly Generating Station, built in 1914.

Hovering like sentries over the surrounding communities, Kelly's large cooling towers can not only be seen but felt by anyone walking alongside them down 2ⁿᵈ Street towards Depot Park. The spray from the cooling tower's condensate mists through the air, spritzing the walkers below. There was something inviting about this quaint, southern town, which doubles in size with the opening of the University of Florida's fall semester when students intermingle with locals, and old bank buildings and power plants live near the center of the town's heart.

First impressions being everything, there was a palpable spirit in this town to which we felt instantly connected.

While I interviewed with commissioners, Melinda explored the city. She found the abundant arts and entertainment scene quite promising for a small community. As an artist, she liked Gainesville's vibe. However, she did fall prey to Gainesville's quirky, four-quadrant grid street numbering system for the city road system that left her consistently returning to the same part of town. It was as though we were staying at the "Hotel California" versus the Hampton Inn.

It was only after we had talked with Commissioner Budd, did we learn the trick to help us navigate the city. Mnemonics APRL and STD would have alerted her to the east-to-west roads as Avenues, Places, Roads, and Lanes, with north-to-south roads as Streets, Terraces, and Drives. I couldn't help but chuckle about the STD mnemonic being used in a college town.

The interviews were followed by a Meet and Greet where members of the public gathered to mingle and ask the candidates questions. Folks like Harvey Budd, one-time Gainesville Sun reporter turned lawyer Ray Washington, and commission candidate and flying friend of John Travolta, Jay Curtis, all grilled me on how I would solve the problems facing the utility.

Washington peppered me with questions about the possibility of abrogating the utility's albatross of a contract. He was intrigued by my background at Panther Creek Partners, a power facility similar to GREC, and how my experience would be useful in dealing with the GREC PPA. He'd continue our conversation even after I returned back home to Pennsylvania, "You did not mention the possibility of wreaking havoc with GREC's investors' income flow by terminal cycling that would exacerbate fatigue and creep and other stresses on GREC's proven unreliable components. But you made clear that during your time with Panther Creek Partners PPA for Metropolitan Edison to economically dispatch your generator in this manner…"

It was quite apparent that Washington had spent an inordinate amount of time analyzing the GREC PPA. It became my first encounter with the religious fervor which people in the community felt toward the Biomass deal. *Note to self: People are looking for me to wreak havoc.*

On April 2, the commission narrowed the field of six to three candidates—Rob McGarrah the Utility Director at the City of Tallahassee, Charles Dickerson the Director-Performance Management at Pepco Holdings and me.

***

My son, David, quickly focused my attention on the laptop screen once again. He told me it looked as though one of the candidates was dropping out of the competition. I listened as Commissioner Todd Chase detailed his conversations with the candidate, Charles Dickerson. It seemed that Dickerson wanted a contract with more than the state-allowed twenty weeks of severance provision—a deal breaker for the city. In response, Chase recommended removing Dickerson from consideration. With a quick vote, the commission removed one of the top three candidates from consideration. Their option was reduced to McGarrah or me.

The commission's desire for further debate abruptly ended as Mayor Ed Braddy instructed the commissioners to submit their top choices for the general manager position. After administrative wrangling, the general manager selection was put to a vote. By a roll-call vote,

Commissioners Todd Chase, Randy Wells, Craig Carter, and Mayor Braddy all voted for Bielarski, while Commissioners Lauren Poe, Helen Warren, and Yvonne Henson-Rawls voted for McGarrah.

The commission as a body had spoken—a commission, I might add, that was substantially different than the December 7, 2017, group. After engaging with the city for almost a year, the process was over in an instant. By the thinnest of margins, a 4 to 3 vote, I was selected as the candidate with whom the mayor would negotiate a contract.

Empathetic to my wife's concern about moving away from the Lehigh Valley, I looked at her and said, "Of course, I'm not sure if I'm really going to take the job, right?"

Melinda looked at me in the manner that all husbands can appreciate and said, "Oh, we're going, baby." I smiled as I understood our journey was about to begin in more ways than one.

As part of their due diligence toward finalizing my contract, city personnel scoured my social media posts and any other media reports. The Gainesville Sun reported that the investigation uncovered "at least one controversial comment on Facebook" without any details. The commissioners quickly weighed in on the investigation's findings.

Speaking on the record, Commissioner Chase said, "I hope they don't judge everybody by what's written on Facebook, or there'd be a lot of people losing their jobs."

Mayor Braddy delivered stronger comments to the Gainesville Sun, "I think it sends a 'chilling message throughout the organization to know that someone can play gotcha with you. He would be a change agent, and there are people terrified of that."

I wasn't happy that people were already arguing about me, yet, I hadn't set one foot in my new GRU offices.

Despite this bump in the road, on May 21, 2015, the commission approved my employment agreement by a unanimous vote. Soon after, I had my first media interview with Morgan Watkins, a reporter with The Gainesville Sun. "I'm not sure what I may have posted that offended anyone." I told her bluntly, "However, it's a no-win situation, so I think from my perspective, I'm best staying out of that arena."

It would be easier to say, "I'm best staying out of that arena," than actually staying out of that arena. That's a story for a later chapter.

Ω

The Contract Doesn't Pass the Sniff Test

Outside of the GRU Administration Building's imposing brick facade, the ills surrounding the GREC PPA were spreading like a virus long before the COVID-19 pandemic. The public's awareness of the awful deal the utility had executed, as approved by the previous commissions, had grown to a fever pitch. It manifested itself in a series of historic elections that changed the ideological balance of the commission by 2015.

From 2011 through 2014, more fiscally conservative local politicians were elected to the Gainesville City Commission, such as former Navy pilot Todd Chase, businessman Craig Carter, and Republican leader Ed Braddy. These new faces brought voices that openly questioned the GREC PPA, Solar FIT, and the lack of fiscal responsibility often displayed from the dais. Without these commissioners, I would not have become the new general manager.

Before the election of this new breed (for Gainesville) of commissioners, the GREC PPA had grabbed the attention of a host of local critics led by a former member of the Florida Public Service Commission (FPSC), Nathan Skop, local property owner, lawyer, and entrepreneur Jim Konish, along with lawyer and former Gainesville Sun reporter Ray Washington. The trio railed against the GREC PPA during virtually every commission meeting. When not in front of city hall cameras, they'd write editorials, engage on social media, and use whatever means at their disposal to advocate for the abrogation of the PPA or, at the very least, mitigate its impact. At the heart of their claims was that the GREC PPA was not a valid agreement, had been improperly executed, and was never formally approved by the commission.

In addition to his FPSC experience, Skop was an aerospace engineer and an attorney. However, even critics have critics. Skop's detractors would focus on one vote he cast while on the FPSC. On June 28, 2010, Skop and fellow FPSC commissioners Lisa Edgar and David Klement voted 3 for, while Chairwoman Nancy Argenziano and Ben A. "Steve" Stevens III voted 2 against the "Petition for Determination of Need for Proposed Biomass Plant." That vote granted GREC the right to proceed through the remainder of the state's permitting process. Without that affirmative vote, GREC's chance of constructing the biomass plant would have ended. Skop's critics howled—how dare you act so righteous.

To Skop's credit, he consistently defended his vote based on the inherent legal limitations to decide otherwise. He cited Florida's Home Rule Powers Act, which, when adopted in 1973, gave cities like Gainesville "governmental, corporate, and proprietary powers to enable them to conduct municipal government." In other words, Home Rule demanded that no matter how bad the decision, it was the city's right to make it and suffer the consequences.

Skop wasn't playing Monday Morning Quarterback with the Home Rule Powers Act. He expressed his logic during the February 9, 2010, FPSC meeting when he said, "So at least from my perspective, it's not for me to… impart my judgement. At the end of the day, it is really not for me to tell the City of Gainesville what they should or what they should not do."

I thought that Skop was one of the most misunderstood players in the GREC saga. He put himself on the firing line as he accurately foretold the perils of the GREC PPA, meeting after meeting.

Prior to the arrival of Chase, Carter, and Braddy, commissioners lost interest in his rhetoric, however insightful and on-point his comments might have been. He would be pilloried, along with other concerned citizens, as a type of Greek Chorus in classical theater. This Gainesville Greek Chorus would be described by free-lance editorialist Ron Cunningham as "actors involved whose function is to provide their own warped interpretation of what's occurring on stage." *Note to self: Politics in Gainesville was a blood sport.*

Skop wasn't the only member of the FPSC that warned of the challenges with the GREC PPA. David Klement also voted in the affirmative but prognosticated, "So, I think that the Gainesville customers will understand that if they do get in the position, that is possible that they will look at the city commissioners and mayor and say why did you do this? And they will have to defend it. The political price of this will be paid by the city commission and not this commission if this proves to be a bad decision." Rather prophetically, Klement also said, "Unfortunately, new regimes usually cannot void thirty-year contracts." *The future be told, my friend.*

Konish was a lawyer who had built his success on publishing law journals along with buying and leasing properties. He couldn't betray his fondness for the old days— a time when downtown Gainesville was the hub of commercial and social activity. He scorned the westward expansion of the community and the flight from the city's core. Konish would stand at the lectern during commission meetings and verbally spar with the sitting commissioners for what he believed were irresponsible, illegal, and/or unethical acts.

In a private moment, Konish told me he loved actor Raymond Burr's portrayal of Perry Mason in the 1960s television series bearing the same name. He wasn't the only person to be inspired by the fictional attorney. Supreme Court Justice Sonia Sotomayor herself told the Senate Judiciary

Committee in her confirmation hearings that "I was influenced so greatly by a television show in igniting the passion that I have as being a prosecutor, and it was Perry Mason." Over the years, I came to recognize that Perry Mason-style passion in Konish's commission appearances.

Ray Washington was the third lawyer of the trio, although he bore the spirit of a journalist. He earned it because he had played one in real life. Before changing careers to become a lawyer, Washington was a reporter for the Gainesville Sun. From my reviews of his work, Washington could really tell a story and turn a phrase. After I accepted the GM role with GRU, Washington reached out to me on multiple occasions explaining the environment in Gainesville along with his version of critical dos and don'ts for any incoming general manager.

In one such communication, he compared my forthcoming arrival in Gainesville with the premise of the Samuel Beckett play - Waiting for Godot. I had to Google it to find out that the play was a prime example of the Theater of the Absurd—post-World War II plays that focused on what happens when human existence lacks meaning. The play involves two characters who wander around the stage while awaiting the arrival of this mysterious character, Godot, who never arrives. Washington would soon find out that I was no Godot.

These three gentlemen, Skop, Konish, and Washington, were smart, articulate, and relentless. They were Wartime Consiglieres in their own right, simply of a different order. Their dedication would serve to attract other concerned citizens who would carry the no-GREC banner for years to come. At first, they embraced me as their knight in shining armor arriving in Gainesville to rid the kingdom of the scourge of the GREC PPA. However, in the end, it would prove next to impossible for us to find common ground—at least while I was serving as the general manager.

In response to the heightening public outcry over the GREC PPA and the city was shaken out of its lethargy - it was time to take an objective look at what had happened. In late 2014, they engaged independent professionals, Navigant Consulting LLC (Navigant), to investigate what had gone so terribly wrong with the GREC PPA to, in their words, "perform an independent assessment and evaluation of Gainesville Regional Utilities (GRU) and its dealings with Nacogdoches Power, LLP (Nacogdoches) and the long-term Power Purchase Agreement (PPA) entered into between the City of Gainesville (City) and Gainesville Renewable Energy Center (GREC)."

The investigation was completed just before my arrival, and the final report, dated April 15, 2015, was presented to the commission. While the report was only 179 pages long, it was supported by sixty-five three-ring binders full of backup information stored in the cabinets within the general manager's office. The report told the GREC PPA story through the lens of new, crucial information for all interested parties to read. Its thoroughness presented a clear timeline and accounting of GRU's selection of GREC as the vendor up through the negotiations and finalization of the GREC PPA. My intellectual digestion of the full report gave me physical indigestion while I cringed in disbelief.

***

The timeline of the GREC PPA had roots as far back as April 12, 2006, when the commission voted to initiate a process to solicit proposals to meet GRU's electric generation needs. In response, on September 5, 2006, GRU submitted a Request for Information (RFI) "seeking opportunities to either develop additional base load electric generation…"

A year later, on October 8, 2007, the commission approved a Request for Proposal (RFP) for a biomass-fueled electric generation—a formal, competitive, two-round, public-bidding process dictated by procurement rules under Florida Sunshine Laws.

On January 28, 2008, after the evaluation and ranking of the eleven (11) first-round non-binding bids, Nacogdoches sat in third place behind first and second-place leaders Sterling Planet and Covanta Energy, respectively. It looked as though without Covanta and Nacogdoches sharpening their pencils in the final best and final offer (BAFO) bid, Sterling Planet would be the chosen vendor.

Over the next few months, behind the scenes, GRU staff re-weighted the evaluation criteria for the final round of bidding. It would eliminate the need for Nacogdoches to sharpen its pencil and irrevocably change the outcome of the bidding process. "While, in our opinion, the re-weighting of the criteria was not unusual," Navigant wrote. "We noted a substantive, and relatively unsupported, change in the scoring on certain criteria that substantially improved the ratings of Nacogdoches over the other two finalists, especially given that there were not significant changes between the initial (first round)and binding (BAFO) proposals..."

In a dramatic turn of events, when the ranking of the BAFO bids was completed, Nacogdoches' total scoring on its Binding Proposal rose by 27%, while Sterling fell by 10% and Covanta rose a mere 2%. Nacogdoches' Binding Proposal was scored 21% higher than Covanta's bid and 32% higher than Sterling Planet's bid. Without the re-weighting of the scoring criteria, Nacogdoches would not have won the bid process.

Vendor	Non-Binding	Binding	% Chg.
Sterling Planet	363.78	327.42	10%
Covanta	348.42	356.60	2%
Nacogdoches Power	341.50	**432.20**	**27%**

44

Not surprisingly, the episode blew up the public's trust like hurricanes blow through Gainesville—leaving damage in its wake. For the average citizen, it just didn't feel right. It was analogous to having your teacher regrade your essay exam from a C+ to an A+ while leapfrogging you to the head of the class simply by giving you more credit for the answers you got right.

Despite the stunning manner in which the RFP winner was chosen, on May 12, 2008, the commission authorized then General Manager Hunzinger to negotiate a PPA with Nacogdoches Power LLC based on the Binding Proposal. While the questions surrounding the procurement process would forever cloud the selection of Nacogdoches in controversy, a second hurricane could be seen approaching on Dopler radar—ready to be named Hurricane Sticker Shock.

The GREC PPA negotiations began when it was announced that they would be conducted behind closed doors, outside of the public's watch. The reason was that Nacogdoches claimed that the PPA was exempt from public disclosure under the Florida Sunshine Law because their proprietary pricing was a trade secret. While trade secrets are valid exemptions under Florida law, there is controversy as to whether pricing falls under the definition of a trade secret. Rather than challenge the exemption, the city attorney's office acquiesced, which in turn added to the growing negative public perception of the biomass deal.

Over the next year, the GREC PPA was negotiated under this military-style secrecy. Gainesville residents could only guess how the contract was progressing while Hunzinger reported back to the commission during his private one-on-one meetings. There were no public meetings, no public discussion, and no public input.

The finalized GREC PPA made its public debut at city hall on May 7, 2009. Well, not so much of a debut as much as a cliff-notes version of the deal, with pages missing. Over the course of that fateful night, GRU's management team took turns strolling to the lectern to wax poetic about what they had accomplished. Paradoxical to the magnitude of the moment, the meeting was rather perfunctory, with nary a tough question from the commission. In fact, when given the chance, there was outright camaraderie.

After Hunzinger introduced Jim Gordon and Len Fagan seated in the audience, he chided the GREC investors for being Red Sox fans while Hunzinger was a Cardinal fan. Hanrahan joined in on the chumminess of the moment, exclaiming from the dais, "As long as they're not Tennessee fans—or Georgia, for that matter." So much for setting the appropriate tone as you get ready to obligate the utility for the next thirty years without the ability to discuss the price in the contract.

After a brief time, Hunzinger handed over the presentation to Ed Regan, who, along with John Stanton, were the co-negotiators on the GREC PPA. Regan was GRU's Assistant Manager for Strategic Planning and served as the idea guy on renewable energy and greening the utility. He had a bachelor's degree in behavioral science and a master's in environmental sciences. On the other hand, Stanton was a former long-tenured Florida Power and Light (FPL) engineer who was comfortable carrying out his management duties on the deck plates of GRU's power plants. I saw them as the bookends of theory and practicality. Tonight was Regan's show.

Within moments of his introduction, Regan was breezing through the changes to which the parties had agreed. First, Regan said, "It's a thirty-year contract. Here's the first big significant change. When we first started negotiating, it was a twenty-year contract. And it's fixed pricing, which is to the advantage of our customers." There were no questions or interruptions from anyone on the dais, despite the disclosure of the 50% increase in the risk horizon.

That's when Regan disclosed interesting things about the parties now involved in the deal. He said, "A little bit about the company (Nacogdoches); that's changed a bit as well." As Regan explained the change, Nacogdoches was originally a consortium between Energy Management Inc and Bay Corp Holdings. Regan nervously said, "And I am probably saying this all legally wrong, but you get the idea." Regan didn't defer to the City Attorney for assistance. He just moved on. The silence continued from the dais.

Regan dug the credibility hole a bit deeper, "What has happened in the meantime – and there's another company called Tyr Energy. Tyr Energy happens to be a subsidiary of Itochu Corporation, which is a Japanese company. And they have acquired a 49 percent share." He continued his litany of organizational changes, "And frankly, now Tyr Energy has an equity interest in the unit (Biomass plant) as well as an operating management contract."

Regan introduced GREC for the first time when he said, "So we think that was a move to our better. American Renewables will own and operate the Gainesville Renewable Energy Center (GREC)." While I might have been able to get past the organizational changes as necessary for the proper functioning of the project, once again, where there ought to have been a question or two, there was silence from the dais, except for pleasantries.

It was then that Regan casually dropped a bombshell. "Nacogdoches, in those days, came back and said, "Look, you know, we—had this pricing in our proposal, but look, here are the things that have changed." Alarm bells went off in my head when he said, "We just can't do it for that." What would he say next?

Regan said that the parties chose to "share that risk through the index period," using a euro-to-dollar ratio to account for the change in prices. I couldn't believe what I was hearing from Regan. In a period of rising prices, GRU's negotiating team had agreed to amend the Binding Proposal

47

pricing and cover those costs on the oft chance prices would go down. That was economic buffoonery. Why would they accept such a risk?

The commission's approval to negotiate had been conditioned on: "In the event the GM is unable to negotiate an acceptable contract with the highest ranked proposer, the GM/Designee may then negotiate with the next highest proposer." I was waiting for the GRU team to show the assembled audience that they had truly negotiated anything.

Confidently continuing to address the commissioners, Regan cited the next change. "After discussion with the commission, we all agreed to go for 100% of the output, knowing we could market some of the output from this unit in your earlier years to other third parties." He didn't stop there. He continued, "We have three companies that are lined up for this."

What made his comment so maddening was that GRU had a choice to accept 50 or 100 megawatts. A 50-megawatt PPA would have reduced the risk for GRU. Worse yet, a decade later, the decision to accept the 100 megawatts would prove extremely costly, particularly when GRU was unable to secure one single potential buyer for the additional power.

Finally, Regan stated the most damning part of the GREC PPA, "The restructure deal (meaning the GREC PPA) is 100% take and pay contract." He explained, "We only pay for the energy they give us. If they are able to make energy and we don't want it for whatever reason, we do pay—we do make them whole on a part of the cost."

To this day, people in the community don't fully appreciate the significance of Regan's comment. In the power generation industry, there are two types of revenues, energy and capacity. Energy revenue is the revenue for every kilowatt the plant generates, while capacity revenue is the revenue generated for the plant's ability to produce those kilowatts when needed but not yet requested. Think of capacity as reservations on current or future electricity for which GRU pays a fee.

The ugly truth about making GREC whole was that it obligated GRU to pay seventy-four million dollars a year, whether GREC delivered the energy or not. The tagline that GRU would only pay for the energy delivered conveniently dwarfed the material monetary exposure that the utility would have to pay for capacity when GRU didn't need it. Failure to disclose this risk during this commission meeting was inexcusable.

All told, the negotiations produced eight formal revisions between the Binding Proposal and the final GREC PPA. In virtually all the revisions, GRU ended up incurring more costs and/or more risk for little or no benefit. Here are the gory details, one by one:

1) The final term of the PPA increased by 50% from twenty years to thirty years,

2) His right to make a first offer to purchase the biomass plant was given up for a grant of the right of first refusal,

3) The right to terminate the PPA for convenience were lost in negotiations,

4) The potential increase in construction costs were accepted through an obscure Construction cost adjuster,

5) The responsibility of ad valorem taxes on the project, estimated at approximately five million dollars a year, were accepted,

6) Capacity charges were redefined as available energy payments grew from forty-eight million dollars to sixty-five million dollars a year, resulting in,

7) Overall fixed costs of the PPA increased from 936 million dollars to $1.9 billion.

Despite these facts that should have been disclosed to the commission, as the presentation was nearing its conclusion, not one commissioner rose in opposition to the GREC PPA. In fact, the total acquiescence was demonstrated no better than when Hanrahan quipped, "I'm just sitting here wishing you guys had negotiated the contract between the County and Shands." The GREC PPA was approved unanimously and ratified two days later.

As poorly as the GREC PPA had already been procured, negotiated, executed, and now approved, there was yet another substantial transgression even after its approval. The transgression had been unceremoniously touched upon by Regan during the May 7, 2009, presentation. He told the commissioners that the plant "wouldn't need advanced scrubbers." While the statement may have slipped through the collegial air, it was a crucial element of the approval of the GREC PPA.

That element would be called into question just five days later during a meeting with the Florida Department of Environmental Protection (FDEP)—attended *only* by GREC staff and FDEP engineer Alvaro Linero. GREC staff learned that the plant's planned use of Selective Non-Catalytic Reduction technology (SNCR) for capturing NOx was not acceptable. The Navigant Report wrote: "Linero suggested for the first time that GREC would need to make a very strong argument if it wished to persuade FDEP that the utilization of SNCR is BACT (Best Available Control Technology)."

SNCR technology is a type of aqueous ammonia injection system. It is a less stringent and less costly method to capture the plant's NO2 emissions. In Linero's opinion and, therefore, the FDEP office, SNCR technology simply wasn't up to their gold standard of BACT. Instead, Linero envisioned a Selective Catalytic Reduction system (SCR), or scrubbers, as satisfying the BACT requirement in the plant's air permit, known as a Title V permit.

Linero's suggestion would have made GREC the only biomass-fired facility in the United States that would be required to use an SCR control device to control NOx emissions. In my opinion, Linero's suggestion was a step too far.

Linero gave GREC a window of opportunity to present an argument that the SNCR was BACT. However, GREC didn't seize upon that opportunity. There's no evidence that at a second meeting with Linero on June 24, GREC presented an argument against the SCR. There was evidence that the meeting was once again conducted without anyone from GRU in attendance. Despite having no formal ruling FDEP on this matter, GREC made the decision to redesign the NOx system to an SCR.

By August 2009, GREC entered discussions with GRU management over the legal and financial consequences of what was deemed a Change in Law, under the provisions of the GREC PPA, along with how much it might cost. Once again, GRU management offered little pushback, as evidenced by Regan reporting back to GREC in that same month "that this change from an SNCR to an SCR was appropriate and necessary, would constitute a 'change in law' under the terms of the PPA, and that some re-evaluation of the Contract Prices between the Parties would need to occur at some point in the future."

Not everybody at GRU was drinking the GREC Kool-Aid. Stanton stood up and informed Hunzinger, in writing, that while he was supportive of modifying the air permit to the SCR, he wasn't agreeable to GRU paying for it. He wrote that he was "not convinced that we need to pay for anything. I think we should really be playing hardball on the change of law thing." The 2015 Navigant Report sided with Stanton when it concluded that "we have identified no evidence to support the conclusion that the change to an SCR should have been treated as a Change in Law under the contract."

Stanton's argument against the technology change being a Change in Law fell on deaf ears. In a spiraling series of mind-bending events, on March 16, 2011, GRU executed the Equitable Adjustment for Change of Law (Equitable

Adjustment), which cemented GRU's acceptance of the technology change as a Change in Law.

Adding more fuel to the public fire, the Equitable Adjustment wasn't even signed by Hunzinger. Its signing was delegated to GRU's CFO, Jennifer Hunt, upon Hunzinger's granted approval, while Hunzinger wasn't even in the office. With Hunt's signing, GRU would be obligated to pay for the 105 million dollars of costs to install the scrubbers, paid for as an additional $4.40 per megawatt hour on the Available Energy Payments.

On April 6, 2011, three weeks after the execution of the Equitable Adjustment, GREC advised GRU that it no longer claimed confidential treatment for any portion of the PPA. As part of the removal of the confidentiality requirement, a GRU e-line news release was sent via e-mail to the commission and the news media.

In addition to hailing the release of the unredacted GREC PPA, the news release also stated that "GRU was able to release today an adjustment to the power purchase agreement that addresses negative costs associated with recent changes in federal environmental regulations and state permitting requirements." Hunzinger went on to say that the changes would have minimal impact on customers. The statement was as baffling as it was outrageous.

If one lets it, the timing of that announcement can take one down multiple rabbit holes, with good reason. What we know is that the Equitable Adjustment wasn't brought before the commission for approval, ratification, or discussion despite it adding over one hundred million dollars in costs to the GREC PPA. It was only publicly discovered in October 2013, only after the biomass plant had already gone into commercial operations. It proved to be the primary reason for Hunzinger leaving GRU.

I was astonished at the sheer weight of the adverse negotiation outcomes. In return for all the concessions, GRU received nothing of any consequence. It was as if there had been no quid pro quo. Instead, it was a quid pro GO! The GREC PPA had obligated GRU to pay GREC up to seventy-four million dollars a year, whether they generated electricity or not. Over the expanded thirty years of the GREC PPA, GRU was faced with over 2.2 billion dollars of future payments. This hadn't been a negotiation! Rather it was a confiscation!

With this staggering sum of expanded revelations reduced to one central repository, the Navigant Report would serve as the foundational blueprint of everything that went disturbingly wrong with the GREC PPA but found no one to hold fully accountable and no other recourse for the utility but to operate under what was deemed a valid, binding PPA.

Instead of placing a sense of closure on any transgressions, the Navigant Report served to incite more discussion and outrage over the contract's details, which had been kept secret for so long. The assembled critics and other skeptics also cried foul because the report was not the forensic audit they thought was going to be conducted.

The report provided conclusions that served as breadcrumbs to follow in my pursuit of the truth. "We understand that a prolonged permitting process was a significant concern for both GRU and GREC and that such a process may not have been beneficial to the mutual interests of both parties given the proposed timetable for the facility and the desire for federal and/or state tax incentives."

"In hindsight, the negotiation of the PPA and the subsequent permitting and Equitable Adjustment appears to have been guided more by accomplishing a perceived mandate by the commission, rather than an objective analysis and assessment of GRU's needs, costs, and risks."

The report stated that "the decision-making appears to have been more influenced by the drive for a 'biomass-fueled energy source, and the city's desire to comply with the Kyoto Protocol, rather than sound business and risk analysis, and concerns about customer rates." Those are pretty damning conclusions.

The commission set a tone for the process that hogtied the utility's negotiating team. No better example of that was the grant issued from the American Recovery and Re-Investment Act passed through Congress. Forever linked to President Obama's term, "shovel-ready projects," the GREC biomass plant became the proud recipient of almost eighty million dollars in grant money as a result - money that flowed to GREC, not GRU. In one last cruel irony, GRU management sped up the process to mitigate GREC's capital costs.

It was under this historical umbrella that I voiced my first public thoughts concerning the GREC PPA. During a July 20 City Commission's evening session, in response to a question from Jim Konish, I said, "The contract (GREC PPA) doesn't pass the sniff test. I'm sorry." After an audible gasp, you could hear a pin drop. Packed into that comment was the validation to the community that I, indeed, questioned the way in which the GREC PPA had been negotiated and foisted upon them. It was my emperor wears no clothes moment.

Before that night, no one in Authority at GRU had ever publicly admitted the folly of the GREC PPA, at least not in such an unvarnished way. GRU management had remained silent behind their three-story bastion of an administration building offering virtual no-comments to the world. With those words, the Bielarski-era at GRU began. And with it, I would challenge the legacy of the person who had presided over this debacle of a contract, former mayor Pegeen Hanrahan.

Ω

Pay No Attention to the Woman Behind the Curtain

In the city elections of 2004, Gainesville elected a young, vibrant, Hillary-esque figure, Pegeen Hanrahan, to the high office of mayor. As "a vegetarian, bike-riding environmentalist," she was a true believer that Gainesville, through GRU, had to lead the nation, maybe even the world, in a crusade to rid it of man-made, green-house gases. She wasn't alone in that belief. Hanrahan galvanized her political power base through the support network of dyed-in-the-wool environmentalists within the vast University of Florida faculty as well as among other like-minded liberal-leaning people. There was little argument that Hanrahan and her army exerted a dominant hand in guiding the utility.

During her reign, GRU was transmogrified from a cost-conscious municipal utility that delivered low-cost, safe, and reliable service to a high-cost utility that subsidized major city projects, a small portion, if any, which benefited its customers. No matter the cost, GRU would lead the way in saving the world, one project at a time.

The first of these major projects was the restoration of Depot Park. The Depot Park site was not really a park, as much as a repository for the waste byproduct of converting coal tar into gas for commercial use. The site was owned and operated by the Gainesville Gas Company until GRU acquired the company as a way to expand its natural gas footprint. Decades of serving as a rather nasty industrial site had left Depot Park as an environmental cesspool, no pun intended.

The commission decided to restore the site, not to a simple brownfield, but an improved greenfield location which would become Gainesville's Central Park—a new downtown destination. Once completed, the expanded restoration of this site would cost utility customers over twenty million dollars. To Hanrahan and her army, the sizeable expenditure was not only worthwhile but necessary because, after its restoration, the abhorrent industrial site would become the crown jewel of Gainesville's southern gateway, or as some called it, Gainesville's Emerald Ring. Depot Park would later serve as the home to the Cade Museum (named for Professor Cade, the creator of Gatorade), an accessible children's area with innovative activities, and the local's favorite, First Magnitude Brewery.

GRU's participation in the Depot Park project was a landmark decision because it set the philosophical template for the way in which the commission would come to view the utility and its resources—if the city cannot afford it, GRU customers surely can. The template was arguably the primary renewable fuel source in Gainesville. Unfortunately, instead of powering GRU's power plants , it ignited anger and division. Even so, for a mayor that wanted to save the world, GRU's financial power was, ironically, a non-renewable resource too good to pass up.

After my arrival, in September 2015, during the Depot Park's ground-breaking ceremony, I was seated next to Hanrahan. I immediately sensed the paradox at play. Obviously aware of my reputation and mandate to deliver us all from GREC's PPA evil, Hanrahan barely spoke to me as, one by one, the speakers took to the lectern to speak to the enormity of the occasion. After what seemed to be an eternity of silence between us, Hanrahan arose to take her rightful place at the lectern. She looked upon the crowd and waxed poetic, in overwhelming detail, over her years on the commission and how rewarding it was to see her vision come to life. She spoke long past the sale and, in doing so, took away from my upcoming speaking time. I was fine with it. I understood that this was her moment.

As Hanrahan ended her speech and slowly drifted away from the stage, I arose to slowly move to center stage. After thanking Hanrahan and all those that made this day possible, I leaned into the microphone and said in a low tone, "I just want you all to know I had absolutely nothing to do with this project." My attempt to grab people's attention drew as many laughs as side-eye stares. It was true, I had only arrived in Gainesville when the Depot Park project had been completed. It would have been presumptuous to accept the appearance of greater involvement.

My comments were also my way of making it known that I was not the type of leader that would be afraid of saying exactly what I meant. I would not have been an advocate for spending more than 20 million of GRU dollars to build the city's version of New York City's Central Park, no matter how beautiful it turned out to be. Finally, GRU shouldn't be in the business of building parks when the city has its own parks and recreation department and funding.

I sprinkled in a faux-Letterman routine, in which I offered my top ten reasons I considered Depot Park to be a great project. The routine had its intended effect. The crowd returned to a celebration. I ended with my number one reason Depot Park was such a great project. I declared, "We rehabilitated a really cool old train station. Now who doesn't love train stations?" *Coo coo ca choo—choo. Sorry, Paul and Art.*

It wouldn't be my last encounter with the political powerhouse. Hanrahan and I tangoed in social media conversations over the years, during which she regularly affirmed her disdain for me. On one such exchange, Hanrahan told me, "Even if we assume Karen Johnson, Bob Hunzinger, Kathy Viehe, Ed Regan, John Stanton, and a host of lawyers and consultants, PSC staff, elected officials and others were a bunch of complete bone heads and we're so lucky that you rode on your white horse to save us all from ourselves, being gracious in victory would be a better long-term plan." I was surprised Hanrahan didn't know that a Wartime Consigliere wouldn't be caught dead on a white horse. No, only a black horse or late-model, black BMW would do.

Hanrahan and her army encouraged, cajoled, and legislated GRU into borrowing and spending more dollars to elevate economic development in the community. On the surface, not such a bad policy. In practice, it led to a host of unintended consequences.

***

In the area adjacent to Depot Park, known as the Power District, rather than rehabilitate, repair, or just make do with its operations and maintenance shops, GRU abandoned the property to head north in the city to construct what would become its Eastside Operations Center (EOC). The move served multiple purposes, the first of which was to improve the working conditions and space for GRU employees. It was seen as a first step in converting the Power District into an area of affordable housing and retail shops. The development of Power District combined with Depot Park was planned as a physical gateway from Gainesville's southern border into downtown, as well as extending the city's urban core.

GRU would end up spending over seventy-five million dollars to construct the EOC and untold millions more in ancillary expenses. The unintended consequence of the Power District's actions was the loss of hundreds of potential customers (GRU employees) in the downtown core. With no coherent direction, the Power District stands largely vacant today after multiple failed development attempts and no visible path forward.

***

The Hanrahan-led commission also shied away from utility-built, commercial solar power farms. She was enamored with the European-style solar customer feed-in concepts which Regan had witnessed in his trips to Germany. Under Hanrahan's leadership and Regan's stewardship, GRU was led down a path of promoting customer construction of behind-the-meter and roof-top solar arrays through a new solar feed-in tariff program labeled the Solar FIT.

GRU's program granted long-term contracts to select participants through a public bidding process in exchange for the participant's installation of roof-top solar units. Four hundred participants were chosen who had the financial wherewithal to spend $25,000 to $100,000 to install their roof-top solar panels and granted long-term contracts up to twenty years. The overall costs of the program would be shared by all the retail GRU customers as a relatively small sum—100,000 electric customers would pay 4 or 5 dollars a month to fund the program.

The program was built on a process known as *peak shaving*. These new rooftop solar arrays would produce additional power during the day during the hottest days of the year—thereby shaving the peak electric load of the utility and possibly eliminating the need to build additional power plants. Once again, in theory, everybody would win.

The Solar FIT program was an immediate hit with customers who were successful in being granted a contract. Even Hanrahan herself became a Solar FIT customer. *Of course, she did.* GRU solar program manager Rachel Meeks said, "Everybody was rushing to try to be the first in line." Meeks, I would add, was still at GRU when I arrived. If anyone was going to control the people rushing to be the first in line, it was Meeks. No shrinking violet, Meeks spent her off hours as a member of the Roller Rebels, Gainesville's Rollerball team, aka Rowdy Dangerfield...

Sara Peach, a writer from the Yale Climate Connections Newsletter, lauded the city: "Gainesville, it seemed, had found an approach to addressing climate change that could have widespread appeal."

Fellow believers, such as Charlie Coggeshall, Renewable Energy Manager at the Southern Alliance for Clean Energy, said, "The city was the golden child for this whole industry for a year or two."

Hanrahan joined in and crowed, "It has become a point of civic pride."

By the end of Solar FIT applications in 2013, 18.1 megawatts of solar capacity were added in GRU territory, as a baseline, that amounted to between 4 to 20% of GRU's daytime electric load at any moment, being served by solar installations on residential homes and commercial businesses.

After gaining commission approval for rate increases to cover the program's costs, Regan said, "It was the easiest rate increase I had ever passed. I was kind of stunned." Regan didn't stop there. He went on to say, "Solar is sexy. Solar is like magic." Sexy or not, the reality was, as with programs of this type, the devil was in the details. I discovered that the Solar FIT housed more than its share of demons.

Solar was certainly magic to those four hundred participants in Solar FIT who had been chosen to be the recipients of the contracts. The program was an annuity on which one could feather their nest and retire—not so much for 99.99% of GRU's customers that failed to benefit from Solar FIT and were forced to subsidize those other four hundred participants' twenty-year contracts. Boy, did they pay?

CY	MWh	FIT payments	$/kWh
2009	368	$101,627.43	$0.276
2010	1286	$411,606.40	$0.320
2011	7269	$2,230,348.47	$0.307
2012	15839	$4,605,954.40	$0.291
2013	19021	$5,319,909.84	$0.280
2014	23329	$5,797,811.48	$0.249
2015	23125	$5,792,714.13	$0.250
2016	24725	$6,178,357.55	$0.250
2017	23373	$5,869,617.42	$0.251
2018	21359	$5,394,071.07	$0.253
2019	21042	$5,247,411.13	$0.249
2020	18618	$4,675,029.86	$0.251
	Total MWh	*Cost of FIT energy*	*$/MWh*
	199,354	$51,624,459.18	$258.959

While the original four hundred participants have since fallen to 258 in 2021, GRU paid these Solar FIT participants over fifty million dollars for generation from 2009 through 2020. It would have cost GRU less than six million dollars to produce that same level of generation.

At $259 a megawatt, these four hundred customers ended up being paid almost ten times more than the market price for power—GRU's cost of generation was between $25 and $35 a megawatt. I repeat, ten times the cost.

I describe the Solar FIT program as a Reverse Robin hood scheme. As graphically defined by The Urban Dictionary, it illustrates the point. "Taking money from the Poor and giving it to the Rich. I get 5% Cash back on my Discover card... They get that cash back money from the poor fucks that get charged with the interest rates because they can't pay their bills, then give it to me for paying on time."

You see, the remainder of GRU's electric customers, who couldn't afford to install roof-top solar arrays, had to foot the bill for the forty-five million dollars of excess costs over the past decade (fifty-one million dollars less the six million dollars). By the time the program ends in the next decade, those excess costs of the Solar FIT will likely reach one hundred million dollars. When all is said and done, I believe the Solar FIT program will be remembered as a huge transfer of wealth from those that could least afford it to those that can most afford it. Yet, the commission continued to virtue-signal with talk of equity and inclusion.

Despite the economic disaster of the Depot Park project and the Solar FIT program, Hanrahan's stature was elevated from a "vegetarian, bike-riding environmentalist" to a grander level. Maybe that's why she was simply called Queen Pegeen by some. And why not? She was successfully shaping the city's political and social landscape. Under Hanrahan's reign, GRU grew from the city's financial engine to the city's laboratory for green energy. The commission was seeking the utility's compliance with the Kyoto Protocol and Paris Accord to promote carbon-less energy.

***

Fun fact #1: the reason the term treaty isn't used is that neither of these deals binds the government of the United States as a treaty requires. Yet, here Gainesville was, binding itself to international protocols and accords. *Yikes!*

Fun fact #2: the biomass plant produced as much carbon emissions per kilowatt as GRU's coal-fired plant. The only difference was the magic of USEPA thinking. Since the biomass plant only used waste wood such as trees with no commercial value that had been cut down, or debris from tree harvesting, and storms, the USEPA proffered that the biomass plant was not adding any *additional* CO_2 to the environment. Afterall, the dead trees and tree debris would decay and emit CO_2 into the atmosphere anyway. The bottom line for the USEPA was that burning waste wood in a controlled environment was better than having it be left to decay or be burnt by in the fields. Thus it was deemed carbon neutral.

***

Depot Park and the Power District were intended to serve as a physical, green, emerald gateway into downtown Gainesville. The Solar FIT served as the city's philosophic, gateway into its next green energy quest. The piece de resistance of the Hanrahan era would be the zero-emission (by EPA standards) biomass plant.

No matter the reality, Hanrahan's almost decade-long tenure in office had reached its crescendo by 2009. The sum of her political will and capital, perfectly captured Gainesville's zeitgeist during the early 2000s. It made building the biomass plant inevitable.

What was just as inevitable was GRU's depleted financial power. To pull off the crowning environmental achievement would require the construction of a costly biomass plant embedded in a power purchase agreement (PPA). For Hanrahan and her army, that's when their master plan would turn into a master money pit. The Hanrahan era projects doubled GRU's debt load by the end of her tenure and doubled it again even after she left. The utility no longer had the capacity to borrow the funds necessary to construct a biomass plant without negative impacts on its bond ratings. GRU was tapped out. They had to find a way to get it built without any balance sheet impact—in a process called off-balance sheet financing.

Investopedia defines off-balance sheet financing as "an accounting practice whereby a company does not include a liability on its balance sheet, and it is used to impact a company's level of debt and liability."

Investopedia also noted: "The practice has been denigrated by some since it was exposed as a key strategy of the ill-fated energy giant Enron."

In GRU's case, the GREC PPA was anticipated to be granted off-balance sheet financing treatment. Maybe it was just wishful thinking because, in the end, under generally accepted accounting principles (GAAP), the GREC PPA was ultimately classified as a capital lease or debt on GRU's balance sheet. Rating agencies recognized the GREC PPA as a debt obligation with all the negative implications.

Wishful thinking or not, in 2010, during the Florida Public Services Commission (FPSC) Determination of Need Hearing, Hanrahan testified that "the additional costs that would be incurred as a result of this project (GREC PPA) are not considered a debt of GRU since the proposed GREC project is structured as a purchased power contract with no obligations to GRU in the event the power is not produced." Consider the gravity of the statement Hanrahan had made under oath. In front of the government authority delivering a determination as to whether the biomass plant would be allowed to move forward, Hanrahan had boldly asserted that the GREC PPA would not be considered debt. Doubling down on her assertion, just like she had forced GRU to do with its debt, she also claimed that there'd be no obligation if no power were produced. If this had been the *Gong Show*, Hanrahan would have been escorted off stage.

Hanrahan testified before the FPSC that "the perception of credit rating agencies is that the excess contracted power is very marketable and would easily be sold." *What? Which contracts and when?* I know from my extensive work with the bond rating agencies that they are extremely unlikely to opine on the marketability of individual contracts, particularly when no counterparty has been identified.

Hanrahan also said, "The credit agencies expressed concerns about GRU's reliance on fossil fuels with regard to carbon regulations."

I saw Hanrahan's assertions about the bond rating agencies as exaggerations. If these agencies had made such a statement, my experience assured me that comment was placed under a smaller contingent category of risk. The power industry had been faced with impending carbon tax legislation for over thirty years, with no action yet to be taken.

More falsehoods flowed when in a March 16, 2011, editorial in The *Gainesville Sun*, Hanrahan told the community: "In fact, the entire contract was negotiated by GRU staff and reviewed by elected officials. We only pay for the energy generated. The financial interests of ratepayers and our city were represented aggressively throughout." Once again, Hanrahan had misinformed people of the authentic manner in which the GREC PPA operated—GRU paid dearly for both energy and the capacity provided.

The Navigant Report put the very foundation of Hanrahan's arguments to rest, making her declarations appear to be the fake news of the day. She may have been ill-informed, unable to comprehend, distracted, or any number of things. One thing was certain, if the interests of the ratepayers and the city had been as aggressively pursued as Hanrahan declared, the Navigant Report failed to uncover that pursuit.

Years later, when I confronted Hanrahan with her statements that GRU would only pay for the energy generated, she took the opportunity to tell me: "Whether they ran the plant or not is a very interesting phrase. Contrary to what I believe that statement implies, the decision as to whether to run the plant was in the hands of GRU, not the hands of GREC." *Huh?* Hanrahan's bewildering explanation was reminiscent of President Clinton's response to a reporter asking a question during his impeachment trial: "It depends on what your definition of is, is." The bottom line for me was I had never seen a contract written in such a one-sided manner with so little understanding of its consequences from its governing board.

Despite what GRU's chairman of the board said, it was a fact that GRU would be responsible for 74 million dollars of Available Energy payments, whether GREC generated the energy or not, along with payment for the energy produced. It was also true that the GREC PPA would be classified as debt on GRU's books and viewed as a debt by the rating agencies.

I was astonished by the magnitude of Hanrahan's unchecked assertions, particularly ones that came under oath. That surprise disappeared when I came to realize that Hanrahan was more than the city's first two-term mayor. She had methodically built a cult of personality in Gainesville. She was the absolute leader of this blue island's progressive activism.

I witnessed the power of Hanrahan on the night of December 7th, when I was prosecuted by three of her mentees, the three musketeers—the next generation of Hanrahan's army built to maintain power over politics in Gainesville. To avoid termination, I would have to withstand the pressures they would lever against me. I would need to cautiously lead the utility while "counting noses," as Mayor Poe had said. I didn't mind counting noses. It was the idea of *cautiously* leading that seemed untenable.

Hanrahan's legacy is quite remarkable. She had led a commission that approved the ultimate quadrupling of GRU indebtedness from approximately 450 million dollars to almost 1.8 billion dollars when the GREC PPA was rightfully recorded on GRU's books as a capital lease. No other comparable municipal utility in the state had experienced close to that level of astronomic growth in their debt during the same period. When Hanrahan took office, GRU had some of the lowest electric rates in the state. During her two terms, GRU's rates for its electric customers increased dramatically. In fact, it was Hanrahan's environmental focus that set the match under GRU's skyrocketing electric rates. When I came on board, those rates were projected to drive bills for residential customers over 50% higher than the state's average!

The financial obligations of the GREC PPA had virtually broken the finances of GRU's electric system. The remaining minimum payments under the GREC PPA were estimated at over 2.2 billion dollars, even if GREC never produced another electron of electricity. For whatever power GREC did produce, GRU paid them another above-market-priced energy charge. What small to mid-sized electric utility could absorb that level of costs just to have a power plant ready to generate electricity?

Even worse, the mechanics of the GREC PPA had placed GRU's electric system at additional risk as well. The introduction of the biomass plant and its conditions of operation under the GREC PPA changed GRU's entire fleet operating conditions. GRU's inability to shut down the biomass plant forced GRU's assets, like the Kelly gas plant and Deerhaven coal plant, to ramp up and down, causing expansive thermal cycling (rapid heating and cooling of equipment and refractory). The imposition of the GREC PPA battered and bruised our older plants creating metal fatigue and wear beyond their years.

Even with all the information to the contrary, on December 19, 2013 (ironically on the same day the Solar FIT application process was finally suspended), an out-of-office Hanrahan arose like the Phoenix and proclaimed, "I do believe that over the long course of time, these both (meaning the Solar FIT and GREC PPA) will turn out to be good public policies and ultimately good financial decisions, as well."

It was as though she had read Winston Churchill's personal notes to General Montgomery: "Never give in, never give in, never, never, never, never, never—in nothing great or small, large, or petty—never give in, except to convictions of honor and good sense. Never yield to force, never yield to apparently overwhelming might of the enemy."

It goes without saying that I've never confused Hanrahan with Churchill. For me, a better analogy was the Wizard of Oz operating the controls behind the Emerald City. To this day, I laugh aloud thinking of Hanrahan as the Wizard in the scene where he implores Dorothy: "Pay no attention to the man behind the curtain." Unafraid, Dorothy's dog Toto opens that green curtain only to find a man operating the controls for the Kingdom of Oz.

Hanrahan was the all-omnipotent Wizard of Gainesville, governing the utility and the rest of the kingdom behind her grand green energy curtain. That is until I came to town as Toto and doggedly pulled back the curtain on the GREC PPA, the Solar FIT, and the Depot Park costs. *Indeed.*

Even with all this baggage, Hanrahan would repeatedly seek to have the last word with me. In one exchange, she expressed her feelings about my statement that the GREC PPA failed to pass the sniff test. As if she was threatening me, Hanrahan wrote: "As long as you go around publicly bad-mouthing your predecessors, though, you are building unnecessary enemies both inside and outside GRU. Those people, in some cases, gave their entire careers to GRU. I gave twelve years of my life to the city. Your unnecessary personal criticism is not kind."

I have always been surprised when people attack others for simply pointing out the truth. I find nothing unkind about expressing the truth when the truth is under attack. My comment that "the contract simply didn't pass the sniff test" was a long overdue acknowledgement that the GREC PPA had been negotiated, amended, and operated in ways that, circumstance after circumstance which, benefited GREC, not the city. I hadn't burdened the utility and its customers with thirty years of excessive payments. It was my job to speak the truth about the GREC PPA to a community searching for answers. Speaking truth to power, they call it. It would become a pervasive theme during my career.

Ω

GRU Wasn't My First Rodeo

My proclamation to the people of Gainesville that the contract didn't pass the sniff test wasn't hyperbole. It wasn't political posturing. It was an unvarnished judgement, largely based on my over twenty years of experience managing a marvelous little power project named Panther Creek Partners, which I simply refer to as Panther. The level of knowledge I had gained in my wild and woolly journey in the then-new world of power generation, power politics, and power plays was the reason I knew that I could do the job in Gainesville.

My journey began on an October morning in 1992 as I ascended interstate route 81 into the foothills of the Pennsylvania coal region. Driving along in my blue Volvo 240 station wagon, the iconic yuppie-mobile distinguished itself from the American-made cars and trucks that filled the freeway around me. It was easy to recognize that this region of the world was quintessential blue-collar America, where people bought American and bled red, white, and blue. Of course, I already knew that. This was the land where my family settled when they came to America.

It was to be my first day on the job of a new breed of power plant, a waste coal-fired, small power production facility. My arrival was one week later than anticipated. An unfortunate encounter with an unidentified flying object delayed my arrival. While playing one last round of golf with a buddy, another golfer's errant drive off the tee smacked me squarely in the face. Luckily, I had chosen glasses over contacts for the morning round. The frames cushioned the blow of the dimpled Titleist as it struck me just below the eye. As startling as it was for me, my playing partner, Jack Winter, was visibly shaken when he saw the blood streaming down my face. Jack was an older gentleman and a heart attack survivor. I was scared he'd have another.

Thankfully, when the bleeding stopped and I could talk again, Jack began to recover. A pinkish color returned to his face when he looked at me and said, "Are you okay?"

I responded with, "I think so."

Jack responded in his typical deadpanned way, "Good, because I think they want to play through." I laughed aloud at the memory.

Alone with my thoughts on my three-hour drive, I contemplated this new world of energy generation. These new waste coal-fired, small power production facilities would not have been built without the efforts of the Carter Administration in response to the 1973 oil embargo crisis. The embargo's crippling impact on the nation's infrastructure had delivered a historic wake-up call to the country's leaders. President Carter responded quickly to the crisis, working with Congress to develop legislative policy to sustain the nation's economic vitality during a period of energy resource scarcity and volatile pricing. In 1978, Congressional action resulted in the National Energy Act (NEA) being passed into law. Comprised of five separate statutes, the NEA's most impactful and, in many ways, controversial statute was the Public Utility Regulatory Policies Act (PURPA).

Little known to the public, the new PURPA statute could easily be argued to be the first federal legislative movement away from the traditional regulated utility monopoly model built on the monopoly power of a regulated utility to decide when, where, and why to develop and construct its generation sites. In the past, these utilities had been regulated by individual state public service commissions who granted site selection and rate increases that they alone deemed reasonable.

PURPA forever changed this traditional regulated utility model by establishing a new type of power generation facility that, as the Federal Energy Regulatory Commission (FERC) wrote, would receive special rates and regulatory treatment. The broad class of these generating facilities would be called non-utility generators, or NUGs. They were more commonly referred to as qualifying facilities, or QFs. Under PURPA, regulated utilities were mandated by law to acquire and pay for all types of alternative power generation, including, but not limited to, renewable energy, cogeneration energy sources, and combined heat and power applications. While the PURPA statute has its detractors, the country was better off with a path for smaller, more entrepreneurial energy companies developing energy alternatives which could be brought to market, financed, and constructed. This was Panther's power plant lineage, borne out if this PURPA statute and classified and operated as a QF.

In the late 1980s and early 1990s, companies teamed up to start investing in these small power production facilities, or QFs. The evidence of PURPA's success became more evident the further I drove. One by one, off in the valleys, I caught sight of these QFs, which I came to call PURPA Plants, as they literally filled the Pennsylvania coal region's landscape.

***

Almost six years prior to my start at Panther, another young man had discovered the significance of the PURPA statute and the type of power projects which fit under its regulatory umbrella. In 1986, that young man, Jim Gordon, founded Energy Management Inc. (EMI), which would develop, construct, and operate a 15-megawatt wood-chip powered power plant in his own backyard, Alexandria, New Hampshire.

In 1986, while in my early thirties, I started two corner grocery stores, doing business in the Middle River and Chase sections of Baltimore, where my dad would work after he retired. While the business didn't generate a fortune, it elevated my wealth to another level. Interestingly, Gordon's dad owned two corner grocery stores, as well, in the Allston-Brighton section of

Boston, where Gordon would work after school and on weekends. Our experiences in these stores would be foundational to our lives.

It was written that Gordon understood: "The little stores were open 365 days a year, from 7 A.M. until midnight. Working there, Gordon learned that people who ran their own businesses did not work eight-hour days, did not take vacations, and did not have much leisure. They worked hard and unpredictable hours, but they did have the opportunity to manage their own lives." Ultimately, Gordon decided: "Like his father before him, he wanted to start his own business."

By the time I arrived in Gainesville, Gordon had already made a fortune as an owner/developer of power plants. I simply made a living. Don't get me wrong, we weren't exactly the Rich man, Poor man of the energy industry. To be fair, I earned a handsome salary and annual bonuses, but it was Gordon who became rich—exceedingly rich. I like to think of the impending future battle between us more like white collar man, blue-collar man.

***

Traveling along my own yellow brick road, I couldn't help but notice the businesses created to serve these new power plants. I admired the abundance of industrial buildings with large conveyor belts processing waste coal products to be blended into higher-grade fuel. Seemingly, just off each exit, there were trucks hauling waste coal products in and around little towns that housed the industry's workers. I glanced at the signs along the road naming these various towns, Pine Grove, Mt. Carmel, Girardville (pronounced jarred vill), Ashland, Pottsville, finally my exit for route 54 towards Mahoney City.

The beauty of the new power plants was how they used discarded by-products of a half-century of anthracite coal mining to generate electricity. Rocks, lower-BTU material, and other non-commercial products that had been piled on abandoned land and mine-sites, left to leach heavy metals into the ground water and aquifers were granted new life as an energy source. The power plants also restored thousands of acres of land and cleaned miles upon miles of streams.

***

The drive was quite familiar to me as I recalled taking the same route when my father took my mother and I to visit aunts, uncles, and cousins in and around his hometown of Ashland. Dad was the youngest boy among nine siblings, and all the boys worked in the coal business at some time in their lives. Dad was the smallest of the Bielarski boys at 6-foot one-inch tall while weighing in at two bowling balls over two hundred pounds. Standing in the opposing corner, his older brothers were 2 to 3 inches taller while weighing up to a small rack of bowling balls heavier than the 200-pound benchmark. As one of my cousins, Wendy would later tell me, "The Bielarski men were some sturdy Polskas."

Dad had lost his father to a stroke when Dad was still a young man. Hauntingly, he'd tell me the story of his brothers carrying their dying father up the stairs to his bedroom only to wait for hours for the local doctor to make a house call. In that place and time, there was no nearby hospital, no ambulance service, just an overwhelmed family physician who, upon arrival, could only pronounce their husband and father dead.

Life got in the way of my dad's dreams of finishing high school. He needed to work to support the family. With jobs in short supply, he really didn't have any choice but to work under back-breaking conditions with his brothers in renegade coal mining operations (known as bootleg mines). His circumstances weren't unusual for other boys in the region. Life was harsh. Given the circumstances, Dad never really had a chance to enjoy his youth. Work became a dominant part of his life. There was always a chore or project to complete. As his only child, I suspect Dad found working together was his way of enjoying life with me.

Despite all the pain and sorrow he had endured as a young man, ever the eternal optimist, Dad had fond memories of those challenging times. He'd make me laugh at stories about hauling coal from the coal hole (slang term for a small coal mine) down a narrow, twisting mountain road as he jammed on the brakes. Some of the trucks had wooden wheels and brakes. He'd tell me, "You laugh now, I was praying then. The trick was to make sure those wooden wheels didn't have termites."

My father's older brother, Amil, was the leader of this band of Bielarski brothers, setting up the mining business, making deals, and managing the brothers who hadn't already left to work in the big city, most called Philly. In many ways, Amil became a father to his younger brothers, including my dad. Amil's bootleg mining operations bordered on the town of Centralia, which became infamous for a massive underground coal fire. As reported by the local newspaper, the Press-Enterprise, in 1988: "He (Amil) was chased out of his bootleg mine operation on Buck Mountain by an approaching underground mine fire in 1969." The fire broke out in 1969, and all told, after burning for almost 60 years, hundreds of acres were abandoned as the fire opened expansive caverns under the earth. The valuable seams of coal have gradually disappeared as they slowly smoldered away in the "underground furnace." Amil predicted it would eventually reach Route 54 before it burnt itself out. Over a decade later, he would be proven right.

By the time Amil passed away in the spring of 2007, the underground fire was still burning. After attending his funeral, Melinda, Dad, and I visited the scene where the massive underground fire still smoldered. Getting out of the car in the mist of the late morning, you could smell the sulfur in the air and feel the heat beneath your feet. Kids had spray-painted graffiti all over the road as though it was a long skate-board park. The roads and town itself had long been abandoned by its residents. The steam continued to rise out of vent pipes and the fissures in the ground. It was an amazing spectacle.

In a book about his recollections about the coal region, a distance cousin of mine, Harry Bobonich, a retired Pennsylvania State professor and Ph.D., wrote: "Ironically, the anthracite coal, which was the reason for Centralia's birth is now the cause of its death." In Pennsylvania's coal region, there was always a thin edge between life and death, and neither side was ever far from sight. People lived hard and unfortunately, many died hard as well.

Bobonich re-tells an old story about how the first Roman Catholic priest in Centralia, Father Ignatius McDermott, denounced the Molly Maguires from his pulpit in 1869. The Molly Maguires were a secret Irish society that came to prominence in America as they fought for coal workers' rights in Pennsylvania. Bobonich wrote that "the angered Mollies, known for getting even with those who oppose them, gave the priest the beating of his life for his comments against them." Afterwards, "Father McDermott called his congregation together and told them that this day forward would be the curse on the community of Centralia—condemning it to destruction."

***

As I passed through the small town of Barnesville, I recognized a sprawling landscape through my driver's side window - the once famous Lakewood Park. During his formative years, Dad spent weekends at the park helping his mom sell her homemade foods at the family concession stand. He told me that when the customer traffic slowed down, he'd sneak off to swim in the lake, leaving his father to mind the store. Behind that small stand, his father discreetly peddled homemade moonshine. Some nights, he imbibed too much of his own product, and Dad was recruited to get behind the wheel, at far too young an age, to drive the family home.

In its heyday, after the Depression and World War II, Lakewood Park housed popular venues in its beautiful Ballroom. The massive Ballroom brought celebrated acts to the region, such as jazz legend Louie Armstrong, bandleaders Tommy and Jimmy Dorsey, and Dick Clark. Promotors also celebrated the ethnic groups that built King Coal (the name afforded the coal industry respecting its significance to people's lives) with Bavarian Summer Festivals, Lithuanian Day, as well as festivals for the Poles and the Welch.

Lakewood Park expanded in the late '40s to include a playhouse where Lana Turner, Dorothy Lamour, and Veronica Lake performed. Sadly, on this day in 1992, Lakewood Park was past its prime. It had been reduced to a shell of its former glory, left to promote smaller venues such as local boxing bouts and small community events. I couldn't help but think about the parallels between King Coal's future and Lakewood's past.

As I passed through a crossroads in Hometown, I looked up to catch my first sight of the massive stacks of Panther in the distance. I felt as though the newly built 80-megawatt Panther Creek Energy Facility was guiding me like a beacon. I laughed when, in the same instant, just out of the corner of my

76

eye, I saw a diner by the side of the road named The Beacon Diner. Certainly, built long before the power plant, I was impressed with the restaurant owner's prognostication abilities.

Pulling onto Industrial Road, I held the plant fully in my sights. I sensed the strength and power of the hulking giant of a facility looming over the valley. The area's natural landscape was hidden by sprawling piles of prepared waste coal products fresh off the preparation plant's decks. Several oversized bulldozers were groaning as they pushed the product into even higher piles by the fuel lay-down area. I could feel a symmetry to it all. I felt a twinge of pride as I thought about taking a virtual handoff from my uncles. I could only imagine my Uncle Teddy, Amil, and my dad extracting those black diamonds out from the coal holes in which they labored.

I envisioned Panther correcting some of the environmental sins of the past. Panther was the first generation of clean-coal technology, which would reclaim thousands upon thousands of abandoned mine lands, clean up rivers and streams, and turn waste coal products into energy. I was proud that Panther would be the place where I started my power industry career. It was the type of pride that Gordon must have felt when he talked about his potential victory on the Cape Wind project. Talking to a reporter, he said, "For me, the victory celebration will be walking on the beach that my dad used to take me and looking out and hoping that it's a clear day, so I can see it in the first place." The way Gordon painted a picture with his words, I knew that Gordon had a deep emotional connection to his past and a reverence for the father who helped to get him to his future.

Panther's very existence was borne out of the successful negotiations of another crafty developer, not named Jim Gordon, with a regulated utility, Metropolitan Edison (MetEd), a wholly owned subsidiary of GPU Energy, which would extend for twenty years. In my Panther journey, ironically, I sat in a seat as the beneficiary of an above-market PPA, not unlike Jim Gordan's PPA with GRU.

The world I was about to enter was a world apart from my previous work experience. Panther was more of a project, not a business, and it revolved around a convoluted network of owner participants, subordinated participants, equity owners, and other legal entities. It had been established as a special-purpose entity for the sole purpose of developing, owning, and operating the Panther Creek Energy Facility. Being a special-purpose entity provided the underlying partners with a legal separation between the project and its creditors in the event of a business failure. While the two partners of Panther Creek Partners were, in fact, Fortune 500 energy-company Constellation Energy Group (Constellation) and worldwide boiler manufacturer A. Ahlstrom Corporation (Ahlstrom), which was headquartered out of Finland, their assets were protected behind a host of unrecognizable limited partnerships, indirect subsidiaries, and limited liability corporations, further below the ladder.

The project team nor I were even employed by Panther. Rather, we were either employees of Constellation or Ahlstrom, whose financial stature afforded us better pay and benefits than what an obscure special-purpose entity might provide. Both Constellation and Ahlstrom would assign employees to the project, in practice known as seconding employees, and bill the project for their services. It was an unusual relationship and organizational structure. In certain ways, it fostered a sense that everyone on the project was a consultant. I share this information because the project-based organizational structure of Panther laid the foundation for how everyone would approach their jobs. It would also provide me with valuable insight into how GREC's organization was built. *A hint: GREC's structure was built the same way.*

In a world where things weren't always as they appeared, I soon discovered that the Panther Creek Energy Facility was somewhat of an illusion as well. It wasn't really located on

Panther Creek or in Panther Valley. Due to a contractual dispute with the original landowner, the plant site was relocated from the Panther Valley to the Nesquehoning Valley on land along Nesquehoning Creek—land owned by Sonny Kovatch. The contractual dispute proved to be my good fortune because Sonny, as the locals knew him, was a larger-than-life figure in the community.

***

As a young man, Sonny had started a small, one-bay car repair shop in town and grew it organically, year after year. To Sonny's great fortune, in 1985, in nearby Macungie (a town Regis Philbin jokingly said sounded like a disease during a broadcast of Regis and Kathy Lee), international truck manufacturer, Mack Trucks, decided to end its production of fire truck bodies during the midst of a poor economic climate. Ever the opportunist, Sonny acquired Mack's business and relocated its operations to Nesquehoning. Sonny built his new company, Kovatch Mobile Equipment (KME), into the largest family-owned fire truck manufacturer in the world. The jobs he brought to this small, former mining town made him a savior and local legend.

Sonny understood that land never went out of style. He purchased a lakeside community known as Hauto Valley Estates in 1963, and he added another eight hundred acres of land along Broad Mountain less than 5 years later. Before the Panther Creek Energy Facility was constructed, he had acquired approximately another 4,000 acres along Broad Mountain and the Nesquehoning Valley. That land included abandoned waste coal sites from which the Panther Creek Energy Facility would produce its fuel, along with the site for the plant itself. Sonny was truly a visionary and played the long game. A trait not unlike the other lords of King Coal country.

These lords were tough, hard-nosed businessmen right out of America's Iron Age, not far removed from the Molly Maguire era. One of those owners, John Rich, the head of Reading Anthracite, was described by locals as a guy who believed the signing of the contract was the start of negotiations. Legend had it that any number of his deals were completed on the courthouse steps. Another tough businessperson, Chuck Parente, the president of Pagnotti Enterprises, was a CPA, who started one of the largest privately-owned accounting firms on the east coast, Parente Randolph CPA's. He was also an owner, investor, operator, and board member for broadcast television stations, construction, and real estate organizations, as well as banks and insurance underwriters. Even among those men, Sonny stood tall as one of the toughest negotiators I would ever meet.

Sonny's financial fortune blasted off when he executed a twenty-year lease with Panther for the site and its fuel. Earning over two million dollars a year with 6% annual escalation clauses would have satisfied most businesspeople. Not Sonny. Sonny's good fortune didn't stop him from initiating head-to-head battles over virtually every aspect of the power plant's operations and every minute detail under our lease agreement. He'd take his wife on Sunday drives in an old Dodge pickup truck—to ensure we were remediating his site to the proper contours. He demanded that the roads be built to his standards on the site in anticipation of some unknown future use. Above all, he wanted a level site. "Like a pool table," he would say. There was no detail too small for Sonny.

No one else on the project team knew of Sonny's plans, so in jest, they'd say Sonny was going to end up building a housing development known as "Ash-hole Acres." Sonny would be in ear shot for the wisecracking. He'd peer over his out-of-style, oversized glasses and reply, "Bah." I knew he was thinking, "I'll get the last laugh."

I recall a meeting in Sonny's corporate conference center in front of dozens of his executives. In response to my unresponsiveness, Sonny pounded the table telling me that I just didn't understand my obligations under the lease. Sonny bellowed, "You are not fulfilling your obligations, Ed!" I calmly looked at Sonny and quietly replied, "Sonny, no matter how many times you tell me, it doesn't make it true." I had found that tough negotiators used this technique often—repeating falsehoods over and over until the argument was simply accepted.

There was no doubt Sonny was a visionary, an entrepreneur, and a skillful businessman. He also happened to be a real bully. Luckily, my dad had taught me that the only way to deal with a bully was to punch him in the nose. Not literally, of course. Every now and then, Sonny and I would get into a battle, and I'd have to, figuratively, punch him in the nose. I came to believe Sonny respected me for standing up to him. Respect doesn't mean agreement. In fact, in some cases, respect means one should disagree. Truth matters. In his future airing of grievances, he changed his approach and softened his language. Sometimes, rather than argue with me against his better judgement, he'd just delegate by saying, "I know you're not going to agree with me, so let's have your engineer talk to my engineer and keep us out of it."

Sonny passed away shortly before my Panther career had ended, but I will always remember him for the complex character he was. He was a flawed man prone to pressure anyone that stood in his way as he tried to get his way. On the flip side, he'd also donate hundreds of acres to the community and worked tirelessly to attract businesses to better serve the community.

Before his death, Sonny made clever use of Panther's reclamation work on the abandoned waste coal site that he and his wife would inspect every weekend. He built a solar park on the land, one of the largest in the state. In the end, Sonny had been the impetus for converting the devastating remnants of coal mining into a solar park that produced clean energy. He brought good paying jobs to the coal region and improved the community's standard of living. Unlike Hanrahan, Sonny left a proud legacy of green energy and *economic sustainability.*

***

My love affair with the power industry started while at Panther. I discovered that most power company employees, whether working for investor-owned or municipal utilities, were driven to do the right thing. They were solid, disciplined workers. The industry's mission was clear: deliver, supply, or produce safe, reliable, and competitively priced power to those who demand it. I enjoyed being involved in providing an essential service. I was also fond of the fact that the electrons we produced were the same between one generation facility and another. In many ways, the goal wasn't about producing a better electron but making the best use of the resources you had. There was something inherently admirable about that concept.

I came to recognize that I was a different breed of power industry employee. I liked that I was wired differently than most of the people in the industry. I observed that many power industry careers were built on earning an engineering degree, working in the plant, and understanding mechanics, but not finance or economics.

I was also an entrepreneur, built to seek opportunities, arbitrage, and evaluate risk. I absorbed the experience like a sponge, soaking up every nuance, every opportunity to learn more about the industry. That made me a valuable commodity. Armed with an entrepreneurial skill set made me unique in an industry that had been insulated from change far too long. My skillset fits well with the PURPA world, where every project was a considerable risk. Even if a PURPA Plant could negotiate a favorable PPA, like Panther had done, the financial fragility of these projects made traditional financing difficult and risky. One's career could quickly become a short-term proposition.

The Panther experience is the reason I could laugh when Pegeen Hanrahan told me later, "It's clear that you think you know way more about PPAs than anyone else who's ever been involved, and I have no basis from which to dispute that." *Sorry Pegeen, but I earned it.*

From the moment Panther began operations, the project team understood that acquiring fuel supplies from the mine sites around the region would be a major challenge. Developers had assumed that mine owners would welcome these QFs using up this burdensome byproduct. They projected the waste coal would be free, with the only added cost being transportation and handling. Wrong! Since, technically, there wasn't a market for waste coal, the systematic construction of these QFs built a new expanding market – one in which mine owners used to their advantage.

Unfortunately, Panther had no choice but to deal with these mine owners. We didn't have access to high BTU value, expensive anthracite coal, known as black diamonds, used in other industrial processes. The project was restricted to the *spoils* of past mining operations. Our fuel supply would have to come from disparate abandoned mine sites, silt ponds, and culm piles (name of anthracite waste coal piles). Even the culm banks that we leased from Sonny were simply waste material, and as we soon discovered, not as much as we thought.

***

A high-level engineering report had alerted Panther's project team of a substantial shortfall in the useful life of our anticipated sources of waste coal, most particularly the Kovatch waste coal banks. Aware of the financial implications, we were obligated to tell our partners and investors the unwelcome news. We were less than a month away from closing on the sale-leaseback. Hell, we had already begun commercial operations of the plant. An all-hands-on meeting was needed, soon.

Sonny was more than happy to accommodate us with his conference room to house such an important meeting on this winter's day. After all, he'd garner a ring side seat on the action. Never mind that it was Sonny's own culm banks that were partially the cause of our crisis.

As the morning sun melted the dew off the culm banks, one by one, owner representatives from Constellation and Ahlstrom filed in, grabbing coffee and a tasty item off the breakfast buffet. Partner representatives had flown in from San Diego, Baltimore, and elsewhere to see how their investment had hit a snag. The morning meeting was also being attended by a fuel consulting group that the project team had recently retained, Miltech Energy Services, founded by Frank Miller and operated along with his son Brian Miller. Frank was a product of the Bethlehem Steel organization, for which he had traveled the world. For all his experience, Frank was still a no-frills, "get-r-done" kind of guy.

Frank had come on-site to take a closer look at the fuel operations for us. He didn't like what he saw. On one occasion, Frank tried to determine why one of our equipment suppliers had so many vehicles in disrepair or inoperable. He was getting steamed as he talked with the operator's principal owner, Nino Logan, on the telephone. Frank yelled at Logan, telling him to

83

get the vehicles we needed, or he'd replace him. Logan replied, "Who the fuck are you?"

Frank yelled back, "Me? I'm fucking Frank Miller, that's who. Who the fuck are you?" Needless to say, Logan's services were halted in short order and replaced with other firms.

Frank's exchange with Logan wasn't lost on me. It was a textbook example of how an independent contractor can conduct work in a way that employees and managers cannot. With Frank's success, Miltech Energy Services would go on to restructure and reorganize the way Panther acquired its fuel and how it would operate the fuel sites. This philosophy would be a template for the one I envisioned using at GRU.

Everyone in Sonny's conference room was braced to hear the bad news. Trying to break the tension, Brian started the conversation with a joke as old as the hills. He started, "A gentleman is returning home after a long trip and is met by his servant at the train station. They had a conversation on the way back home. The gentleman asks, 'so has anything happened while I've been away?' The servant replies, 'No, sir, I can't think of anything at all worth mentioning.' The gentleman replies, 'come on, I've been away for weeks. Surely something must have happened.'" By this time, the gathered group is waking up from the caffeine.

Brian continued, "The servant replies, 'Well sir, come to think of it, your dog died.' The gentleman gasps, 'My dog died. How awful! Still, he was getting on in years, and I suppose it had to happen at some time. How did he die?' The servant hesitates and says, 'The vet says it was from the rotten meat.' Surprised, the gentleman asks, 'The rotten meat? Since when do we have rotten meat lying around?'"

The group starts to listen more intently. Brian trudged along further, "The servant says, 'Well, it was the horses, sir. They'd been rotting for some time after the barn burned down.' Aghast, the gentleman answers, 'Good heavens. How in the world did the barn burn down?' The servant calmly says,

'It must have been from the embers that blew over from the house, sir.'"

The audience started to chuckle as they anticipated the ending. Brian continues with his story, "The gentleman crushed, asks, 'The house? How did the house burn down?' The servant responds with another calm answer, 'Well, sir, we think someone must have blown the candle over.' Perplexed the gentleman says, 'Wait a minute. We don't use candles to light the house.' The servant replies, 'They were there for the wake, sir.'"

Now Brian has everyone's attention. He says, "The gentleman cries, 'The wake? What wake?' The servant says, 'Your mother's sir. She passed away quite suddenly.' Almost in tears, the gentleman mutters, 'Oh, my Lord. Mother is dead. The house is gone, along with the stable. Even my dog is dead. What did mother die of?' The servant slowly states, 'It must have been the shock, sir,' to which the gentleman says, 'Shock?' The servant ends the tale of woe with, 'Yes, sir, when your wife ran off with the handyman the day after you left, sir. But aside from all that, it's been fairly quiet while you've been away, sir.'"

As the bigwigs were laughing, Brian looked at them and said, "I'm here to tell you that your dog has died." The laughing soon ended. Brian's point was well taken. For years, even decades after that moment, the Millers and others associated with Panther would talk about the day they learned the dog died.

***

While Panther was long on characters, there was no shortage of challenges. As we focused on the fluidity of fuel supplies and the plant's mechanical break-in period, the higher costs of our PPA had not gone unnoticed by Met-Ed. Along with several other regulated utilities, Met-Ed responded with a rather clandestine program dubbed "MUG-a-NUG" - Panther and other NUGs were subjected to strict enforcement of the more stringent provisions of their PPAs. This was the program

Ray Washington had been so curious to understand when we met in the GM Meet and Greet.

Panther's PPA and that of other NUGs didn't arm regulated utilities with economic dispatch capability, meaning they couldn't take NUGs offline just because their power wasn't economical. NUGs could only be taken offline for system emergencies, so, in most events, Met-Ed would inform our control room of such a system emergency, sometimes called a Minimum Generation Emergency (Min-Gen). We suspected that "MUG-a-NUG" actions were meant to be an attempt to run NUGs under economic dispatch provisions— a clear overreach by MetEd in their interpretation of the contract. An overreach predicated on Met-Eds expectation that Panther didn't have the resources to wage an expensive and protracted legal action.

Thankfully, the "MUG-a-NUG" program withered on the proverbial vine as Panther and other NUGs pushed back against the predatory Min-Gen practices, demanding evidence to support these Min-Gens and shutdown demands. The secretive program disappeared almost entirely when in 1996, the Commonwealth of Pennsylvania enacted the Electricity Generation Customer Choice and Competition Act (Choice Act), providing for a fundamental restructuring of retail electric services. "MUG-a-NUG" was effectively replaced with a mug and an electric customer.

**

Soon after my experiences working through "MUG-a-NUG," I would face a business challenge from a rather unlikely source—William Dimeling. Dimeling was a Keystone State original. No stranger to controversy and politics, his antics caught the attention of a *Philadelphia Inquirer* reporter, Joseph DiStefano, who wrote about him in a 2003 article entitled "An Investment Joyride."

DiStefano tells us that Dimeling "descended from rail, mine and lumber barons, wagon-train pioneers, and Civil War financiers, Governor Bill "the Raftsman" Bigler, and other giants of Pennsylvania's vanishing industrial frontier." However, now he "lived in less heroic times." A larger-than-life figure, Dimeling had grown up in western Pennsylvania, in a town named Clearfield, where "the tallest building in town was the Dimeling Hotel, the boroughs up the valley were named for his great-grandfathers, and Dimeling grew up with the confidence that comes from being part of the hometown elite." Dimeling "was the class for whom school ties and the whiff of former fortunes could still open doors to prosperous careers as investment bankers and corporate lawyers in the big cities east of the mountains."

Dimeling was the antithesis of Ed Bielarski Jr, whose father hadn't completed high school. There were no Bielarski Buildings in Ashland, Pennsylvania, or anywhere for that matter.

Dimeling was the product of military boarding school (Culver Military Academy), Ivy League education (Yale), three years of active duty as a Lieutenant aboard Navy destroyers, and the University of Pennsylvania Law School. It seemed that he had it all. Ready to embark on a career with a prestigious Philadelphia Center City law firm, people's vision of having it all wasn't all Dimeling cared about. He gave it all up. "Bill wasn't going to work for any law firm,' said Dimeling best friend, Philadelphia lawyer David W. Marston. Instead, Dimeling in 1982 formed a Dickensian 19th-century throwback—an unincorporated general business partnership, Dimeling, Schreiber and Park (DSP), based in a restored Locust Street mansion in Philadelphia and engaged in the dicey business of buying, fixing, and selling bankrupt industrial companies across the United States."

One of DSP's acquisitions was a mining concern in Mount Carmel, Pennsylvania, which Panther had leased for $15,625 a quarter to potentially use the waste coal reserves. As part of the deal, Panther had a ten-year option to buy the property for $625,000.

As unlikely as the Dimeling connection to coal mining might seem, it was all part of his overall vision. That vision was described by DiStefano: "Over 20 years, Dimeling, Schreiber and Park raised a billion dollars from private investors, giant corporations such as General Electric and the Episcopal Church's pension fund and spent it like a merry band of Rust Belt opportunists. Dimeling trolled for troubled plywood mills and coal mines, railroad shops and aircraft assembly lines—the bankrupt inheritance of the Industrial Revolution, derelict places where Dimeling believed that, with relentless negotiation, other people's money, tax sheltering, and Philadelphia lawyering, he could find gold the less diligent had overlooked."

Dimeling had skillfully negotiated the contract with Panther. He made sure that the $625,000 option price was secured with an irrevocable letter of credit, meaning that if Panther were to default, Dimeling could take the letter of credit to any bank and redeem it for a check in the amount of $625,000—a provision that would prove to make Panther an easy mark for mischief.

Long after the contract was executed, I was notified by Panther's letter of credit bank issuer that Dimeling had cashed in the $625,000 letter of credit. They had no choice but to honor it within three days. It made no sense to me. I checked and saw that Panther was mere days late on its $15,625 payment but still within its cure period. Dimeling's action was clearly an illegal move. I immediately called Dimeling, who simply told me, "I warned you if you were late on my payment, I'd make you pay. Now you lost." The phone clicked silent. Wow, had I underestimated the tenacity of one, Bill Dimeling. He had just picked up $625,000 for a property Panther would probably never use, nor would he.

Not sitting still, the project's attorney sought the granting of an injunction. Within two days, we were in Center City Philadelphia, expecting to make a short order of the dispute. Our position: Dimeling had his quarterly rent of $15,625 in hand, and he should not be allowed to unjustly enrich himself by drawing on a $625,000 letter of credit redemption.

While in court, I kept in communication with the bank, knowing that a 4 o'clock deadline had been set for honoring the redemption. While the judge calmly listened to our plea, I could sense that Dimeling had some influence. The judge spoke to him on a first-name basis and was reluctant to hear our side of the dispute. After ten minutes, the judge instructed both parties to recess. "You ought to try to settle this yourselves," he said. With no rooms available, we convened in the crowded hallway of the courthouse. It was like a scene out of a television crime show. As we discussed rescinding the drawing on the letter of credit, Dimeling droned on about personal responsibilities. As I tried to engage in a meaningful dialogue with him, I noticed that Dimeling kept glancing at his watch. I came to realize the son-of-a-bitch was filibustering us. I grabbed the attorney by his arm and implored him to get in the court room. Dimeling just stood there smiling like a Cheshire cat.

By the time we were placed in front of the magistrate, the funds had been wired out of our account. There was no need to rule upon our injunction request. The issue was moot. As we left the courtroom, Dimeling smiled at me while I stewed with anger.

It wasn't until years later, in the months before his untimely death from, of all things, pancreatic cancer, that I learned the scope and depth of Dimeling's connections within state and national politics. As part of his resume, Dimeling had been appointed by former Secretary of Transportation Drew Lewis in the reorganization of the Reading Railroad and, later, served on the successor entity, Conrail's Board of Directors. He led efforts to create the Philadelphia Convention Center and the Reading Terminal Market.

Dimeling had also left hard feelings that lasted after his death. DiStefano wrote that "some of the people that he faced across the negotiating table—or the courtroom—still won't talk about him on the record." Anonymous quotes included: "He approached life with reckless abandon. I really don't think he himself knew what he was going to do next; he seemed bent on following the dollar, regardless of the casualties there might be along the way; Dimeling beat us in court. Of course, he beat us. He was extremely politically connected."

I had been ill-prepared and naïve in my fight with this politically connected business titan. No one had gotten the better of me in my career like Dimeling had. In a weird type of way, I appreciated that it was someone with Dimeling's style that had done so. *Note to self: Never allow myself to be unprepared again.*

I last talked to Dimeling late in 1999. Our conversational tone had totally changed. We talked about what had happened between us, and he shared the details of his medical treatments. He expressed hope. I told him that if anyone could beat it, it would be him. I couldn't be angry at him any longer. I remember hearing the courage in his voice but knew that it masked a deep fear of the unknown. Part of that unknown was his life. The other part was the lengthy list of business deals that he knew would begin to unravel upon his death.

On October 18, 2001, my old nemesis, William Dimeling, passed away quietly at his home in Chestnut Hill, an elite section of Philadelphia. On October 25, he was buried, which was the same day, albeit a different year, that Melinda had her life-saving pancreatic cancer surgery. It was amazing how the dates of major events in my life kept repeating themselves.

Years later, I thought about my relationship with Dimeling while I waited for Melinda to come out of surgery on that October 25, 2017, day. It scared me that this larger-than-life figure had gone up against pancreatic cancer and lost. He was healthy, then hopeful, after which he simply was gone. My experiences with Dimeling made Melinda's battle all too real.

Knowing that he was dying, DiStefano wrote that Dimeling planned his funeral with his wife. "His best friend David Marston would say of him, 'Bill Dimeling is either going to be mayor of Philadelphia or he's going to be hung as a horse thief. My problem is I don't know which.'" Dimeling apparently approved.

***

On January 1, 2000, I was elevated to the role of General Manager of Panther. Three hundred miles away in Boston, Jim Gordon was waiting for inspiration on what to do next with his career. His firm, EMI, had placed his remaining five power plants up for sale during the summer. He had achieved his goals, making the right moves at the right times. He was rewarded with a small fortune, which he used to purchase a 3-million-dollar home on Beacon Hill overlooking his old neighborhood and two $80,000 parking spaces. Not yet fifty years of age, some would call Gordon rich. Whatever he was, Gordon needed something to do. That something would be the Cape Wind deal and biomass power.

***

Life as the general manager of a waste coal-fired power plant had me engaged in high-level legislative and regulatory issues. While I served as the Vice President of the industry's trade association, the Anthracite Region's Independent Power Producers Association, or ARIPPA, I regularly met with Pennsylvania legislators. Their support was instrumental in the industry's fight against a growing environmental movement based on ending the long-standing practice of using coal ash as a soil supplement, known as the beneficial use of coal ash. It would be a life-or-death struggle for Panther and the other PURPA plants.

Beneficial-use of coal ash had been utilized by PURPA plants for over twenty years and had been one of their central, over-riding, environmentally friendly practices. The practice was simple and effective. The power plants would blend the coal ash produced from burning the waste coal in their boilers with reactive limestone. Hauled off the site in dump trucks, the beneficiary's ash was used as mine fill product to mitigate acid-mine runoff and the leeching of harmful toxins into the

91

aquifers and headwaters of the commonwealth. This successful practice was being jeopardized by a new EPA Administrator, Carol Browner, when in the spring of 2000, her agency issued proposed rules which would classify the coal ash product as hazardous waste. Instead of mitigating acid-mine runoff from abandoned mine sites, Browner would have the coal ash to be dumped in lined landfills. *What a waste!*

Pennsylvania State House Representative David Argall and I took our story to the media and pleaded our case. I informed the *Hazleton Standard-Speaker* that "if the EPA classifies coal-waste ash as a hazardous material, then our record of environmental accomplishment may end." That accomplishment "over the past eight years has prevented almost three billion gallons of drainage (acid mine drainage) containing 4,000 tons of sulfates, twenty tons of aluminum, and forty-eight tons of iron from reaching the Lehigh River watershed. This accomplishment has earned Panther Creek Partners recognition from the Wildlands Conservancy and Lehigh River Watch."

Working as a well-oiled machine, ARIPPA along with state and national officials lobbied Governor Tom Ridge, Pennsylvania's US House delegation, and US Senators Rick Santorum and Arlen Spector. The industry's story ultimately proved so compelling that the EPA stood down from its more onerous classification of our coal-ash as a hazardous material. Little did we know the fight was just beginning.

In early 2003, a scientist and Tamaqua resident, Dr. Dante Picciano, elevated the beneficial use of coal ash from the local stage to the national arena. Starting an organization under the name Army for a Clean Environment (ACE), Picciano waged a battle against the filling of a local coal pit, called the Springdale Pit, with a new mixture of coal ash, dust from cement and lime kilns, and river sediments dredged from the harbors and shipping lanes of Philadelphia, Baltimore, and New York.

This proposed new practice being considered by the Pennsylvania Department of Environmental Protection (PADEP) had not been tested as vigorously as the PURPA Plant's two-decades-old practice of the beneficial use of coal ash as mine fill material. It was the perfect storm under which Picciano could reuse tactics from a different era.

***

Picciano was one of the original environmental justice warriors of the late 1970s. While working for Biogenics Corporation, he had gained national attention for the study he co-authored with Dr. Paigen in which they observed chromosomal aberrations in residents living at Love Canal. The Love Canal community became a dump site for municipal waste from the City of Niagara Falls in the 1920s and its canal would be purchased by Hooker Chemical in the 1940s. For over a decade, Hooker Chemical used the canal to dispose of chemical byproducts.

After decades of allegations about the poor health outcomes for residents living in the community around the canal, Biogenics Corporation was engaged and Picciano and Paigen's study was undertaken. They concluded that eight people in a thirty-six-person study had a rare aberration called "supernumerary acentric fragments." The study and the events that followed at Love Canal led to Hooker Chemical being found liable for damages and resulted in the establishment of the Superfund site designations by the EPA. Picciano's work made him a legend of sorts.

***

In the current battle, Dante's Army employed misinformation, fear, and intimidation to blur the differences between beneficial use and the new, untested practice. They attacked legislators, businesspeople, and anyone critical of their mission. The anti-coal ash environmental cause gained momentum and resulted in some wide-spread media coverage. It was being reported not only by the *Times News of Tamaqua* but the *Associated Press.*

Michael Rubinkam, an *Associated Press* reporter, released an article, "Environmentalist Back Plan for Mine," in which he wrote: "A pit at the edge of town is at the center of a scientific and political debate over what to do with thousands of

93

abandoned strip mines that pock the Appalachian landscape, turning streams and rivers into orange-tinted dead zones and scenic areas into eyesores." Pulling at the reader's heart strings, the *AP* article ended with a resident saying, "The DEP and EPA are not here for us. They don't give a damn if we die here." The comments could not offer a more vivid display of how emotional the issue had become for some residents.

As with most legends, there was some fact and there was fiction embedded in the story of ACE's environmental hero. Further scrutiny, not by me but by others, reported to have discovered unsettling facts about Picciano's previous work. There were credible sources that claimed significant inconsistencies in Picciano's discovery of supernumerary acentric fragments at Love Canal. It seems that the scientific acceptance of the study's findings has diminished over time.

In one of my first efforts to change the public narrative, I wrote an editorial in the *Times News* entitled, "Picciano—white knight or someone with agenda?" In it, I cited Michael Brown, who wrote a follow-up piece to the controversy in the July 1989 issue of the *Atlantic Monthly*: "In 1980, a special panel headed by Dr. Lewis Thomas, then chancellor of the Memorial Sloan-Kettering Cancer Center, in New York City, and a best-selling author, described the report issued by Paigen in 1979, which claims to have found a multitude of disorders among the canal-area residents, as falling far short of the mark as an exercise in epidemiology, inasmuch as it relied on largely anecdotal information." Brown continued: "A follow-up chromosome study conducted for the US Department of Health and Human Services from December 1981 to February 1982 on 46 neighborhood residents—including 17 whom Picciano had tested—failed to confirm Picciano's claims of supernumerary aberrations."

If this wasn't enough, Brown reported Michael Bender, a senior scientist in the medical department at Brookhaven National Laboratory, as saying, "We should have known at the time he used the term supernumerary acentric fragments.

Several papers from the 1970s had noted similar phenomena. We just never had seen it put in those terms and, unfortunately, failed to recognize what we were dealing with, partly because we never got to see Picciano's material. If we had, I think we should have immediately known. Such aberrations are a natural phenomenon, which is seen particularly in females and increases with age. They appear in the form of extra X-chromosomes, which have no more known association with exposure to anything nasty. It's just something that happens as an odd spontaneous event."

Armed with this previously undisclosed information, I challenged Picciano stating: "For months, Dante Picciano and his army have personally attacked government officials and other private citizens concerning their veracity over the fly ash and river sludge issue. Day after day, people's credentials and intentions have been questioned, as though Dante and his army can only speak the truth, amen (see Army for a Clean Environment newsletter invoking biblical reference from Matthew 12:30). Now, when the lead questioner is asked to be brought out in the light of day, he responds that Love Canal has nothing to do with the current controversy and, in addition, invokes the fifth, as advised by his attorney."

Throwing down the gauntlet, I wrote: "Dante Picciano was at the heart of one of the nation's most controversial environmental battles with a scientific study. Now, out of nowhere, Dante Picciano places himself in the forefront of the fly ash/river sludge controversy. Is he a white knight, a concerned citizen, or a spokesman for an unnamed environmental group with a national agenda?" It was important to put Picciano on notice that I wasn't afraid of his threats or unsupportable claims. My decision to directly confront Dante's Army with facts would serve to turn the tide of public opinion. I wouldn't allow Sonny to spread falsehoods without rebuttals. I wouldn't allow Picciano to spread his own mistruths, either. That experience proved to be one of the most valuable leadership lessons I ever learned—don't ever allow false information to prevail. During the same time I was learning to speak the truth to agenda-driven icons, Jim Gordon was doing the same to his foes.

***

In October of 2002, the *National Public Radio* show, *The Connection* broadcast a debate between Bobby Kennedy, the son of former presidential candidate Robert F. Kennedy Jr, and Gordon. It was intended to be an hour-long gentlemen's discussion about Cape Wind. Kennedy turned out to be no gentleman.

The ordeal was memorialized in *Cape Wind*: "Jim Gordon was caught off-guard by the emotional onslaught. He had known Kennedy would be on the radio show, but he hadn't realized the show would be done in debate form. As he wondered how to respond to the barrage of statements made by Kennedy, he looked through the glass window separating the interview studio from the head-phoned producers. They, too, were shaking their heads in amazement."

Later, in a more private setting, Kennedy told Gordon's lawyer, Dennis Duffy, "Oh man, I can't believe you think you're going to do this. I learned to sail out there. You're going to have a fight every step of the way." And so, it would be for Gordon and me, as we prepared for our own battle.

The GREC debacle turns out, wasn't the first rodeo for either of us.

Ω

The Great Allentown Water Fight

In the fall of 2012, I left the rugged hills of Pennsylvania coal country as a turbulent, exciting, and beneficial chapter in my work life had concluded. Panther's project lease had ended, and its general partners had both been acquired by other companies. Neither of these two firms had any desire to buy the plant from its owners. The underlying PPA had also expired, leaving a 20-year-old plant with no sustainable economic engine to compete on the open market against newer combined-cycle natural gas plants. The owners reverted to scuttling operations, only dispatching it during high power demand periods.

With the knowledge that my Panther days were ending, I had been able to position myself to join the Lehigh County Authority (Authority) as its Chief Financial Officer and later its Chief Operating Officer. While I was totally unaware at the time, my work with the Authority would prove to be instrumental in the work I would undertake at GRU. Without the Authority, there might not have been a GRU on my resume.

For all but two years of my 20-year career with Panther, I had lived in Allentown while working in Nesquehoning. The long and tedious commute was exhausting but necessary since the coal region lacked the educational infrastructure provided by the Lehigh Valley schools my children would attend. I was looking forward to working and living in the Lehigh Valley rather than just living there. The change would provide me with a better opportunity to play old-man basketball with my buddies at the Allentown Jewish Community Center (JCC), where Melinda volunteered in co-chairing its Nearly New sales.

The Nearly New sales were a big deal for the JCC, serving as its largest annual fund raiser. Neither the sales nor the JCC would have been possible except for Max Hess Sr, along with his brother Charles, founders of the Hess Department store. Over the years, the Nearly New sales events received a nice nudge from the trendy downtown department store, in which Hess had brought Paris, London, and Rome to blue-collar Allentown residents. Hess would donate his overstock to the JCC to juice up the event.

Why is this mention of Max Hess Sr so important to my story? Well, he's not, but his son is. Max Hess Jr caught people's eyes in Allentown and surrounding communities. Anyone living in Allentown for any time knows the stories about the younger Hess's grandiosity and splendor. He was a master showman, like a Broadway producer. He built a Beverly Hills-style mansion with a nightclub. Famous celebrities such as Bob Hope, Zsa Zsa Gabor, and *Superman's* George Reeves would attend Hess's parties. So extravagant were his affairs, he once transformed the mansion into a jungle, including stocking live alligators in the swimming pool. Hess also went on to gain national attention when he brought topless women's bathing suits to Allentown. He didn't sell a single swimsuit, but the salacious swimwear had folks from all over the area talking about the Hess Department Stores. Others would trek downtown and, invariably, buy something less bold but buy, nonetheless.

Hess was an over-the-top personality. I couldn't help but admire the way Hess controlled the narrative about himself and his stores. If my cousin Buddy Bielarski had played to his NASCAR crowd, Max Hess had done the same to his retail audience. Almost 50 years after his death, locals still talk about the great Max Hess, in B.C. Forbes and Sons 1953 book, *America's Twelve Master Salesmen,* Hess is listed as its number two salesman. I really loved his store's three principles: "Be best, be first, and be entertaining." These were principles to which I would ascribe.

Although the Authority was no Hess Department Store, since its formation in 1969, it had grown to be successful in providing water and wastewater services to the suburban communities of the Lehigh Valley (outside of the City of Allentown) while working with builders and developers to expand the overall footprint of the region. It started that expansion through attracting companies like Kraft Foods and Schaefer Brewing Company to the region, followed by the construction of an industrial wastewater pre-treatment plant. The pre-treatment facility allowed the Authority to continue adding industrial customers as it recruited the likes of Coca-Cola, Boston Beer, and Ocean Spray. The Lehigh Valley was becoming a mecca for beverage companies. However, the growth in customers was outpacing the infrastructure of the region.

The challenge for the Authority was that the entire region's water and wastewater service territory was a network of separate municipal utilities. All told, the entire Lehigh Valley had twenty-two separate water and wastewater providers. These twenty-two entities operated under a host of service agreements and operating arrangements, which had been executed decades upon decades ago. Weighted down by these twenty-two governmental bodies and a host of political demands, the harmony upon which the symbiotic relationship was built was being threatened.

These twenty-two entities could not accept the financial commitment needed to mitigate the failures at the City of Allentown's aging Kline's Island Wastewater Treatment Plant, which serviced the entire Lehigh Valley. So egregious were the plant's failures that heavy rain events resulted in raw sewage mixed with storm water overflowing from manholes, pumping stations, and leaky pipes. It was an environmental cesspool, pardon the pun. These documented failures had not escaped the watchful eye of the US Environmental Protection Agency (USEPA).

Without any action forthcoming, the USEPA placed all the municipal utilities, including the city and the Authority, under the demands of a consent decree. This consent decree had the force of law to require the city, the Authority, and the other twenty municipalities to develop a comprehensive plan to address the fall-out of these storm events in a timely manner, no matter the cost. Despite their fiefdoms, municipal leaders from all corners were forced to consider the consolidation of the disparate water systems. A one-region solution was ripe for the picking, not to be confused with the Hayes-Santos' one-city solution.

On July 19, 2012, then Mayor of Allentown, Ed Pawlowski, picked the ripe fruit and dynamited the decade's long regionalization impasse with the announcement of a plan to lease the city's water and wastewater systems to the highest bidder. The issuance of the Request for Qualifications (RFQ) for potential bidders exposed the possibility of a consolidated regional network. It also presented an excellent opportunity for privatizing the network. There was little doubt that Pawlowski knew it was a double-edged sword. In my mind, that threat was the genius of his plan. With the announcement, the Authority was thrust into the spotlight.

Unfortunately, Pawlowski would make a colossal disaster in his personal and political life. Years later, he was investigated by the FBI and convicted on forty-seven charges in a pay-to-play scheme involving conspiracy, attempted extortion, bribery, making false statements to federal officials, along with fraud.

During his years leading the City of Allentown, Pawlowski still found time for notable achievements. He was a fiscal hawk, a crafty streamliner of city bureaucracy, and, of course, the brainchild of the plan to lease the city's water and wastewater systems, known later as the Concession deal. Pawlowski was also known to have a sharp tongue which he'd use to slice and dice those around him with snarky comments. Make no mistake about it. The driving force behind the Concession was quite a confident man, maybe too confident. That confidence, combined with a high level of arrogance, may have, in the end, led to his downfall.

As the City of Allentown's RFQ spelled out: "The main purpose of the concession lease is to generate upfront proceeds to address Allentown's various long-term liabilities." Those long-term liabilities represented the City of Allentown's over 160 million dollars in unfunded pension liabilities that were threatening to collapse their budget or drive property taxes dramatically higher. So, threatening were these unfunded pension liabilities, Pawlowski was quoted as saying, "In less than twenty-four months, Allentown would be just another Pennsylvania city making very ugly headlines about bankruptcy and its leaders lacking the political courage to address its fiscal problems."

The RFQ was well received by the investment community. Even before my arrival, on August 31, 2012, the Authority, along with six other private entities, were notified they had qualified to bid on Allentown's Concession agreement. We learned that the heavyweights of the industry were looking at this transaction, such as American Water, United Water, and Macquarie, who were all known to feed on these small to mid-sized cash-generating water systems.

On October 1, 2012, I joined the Authority armed with the details of the highly unusual 50-year Concession agreement along with books of financial and operational information from the city. I worked behind closed doors for the next several months developing a model to support a potential Authority bid, expected to be delivered on March 21, 2013. Like Pennsylvania's famous groundhog, Punxsutawney Phil, I would poke my head out at just the right time to meet with city officials in a series of meetings on the beautiful Muhlenberg University campus on the west side of Allentown. Under towering trees on a plateau overlooking Allentown's southern working-class city council wards, the campus provided the appropriate level of solemnity to the process. I would joke that you couldn't turn around without bumping into a lawyer or other consultant as we met during day-long sessions conducting page turns of the evolving draft Concession agreement.

The drafting of the Concession Agreement provided the first field of battle. The agreement was meant to be tailored to each individual bidder so their bids could optimize the value to the city, as well as its other bidders. The city staff would spend hours negotiating separately with each of the seven bidders, unilaterally deciding on which provisions to accept and with whom. While the contents of the agreements were up for negotiation, it was made quite clear that there would be no negotiation over what the city was looking for in everyone's final bid.

The City of Allentown's Director of Finance, Gary Strathearn, proclaimed that they would require only two numbers to be delivered in each party's bid package. Looking at us over his reading glasses, Strathearn declared there would need to be an upfront payment in an amount no less than $150 million, along with an annual concession fee. He said, "Nothing else will do." The bar had been set. The city's rigid approach left the Authority with one tool in its toolbox—the flexibility of modifying the Concession agreement.

My main concern was as a municipal bond issuer, the Authority couldn't easily or economically secure committed financing through a date certain in the future. Instead, we'd have to go to market with a bond auction prior to the actual closing of the Concession deal and take our chances. There would be several months during which time we'd have a binding, executed Concession Agreement awaiting financing. That monetary risk had to be shared in a reasonable way between the city and the Authority—we would need concessions (small c) from the city surrounding the bond financing we would have to undertake.

102

As a solution, I envisioned a protective financing clause which could be inserted into the agreement providing the Authority with a potential economic reduction in the upfront payment if there was an upward shift in the municipal bond market index. In simple terms, the financing clause was a homebuyer's equivalent of a financing contingency on a real estate purchase. Typically, a homebuyer will make an offer contingent on securing a mortgage with a certain amount of down payment and at an interest rate not to exceed a specific level.

Strathearn fought hard against the concept, which we called the interest-rate provision. In response to my requests, Strathearn repeatedly offered his one-word response, "No." Sometimes, he'd say, "No, Ed." Other times, it was a negative nod of the head. We continued talking for hours through multiple afternoons as Strathearn looked as bored as he was quiet. You get the point.

Finally, I presented the idea to Strathern as a deal-killer if the city failed to incorporate the clause in the agreement. As the meeting was ending and after consulting with his legal team, Strathearn told us that the city would agree to an interest-rate provision only if that provision worked both ways. He said it would have to include a mechanism to increase the upfront payment when interest rates fell. It was a fair request, as was the counteroffer I had prepared in anticipation of the city's pushback.

With the right amount of hesitation, I informed our team that we should agree. Given the current forecast for municipal bond rates, our acceptance of the added condition was akin to the popular business analogy of offering the city a sleeve off our vest. The interest-rate clause provided that the final upfront payment in the Concession would be increased or decreased based on the final borrowing rate while being capped at 4% of the upfront payment in either direction. The obscure provision would be lost in the litany of provisions within the Concession agreement, virtually hidden in the clear sight of the public and other bidders. It wouldn't be until the very end of the process that its importance would truly be understood.

Meanwhile, back at Allentown City Hall, officials were being bombarded with complaints that the city was giving away its most valuable assets, leaving its citizens at the mercy of another entity. People were worried that their water and wastewater bills would skyrocket. Mayor Pawlowski stayed on point in all his public meetings with the message that the city's unfunded pension obligation needed to be resolved. The only viable way to do so was directly through the Concession deal, Pawlowski declared.

Just like the city only had one path to solve its crisis, the Authority only had one way to bid on the Concession. The Authority's path to delivering its bid would require avoiding another bump in the road—the Authority only had 36 years left on its charter granted by our ultimate governing board, the Lehigh County Board of Commissioners (LCBC). The Authority couldn't own or mortgage a property for longer than its legal existence allowed. To compete in a bid to acquire the Concession, the Authority would need to formally request the LCBC for an extension of its charter to 50 years. Not a problem, I thought, given the fact that there was no magic to the 36 years or 50 years. We will just go to the LCBC and ask them to extend the Authority's charter. *Easier said than done.*

On February 27, 2013, the Authority was scheduled to go before the LCBC with a request to extend the Authority's charter to 50 years. In anticipation, Arndt met privately with the individual members of the commissioners with the following messages: 1) the Authority was the best organization to execute a Concession and minimize the rate impact to the suburban customers; 2) the Authority's very history and mission was to minimize rates for the suburban customers; 3) the Authority would not use the Concession to subsidize the city customer rates from higher rates out of its suburban customers. Arndt assured the Authority's Board of Directors

104

that he had the votes to secure an extension from the county commissioners.

On the day of the LCBC meeting, conservative member Scott Ott said, "It's getting comical how little information we're getting on such a big decision." He added that he would like a quid pro quo for approving an extension—the grant of more LCBC oversight in the Authority's decision-making. Ott wasn't alone in his thoughts. Conservative LCBC commissioners, Scott Ott, Vic Mazziotti, Lisa Scheller, and Mike Schware, envisioned that the Great Allentown Water Fight could provide a window of opportunity to grab power over the Authority.

The meeting proceeded to reflect on how, over the past several decades, the love-hate relationship between the LCBC and the Authority had shifted towards hate. At the heart of that emotion was that, although the LCBC had the sole authority to grant extensions to the Authority's charter and work with the county executive to appoint members to its board, it could do little else.

The LCBC's helplessness was reflected when fellow conservative Vic Mazziotti bemoaned, "At the last meeting, we were told that information would be shared with us. What I was told was, give us an extension and you're not going to receive any additional information. I was very uncomfortable with that." Sorry, Vic, the Authority had its own board of directors who retained governance over the organization.

On the other side, LCBC commissioner, Dan McCarthy, understood the middle ground required, reminding the commissioners that the Authority was established to insulate the system from political wrangling like this. McCarthy said, "I don't believe that's our role as county commissioners."

By the end of the meeting, the polarized LCBC was at an impasse, as the *Morning Call*, Allentown's paper of record, wrote: "The LCA's ability to bid on the Allentown water and sewer lease remained in doubt Wednesday night after a deeply divided county Board of Commissioners pushed for more oversight." The easy decision was postponed to another date. *Note to file: Expect more of these types of maneuvers when you get to Gainesville.*

Arndt and I responded to this public shakedown with another series of meetings held in executive session with up to three commissioners at a time. Under Pennsylvania law, the Authority was allowed to conduct these shade meetings with a minority of the commissioners. In these private meetings, I presented the commissioners with the results of my model along with an analysis as to how the Authority could be quite competitive in the bidding process. The numbers I was projecting were staggering. Under conservative assumptions, the Authority could generate over one billion dollars in free cash flow.

Armed with this valuable insight, the commissioners seemed to have left the meetings happy, with the understanding that the Authority had the ability to finance and close the deal. Most importantly, both Arndt and I made the point that if not the Authority, the community's water system would likely fall into a private company's control. That would be politically harmful to the LCBC and, certainly, not in the customer's best interests either.

Once again, the positive impressions were short-lived when on March 13th, the LCBC rejected the request, leaving, what most thought, an end to the Authority's goal of bidding on the Concession. In celebration, the LCBC expressed satisfaction that they had dashed the Authority's hopes of ever submitting a bid. They reveled in the Authority's defeat.

The next morning, during our debriefing of the previous night's loss, I was surprised at the level of depression I felt among the group. I told them not to fear. I informed them that I had anticipated the county's pushback and developed a pivot strategy. As part of that pivot, I had already truncated my model to reflect a thirty-six-year lease, not the full 50-year Concession. The pivot strategy hinged on the net present value of the monies received in years thirty-seven through fifty, not being the biggest drivers of the deal. In simple terms, the money you receive thirty-seven to fifty years from now is far less valuable than the money you receive today. I concluded, "Let's just bid on a 36-year value?"

Michael Jarmin, our lead attorney with McNees, Wallace and Nurick (NWN), looked at me, politely smiled, and said it wasn't that easy. However, the more we talked, the more Jarmin's mind churned. At one point, he tilted his head as he started to ponder this novel approach. After bantering the idea around for a while, Jarmin abruptly suggested that, indeed, it might just work. Thinking aloud, he said the strategy would hinge on getting the city to grant a modification to the Concession agreement. We all agreed the city would have to limit the term of the Authority's Concession agreement to the shorter of the Authority's charter-granted life, or fifty years. Yes, that would do it. He recognized that the Authority still maintained a substantial advantage.

The city's legal team understood the magnitude of the LCBC actions of the night before. Proceeding with the bid process without the Authority's involvement would have cast a negative shadow over the entire process. The city needed to show the concerned public that a partnership with the area's other non-profit water company had been carefully considered. As a result, and not surprisingly, the city agreed to insert the language the Authority needed to bid for the Concession.

The underlying beauty of using thirty-six years as the Concession term was that for the Authority to exist, the Authority's charter would have to be extended sometime within the 36 years. Without an extension, the Authority would have to be simply dismantled. That was highly unlikely. No, if we were successful in our bid, the LCBC would have thirty-six years to agree to an extension of the life of the Authority. It would be foolish for them to wait or fail to deliver the extension.

In another twist of fortune, bidding on the thirty-six years meant the remaining fourteen years of the Concession could generate huge profits at no cost to the Authority. If we won the bid, the fourteen years of profit would be free to us. *Cool.* I thought it was an eloquent solution. Jarmin thought so as well.

On March 20ᵗʰ, Goldman indicated that through the merging of our two models, they conservatively believed the Authority could deliver a bid north of two hundred million dollars for an upfront payment to the city. The lofty number was well above the city's expectations expressed by Strathearn during the Muhlenberg meetings. Better yet, the higher bid range was based on conservative assumptions such as borrowing at a "BBB+" rating in a stable municipal bond market and stepping into the city's position on its agreements with the surrounding municipalities. I thought, *"This is getting exciting."*

The next step was to present final bid options to our board members and request their approval to deliver a specific bid package on the Concession deal. Over the weekend, I e-mailed our board members a summary of the most recent bid forecasts. In my summary, I wrote: "The 1.5 billion dollars (of net cash flow in year 50) represents future cash, above and beyond the assumed two hundred million dollars bond borrowing and carrying costs (interest over the life of the bonds). The 1.5 billion dollars is a cushion, for want of a better term, against uncertainty, such as lower efficiencies. The two hundred million bond borrowing is far below the net present value of those 1.5 billion dollars."

The next day we received the encouraging news that S&P issued us an A-bond rating, one notch up from the projected BBB+. The A-rating meant we'd be looking at slightly lower borrowing costs and marginally higher bidding capacity. The pieces were falling into place. I was prepared to recommend an upfront-payment limit of 230 million dollars and an annual $

500,000 Concession fee to be paid to the city. All I had to do was gain the board's approval.

On Tuesday, March 26th, the Authority Board held consecutive public and executive sessions spanning a total of 5 hours. In the executive session, legally kept out of public viewing, Goldman's team presented a full exploration of the risks and rewards of borrowing structures for the Concession. On hand was Jill Toporek, a long-time Managing Director with Goldman Sachs, whom I had worked with in my years at Panther. With more financing deals under her belt than almost any Wall Street underwriter, Toporek's presence added a great deal of credibility to the team. The executive session ended with the board granting the Authority the option to offer up to 230 million dollars in an upfront payment with $500,000 a year over the life of the concession. The numbers were too compelling not to.

During the public session, the Board voted 6 to 1 in favor of making an offer on the Concession. *The Morning Call* issued the headline, "Lehigh County Authority to bid on Allentown water, sewer lease." Reporter Samantha Marcus wrote, "The LCA, which jumped through hoops for the chance to bid on the Allentown water and sewer lease voted Tuesday to make an offer on the system." Authority Board member, Richard Bohner, offered his reasoning for voting yes. "I agonized over this for a considerable period of time. I finally convinced myself there was no way I could change the circumstances. I believe that we are the best entity to respond to because of our background, our no-profit philosophy, and our continued desire to provide service to the people of Lehigh County."

Chairman of the LCBC, Lisa Scheller, continued her campaign against our bid saying that she was disappointed LCA chose to be complicit in Allentown's plan to bail itself out of a pension crisis. For Scheller and the rest of the LCBC, this vote would be a source of future quid pro quo appointments to the Authority board.

While the board had approved an upfront payment of no more than 230 million dollars, I spent the next two days working with Goldman to refine our opening bid. The bid process would be conducted under the rules of a best and final offer or BAFO process. Under this BAFO process, the top two bids would be selected to move into the next round, where they would submit another bid in a final selection. Through reverse engineering of similar bid processes, I determined that the best upfront payment offer other bidders could put on the table would be 190 million dollars. However, I suspected these bidders would sweeten their annual payment offers with a 2.5-million-dollar annual fee, higher than our $500,000. The combination played to our advantage.

Since the bids would be scored on their net present value (NPV), using a 6% discount rate, the higher upfront payment was more valuable. Not wanting to overpay, the question was, "What amount should we offer to get to the BAFO round?"

I extrapolated a first-round offer from anyone other than the Authority would be a 170-million-dollar upfront payment with an annual fee of 2.5 million dollars. That bid would result in a scored NPV of 203 million dollars. I called it Bielarski's Guess—First Bid.

I recommended the Authority submit an upfront bid of 205 million dollars, staying with a $500,000 annual. That would generate an NPV of 212 million dollars and a cushion of 9 million dollars. After discussions with Arndt and Toporek on Thursday, March 28, they agreed with my analysis. I submitted the initial bid for the Concession.

Just before the end of the business day, we received the call that the Authority was selected as one of the top two bidders!

Although I wanted to celebrate, I knew that it was like going to the Super Bowl. It's great to get there but now you got to win. Nobody remembers the loser of the Super Bowl. My mind raced with thoughts about who we'd be competing against in the next BAFO round. Without any information as to who was the high bidder, both bidders were asked to reconsider and submit their BAFO four days later, on April 1st.

Over the Easter weekend, I finalized the Authority's final bid—205 million dollars upfront with a $500,000 annual fee, netting out at 227 million dollars in NPV. I estimated the best our competitor's best and final offer was an upfront payment of 190 million dollars and a 2.5-million-dollar annual fee which would deliver a net present value of 223 million dollars. A slim 5 million cushion. If it proved to be the winning bid, I would have saved the Authority 15 million of what the amount board approved—230 million dollars. I submitted the bid.

On April 2nd, I felt a Zen-like calmness as the entire organization awaited the results of the final bid. I just had to wait. Then the call arrived. We were notified that we had outbid American Water to win the bid. I marveled that American Water had bid a 189 million upfront payment, a mere one million dollars less than I predicted. They also bid the 2.5-million-dollar annual payment like I expected.

	Authority Bid	American Water	Bielarski's Guess American Water
First Bid:			
Upfront-payment	$ 205 mm	$ 176 mm	$ 170 mm
NPV of City payment	7 mm	33 mm	33 mm
Total scored bid	$ 212 mm	$ 209 mm	$ 203 mm
BAFOS bid:			
Upfront-payment	$ 220 mm	$ 189 mm	$ 190 mm
NPV of City payment	7 mm	33 mm	33 mm
Total scored bid	$ 227 mm	$ 222 mm	$ 223 mm

Even in my state of low-key euphoria, I recalled that with interest rates rising, the small, interest-rate provision I had pushed for, might just come into play before we planned to close the deal. I smiled as I thought about the insertion of the clause into the Concession agreement while negotiating with the city at the Muhlenberg College campus. I was happy I had stood my ground and fought for its inclusion in the Concession agreement. It might prove to be incredibly valuable.

Jarmin e-mailed me, almost immediately, with the comment: "You are some steely-eyed missile men, Ed!" Authority Board member Richard Bohner wrote, jokingly, in an e-mail: "I am extremely pleased with the outcome and congratulate Ed on sound predictions leading to the final bid. With such sound predictions, I am almost inclined to recommend the formation of a sports book to enhance our revenue flow."

My work also impressed the Authority's Chief Administrative Officer Liesel Adams so much that she was compelled to tell me, "Been thinking since your last visit to my office and have come to the conclusion that you, Goldman Sachs and McNees, Wallace and Nurick are the primary reasons we won the bid, mostly you in my opinion." *Not too shabby!*

The words were as rewarding a validation of your professional success as you can get. However, it was still not over. We still had to gain the Allentown City Council approval and the actual signing of the Concession agreement. The final celebration would have to wait a little longer.

On April 25th, the council met to decide whether to authorize Pawlowski to execute the 50-year Concession agreement with the Authority. City hall was packed with people lined up and down the sides of the room. Of the over one hundred people, forty-six eventually got up to speak in the microphone. This would not be a polite exercise in democracy. There were more jeers than cheers as the mayor climbed out of his usual character to respond to the more egregious public accusations. You could see Pawlowski growing tired of people not understanding what he knew. He had worked this Concession arrangement out in his mind with a bevy of financial advisors and attorneys. There was an air of, how dare you question me?

At the end of the evening, the council voted 6 to 1 in favor of the motion to authorize Pawlowski to sign the Concession agreement. City Council President, Julio Guridy, said of the matter, "It was contentious, but the majority of people knew it was the right thing to do for the city. We got $220 million from the deal."

On May 1st, the Authority and the City of Allentown executed the Concession agreement from which we had a 90-day transition plan to closing. Within that 90-day window, we would have to finance the 220-million-dollar upfront payment along with the over eighty million dollars of reserve funds required by the future bondholder and the city. This required bringing in an underwriter, engineering consultant, as well as bond and transaction counsel. Of course, I had engaged Goldman early in the process, along with various very experienced legal counsels knowing that they'd need to be engaged throughout.

On July 31st, Arndt and I drove into New York to meet with Goldman Sachs as the sole book runner on the bond offering. As the sole underwriter (or book runner), Goldman sold over $307 million of bonds in a live auction of the various series of bonds, pricing and accepting offers. Despite Arndt's earlier reservations, Goldman had delivered as the underwriter in this historic deal and secured the financing that was to take place. The Authority had the money to close the Concession deal, or so we thought.

There would be another unfortunate speedbump before the Authority could close on the Concession. At the end of July, the city's attorneys alerted the Authority that a lawsuit had been filed against the city, in May, no less. A minor lawsuit that, if we had been alerted to its existence, would have been vetted already. However, due to its late disclosure, the need for disclosure counsel to opine, and with the short window, the lawsuit would require a one-week extension of the original July 31st Concession closing to August 7th.

Incredibly, along with the disclosure of the lawsuit, the city demanded $ 132,000, representing one week of interest on the debt.

In response, one of our board members, Brian Nagle, had an electronic meltdown over the mayor's demand and sent an e-mail on July 26th in which he demanded: "On behalf of City ratepayers and my own conscience I can't accept the recommendation without specific, legitimate reasons why LCA should pay the city over $ 132,000 for a closing date extension that was caused by the city's failure to notify us in May of the legal action being taken concerning the Concession Agreement." On a roll now, Nagle wrote, "I think it is time to play hardball with the city and let them know that we will not tolerate such behavior on their part."

Arndt had inadvertently set this meltdown in motion with an e-mail he had written the day before, July 25th. "Attached is a proposed closing extension to August 7th, which was developed by the city's and LCA's attorneys. I don't like it for multiple reasons, not the least of which is that we did not act or failed to act on something that caused us to miss the original closing date. In addition, this leaves open, unresolved issues and little leverage in any negotiation."

In one last effort to keep the Concession from falling apart, I wrote to the Board: "As much as I want to teach the mayor a lesson and set a tone in our relationship, I am concerned with protecting the 10-million-dollar letter of credit, reducing the possibility of litigation in the future, and securing the financing." I followed with a solution suggested by Toporek, our "expensive underwriter." Understanding the gravity of the moment, Toporek negotiated a reduction in its counsel fees, delivering a tidy savings of $122,000.

It was an elegant solution to a hot-button item that threatened to sink the 300 million-dollar, historic consolidation of the region's water and wastewater resources. The Authority's chair and County Chief Executive, Tom Muller, wrote back, "I agree with your logic. There is no right way to do the wrong thing."

With another crisis averted over a minor $132,000, at midnight on August 8, 2013, the Authority took control of the city's water and wastewater systems. In an interview with the *Lehigh Valley Business Journal*, I spoke with Brian Pederson about the transition. "For me, it's really rewarding because I believe as a public entity, without a profit motive, we are the best option for the city. I believe it's a win for the little guy." That really summed up the whole experience for me.

That's when my early work saved the Authority a cool nine million dollars.

The Morning Call reported that "a little-known provision in the contract" had been invoked—the interest-rate provision I had negotiated into the Concession agreement during the early negotiations. In a weird twist of contractual artistry, the Authority had won the deal with a 220-million-dollar upfront commitment, only to have it lowered to 211 million dollars because of my contingent adder. The 211 million dollars was *lower* than American Water's BAFO bid of 215 million dollars in the end—but there was nothing they could do about it.

City officials, behind closed doors, were furious. Pawlowski voiced his desire to void the agreement, threatening to offer the deal to American Water. Of course, cooler heads prevailed. The city's response was best publicly expressed by Councilman Jeff Glazier, who said, "I'm sure we all would have been happier at 220 million dollars, but this is what it is. The rate environment has changed." They would have been even happier if interest rates had gone the other way and the city was the recipient of more money.

If there was any doubt about the extraordinary value, sophisticated nature, and elegant complexity of the Concession deal, it should have vanished when *Bond Buyer* awarded the Authority the "Deal of the Year" for the Northeast Region. *Bond Buyer* recognized that the Concession; 1) had been the country's first-ever, publicly bid concession arrangement between two public entities to reach completion; 2) successfully merged the City of Allentown's water/wastewater system operations with that of the Authority; 3) was instrumental in delivering hundreds of millions of dollars to spearhead Allentown's downtown development.

The Concession was the financing vehicle providing the impetus for changing that old image of Allentown. It was such a landmark arrangement that folks in Allentown would no longer need to wait for the "Pennsylvania they never found," as Billy Joel had sung. The time had come for Allentown's self-discovery. The Authority's upfront lease payment of over $200 million went into the building of a downtown hockey arena and events center. New public places sprung up around Allentown and the neighboring communities. A downtown events and hockey arena was built along with a baseball stadium housing the Triple A franchise, the Lehigh Valley Iron Pigs. *Oink, Oink.* The Concession funding began an urban renewal process that continues to this day.

Full of pride and a sense of a job well done, on December 6, 2013, Arndt, Liesel Adams, our Chief Administrative Officer, and I travelled to New York City to accept this prestigious award. The City of Allentown was a co-awardee with the Authority, with Mayor Pawlowski and members of the city team in attendance. When the award was announced, Arndt, Adams, and I were escorted on stage, with Arndt taking center stage.

As the room grew quiet, Arndt looked out over the sea of financiers, investment bankers, and Wall Street municipal bond players. Holding the award, he peered through the lights and said that he didn't know whether to be happy or sad about receiving the award because he saw the award as rewarding the bad behavior of borrowing money. Leave it up to Arndt to stick the proverbial pin in the balloon of joy. There were members in attendance that laughed while others stared at him in disbelief. Others lightly applauded. Toporek rolled her eyes as she looked my way. *Rewarding bad behavior, indeed!*

Despite Arndt's suggestion of rewarding bad behavior, more complimentary reviews came in on the deal. Paul Burton, writer/reporter for *Bond Buyer*, penned a column: "Water Deal will save City," in which the Authority's Chairman of the Board, Tom Muller said, 'LCA is only focused on two things: water and wastewater, nothing else. Whereas the city's got a million other things to worry about."

Standard and Poor's Rating Services issued a modification to the City of Allentown's bond ratings, increasing it three notches from BBB+ to A+. It was a historic and dramatic one-time rate increase, and it was due to the city's "significantly improved budget flexibility, as a result of its water and sewer system lease-concession agreement."

John Tierney headlined an *Atlantic* article, "The City that turned its water into cash," in which he wrote: "The money for the city's new reconstruction effort came from an innovative and practically unique tax recycling deal." The awards and headlines were well-deserved.

***

While I was savoring my victory, Jim Gordon was methodically waging his battle to bring wind power to Nantucket. Unfortunately for him, a new, well-funded combatant had joined the opposition forces—Bill Koch. Under the headline, "Koch Brother Wages 12-Year Fight over Wind Farm," on October 22, 2013, the *New York Times* wrote: "Mr. Koch, a billionaire industrialist who made his fortune in fossil fuels and whose better-known brothers underwrite conservative political causes, has been fighting the wind farm, called Cape Wind, for more than a decade, donating about $5 million and leading an adversarial group against it. He believes Cape Wind's 130 industrial turbines would not only create what he calls 'visual pollution' but also increase the cost of electricity for everyone."

Koch really knew how to get under Gordon's skin, which after twelve years must have been wearing thin. In the spring of the year, *Commonwealth Magazine* conducted an interview with Gordon, in which the reporter, Bruce Mohl, asks him, "Koch praises you. He says you're brilliant and he'd like to hire you."

Gordon replied, "I'm not working on the plantation, sir." *Ouch.*

By December 2013, Gordon would be engaged in a two-front war. The biomass plant would start commercial operations, as it started delivery of the same high-priced power to GRU that Koch was afraid Gordon's Cape Wind would deliver to New Englanders.

Ω

A Swamp Yankee

Unlike the fictional Godot, on June 22, 2015, I appeared on the Gainesville stage, where I was thrust into a hot bed of internal GRU dynamics, city politics, and strange alliances. Despite my credentials, there were people within the community that were unhappy with my hiring. There were even people in the hallways and alcoves at GRU that were dispirited with the commission's choice. Others told me there were people gunning for me. It wasn't surprising.

During the public interview process, I was on the record questioning the motives, strategies, and tactical decisions in executing the GREC PPA. I leaned into the challenging circumstances. What surprised me the most was there were people that just didn't like a northerner, a Yankee, running the city's utility.

I wasn't just some Yankee. I was a Swamp Yankee—a more countrified, stubborn, independent, and less-refined sub-type of your plain old Yankee. I was the *Columbo* of Yankees. Being labeled as a Swamp Yankee also sounded a whole lot like I belonged on the Florida Gator's campus, so I made it my unofficial title, armed with the necessary common sense and confidence to take on the challenge and save the utility.

***

I wasn't the only outsider to ever have been hired as GRU's top dog. In March 1950, city residents voted on a charter amendment that established the utility as a separate department of the city—Department

119

of Public Utilities. Two days after a 19-vote victory for the amendment (out of more than 1,700 votes), the commission appointed Walter A. Furst as the city's first director of utilities. He was a 35-year veteran of the utility business, with experience as a Westinghouse engineer travelling the country installing and trouble-shooting equipment. The commission paid Furst $12,000 a year to start.

Unfortunately, Furst was said to be better at installing and trouble-shooting turbines than managing a utility. After disappointing results, the commission unabashedly reduced Furst's salary to $10,000 the next year. During 1951, the commission continued to lose confidence in the industry veteran. Steps had to be taken.

In a 1990 memo, City Commissioner Jim Richardson retells the story that in September 1952, during a round of golf at the Gainesville Golf and Country Club, a foursome comprised of three commissioners started discussing Furst's performance. Of course, this was before the strict requirements of the Florida Sunshine Law. One commissioner stepped up and urged the other two commissioners in the group to "fire Furst and hire John R. Kelly."

John R. Kelly had been the utility superintendent starting in 1946, prior to the amendment vote, and was well-liked. He came up through the utility ranks. Beginning in 1929, while laying off a semester from the University of Florida's Engineering School, he was hired by the utility to sweep floors and clean the plant. By the time the Great Depression hit Gainesville, he was making $19 a day, working 7 days a week. In an interview in 1987, Kelly told the reporter, "If you missed a day of work, someone would walk in off the sidewalk and step right into your job."

In response to the proposal, another commissioner said, "If I make this next putt, I'll vote for it." Everyone agreed that whoever made their putt would agree to the proposal. The putts were made, and in the afternoon, Furst resigned and J R. Kelly was hired. It wasn't until days later that the action was approved at a commission meeting.

John R. Kelly would go on to be known as one of GRU's greatest and most influential general managers. Kelly would end up serving the utility in multiple capacities for a quarter of a century. He would supervise the installation of 144 megawatts of nameplate capacity on the power plant that bears his name (JR Kelly Generating Station) and another eighty-one megawatts at the Deerhaven power station.

***

I started my first day expecting the unexpected. Armed with coffee and a few ideas, I ambled towards my conference room to attend my inaugural leadership team meeting. As I grew nearer to the gathering, I couldn't help but hear the drone of people's chatter. As I walked through the door to take my seat at the head of the board table, that chatter fell meekly into silence.

That is, apart from John Stanton, who continued a discussion with another employee. The employee looked at me helplessly as though he wanted Stanton to give up the floor to me. With no sense of urgency, Stanton slowly and loudly finished making his points as I casually reclined in my chair. As Stanton and I eyed each other, I could sense that he was going to challenge me from the start. *Not to self: Keep an eye on Stanton.*

I scanned the room full of assistant general managers of departments, directors, and other leaders. It was no small gathering. There weren't enough seats in the room to hold the cadre of people reporting to me. More chairs had to be brought in from the reception area to accommodate the standing-room-only crowd. I had a visceral reaction - a smaller, more manageable executive team pushing a more focused direction was in order.

I was also struck that I was being met with the very same eyes when I was interviewed to become the general manager. This morning, these eyes were not as confident as when I wasn't their boss. You could see fear in their eyes—a fear of changing the status quo. That was a disconcerting thought to have about one's new leadership team. I told myself to give them time. It had been a rocky time at GRU.

In the days, weeks, and months that followed, there were hundreds of meetings, presentations, and hallway discussions. However, there were those meetings that were so important they shaped the path forward, no unlike the stacks on the

121

Panther power plant that guided my path to its doors. No matter the noise and distractions, I kept my sights on those stacks.

One of my most important meetings was a June 25th get together with Interim Chief Financial Officer David Richardson. Immediately upon arriving in my office, Richardson plopped a sheet of paper on my desk for me to follow along with—a copy of Richardson's May 4th memo sent to my fellow charter officer, City Auditor Carlos Holt. As I started to glance at the contents of the memo, Richardson explained how Holt had challenged him on the viability of withholding payments from GREC. In response, Richardson had prepared this memo entitled "Talking Points for Carlos Holt."

Holt had been selected by the same conservative commission that selected me. We were the one-two punch of charter officers the new commission had hired with the intent on righting the city's financial affairs and mitigating the high costs of the GREC PPA as quickly as possible.

Richardson told me that if I harbored any thoughts about withholding payments to GREC, he wanted me to read the memo first. He'd highly dissuade me from withholding such payments. I had to give Richardson credit for his directness. He wanted no part of withholding monies from GREC. I wondered how he felt about challenging the status quo.

After issuing his warning, Richardson allowed me time to read the memo: "I've had some time to think about the impacts of refusing to pay the GREC PPA." A string of what-ifs followed, such as, "Stopping payment to GREC consistent with the current contract would have serious immediate and long-term consequences. GREC would immediately bring suit against the City for breach of contract. Rating agencies would be concerned and want to know the basis of the suit."

I smiled, as I couldn't help thinking about the "Dog-Died" joke as the memo addressed one bad result after another. Richardson looked at me quizzically as I smiled. He had no idea what I was thinking. The memo continued: "If we were alleging that GREC was in breach of contract, there might be no rating impact or a small rating impact. If we say that we don't like the contract and are refusing to perform under the contract, rating agencies (and others) will be very concerned that we are unreliable counterparties."

The memo ended ominously when Richardson wrote, "If I'm asked, I'll lay out the potential consequences." *Was this a threat? Had Richardson ever been asked not to lay out other consequences at another time? Am I missing something here?* I was surprised with Richardson's apparent need to deliver such an over-the-top letter first to Holt and now to me. I guess in hindsight, it was the typical CYA strategy—Cover Your Ass. However, what bothered me was Richardson's strong expression of what I *ought not to do* regarding the GREC PPA. When I asked him about a buyout of the GREC PPA, he said it had already been tried. He offered nothing new in terms of potential avenues of what we *ought to do* to reduce the costs of the GREC PPA.

It was then that I recalled Richardson having formerly served as the utility's Director of Water and Wastewater for many years. To his credit, he had stepped up to serve as the Interim chief financial officer after Hunt had left the utility. However, if I wanted more financial savvy from my chief financial officer, it looked as though I would have to search outside the utility.

On that same day, John Stanton joined me for a briefing on GREC and other energy supply issues. Stanton was the guy that had already tested me in a subtle alpha-dog display of power during the leadership meeting. I was intrigued with what he'd do for an encore.

Stanton had joined GRU after retiring from a lengthy career at Florida Power and Light (FPL). As the adage goes, "Timing is everything," Stanton arrived just in time to serve as a co-negotiator on the GREC PPA. I remembered his courage in speaking out against the Equitable Adjustment. He lived through the ballooning of GRU debt and managed the operational impacts of North America's worst PPA. Given his experience, I thought Stanton would have a clear view of the situation with GREC.

As we talked, I couldn't help but notice how matter-of-factly Stanton spoke, reminiscent of my former plant managers while I worked at Panther and the Authority. I quickly likened Stanton to a fictitious Joe Friday, the Los Angeles detective in the old television series, *Dragnet*. Friday would enter the scene with his notepad and pencil, deadpanning the line, "Just the facts, please." One by one, Stanton rattled off his facts, just like Joe Friday.

Most interesting, Stanton revealed that the GREC plant was technologically suited to operate as low as fifty-five megawatts, not the 70 megawatts negotiated within the GREC PPA. Stanton seemed encouraged that we'd be able to gain a concession from GREC to do so. While the lower operating level would bring cost savings to GRU, Stanton's optimism was a little surprising to me. GREC was under no obligation to do so. When had they ever acquiesced before? What made him think they'd negotiate now?

Easily shifting his focus, Stanton offered insight into GREC's ownership structure. The owner of a series of hotel chains, Starwood, had recently become a new 40% owner of GREC. Starwood was a sophisticated investor. That was an interesting development which could impact future negotiations if there were to be any. It got better. Stanton threw in another nugget—Jim Gordon's company, EMI, was also getting out of Cape Wind.

I jumped in and asked Stanton about getting me the amended and restated PPA. Taken aback, he told me that although the GREC PPA had been amended multiple times, it had not yet been reduced to an amended and restated PPA. After a little prodding, Stanton offered that he had been working on a consolidating document himself, so things like the Equitable Adjustment were placed in the proper context. I asked him to prioritize this process of amending and restating the PPA as soon as possible because I would need it to properly navigate the entire GREC PPA.

While on the surface, the failure to consolidate the documents doesn't sound like anything that's terribly important, it was a sign to me that the organization's scrutiny of the GREC PPA was over. Just a sense I was getting. It was also tone-deaf. An amended and restated agreement would have been the proper merging of all the amendments and modifications to an agreement into one document. How could anyone allow any more misunderstandings of such a controversial contract?

Stanton pounced on the opportunity to tell me about the Equitable Adjustment. As a reminder, the Equitable Adjustment was anything but equitable to GRU. It should have been titled the Inequitable Adjustment. Stanton's pursuit of the Equitable Adjustment, at this time, seemed curious to me. He seemed intent on amending the agreement to allow for a recalculation of the actual capital costs of the environmental controls in what he called a true-up. However, it was a thorny issue, and that thorn was still in the paw of the lions of the community, including Stanton, it appeared.

By the end of our meeting, I was truly fascinated with the manner of Stanton's update. He was forthcoming in an unforthcoming manner if that's even possible. He was quite an enigmatic engineer. I wondered if it would be fun to try to figure out which of his comments were important and which were not.

One thing for sure, Stanton and Richardson had seemingly co-authored the script from which to speak. Stanton reiterated Richardson's point that GRU had taken a serious yet unsuccessful attempt at buying out the GREC PPA. He optimistically said I might have something new to offer. Nice try, but his tone betrayed him, as I sensed an underlying message: *"Don't think we haven't tried everything you could have ever thought of."*

One day later, on June 26th, Richardson met with me once again to discuss GRU's financial situation in preparation for a budget meeting with Commissioner Chase. He had an unusual energy as he sat down in my office to work from a chart he had placed before me. The chart illustrated the growing gap between GRU's electric rates and that of the other Florida utilities, which he called the Competitiveness Gap.

The chart demonstrated that GRU was currently collecting twenty-four million dollars a year more from its electric customers than the average Florida utility. A 24-million-dollar gap in revenues wasn't a good thing. It was the direct result of the additional costs of the GREC PPA, which meant GRU wasn't earning any profit from those additional revenues. It was just passing along the additional costs to its electric customers. I found the chart depressing.

What was even more depressing was that the projected separation between GRU's electric rates and the average electric rates for the state never diminished. It grew larger and larger every year. It was a stark reminder of the dramatic fiscal impact the GREC PPA had on the utility.

My emotions moved from depressed to disturbed when Richardson offered no options to close the gap. Instead, I heard him reiterate that the previous attempt to buyout the GREC PPA had failed, as though he was telling me not to try a buyout again. *Why?* The GREC PPA forced the utility to run the biomass plant at levels that placed its own power plants at risk, and the utility had reduced staff to a level below that of a decade before. Mr. Doom was in town while Mrs. Gloom was fast approaching.

Looking back on my first week, the takeaway was easy—I had been informed, by my two most influential and important leaders, GRU's Chief Financial Officer and its Assistant General Manager of Energy Supply, that they had marginal insight into how to mitigate the blossoming, full, onerous costs of the PPA. My most urgent to-do was to build a team of trusted staff around me that were supportive of doing the right thing, wherever it took us, whatever actions were needed.

On June 29th, I discovered that Richardson's conversation with me on June 25th wasn't enough to assure him that I wouldn't side with City Auditor Holt and refuse to make the GREC PPA payments. At 6:33 PM, I received an e-mail from my stalwart interim CFO in which he wrote: "In early May of this year, Carlos Holt had mentioned the idea of not paying GREC in accordance with the existing PPA as a potential method to obtain more favorable terms and conditions." Richardson then included the contents of the Holt memo once more. Richardson was more scared of what I might do than what the GREC PPA had already done to the city. It wasn't an attitude that I expected a CFO in this position to have. I was also shocked that Richardson had this need to put this in writing, not once, but twice. *What was he scared of?*

In response to my prior week's questions about Stanton's understanding of the GREC PPA, he dropped off a paper reflecting those sections of the PPA he had drafted. Those sections were Section 10-Dispatch and Scheduling, Section 11-Pre-Operational Commissioning and Testing, Section 12-Operations, Maintenance and Performance Standards, along with three appendices.

I was reminded of Regan's comments during the May 7, 2009, commission meeting; "In fact, we don't pay anything until the plant not only comes online but makes Mr. Stanton here happy that they've met all the obligations under the contract for proof of firm capacity. And that's in a—I must say, I want to compliment John on that. He added value to the whole process on that. And it was really done in the weeds, and I was pretty impressed."

Later in the day, I met with City HR Director Cheryl McBride concerning a variety of issues around human resources. She told me that her staff's review of the chief financial officer's job description led them to the understanding that Richardson wasn't qualified to be a

127

candidate for the GRU's permanent CFO opportunity. Caught off guard, I asked McBride how he had been able to become the interim. She told me that interim employees aren't held to the same standards under the city's human resources policies. *Another note to file: I need a better understanding of the city's HR function.*

Before ending the day, I placed my first call to Jim Gordon. It was becoming evident that if anything could be done to get GRU out of this GREC PPA, I'd have to do it. I didn't see any inspiration from Richardson or Stanton.

Sitting on the dais at my first city commission meeting was quite different from that day in May when my family followed the governmental proceedings live-streamed from my laptop. Tonight, July 2nd, was more raw, real, and intense. With a heightened sense of responsibility, I gazed out from the dais through the bright lights towards the audience. I felt like a television anchorman—one without a script.

I had an opportunity to meet State Representative Keith Perry, who came to speak about a new GRU governance bill he was sponsoring in the state capital, Tallahassee. His words would foreshadow a multiple-year struggle between the commission and his office concerning the city residents voting on a new governance structure for the utility. Instead of GRU reporting to the commission, Perry's plan would appoint an independent board—an approach in complete opposition to Hayes-Santos' one-city concepts. Little did I know, when Commissioner Carter introduced me to Perry, I was being introduced to a future adversary.

On the lighter side, the night ended with Commissioner Goston using a phrase he'd later repeat. In response to what he thought were crazy ideas expressed during public comment, Goston said, "That guy needs a checkup from the neck up." I couldn't help but laugh. *Note to self: Checkup from the neck up is a funny line. I need to find ways to use it.*

I was sitting on Day 17 with the utility. It reminded me of the news reporting during the Iran hostage crisis that started on November 4, 1979. During an era when everyone sat down to watch the evening news after work and before dinner, each broadcast would start with the number of days America had been held hostage. With little progress on the GREC PPA, I was feeling helpless as the days ticked by.

I sensed it was time to test Stanton and his team's positions regarding the GREC PPA. It was time to crack a few eggs. I sent Stanton an e-mail reading: "Unless you can present a convincing argument otherwise, I'd like to keep GREC at full load throughout the summer months. Given the incremental operating cost of the extra thirty-two megawatts, it seems to be a better strategic plan for GRU." I looked forward to his reply

Later the next day, I stopped by Stanton's office to see if he understood the e-mail from the previous day. I told him that I was a numbers guy, and I simply wanted to better understand the costs to GRU of running GREC full out at 102 megawatts, or at a minimum load of seventy megawatts, or under our economic dispatch, compared to the status quo. Stanton just stared at me.

I laughed as I told Stanton that there were those that thought GREC couldn't run at full load for long because it would break down. I told him, yes, I was well aware of the "Break GREC" crowd. That's exactly why, from my perspective, it would be nice to run GREC at full load to end the myth that the GREC plant was a "bag of bolts." I also said, "You, more than others, understand the pressures of dealing with the GREC PPA, so let's make sure we have firm numbers here." Stanton was quiet for some time.

Although he said he'd work on it, Stanton looked confused about my request. I explained to him that I came from a business world in which we always explored options. We called that exploration developing optionality. I said, "Without optionality, we'd have no strategy since there's nothing to choose from."

On July 20th, during our regular one-on-one meeting, Stanton delivered his staff's alternate production cost models (on the proprietary software named Gentrader) for the months of July, August, and September. In it, Stanton and his team analyzed what-if scenarios, including 1) setting GREC to full load, 2) keeping GREC offline but available, and 3) economically dispatching GREC. Comparing each one of these scenarios to the status quo, Stanton placed the paper in front of me and proceeded to explain how dispatching GREC to full load would cost GRU more than $800,000 over the three months of July, August, and September. He wanted me to see that the exercise had affirmed his team's actions in managing GREC.

What Stanton may have seen but clearly didn't focus on was that GRU would save almost two million dollars for those 3 months if the GREC plant were to be shut down and remain on standby or ready to generate power only. Those models also showed that running the GREC plant under economic dispatch, as is the best practice for a utility, would save GRU almost 2.2 million dollars a year. Stanton, surprisingly, said that both scenarios in which GRU could save money were "for comparison only." The GREC PPA prohibits GRU-directed shutdowns during the summer period, and the overall restrictions on on/off cycles prohibit true economic dispatch. I wondered what constituted non-GRU-directed shutdowns. I didn't ask and Stanton didn't offer any explanation.

Stanton also said that dispatching the GREC plant to full load would dramatically reduce generation at our lowest cost generation at Kelly and increase our highest cost generation at Deerhaven Unit 1. Finally, he said the Kelly plant would fall out of NOx environmental compliance if GREC were taken to full load over a prolonged period. *Boy, Stanton really did appear to be reluctant to change the status quo.*

Stanton seemed quite pleased with shooting down my arguments. I suspect he thought he had disarmed my request to dispatch GREC to full load. Of course, he would. However, he didn't know it was just a test. I didn't think we should dispatch them to full load, either.

130

I believe Stanton saw me as an unworthy successor to GRU's previous general managers. It wasn't hard to imagine Stanton thinking of me as strictly a financial guy, just a bean counter. I wasn't an engineer and therefore wasn't qualified to manage him. He just had to prove it to himself, followed by the rest of Gainesville.

After finishing his presentation, Stanton moved on to talk about the actions he felt would help the utility; 1) negotiating a lower minimum operating load into the GREC PPA; 2) negotiating a new Available Energy charge; and 3) employing a true-up of the Equitable Adjustment costs. I responded that I'd be receptive to discussing any of these options if they provided an overall benefit to the utility.

I pointed out that it was my understanding that each of these items had already been negotiated, albeit poorly, particularly the true-up to the Equitable Adjustment. Any discussion would have to be considered in the entire context of the GREC PPA. I said, "Be careful trying to pull on one thread. The entire piece of clothing might be ruined."

Undaunted, Stanton remained fixated on the concept of a true-up of the Equitable Adjustment costs. Given his compelling arguments against it at the time it was executed, I understood his feelings. He wanted to correct a wrong. He needed to correct the wrong. I also assumed he desperately wanted to be more relevant and respected. He had been personally hurt by being "criticized by members of the City Commission and the public for terms of the PPA, whether they were his responsibility or not."

The bottom line was I found it unacceptable to ignore a potential 2-million-dollar potential savings over the three summer months and/or fail to develop a plan to capture those savings. I understood the potential savings were not the silver bullet we were looking for. However, compared to the 24-million-dollar Competitiveness Gap, it would set the right tone for any future negotiations with GREC. The situation reminded me of one of my favorite expressions: the only way

131

to eat an elephant was one bite at a time. However, this elephant would require my special sauce. *Munch, munch.*

Out of the blue, towards the evening of the same day, Stanton delivered a memo to me that he had previously written to one of the commissioners back on April 2, 2015. In the memo, written almost 3 months prior to my arrival, Stanton answered a question from a commissioner about his desire to better understand one of the GM candidate's stories, namely me.

Stanton described the commissioner's story as "about the off taker of the power for the NUG plant dispatching in such a manner as to increase the number of forced outages, i.e., cycling it broke the plant." He wrote that he had told the commissioner: "You asked me about our ability to do the same to GREC. I recall asking rhetorically, why would you want to (try and break GREC)?" The reason Stanton gave for writing the memo was their conversation was interrupted by the call-to-order of the Commission meeting. The memo served to "provide some additional facts and opinions for your consideration as you think on this topic."

I paid particular attention when he ended the memo with, "Therefore, and again in my professional opinion, even if there was a success in damaging GREC, it might cause GREC significant cost to maintaining reliability, but it won't give GRU customers much relief from Available Energy charges."

It all hit me like a ton of bricks. Stanton thought I was part of the group that wanted to "Break GREC." It was also a maneuver right out of Richardson's gameplan when he had warned me about withholding payments from GREC. *How stupid does he think I am?* You can't break a plant. You can make it harder to manage the ups and downs of cycling, but it doesn't break a plant. These difficulties can stress the plant but don't break it. The term break was being used to illicit emotion, not facts.

As a result of our exchanges, I realized how little Stanton trusted me. If I had genuinely wanted to damage the GREC plant, as Stanton thought, I'd be requesting dispatching them on and off for the full sixteen occasions allowed in the winter period under the GREC PPA. I hadn't requested that be done. Instead, I had asked about letting GREC prove themselves worthy of running at full load over an extended time. I shook my head with the knowledge that Stanton had failed my tests.

I celebrated my thirty-day anniversary on the job with the declaration that "the contract doesn't pass the sniff test." If that wasn't enough, it also was the day I decided on my top ten initiatives moving forward. The most important of these was that, before the end of 2015, I needed to hire four new people to form a streamlined executive team. I needed to reduce the leadership team from eleven pairs of status quo-preserving eyes to four eager pairs of eyes of hope, change, and ready to support my goals.

I began by creating a Chief Operating Officer position to manage the utility's five services. Before years end, I hired Tom Brown, whom I had worked with during my Panther days. I had personally witnessed Brown's ability to do the right thing - standing up to owners and investors who looked to profit from laying off workers in Pennsylvania's coal patch towns. Like me, Brown was the general manager for another one of the area's waste-coal-burning power plants. We have worked jointly on fuel supply arrangements and other alternative ways of driving down fuel costs.

Behind Brown's calm exterior, there beat the heart of a doer - he had built his own airplane, including tooling some of his parts, in his spare time over seven years. Not only had he ended up regularly flying across the countryside while living in Texas, but Brown had also used that plane to actively participate in aerial mock dog fights. That was just too cool (a phrase Brown was apt to use). The way things were going, aerial cover might also come in handy...

Brown was a man to be trusted, and he was a man with incredible insight into the power industry, including a superior knowledge of the inner workings of power plants. I envisioned

Brown as a foundational component of my new executive team. He'd serve as the technical guy driving an essential transition away from status-quo thinking. Just as Frank Miller and his Miltech firm had facilitated changes to Panther's fuel plans, so too could Brown deliver a fresh look at GRU's energy plan. I couldn't help laughing as I thought about Brown as my new Frank Miller, just without the cursing. I knew Brown could provide the type of leadership I needed at GRU. As a result, Stanton and the other operational officers would report directly to Brown, not me.

I also hired a new Chief Financial Officer, Justin Locke, who had the right kind of knowledge base, confidence and professionalism. He had solid connections with the bond rating agencies we would need to impress. Locke would be instrumental in upgrading the CFO position to the level I needed to support the goals I had set. Richardson had served admirably as an interim CFO, but he just didn't have the qualifications needed to do what had to be done going forward. He wasn't a Justin Locke. I still remember Richardson's disappointment when he left the Interim CFO assignment to return to his old post. In frustration, he told me, "I hope you didn't expect me to do backflips over it."

I also created a new Chief Information Officer role, under which all the information technology and operational technology would be managed. Prior to its creation, the utility had IT directors and information management was decentralized throughout the organization. With the new role, I centralized all information technology management. With the new role, I found the perfect fit, Walt Banks.

Banks brought a wealth of experience in municipal information technology and had a dynamic personality and style, which I believed would drive change within the utility. Banks replaced not a single IT Director but three IT Directors, who had been rotating in and out of the position every six months. It seemed that rather than choosing one director, prior GRU management thought it easier and fairer to allow three people to share the role.

Banks was ex-military, Army to be specific, and he loved order and structure. He was his father's son, who respected his late father by quoting his words of wisdom to us. We called his words of wisdom, Walt-isms, and Banks would launch into them in a New York minute or sooner if needed.

Finally, I created a Chief Change Officer role which would serve to channel the organization through our period of transition and self-evaluation. I wanted to make the art and science of change an executive-level function within the utility. I hired the right person, a young professional, M Smith, who was a lawyer, a motorcycle enthusiast, and a performance bodybuilder. Smith would prove to be yet another formidable change agent.

I met Smith while attending a Meet and Greet after she interviewed for the Director of Equal Opportunity position with the city. She was vibrant, smart, and especially attuned to the City and GRU's situation. I hired her as a temporary, full-time employee to place her quickly on board to assist the organization in adapting to the challenges ahead.

Both Banks and Smith were accomplished, Black professionals. In a town that had been referred to as a Sundown town by Commissioner Goston, I took the advancement of minorities within the leadership team very seriously. A Sundown town was one, as Goston had explained, where Black folks needed to be at home before sundown or otherwise be held on suspicion of being involved with criminal misdeeds. Goston told me that as a young boy, he would go into town with his uncle, and, as it was getting late, he remembered certain white folks looking at them and calling out something like, get along home, you little n——. We don't want you around these parts. Yes, I was committed to creating opportunities for those stripped of their humanity.

The Business Report of North Central Florida recognized the restructuring with the following headline, "GRU Shakes

Up Executive Team." In the article, I am quoted as saying, "The CIO, along with the newly established CCO and COO positions, will work together with the rest of our executive management team and other senior leaders to ensure that we are utilizing our current assets in the most efficient way possible and to identify what changes need to be made to decrease upward rate pressure while maintaining the high quality of service our customers rely on."

The demotion of the former leadership team to a level beneath my new executive team did not sit well with my longer-tenured employees. Nobody took it more personally than Stanton, who, prior to my arrival, had been granted significant authority by Interim GM Kathryn Viehe. Whatever differences Stanton and I had rose to a higher level when on August 6, 2015, during a commission meeting, Stanton hand-delivered another memo, this time to all the commissioners.

Unaware of the memo's existence, I was informed by Commissioner Chase that the memo had arrived in his mail basket with the subject, "Possible opportunity to reduce GREC fixed cost." The contents of the memo addressed what else but the Equitable Adjustment. I was stunned that Stanton delivered the memo directly to commissioners, fully outside of organizational protocol, which required correspondence to be vetted by the executive team. Chase laughed as he told me not to worry. He was just sorry the memo wasn't Stanton's resignation letter. I looked at him and said, "It could be."

While I had explained to Stanton that the ship had sailed on avenging the agreement, he couldn't help himself but to write his rambling, private interpretation of how to correct the injustices of the Equitable Adjustment.

As if to make sure I didn't garner any credit for his ideas, Stanton began the memo: "With the recent change in leadership at GRU and the recent change in the makeup of the Commission, I would like to suggest a possible avenue to reduce GREC fixed cost that I have previously offered without success in making my case." In total, he meandered through three pages ending with, "I was unsuccessful in convincing Mr. Hunzinger not to enter into the Agreement. To date, I have been unsuccessful in convincing anyone to initiate action to force a true-up. I will not speak for the City Attorney's Office, but I am informed that counsel does not see merit in the position I take nor the argument I make… I recognize that what I see as intent of the Parties and a rationale for a true-up may not be reflected in the legal language of the Adjustment."

While I was furious over Stanton's actions, I realized he had just provided me with an unexpected glimpse into his real thoughts. I honestly believed that Stanton had tried to dissuade Hunzinger from entering into the Equitable Agreement in 2011. The Navigant Report documented as much. It made sense. Now, however unfair, Stanton would be forever the co-negotiator of the historically onerous GREC PPA. I understood his need to distance himself from it. What better way to do it, but to express his desire and offer a solution?

Sadly, Stanton had approached the situation in an unprecedentedly poor manner. He didn't vet the letter or his position with the city attorney or me. He tried to force his message past me to make himself more relevant. His actions forced me to call him in for a meeting in my office at 11:00 AM on August 7th.

I asked Kathy Viehe and Lewis Walton to attend my meeting with Stanton, knowing full well that there would be difficult conversations that would need to be witnessed. I started the meeting by expressing my primary concerns to Stanton as; 1) the memo related to subject matter under an opinion from our own city attorney and I; 2) hand-delivering the memo was awfully close to an attempt to violate Sunshine Laws; 3) the perception that going directly to the commission was a direct assault on my leadership and poor optics for an officer of GRU.

Stanton said he sent the letter as a result of the attacks on his credibility. He wanted to address those in the community that implied he hadn't had GRU's best interests in mind. He wanted to show them that he had attempted in the past to point out ideas to improve things. Finally, he said he also didn't want "to go Dad" to solve his problems (referring to me).

I told Stanton that his actions had brought about unintended consequences. I told him that as the co-negotiator on the GREC PPA, he never went around Hunzinger to tell the commission it was a bad deal. Yet here we were. He was quite comfortable going around me. Stanton responded that it was his job to tell his boss (Hunzinger) what he thought of the contract, which he had done several times. I looked at Stanton incredulously. Did you really say that to me right now, John?

The bold way I confronted Stanton visibly shook Viehe and Walton. I suspected that such direct conversations were not standard practice here in Gainesville. The conversation was long overdue. I had spent forty-five days as a Swamp Yankee in the swamp, and I wasn't about to let Stanton keep me from my mission.

I told Stanton to take the weekend to consider offering me his resignation, given the weight of the circumstances. Stanton looked at me and said that I could not terminate him without cause and there was no cause—he would be the best Energy Supply guy he can be.

I shook my head as I listened to Stanton. I responded, "John, you need to seriously consider resignation. I need to consider my options." The meeting ended with the expectation that the weekend would be filled with Stanton's self-reflection before resigning on Monday. It was hard to admit, but in many ways, I empathized with Stanton. From all I knew, he was simply a hard-driving company man whose extensive career was filled with accomplishments. Like the tragic hero from Greek literature, his fortunes abruptly changed because of that fatal flaw—being the co-negotiator of the lamentable GREC PPA.

Ω

An Act Of God

Before going home for the weekend, I reflected on how my conflicts with Stanton were overshadowing the traction I was gaining in creating my own chaos under the GREC PPA. I use the term chaos because the relationship between GREC and GRU had been too cozy for my comfort. Chaos and conflict are the battleground of change, not maintenance of the status quo.

***

As I began my second month on the job, I speculated that the contract language of the GREC PPA related to the dispatching and scheduling of the biomass plant might have untapped negotiating value. While there was rather tight language surrounding the number of times GRU could shut down the biomass plant throughout the year, dispatching the plant back online wasn't so straight forward. The way I read the contract, in theory, if GREC went offline for any reason other than GRU's dispatch command, it could be kept offline for the remaining twenty-seven years of the PPA. Holy loophole, Batman. *Of course, GRU would still be liable for the $2 billion of available energy payments over that period of time, unless...*

Maintaining a 102-megawatt biomass power plant in standby mode for twenty-seven years and not actually being dispatched to run would be quite unusual. During that time, in order to receive the $2 billion of available energy payments, GREC would need to keep its crews on site 24 hours, 7 days a week, to ensure they are able to call in every day to notify GRU's system control of its availability. All the required maintenance and exercising of equipment would need to occur on a

139

scheduled basis. Finally, every summer and winter period they'd have to demonstrate the ability to reach their rated electrical output.

It was the beginning of a strategy, using the shortcomings in the GREC PPA to GRU's advantage. From my experience, keeping a power plant in standby mode for a long period wouldn't be easy. might be the leverage I had been seeking.

I promptly scheduled a meeting with Brown and Stanton to discuss my epiphanies. I also brought in GRU's Utility Attorney, Shayla McNeil, who was well-versed on the topics. As we batted ideas around, Stanton told us, in a matter-of-fact manner, that he had been aware of GRU's ability to keep GREC offline. Stanton said that it wasn't a new idea. I stared at him in disbelief as I asked him why he hadn't exercised that option. In all our meetings, Stanton had made no mention of it.

I understood that, prior to my arrival, GREC had tripped (an industry term for a plant coming offline) on multiple occasions and, on each occasion, been quickly restored to their minimum load of seventy megawatts. Stanton informed me that wasn't true. He cited a case when, most recently, GREC had tripped days before an outage, and he had held them offline, given the proximity to the start of the outage. I listened intently. In the case Stanton discussed, I realized that his actions had resulted in benefiting GREC, not harming them. I was also sure that GREC had seen it that way. Being left offline allowed them to avoid the additional costs of ramping up to a minimum load, only to be shut down for the outage soon afterwards. C'mon, man.

It was obvious that Stanton saw the world primarily through an engineer's prism. While it was true that natural gas prices had not fallen far enough to make it economical to keep the GREC plant offline, it was also true that the GREC PPA didn't require GRU to economically dispatch the biomass plant, as Met-Ed had required Panther to do. In my brave new world of imposing more stringent standards upon GREC, I needed Stanton to consider the entire range of costs imposed on our other power plants before keeping GREC online. How could he not?

I recalled my days at Panther when Met-Ed employed quasi-economic dispatch of the power plant. Their bold actions had placed our plant on its heels. They were tough businesspeople ready to ask for forgiveness rather than ask for permission. I didn't see toughness in my leadership team

140

unless the toughness was being directed at me. I didn't suspect Stanton's timid management of the GREC PPA was the right style for what I had planned. At a 30,000-foot strategic level, Stanton seemed unable to see any of these issues as leverage towards negotiating the utility out from under the GREC PPA. Stanton's action, or inaction, concerned me.

As the meeting progressed the more my emotions regressed. I was being drawn into uncomfortable thoughts. Stanton and his team were allowing GRU to absorb huge, damaging costs of their power plants being cycled on and off, on and off, multiple times each week, sometimes daily. They were simply accepting their fate. I needed a plan of action that provided a means to recover GRU's electric generation flexibility that had been shattered with the introduction of a 102.5-megawatt power plant required to run at a minimum load of seventy megawatts.

Running the GREC plant at 70 megawatts was analogous to driving a car on Gainesville City streets, unable to go no slower than forty miles per hour, and at times never being able to come to a stop. The more fitting analogy was from the movie Speed, *where passengers are trapped on a bus armed with a bomb set to explode if the bus's speed falls below 50 miles per hour. Whichever the comparison, we needed to get out of this precarious position.*

I demanded then and there that upon the occurrence of any non-GRU-initiated event that took GREC offline, GRU's system control would deny the plant's return, requiring the unit to be kept in standby mode. Furthermore, GREC would still have to stand ready to fire their boilers upon request and immediately start to return to full load. As if to defy my authority once again, Stanton gleefully told me that his team had already been operating under this strategy. "I don't have a problem with that," he said.

Stanton was wrong. His group had not been operating under the full-scale implications of the strategy I had in mind. Frankly, under my leadership, it would be a cold day in hell if and when GREC would be called back into service after being taken offline. I was determined to act on contract in the best interests of the community. I looked at Stanton and just smiled.

On July 24th, I retained a new law firm, Winston and Strawn, led by a former associate, Jonathan Birenbaum. Birenbaum had been

Panther's outside counsel during my tenure, and he was one of the best lawyers in the power business. He was also a New York City kind of guy and had the state of mind Billy Joel would sing about. After Birenbaum flew down to Gainesville to meet with my team, we reminisced about the good old days during lunch at Gainesville's best barbecue rib joint, Mojo's downtown.

Mojos slowly cooked its meat, and I wanted to treat Birenbaum to our southern gastronomic hospitality. Sheepishly, Birenbaum confided with the group that he had never partaken in a southern barbecue. What? Hearing that, I told him that this trip would include a bunch of firsts. After the southern barbecue, I exclaimed that I would treat him to the worst PPA ever written in North America, the GREC PPA. Granted, Birenbaum had seen his share of PPAs, but I was certain that he'd never seen one quite like this.

By the end of the day, Birenbaum and his associate, Lisa Cottle, confirmed my interpretation to keep GREC in standby mode upon a non-GRU-initiated shutdown. They also confirmed that they had never quite seen a contract written so poorly and so one-sidedly. I had gotten what I needed.

After enjoying our expertly cooked brisket at Mojo's, I introduced my own style of cooking as I turned up the heat on Gordon by sending him a letter stating it was time to sit down to negotiate added terms for the PPA. I didn't have hope for a productive response. My e-mail had an ulterior purpose—to keep the public focused on the primary reason for GRU's higher rates. It wouldn't hurt GRU's public perception to have the new general manager seen as taking the game to Gordon. We had serious challenges with the GREC PPA. As I said to the Gainesville Sun, "The biggest reason our costs are high is the GREC contract, so we are looking to mitigate those."

The process of memorializing my thoughts and actions in e-mails, letters, and other correspondence was a tactic that I had used elsewhere. In Florida, that tactic took on more significance. Sharing this correspondence directly with the commission made them public documents, which made them accessible to the public through the city's website portal, or through public records requests. While others had seen the Florida Sunshine Laws as a detriment, I saw these laws as my secret weapon. Since the state demanded transparency, I thought, why not use that transparency to gain a strategic advantage? It was the perfect vehicle to keep the entire community aware of the efforts my team and I were undertaking. It was also the perfect way to message Gordon and control the narrative. Note to self: it's always a win when you can turn a perceived weakness into a strength.

On August 6, 2015, I, along with Holt, conducted a meeting in GRU offices with GREC point man Al Morales. The issue at hand was the Construction Cost Adjuster, which Holt thought was being misapplied. Despite Richardson's warnings, Holt had conducted an audit and discovered the basis to withhold payments from GREC for approximately $200,000. The city attorney responded, suggesting a vetting of the issue with GREC management was in order.

Morales played the circumstances surrounding the Construction Cost adjuster and the dollar-to-euro index close to his vest. In short order, he indicated that he hadn't thought about the index but would investigate it. Okay, I thought if you want to play poker, let's have it.

While we were at the table, seeing that Morales wasn't going to offer any information on the primary topic, Holt decided to explore Morales' understanding of the Equitable Adjustment. Morales indicated that he was aware of questions about the validity of the agreement. However, GREC's attorneys told him otherwise. I laughingly told Morales that it was unfortunate that "he got to see ours while he didn't show us his." Morales did not find my comment humorous in the least. Morales could not hide his frustration with me. Touchy, I thought.

At this point, I decided to have a little fun with the less then fun-loving Morales. In my world, if you don't have a decided advantage, or any advantage for that matter, being unpredictable can be a game changer. Morales told us that the constant chatter from commissioners decreased our ability to work together. He said, "Lenders and investors are watching."

I quizzed him as to why GREC's investors were so upset about what was said at commission meetings. I asked, "If you're okay with your legal position, why do you care?"

Morales snapped back, "We always care."

Sensing his passion for having the last word, I hit Morales' launch button by asking if there was something more for GREC to lose, "Like a refinancing or something?"

Visibly upset, Morales declared, "I hope that you aren't trying to harm GREC."

I told him simply, "Tortious interference was not anywhere on my mind." Gordon's point man was furious. We stared at each other in complete silence as Holt coughed nervously while trying to return the conversation to normalcy. Of course, I was testing Morales as much as I was having fun. I wanted to see what type of individuals Gordon would surround himself with. I wanted to assess the people who would be giving him advice. I got my answer; Gordon must be one serious dude.

During later discovery work, Morales was found to have written e-mails to himself, labeled as memo-to-file, which memorialized important conversations, such as this testy conversation. Recounting it, he wrote, "I took his words to mean that they (GRU) were aware we were contemplating a refinancing of GREC, and that the city was deliberately creating a public ruckus in order to make accomplishing that refinancing difficult for GREC." I must admit, it's the first and only time in my life I was ever accused of creating a public ruckus. Note to self: learn to stay away from any public ruckus.

***

On the evening of August 7, 2015, hours after the meeting in which I asked for Stanton's resignation, the impetus I had been waiting for happened. At 8:09 PM, during an evening thunderstorm, the GREC Plant was struck by lightning and forced offline. At precisely 8:22 PM, I received an e-mail from Stanton in accordance with my instructions. "FYI, as we have discussed, Production Cost Modeling shows savings to our customers if GREC remains offline. As such, we have told them to go into Standby when their Forced outage condition has cleared. As part of our obligation under the PPA to use 'good utility practice,' we will advise them (and you) when we expect them to be dispatched back on economics. We will get to that next week. Please be advised that a loss of any GRU asset may require GREC to return to service for reliability rather than economics. I will keep you advised."

It was only 10 hours later when the biomass plant was ready to return to service. At 6:27 AM, upon resetting their instrumentation, GREC personnel called GRU's system control, informing them the plant was available. GRU's system control stated my new direction that GREC was to remain in standby condition. With that, the magic words were spoken— GREC is to remain in standby condition. The biomass plant was offline, and it was now in GRU's hands to determine whether or when GREC would be returning to service.

The power between GRU and GREC had shifted. We had our catalyst, an act of God, which took GREC offline and shifted the balance of power and control towards the utility. With this latest development, Stanton's precarious position changed as quickly as the lightning bolt that struck the plant. As a key player in keeping GREC offline, I realized that it would be a rather inopportune time to terminate him, given the impending battle that was sure to follow. Obviously aware of his newly elevated status, Stanton decided not to resign while I chose to leave sleeping dogs lie. It was time to keep the pedal to the metal. With renewed optimism, I returned my focus to the GREC PPA.

That night, I wrote an e-mail to Gordon that I also shared with the commission. The e-mail was short and to the point, "GRU elected not to return the Facility to service and instead is operating its own generating assets and purchased power at a more optimal level and at operational savings. At the present time, we don't anticipate bringing GREC back in service until at least October. We will be reviewing our options."

The usual negative coverage of GRU from the *Gainesville Sun* turned upbeat when they ran a front-page article entitled," Power play puts biomass plant on pause." The newspaper accurately reported that GRU might not request that the GREC facility be taken offline during the summer month at GRU's discretion. If the plant goes offline for another reason,

GRU can opt against taking energy from the plant. I was impressed that they had gotten it right.

Mayor Braddy praised me as he was quoted in the *Gainesville Sun* saying, "Mayor Ed Braddy said part of the reason city leaders wanted to hire GRU's new general manager, Edward Bielarski Jr., is because they wanted an interpretation of the city's power purchase agreement with GREC that's more aggressive, in the sense of looking out for ratepayers."

Even Nathan Crabbe, the editor of the *Gainesville Sun*, joined in. "GRU's new general manager wasted no time showing he was going to play hardball when it comes to the biomass plant. For ratepayers, it was encouraging news."

"Whatever you call it, Bielarski's approach is a welcome change."

Crabbe included my carefully crafted quote as well, "I wouldn't call it a strategy to get concessions out of the contract. I'm looking at it as the best way to give value to the customers based on the contract we signed. If they want to negotiate, that's great, but we will do this to get the value out of the contract." Make no mistake about it; value was being derived from keeping GREC offline.

One thing is certain, taking bold and decisive action on the night of August 7th was the first time GRU had drawn a line in the sand and told GREC not to cross it, albeit initiated by an act of God. GREC blinked. Whether legally bound or unaware, their acquiescence provided GRU a green light to buy cheaper power off the grid and operate our own units more efficiently for as long as we could.

Soon after GREC's shutdown, realizing that I was serious about keeping them offline, GREC staff communicated through Stanton that they'd consider reducing the minimum load to fifty-five megawatts, down from the contractual 70 megawatts. I slyly told Gordon that I saw this as a response to my earlier July offer asking that we renegotiate the PPA, and yes, I agreed to his acceptance. In an August 24th letter from Gordon, he said the reduction in minimum load was mentioned as simply a question. It was not intended as his agreement to amend the contract.

The *Gainesville Sun* reported upon the series of events with an article entitled, "GRU in no hurry to buy power from biomass plant." I offered the Sun a quote in which I cast further uncertainty about if GREC would be brought back online, "It depends on the marketplace. It's simply whatever we can do what's best for the customers." I also said that it was not likely, GRU could go an entire calendar year without GREC's power generation.

If there wasn't enough irony in the situation, before the month of August ended, former Mayor Hanrahan received an award from The Friends of Susan B. Anthony in recognition of her work as a civic activist, public servant, and environmental advocate. Protesters lined up in front of the Best Western Gateway Hotel to let people know that Hanrahan was anything but a hero.

A local Gainesville resident, Maria Parsons, said, "We don't understand why Pegeen Hanrahan is getting this award when... as a commissioner and a mayor, she did not protect our city." Of course, Hanrahan remained defiant towards my efforts. She told a local reporter, "I think that if I were in a position of authority, I would work to try to find some changes in the contract or other concessions that would make sense. I don't think the sort of hostile atmosphere that's been creating is facilitating that, though." I laughed out loud as I remembered Hanrahan's demeanor during the May 9, 2009, commission meeting when they approved the GREC PPA. *Hostile indeed.*

On November 5th, the commission agreed to establish a new Utility Advisory Board or UAB. It was largely a defense against Representative Perry's attempts to wrestle control of the utility away from the commission. I wasn't sure how or why a non-voting advisory board would impact Perry's desire to change GRU's governance. I knew I wasn't excited about having to shepherd presentations through two bodies, the commission and the UAB. My staff was already fully consumed by an extensive workload.

Later in November, Anthony Lyons was named as the interim city manager replacing long-time City Manager Russ Blackburn. Lyons told all city employees in his hello letter that, "Russ actually hired or appointed me on four separate occasions, twice as CRA Director, once as Interim Director of Planning and Development Services and most recently, as the Executive Director of the Blue-Ribbon Committee on Economic Competitiveness." Lyons was not your typical city manager, as I was not your typical general manager. I was hopeful that we could work together.

Through it all, the GREC plant remained offline.

As 2015 was coming to a close, unexpectedly, on December 21st, Gordon sent me GREC's Demand for Arbitration on the over $223,000 of payments withheld resulting from Holt's audit. *Crap!* Holt had miscalculated the legal basis of these so-called over-payments. Whether he was simply too energetic in trying to place his mark on the GREC saga, we'll never know, but now it was my problem.

Another controversary surrounding, yet another city misstep, was the last thing I needed during this sensitive process. Aware that the *Gainesville Sun* would elevate Gordon's Demand to a higher level than it really was, I went into action to deflect attention away from the kerfuffle. I crafted a few statements.

"The Commission should be aware that GREC's demand relates solely to the dispute surrounding the Dollar-to-Euro Exchange Rate pursuant to the Construction Cost Adjuster."

"In regard to the limited focus of the Demand for Arbitration, I plan on digesting its contents over the Christmas holiday (along with some holiday food) and exploring GRU's prospects for success as compared to the legal costs in the process."

On the morning of Christmas Eve, I talked with Gordon and confirmed that GRU would remit the $223,000 and forego the auditor's claims. I also talked about engaging in discussions about buying the plant. Gordon was not surprised but cautioned me that he had been tried before with no success. I told him, "Yeah, but not with me." He chuckled.

I followed up with an e-mail to the commission in which I crafted the following ray of Christmas cheer: "In light of this morning's conversation and with a sincere effort to look towards avenues of mutual benefit, supported by our renewed spirit of cooperation and as an act of good faith, I am electing to remit the previously withheld CCS disputed funds, along with withdrawing GRU's claim for CCA funds (hopefully before year-end). As I have said in my previous communications with you, I believe the GREC facility has value for GRU. It's the PPA which is problematic for GRU. Let's see if we can't make this a win-win for both of us."

As I expected, within hours, the narrative shifted from the city's failed attempt to withhold funds to GRU potentially buying the plant—Biomass Buyout. The UF *Alligator* had a headline which read: "City discusses buying biomass plant." In it, reporter Hunter Williamson wrote, "GRU GM Ed Bielarski Jr. said discussions were underway with GREC, which owns the biomass plant, to arrange for negotiations." In a *Gainesville Sun* article, the usually combative GREC representative, Al Morales, was quoted as saying, "GREC has always been willing to work cooperatively with GRU to find ways to create value for mutual benefit."

August 7th became the day when an act of God gave GRU its best opportunity to finally exert a better bargain from the lopsided contract it had negotiated. With it, the potential of a Biomass Buyout made its first appearance.

$$\Omega$$

Know Thy Enemy

Up until the end of 2015, Gordon and I had simply been sparring with each other. Gordon was the face of a burgeoning renewable energy franchise, while I was just the general manager of a municipal utility, who others saw as the new sheriff in town. I would need to chart the right course to be successful.

The first time Gordon and I ever spoke with each other was on that July 1st day when I reached out to suggest we sit down for a cup of coffee whenever he was in town. I told Gordon with a chuckle; we could be Gainesville's version of *Comedians in Cars getting Coffee*. I briefly paused before offering him a brief description of the show. I told him the television show featured comedian Jerry Seinfeld, joining fellow comedians in a unique venue. Seinfeld would start the show by showing off a vintage classic car which he would use to shepherd his guest off to a local coffee shop. A classic car aficionado himself, Seinfeld would select the right car to fit his guest's style. Once in the car in search of that illusive coffee shop, they'd engage in spirited conversation as they discussed their craft. That's when I told Gordon, "So, you see, that could be us."

I could tell Gordon was mystified by my reference to this pop culture phenomenon. Unexcitedly, he did acknowledge that he heard of the show but knew little else about it. Great, I thought, realizing my previous encounters with Morales had accurately pegged Gordon as a serious soul. I imagined

Gordon thinking, who is this guy? Undeterred, I told Gordon that the show came to mind because Jerry Seinfeld reminded me of him. Gordon blurted out, "Me?" In a jovial manner, I quickly responded, "Sure, both you and Seinfeld have more money than God, and I suspect you both get bored pretty easily." Of course, Gordon and Seinfeld, not Gordon and God.

Gordon understood my humor as he laughed. He said that he wasn't sure about driving around in classic cars, but he thought having a coffee together would be fine. He thought we ought to meet sometime soon during one of his trips down south. Today would be that day.

On a sweltering summer Gainesville day, I took a short drive to GREC's modular office building sitting like a country cottage in front of the massive, exposed steel girder power plant. With no exterior walls, the plant looked like an erector set on steroids. Of course, the heat of the south requires power plants like GREC to be built with no outside coverings, lest they become a sweltering spa inside, unfit for human beings. As I entered the lobby, Gordon was standing alone, waiting for me. I was immediately reminded of a passage in the book *Cape Wind*.

"When Gordon, at six foot one and 165 pounds, walked into the room, Mitrokostas was impressed. He saw a man who had to be taken seriously. Gordon's closely cropped hair, athletic appearance, and neat but basic clothing belied his self-made wealth. The guy's substantive thought was Mitrokostas, who had expected someone a bit more flakey looking. He had little patience for environmentalists or ageing hippies, but Gordon had a strong presence and spoke clearly, directly, and sometimes even eloquently."

Within moments of sitting down in the plant's conference room, Gordon went all in on an elevator speech, telling me why his biomass plant was the best thing that ever happened for Gainesville. I didn't argue. I simply listened as I gauged my opponent. Yep, Gordon was as Mitrokostas had described him. He was as serious and on-point as a knife blade.

Gordon politely said, "I am happy operating in accordance with the PPA." I responded that I would be fighting for the rights that GRU had bargained for within the GREC PPA. The one thing we agreed on was that any future success would be built on a platform of trust. I left happy to have a seat at the table with a skilled negotiator and prominent businessperson, albeit as an underdog.

When I returned to my office, I methodically arranged a series of meetings with *WCJB TV News,* the *Gainesville Sun, Business in the Heart of Florida magazine,* and other media outlets. It was time to dial public pressure up a notch. In my interview with Chris Ebersole with *Business in the Heart of Florida,* I used the platform to not only reach the community but Gordon as well. I knew Gordon would read the article. He read everything about his multi-billion-dollar investment. I told Ebersole, "Part of building trust is being able to go out in the community and say what you mean and mean what you say. Building trust doesn't come overnight. You have to work with people over a period of time and build a relationship. Trust isn't just a word; it's a feeling and an emotion." *I heard you, Jim.*

Given the history of the GREC PPA, I had to find a way to let the public in on what I was telling Gordon in private. I knew the upcoming struggle would be fought under the bright lights of public scrutiny. As a result, I took a little literary license and told the local *WCJB Television channel* that Gordon was ready to negotiate. Specifically, I said, "It puts them on the record saying yes, we're willing to negotiate—we're willing to talk about this- because up until now, they haven't really said that." I also laid GRU's problems directly on Gordon's doorstep: "The biggest reason our costs are high is the GREC contract. So, we are looking to mitigate those." Let Gordon dispute my claims.

Interestingly, GREC spokesperson John Brushwood responded on Gordon's behalf, telling the newspaper, "As long as we can find a mutual benefit for both companies and the ratepayer, we're willing to do the hard work and look to find a better deal for the Gainesville ratepayer." *Perfect.*

Before engaging with Gordon in the real heavy lifting of our disputes, I took time to research the man, the myth, and the legend. I would not make the same mistake I had made with Bill Dimeling. Lucky for me, Gordon's previous business successes had not gone unnoticed by the press. Newspaper, magazine articles, and a book about his Cape Wind project added up to a treasure trove of valuable insights into Gordon's business dealings and the man behind them.

The thumbnail sketch of Gordon, as reported by the Boston Globe and others, was that he had been born to Russian Jewish immigrants. He'd never have been accused of being born with a silver spoon in his mouth. Despite his modest upbringing, Gordon had been able to spend his summers in Maine's West End Camp, thinking the experience would build his self-confidence. It worked because, by the age of five, he was nicknamed "Toughie." At thirteen, he grew to be known as "Cool Hand Luke." The phrase I remember the most was, "Gordon never forgot the fun of being the underdog." *Hmmm, that would not be the case here. That would be my role.*

After earning his degree in communications from Boston College, by his own accounts, Gordon had an epiphany while waiting in the long gas lines during the 1970s oil embargo. The experience changed Gordon's early career vision of becoming a filmmaker into being a dealmaker. Energy deals would be his specialty—alternate energy like biomass, natural gas, wind, and solar. But first, Gordon would need to build wealth.

One thing was undeniable about Gordon; he made his fortune the old-fashioned way—he earned it. His first fortune came from selling cable as he "signed so many subscribers that he broke a national sales record, and company executives came from New York to ask whether he would develop a training program. Could he sell?" Gordon recalled his early sales success simply; "What I was saying was what I believed in."

It was apparent to me that Gordon used any sign of disrespect as emotional fuel to drive his engine. If people marginalized him for not having an Ivy League education, throw another log on the fire. Not born into the elite class, well, throw on another two logs. *I feel it getting a little warm here.* I understood Gordon's emotions. I had been known to harbor similar ones.

After his financial success in the cable television industry, he reached out for more. His instincts and research uncovered an opportunity to build low-cost, low-greenhouse gas-emitting natural gas power plants in the New England area, which already had ample coal and oil-fired power generation. I imagined Gordon's spider senses tingled when he recognized the potential of the new combined cycle gas technology. Without hesitation, he formed a new company, Energy Management, Inc. (EMI) and parlayed his profits into the alternative energy industry, starting with the design and construction of a series of natural gas-fired plants from which he built a renewable power empire.

Gordon once confidently told a reporter, "Three of our natural gas plants killed three coal plants." I thought Gordon's words offered a glimpse into his aggressive way of thinking, dare I say business killer instinct.

I laughed when I read him in the same article saying, "This isn't a contest. It's not does Jim Gordon ultimately win or does Bill Koch ultimately win. The real winner is the environment."

His words made it clear to me that every deal Gordon entered was a contest, to beat, or kill the competition. While Gordon admitted to being a true environmental believer, he just wanted to win on both counts, the money, and the environment. I grew to think of Gordon as an elite intellectual reminiscent of the words of the famous American novelist, F Scott Fitzgerald who said, "The test of a first-rate intelligence is the ability to hold two opposing ideas in mind at the same time and still retain the ability to function. One should, for example, be able to see that things are hopeless yet be determined to make them otherwise."

I was amazed at how young Gordon had been when he jumped into the energy field with no industry experience, out of nowhere. As a 2004 *Boston Globe* article wrote, "He had no background in the field, but at twenty-two, the quick study began pouring over energy research. Gordon founded Energy Management, Inc. (EMI) with $3,000 in savings. He would take then-girlfriend Jan Saragoni on double dates with forty-year-old investors." I was impressed with Gordon's unabashed aggressiveness and curious sense of entrepreneurship. I laughed when I read that Gordon's second wife, Meg, describe him as, "a turtle, and he always wins."

Gordon's plant in Gainesville was not his first biomass power plant development. As I mentioned earlier, Gordon had built a 15-megawatt biomass power plant in New Hampshire in 1986, and over two decades later, he secured a PPA with Austin Energy for the power production from a biomass plant to be built in Nacogdoches, Texas. The Nacogdoches PPA was eerily like the GREC PPA. The Nacogdoches biomass plant, itself, was serial number 1 of its kind, with GREC being serial number 2 (which is engineers speak for identifying the Nacogdoches plant as the first commercial design of its kind, with GREC being the second). Before the plant ever reached commercial operations, EMI sold their interests to Southern Company, a huge power company serving the Gulf States.

Contemporaneous with his biomass pursuits, Gordon doggedly continued his fight to bring wind energy turbines to Cape Cod, intent on a prime location off the coast of Hyannis Port, Massachusetts. Gordon started the project, known as Cape Wind, in 2001, when he was only forty-eight. After almost two decades of fighting for wind power off the coast, Gordon's business idea had become an odd quixotic quest.

Instead of flailing away at windmills, he was intent on constructing them.

Gordon's support came from stalwarts of the environmental community, while his opposition formed a political who's—who of foes. Walter Cronkite, Edward Kennedy, Robert Kennedy Jr, John Kerry, the Koch brothers, Scott Brown, and Mitt Romney would all use their influence and money to keep unsightly wind turbine blades from spinning on their expensive, expansive horizon. Gordon once quipped, "There are easier ways to make a living."

The late Ted Kennedy would simply not allow his Hyannis Port compound view to be marred by 130 wind turbines lined up on the horizon like cars in those long lines at gas stations during the 1973 oil embargo. Neither would Bill Koch, a conservative billionaire, who funded America's World Cup, and owned Oxbow Energy. In 2013, Koch bought Bunny Mellon's waterfront estate on Nantucket Island garnering a front row seat to the Cape Wind fight. His strategy of delay, delay, delay would drain, drain, and drain Gordon's valuable resources and time.

Koch's strategy was a perfect counter for someone like Gordon who, as Koch once said, fell in love with his projects—a real no-no for developers and a real insight into his psyche. I believe that due to Gordon's first-rate intelligence—he understood the hopelessness of Cape Wind while remaining determined to make it otherwise. I suspected Gordon's well-documented tenacity would be his downfall. Cape Wind would be his Waterloo.

Gordon's mother, Florence, once discussed the difference between Gordon and his brother with a reporter. Florence said, "Michael, he should rest in peace he would have to have one hundred toys to play with. And Jimmy played with one. That one toy would be his satisfaction. He would do it until he got it right."

CNN quoted Gordon as saying, "When you believe in your heart that you have the right project at the right time you just keep putting one foot in front of the other." Gordon had simply replaced his childhood toys and solitary focus with power plants. Cape Wind was his latest toy.

I perceived the joy of developers like Gordon was to construct their dream, not necessarily operate them. I hoped that Gordon saw GREC PPA's intrinsic value as a way to keep Cape Wind. If so, I believed he'd be willing to part with it for the right price. He just needed the right motivation. Hopefully, I was offering just the right type of motivation through requiring GREC to stand up contractually for the deal GRU had bargained for.

More digging into Gordon's world uncovered another morsel. In 2015, Gordon failed to meet a construction deadline and two local utilities canceled their PPA's with Cape Wind. Gordon was receiving ample motivation to negotiate a deal with me.

With Gordon facing mounting financial pressures with Cape Wind, I had continued to direct his prized GREC biomass plant to remain off-line, placing his income from the biomass plant in jeopardy. By his own admission, Gordon told *Commonwealth Magazine* that they (meaning him and his investors I assume) had invested sixty-five million dollars through 2013. I also assumed he would reach one hundred million dollars before it was over. Gordon's mind-boggling investment left me hearing Bob Dylan singing that Gordon's fortunes were, "just blowing in the wind." *Note to self: my affinity for matching song lyrics to memorable moments might just catch on.*

I wondered if Gordon's quest was more of a need for conquest. I believe that need was on full display when he talked about being able to convince people to change their opinions. He took immense pride in telling others how in two and 1/2 hours with Walter Cronkite he had convinced America's broadcaster to reconsider his opposition to the Cape Wind project. As told by Gordon, he had persuaded Cronkite to see his legacy as a journalist was being betrayed through his failure to analyze both sides of the story. If Gordon could do this to the "most trusted man in America" do I have any chance?

I had attended two Jesuit Universities. If anyone understood the prioritization of competing ethical dilemmas, it was I. If Gordon wanted to go toe to toe with me on the competing interests of mitigating climate change in one town versus imposing backbreaking rates on the disenfranchised, well, let's rumble.

Rumble or not, I read all too often that Gordon was a relentless and dynamic negotiator. To that first point, William Mooman, a professor of International Economics at Tufts University's Fletcher School would say of Gordon's pursuit of the Cape Wind deal, "Jim Gordon has to be one of the most persistent people who truly believes in the goal he's set for himself. Most people would have pulled out long ago."

To the second point, an aptly named Cape Wind opponent, Glenn Wattly said about him, "He's the master at how you spin things."

Gordon was emotionally built for one-on-one negotiations, like a Ferrari was built for high performance. I was no Ferrari. I was built to rethink ideas, overhaul assumptions, and change gears. I was more of a four-wheel drive pickup.

As events unfolded, I would soon learn that I wasn't the only party performing research on the other. Gordon had his sources of information, as well.

Ω

Secret Agent Man

On October 19, 2015, Stanton notified me through an e-mail that he intended to retire from GRU—on April 28, 2017, a whole eighteen months hence. I thought his decision had to do with actions I had taken two months previously, when on August 17, 2015, I notified both Gordon and Morales that Stanton was "*not authorized* to make changes to the four corners of the Power Purchase Agreement or any of the controlling documents. In the future, please direct communications related to these changes to me for GRU's official position and ability to renegotiate." I'm sure this new directive was a devastating blow to Stanton's ego, particularly coming from a Swamp Yankee and bean counter like me.

I had multiple reasons to issue the August 17th directive including Stanton's previous cavalier delivery of the Equitable Adjustment memo to the commissioners, his previous failure to share a letter from GREC's President of Engineering and Asset Management, Len Fagan, concerning a potential reduction of minimum operating load to 55 megawatts, and his ever visible, growing, friendly behavior towards GREC's management. I didn't need these distractions.

On January 7, 2016, with the GREC plant still off-line, I reached out to the community to inform them of my plans to pursue a buyout of the GREC PPA in a *Gainesville Sun* editorial succinctly entitled, "Why buy the biomass plant?"

"In the midst of contract disputes, legal proceedings, perceived overall poor relations, the discussions about GRU possibly buying GREC might come as a surprise to many. As GRU's general manager, I would like to offer an explanation of our reasoning." I ended the editorial by stating: "Rest assured that I will only bring options to the City Commission that make financial sense to GRU customers."

The campaign to buyout the GREC PPA had begun.

Like clockwork, five days later, on January 12, 2016, Stanton interfered with my message by delivering a white paper to the over one hundred employees under his command. Supposedly, the white paper served to answer two questions, *How bad GREC was being hurt by not running the plant, and what would it cost to buy GREC? How dare Stanton put out another public document without the proper vetting, right on the heels of my public announcement.*

In addressing whether GREC would be hurt by not running the plant, Stanton wrote: "It is very likely that GREC will make at least as much money by not running, and perhaps millions more, than if they were actually delivering energy. And they will be doing it with much less operational risk and therefore less risk to cash flow… which should benefit them in refinancing." I couldn't believe it. This white paper was a transparent attempt to harm the underpinnings of my efforts. Worse yet, Stanton's conclusions were wrong.

A power plant, like the GREC plant, which is being kept on standby for an indeterminate period makes bankers nervous, not more receptive towards a refinancing. Stanton's contention that GREC was making more money was wrong as well.

The idea that GREC could forego its outages just because it hadn't been running was ludicrous. In the Florida heat and dampness, a mechanical piece of equipment left idle needs more upkeep, not less. Furthermore, where did he get off writing that GREC had cancelled their upcoming outage?

Stanton brashly plowed through the other question about what it would cost to buy GREC. Without consulting with anyone else of authority within GRU, he proceeded to present the case that the fair-market value of the GREC PPA based on the plant remaining in shutdown was over one billion dollars. *Note to self: Stanton had chutzpah.*

Stanton reasoned that drafting the paper was made necessary to respond to those GRU employees asking the question after reading my editorial. *Nice try.* No, for me, the paper represented a big middle finger pointed directly at me, as he attempted to discredit my strategy over the growing list of disputes. He seemed so blinded by his dislike for me that he would cross the line of propriety.

My emotions aside, my growing concern was Stanton's progressively growing bias against me. I also suspected that Stanton now saw himself as untouchable heading towards a planned retirement. I felt with his latest actions, Stanton had hoisted himself on his own petard—a phrase out of Shakespeare's play Hamlet which means a bomb-maker is lifted off the ground with his own bomb. I intended to keep Stanton close and find the underlying cause of his allegation that GREC had cancelled its outage.

Despite Stanton's intrusions, I was beginning to hit my stride. I was controlling the narrative and keeping Gordon's team on the defensive. I had built a highly qualified executive team to help me achieve utility goals. However, I sensed that Gordon had grown more suspicious of me. Quietly, I wondered if there was something of which I wasn't aware.

Gordon's agent on the ground, Al Morales, continued to send me threatening letters, calling GRU's actions improper, and held the utility responsible for all its unspecified losses. I knew there was something else. Then, it happened. In early February, the long-simmering issues with Stanton came to a head, in a series of e-mails.

***

On February 3, 2016, during the midst of a GREC dispute as to whether they had to conduct a spring outage, Stanton sent me an e-mail, copying the affected parties. In it, Stanton detailed actions he had taken that were in direct contravention of my August 17th and September 13 mandate limiting his authority in working with GREC.

Written in a devil may care, spirited manner, Stanton said, "I have the letter from Len (Fagan, GREC's VP of Engineering) canceling the outage and (I think) my email recognizing receipt of the document. I'll get them next Monday." That was the first time I had heard of such a document. I thought, this is it Stanton, you've gone too far.

He followed that with the comment, "The language about outages and their approval was drafted by me so I absolutely know the intent. GREC is required to use Best Utility Practice to maintain availability/reliability. Nowhere does GRU have the right to dictate means and methods of doing so." Stanton was daring me to tell him that he was wrong.

As support, Stanton forwarded me an October 14, 2015, letter from Fagan, in which Fagan declared, "GREC plans no Maintenance or Planned outages in 2016." Stanton had replied to Fagan via e-mail saying simply, "Thanks, acknowledging receipt." I was shocked. It was the first time I had heard or seen this e-mail chain. I had never been included in Fagan's original e-mail distribution, nor was the e-mail electronically forwarded, or delivered by hard copy to me. Obvious to an elementary school student, Stanton had ignored my August and September instructions to refrain from making any changes to the PPA or controlling documents of which the maintenance schedule was one. It wasn't lost on me that GREC had ignored my instructions as well.

The significance of this series of e-mails cannot be overstated. My own Energy Supply Officer, whom I had given a second chance after multiple missteps, was formally supporting GREC's argument that they needn't take a planned outage—ostensibly destroying our primary argument in the dispute and making GRU liable for four million dollars and much more.

I soon found out Stanton wasn't done digging the hole deeper for himself. He wrote back that same day, "...and furthermore; my receipt and acknowledgement thereof were not just implied approval... I clearly approved on behalf of GRU. If there is any criticism of doing so. If there is blame it should be on me." Now he was just goading me.

Furious with the level of his insubordination, I collected myself and e-mailed him, "Let me be clear; you are not authorized to accept on behalf of GRU, given that it was a contract issue (if you remember I notified you and GREC of that change last year). I really don't care about your rationale in deciding if it was appropriate or proper for GRU to authorize the change. The point is that you took action against my directive, in a clear act of insubordination. This is unacceptable behavior for any employee of GRU, much less the Energy Supply Officer."

That night, in response, Stanton doubled down, when he sent me another e-mail in which he declared, "I (and my team) had been coordinating GREC outages with the outages of GRU's plants since the summer of 2013. I (with my team) had been coordinating maintenance outages for many, many years for all the other facilities from which GRU produces energy. I offered that I felt that nothing is more operational than planning maintenance."

The e-mail chain expanded when I dispatched another e-mail expressing my further displeasure, "With your latest correspondence you continue to show me that you don't grasp the magnitude of the situation, as well as the distinction between GREC's interest in a physical outage and GRU's overall interests. Furthermore, within this process you have effectively made public your opinion that the GREC contract doesn't allow GRU to reject changes to planned maintenance outages. That is way beyond your scope as the Energy Supply

Officer and is without authority, both on a commercial and legal basis."

Stanton had stepped way beyond the cliff. There wasn't any way to bring him back from the fall he was about to experience. Stanton was performing without a safety net now. Stanton's actions clearly constituted insubordination.

As a direct result of his actions, Stanton was issued an employee notice in which he was informed that his actions were cause for termination. He was escorted from GRU's offices. After a series of grievance proceedings, his employment finally ended on April 5th. Like the Energizer Bunny, Stanton would not be deterred. He would soon find a way to introduce himself back into the fray.

**

On Gainesville's political front, in March of 2016, Mayor Braddy lost his reelection bid to former Commissioner Lauren Poe, who, as you may remember, was one of the three commissioners who had voted for someone other than me to be the GRU GM, less than a year earlier. He had been mentored by former Mayor Pegeen Hanrahan, so time would tell if Poe would support me in the same manner as Braddy during the on-going conflict with GREC.

During the same election, one of my supporters, Commissioner Randy Wells termed out of office and Hayes-Santos won the empty commission seat easily against Jim Konish, 4,517 votes to 1,021. I could see the commission's political complexion changing in real time. I envisioned more upcoming shifts in the commission's balance or power. I feared that I would have to tread lightly in the GREC matter. *Damn!*

Throughout the early part of 2016, the list of contract disputes grew, along with Gordon's frustration. The common thread running through the disputes was whether, or not GREC was truly able to deliver Available Energy at those times when they were conducting outages and ramping the plant up or down. As part of that thread, GREC's unilateral decision to forego their upcoming outage took center stage. I authorized the withholding of four million dollars from GREC's payments as that amount represented the reduced GRU costs during such outages.

Through further legal discovery, we uncovered GREC's plant logs reflecting more events when GREC may not have really been available to run, yet declared it was. All told, we had approximately ten items under dispute, and I authorized withholding approximately six million dollars from GREC payments. I laughed as I thought about Richardson telling me the world was going to end if we withheld payments from GREC.

Finally, Gordon had enough of my gamesmanship. He notified us that GREC would bring the dispute to a formal arbitration. With Winston and Strawn already representing the utility, I expanded their role to represent us in the proceedings. As I mulled over my next series of moves, I realized I had one more arrow in my quiver - GREC's filing of an arbitration claim over GRU's withholding of money was an acknowledgement on Gordon's part that that there was a default under the PPA. No matter which party was at fault, it was our obligation under the GREC PPA to notify all parties of the default along with our legal position. I instructed our lawyers to notify GREC's international banking consortium of that occurrence.

I fist pumped as I thought about Gordon getting hoisted with his own petard. His filing gave me the opportunity to engage his bankers in the arbitration now. It was my experience that bankers react to such notifications like a mule responds to being pulled from its feeding trough. They stubbornly stand firm while continuing to eat, afraid of when their next meal will come. Put another way, the bankers withhold funding, continuing to collect collateral, such as cash held in bank accounts. While protected, they "lawyer-up" and wait for courts to decide further actions.

Bottom line: Not only was the notification valid, but it would also place an enormous amount of pressure on GREC's investors to push for a compromise to the arbitration claim.

By the summer of 2016, both GRU and GREC had staked out their substantial claims before a judge in arbitration hearings. Gordon was indeed that turtle his second wife had described. He relentlessly moved along like Father Time. Every time I thought about her words I laughed. My wife's alma mater was the University of Maryland (UM) whose mascot was the terrapin. The UM battle cry was "Fear the Turtle." *Hmmmm, I really like turtle soup.*

Towards the end of July, I was notified that Father Time had been joined in the nick of time with Stanton. GREC had modified its complaint, largely on claims made by John Stanton. *Oh boy, what's this about?*

The *Gainesville Sun* received the details of the modified complaint almost as quickly as we had received it. They reported on it in an article headlined, "GRU, biomass plant battle gets uglier." Sinking their journalistic teeth into the controversy, they wrote: "In the latest row, the biomass plant owners claim in court documents filed in early June that elected city officials and Gainesville Regional Utilities' top boss wanted so badly to get out of what they see as an unfair contract that they've tried to break the plant and monkeyed around in the biomass company's finances, to stop it from being able to refinance loans." *There it was, Stanton pulled the "break the plant" foolishness out of mothballs.*

I informed the *Gainesville Sun* that GREC's claims were "without merit." I said, "GRU does not operate the facility— GREC operates the facility. The extent to which the facility fails to perform as required under the contract can only be attributed to the actions or inactions of GREC."

Given his history, it wasn't hard to imagine my former Assistant General Manager and one of the lead negotiators of the PPA reaching out to Gordon and the team to support them in the arbitration. As the *Gainesville Sun* wrote: "Stanton's

166

recollections of city and GRU officials trying to break the plant and disrupt its finances and cash flow- offered via sworn affidavits as part of the amended complaint-are the crux of GREC's argument."

While I wasn't surprised about Stanton's continued involvement in the GREC saga, I was surprised by the discovery of certain documents that verified Stanton's legacy of less-than-arms-length dealings with GREC management. Copies of e-mails and correspondence unearthed through the arbitration proceedings showed that Stanton had been communicating inside information with GREC staff since at least 2014, even before I had been hired as the general manager. Unknown to Stanton, Gordon and Morales were memorializing their conversations with Stanton with e-mailed memos to their files. Every relevant assertion Stanton told them was catalogued in a contemporaneous e-mail. It was a smorgasbord of deception.

On October 1, 2014, nine months before I had arrived, Morales wrote in his memo to file e-mail: "On a call, Stanton said something to the effect that 'at least some of the Commissioners want to make it hard for GREC to do business.'"

In another e-mail from April 17, 2015, again written prior to my actual hire, Gordon wrote that Stanton warned them: "The utility was going to dispatch us offline for economic reasons, namely because the cost for natural gas has plummeted and they would inform us in the future for operating instructions. He told me things were 'getting crazy' and one of the candidates for the GREC General manager position, Ed Belarski (spelt incorrectly), had told City Commissioners that based on his experience running an independent coal facility, he knew ways to make it operationally difficult for GREC like abruptly starting and stopping the facility and cycling the GREC facility up and down to break the plant." In reality, I had told the commissioners what had happened to the Panther plant, not what I wanted to do to the GREC plant. Big difference.

The information contained in both Morales and Gordon's memos to file was startling. It made it quite clear that Stanton had developed a cozy relationship with the GREC people— way too cozy. On top of that, the information being disclosed was inaccurate. I had never talked about breaking the GREC plant or abruptly starting and stopping it. While those comments were absurd, they made me realize it was no wonder Gordon had been wary of me.

On May 12, 2015, Morales wrote that Stanton told him a commissioner said he's "looking forward to having Ed Bielarski assume his role as the new General Manager of GRU because Bielarski knows how to 'inflict damage on a NUG." Stanton continued, by Morales' account, saying, "The city commission is out for blood."

Just a week before I started, in a June 17, 2015, e-mail, Morales wrote that Stanton said, "He had been spending some time instructing Carlos Holt, the new City auditor, on the ins and outs of the PPA. Holt was 'full of piss and vinegar' and has been sent by the mayor on a 'mission from God' to find something in the PPA they can use to their benefit." For the record, Holt was a marine and served the country during Operation Desert Storm in Iraq. Of course, Holt had been trained to be full of piss and vinegar.

Unbelievably, with less than three weeks after GREC was placed in standby mode, on August 26, 2015, Morales wrote another e-mail in which he describes Stanton "poking his head into the conference room" at GREC while they were in standby mode. Morales wrote that Stanton described my strategy this way, "he said there's a desire to force GREC to the bargaining table using only a stick, instead of a carrot. John added that by taking that course of action if GRU ever does offer a carrot, the other side will only think that it's poisoned. He said this is not the right thing to do in business. John added that the city is making GREC out to be the problem…"

As time went by, Stanton continued to supply the GREC leaders with his understanding of his meetings with me, as well as informing Morales of the organizational changes I had made. He went as far as suggesting I was forcing "low morale upon staff." Morales wrote that Stanton said I "wanted to surprise" GREC, so they could fail a dependable capacity test. The e-mails were colorful and sprinkled with elements of truth. Mostly, they were self-serving on Stanton's part.

By December 2015, Stanton was discussing the operations of GRU plants with Morales, such as when Morales noted in a December 1st memo to file, "They are in the process of negotiating an agreement with FPL to purchase a block of power from them at $27/MWh, delivered." It was a real no-no to discuss power pricing with other parties competing against us.

Stanton had grown so friendly with folks at GREC that he openly discussed the Florida Department of Law Enforcement (FDLE) investigation into Jeff McAdams, who was the former President of the police union. Stanton commented about the salacious details of McAdam's evening at the Lollipop Club. Morales reported him saying, "John said that as he and other people around the office say, 'you can't make this up.'"

On December 14th, Stanton took the time to share his career aspirations with Gordon: "I've given GRU 18 months' notice that I intend to wrap up my career here. April 2017 is a 'no later than' date for me. I'm not 'done'...just done here. In good health and have lots of energy. I'm looking around for other interesting opportunities. I am advising you so that if, on your travels, you hear of someone in need of my skill set, you might pass along my name. I would be willing to commit for up to two years on the right opportunity." At the time, Stanton was still employed by GRU and awfully close to asking the Managing Partner of GREC for a job. *Stanton was way out of bounds.*

Before being terminated, on Thursday, March 10, 2016, at 8:08 AM, Stanton sent an e-mail to Gordon: "Today is the day that you will file for arbitration and requested to restart GREC. I would like to know the status of the latter and the notification when the former has occurred. The filing of the arbitration triggers the next move on my part. Thanks, and good luck." Just the previous week, Stanton had flown to Boston to meet with Gordon. He had forwarded them the flight receipt from Delta Air Lines, expecting reimbursement, while also informing Gordon when he was landing.

I found out that on the day Stanton was finally terminated (April 5th), he cooperated with GREC to build a case against us. He had forwarded our blistering February 3rd e-mail chain that got him fired to none other than Jim Gordon, "Here's what I am referring to. The bold and underlying is mine."

Four days later, Stanton forwarded a copy of our ten-year outage plan, saying, "I'd add that there is an annual plan for each unit for each year, but sometimes the 'plan' is to do no Planned Maintenance on that unit during the year."

If that weren't enough, Stanton had dinner with Jim Gordon and Al Morales at one of Gainesville's more venerated Asian restaurants, Mr. Hans, on April 21st. Morales wrote that Stanton's said: "EB (Ed Bielarski) had fired or marginalized everyone who was there before he got there, and he only consults with his handpicked team (Locke, Brown, Smith). Everyone is afraid to raise any new ideas or do anything that might attract attention to them in any way. He said anyone worth keeping is looking to get out of GRU. In particular, he mentioned that Shayla McNeil and Lewis Walton are looking to get out." Stanton was not finished. Morales wrote: "he said EB appears to have no sort of strategic plan or guiding theme. He focuses all his attention on wanting to harm GREC."

Two weeks after the Stanton dinner meeting with GREC, for some undisclosed reason, he forwarded contact information to Jim Gordon. That contact information included Stanton's e-mail address and phone number. It also included e-mail addresses and phone numbers for former GM

170

Kathy Viehe and former CFO David Richardson. My battle with Gordon was expanding from the inside out.

After reading the memos to file, the events of the past year were lifted out of the fog, and everything seemed clear to me. The blank stares, lack of cooperation, and failures to adequately communicate with me made perfect sense to me now. Stanton had developed an uncomfortably close relationship with the GREC folks. These e-mails and conversations confirmed to me that Stanton had given up on the idea of changing the status quo of the GREC PPA. As he accused me of trying to break the GREC plant, he seemed intent on simply breaking me.

As I thought about Stanton's demise, I couldn't help but recollect the lyrics from Johnny River's 1960s classic, "Secret Agent Man." The crooner sang, "There's a man who leads a life of danger. To everyone he meets, he stays a stranger. Oh, with every move he makes, another chance he takes." Stanton had taken his last chance.

Time was growing near to start depositions and discovery work for both sides—both costly and time-intensive endeavors. I could only imagine having to go back in front of the commission, asking for $250,000 increments to our budget to facilitate the arbitration. I could envision Poe looking at me and saying, "Your time is up."

My dilemma was that although Winston and Strawn were confident about the claims being decided in our favor, they weren't as confident the claims would be sufficient to abrogate or void the PPA. The utility needed to significantly reduce the onerous costs of the GREC PPA, not win a small settlement.

So disquieted by the thought that GRU could win the battle and lose the war, Winston and Strawn recommended a mediation be held in one last attempt to reach a resolution. I agreed. By the next day, Gordon agreed to proceed with the mediation process. I sensed he was in no hurry to enter full arbitration hearings, either.

The GRU team and I met with Gordon and his team in Washington on October 25, 2016 (One year exactly to the day when Melinda would be undergoing life-saving surgery). The day-long, non-binding, confidential mediation in Washington saw Gordon uncharacteristically agitated and on edge.

To the surprise of my fellow GRU team members, late in the evening, GREC offered a series of compromise offers on the ten disputes at hand. Those offers started with GREC putting forth an offer to adhere to a minimum amount days of annual planned outage work, followed by a standard ramp time which would allow them to return to service, and GREC would allow GRU to retain one million dollars of the four million it had retained.

Overall, GREC's offers created an air of credibility to our arguments. Better yet, Gordon had unknowingly quantified the impact of each dispute. The mediation was also useful in that I was given a glimpse of Gordon's mindset on the disputes. He acted confidently, but there was an underlying fear that we might win in arbitration. I saw it as the second of GREC's blinks, with the first being on August 7, 2015, when the GREC team didn't fight against the continued shutdown.

I sensed that for the first time since GREC and GRU executed the PPA, Gordon might need me. He'd never admit it to me, or even himself, or anyone. I knew Cape Wind was not going well. His investors in GREC could not have been happy with the state of their investment. The plant wasn't operating, the parties were embroiled in an arbitration, and the banks had been notified of a possible default. I was liking our position.

In a quiet moment, I asked Gordon if he had been so concerned about the environment, why wouldn't he just sell us the plant so that GRU could operate it in a manner that fits our generation profile. The power plant would invariably run more often. I told him I could re-engineer the plant's financial structure and it was possible. He looked at me and before he could speak, I said, "I'll put something together for you." His facial expression softened when he said he wasn't interested right now. However, I knew that for Jim Gordon, that response was a yes.

My argument hit a sensitive nerve for Gordon. This new wrinkle that GREC's placement of its biomass plant in a condition where it couldn't promptly respond to GRU's dispatch order, returning it to service was a punch to Gordon's gut, maybe even a hit to his wallet. Available Energy was only payable to GREC if the plant could produce it. It was the equivalent of removing your car's tires, putting it on blocks while telling your wife it was still ready to drive. *Sure, but when? That was the key question.*

On November 9th, with the GREC plant still shutdown, Gordon responded, "Ed, the threat of non-payment in your latest letter has significantly escalated the scope of our dispute. This threat contradicts explicit terms in the PPA, as well as the national uniform reporting standards for unit availability referenced in the PPA. GREC requests that you immediately retract the threat of non-payment of your October 31 letter, and we look forward to your prompt response."

As aggressive as the letter was, I couldn't help but wonder when I read Gordon's recital of David Richardson's June 29th e-mail to me in which he reaffirmed the dire consequences of halting payments to GREC. "Finally, you should be aware that GRU's threatened payment failure would pose substantial direct damage to GREC, for which the City of Gainesville would be responsible, as well as broader damage to the city. You were warned of this damage in the attached June 29, 2015, e-mail from GRU's Interim CFO, Mr. Richardson, entitled, 'Potential Consequences of ceasing Payments to GREC' in response to a similarly reckless proposal of the city auditor, Mr. Holt."

I leaned back in my chair as I scanned the sun-drenched landscape. I reflected on the past eighteen months or so. I was fighting for GRU's financial solvency as over six million dollars a month flowed from our customers to various banks and investors around the world.

As part of that fight, I was challenging not only Gordon but my own people. My former Energy Supply Officer John Stanton and former CFO David Richardson's words were being used against us. I realized that it didn't matter. I smiled as I understood that I had gotten what I wanted. In the fine tradition of John Rich, Gordon and I were negotiating on the courthouse steps. This would be the place of GRU's greatest leverage, which up to now, it simply didn't have. Now was the chance I had been waiting for. The hell with these distractions.

Ω

All The World's a Stage

The winter of 2016 in Gainesville provided an extended intermission between the first and second acts of the Biomass play, reviewed by critics weekly in the *Gainesville Sun*, *TV20*, and *UF's Alligator*. We even had off-Broadway performances at Gainesville City Hall every first and third Thursday of the month.

At the end of the first act, Gordon and I had agreed to suspend the arbitration and continue under the comfort of a non-disclosure agreement in an extended mediation. During our four-to-five-week intermission, we stretched our legs, meandered to the restroom, picked up our popcorn, and were again comfortably in our seats, just in time for the dimming of the lights.

The curtain opened on the first day of December 2016, when I responded to GREC's mediation-day offer with one of my own. As with my other actions in the negotiation, the offer wasn't meant to close the deal. It was meant to control the narrative and influence the final deal. The offer introduced a new concept for Gordon to consider.

I asked GREC to agree to a GRU purchase option granting the utility the right to purchase the biomass plant at a future time of their choosing. The option extended from the date of execution of the amendment until the end of 2031. At GRU's election, we could buy the plant for 575 million dollars in 2017.

For every year after that, the purchase price fell by twenty-five million dollars.

I landed on the concept because it served to put a fair number in front of Gordon without fully obligating GRU. It was like the old saying I expressed earlier—we were giving Gordon a sleeve off our vest. On an emotional level, it was an icebreaker for the longer negotiations ahead. On a negotiating level, the purchase option showed Gordon I was serious.

I wanted Gordon to understand that I appreciated the value he had negotiated with the PPA over the life of the contract. GRU was not buying a plant as much as it was buying itself out of a bad deal. I suspected that without a further strategy on my part, Gordon would simply sit atop his catbird seat and crow about the view.

It's important to understand GRU had previously engaged Gordon in potential buyout discussions. In an embarrassing exercise in futility, GRU staff watched as the commission debated the offer in public, intent on delivering nothing more than the value of the plant itself in return for buying out the PPA. The commission approved a lowball four hundred-million-dollar offer, which didn't scratch the surface of Gordon's monstrous PPA value. Not surprisingly, Gordon rejected it, in a meeting in New York City, inappropriately a New York minute.

I would have to suffer the consequences of that failed buyout attempt, which I surmised proved to Gordon the folly of entertaining any future transaction with the city. The whole episode reminded me that an accomplished businessperson like Gordon didn't suffer fools lightly. He didn't waste his time with people who can't make decisions, right or wrong. As former CEO of Intel, Andy Groves, once said to an employee who entered a meeting late, "All I have in this world is time, and you are wasting my time."

As 2016 was ending and the second act was moving toward its close, I considered I had made considerable progress by being able to place a non-binding number in front of Gordon, albeit a low number at 575 million dollars. I knew that any restart of the arbitration proceedings placed Gordon's value in the PPA in jeopardy. Neither one of us could afford an adverse decision, although Gordon was in a much better situation.

During the second act's final scene, on a leisurely telephone call, Gordon told me he wasn't interested in granting a purchase option to GRU. The only transaction he'd consider was an outright purchase. If not, he'd be fine just operating the plant under its current PPA.

For most people, that comment would not garner a second thought. I focused on his words, "The only transaction I'll consider is an outright purchase." Gordon was parsing his words carefully. For me, he had emotionally moved on. Maybe Bill Koch was wrong. Gordon might be willing to sell projects he loved. At that moment, I felt as though Gordon had gone off-script. I felt as though it had been his third blink. Gordon and I had shifted from being the contractual equivalents of the *Hatfields and McCoys* to possible buyer and seller.

Gordon recovered from his monumental disclosure with the condition that GREC partners felt the plant was worth one billion dollars. *Of course, he did.* I knew the value of the GREC PPA. I couldn't forget that Stanton had issued an unsolicited white paper showing that the GREC PPA was worth more than one billion dollars. It didn't matter. I didn't care. This was not going to be a two-act play.

A third act was about to be written and I was ready to get to work. In support of a hard-dollar purchase offer, I engaged with Goldman Sachs to certify the value of the PPA based on a set of assumptions and facts that GRU had developed over the years of GREC's operations. The report would be our scorecard.

I didn't want to directly negotiate the price. I wanted to debate the assumptions from which a price would be decided. Based on what I knew about Gordon, I wouldn't be successful attempting to strong-arm him over price. That was a fool's folly. Instead, I imagined success would be gained through agreeing on the assumptions that would drive the value of his valuable PPA.

Lurking in the shadows, behind the center stage, was a fickle bond market whose current rates were still quite competitive. *But for how long?* If GRU were to buy out GREC, as I planned, the utility would be better served to complete the Biomass Buyout during this period of historically low municipal bond market rates. For every basis point, GRU's purchase price could fluctuate by one to one and a half million dollars, depending on the purchase price.

A basis point is a unit of measure used by bankers and investors to communicate interest rate movements more easily—by 1/100th of 1%, or .01%. For example, a one basis point increase on a 3% interest rate would deliver a 3.01% rate.

The oft-cited Goldman Report of December 21, 2016, showed that if GRU stayed in the GREC PPA until the end of its contract (2041), GREC would have earned between 931 million dollars and 1.3 billion dollars in today's dollars. That 931 million dollars to 1.3-billion-dollar range was built on varying assumptions, including interest rates and worst to best-case operating scenarios. It placed Gordon's 1-billion-dollar estimation of his value in the GREC PPA solidly in the range of expectations.

On the other hand, Goldman's report reflected that GRU could realize savings (relative value) of between 212 million and 740 million dollars if Gordon accepted either a 540 million- or 719-million-dollar purchase price, respectively. It was a very conservative analysis, driven by my own conservative cost assumptions. It was a perfect way to start the negotiations. Six hundred million dollars would be my opening offer, halfway between 540 and 719 million dollars.

On December 28, 2016, I sent the Goldman report via e-mail to Gordon with a comment that the report supported a value of six hundred million dollars which I was now assigned to the purchase of the GREC facility. I recognized that Gordon was assigning one billion dollars to the PPA while the report reflected an amount as high as 1.3 billion dollars. To have any credibility, it was important to increase my offer to six hundred million dollars. It was at that moment that I considered the negotiating range of the Biomass Buyout was set at between six hundred million and one billion dollars. We were four hundred million dollars apart.

Over the New Year's holiday, during another telephone conversation with Gordon, he asked if I was serious about buying the plant. He mentioned he didn't want me to waste his time and that he needed to know I was serious. I listened and waited long enough to recognize that I was truly uncomfortable with my own silence. "Jim, I'm the only guy you've talked to in Gainesville that's ever done something like this. Are you serious?" Gordon didn't immediately answer. After a pause, he said he'd have to talk with his partners.

On January 6, 2017, we reconvened. I was stunned to hear Gordon tell me that his conversation with his partners resulted in being able to tell me, "We can execute a transaction in the high sevens to mid 7's." He also said that the price was contingent on transacting on an "as-is, where-is" basis as a sale of GREC, an entity sale, not an asset sale.

As much as Gordon's offer excited me, his use of a range puzzled me. It seemed amateurish and out of character. All I could envision was someone attempting to sell their used car. When asked what price they'd take for the car, they'd respond, "Oh, between 3 and 4 thousand dollars." Who would then offer four thousand dollars? Certainly not me. Why had Gordon given me a range when he knew I'd fight for the lower number?

After some reflection, I came to realize Gordon's board had initially felt rather good about buying an interest in a bright and shiny renewable project with hefty returns and little controversy. Now they found themselves with an older plant on a nitrogen blanket layup (a process by which the plant's metal tubes are filled with nitrogen gas to avoid oxidation), fighting in an arbitration with a newly minted general manager who had sent their banks a notice of default, all the while having the biomass discussed nightly in the news. While they could deal with soiled reputations, they couldn't accept the possibility of diminished returns. The expression of a range was Gordon's way of signaling to me that his partners weren't aligned on the price, but all of them wanted out of the deal for a price.

My second thought was, why did Gordon drop his price so sharply? While at first, I thought it was Gordon's fourth blink, I realized it wasn't a blink at all. It was more of a test of my mettle. Better yet, Gordon had used another *Godfather* ploy - an offer I couldn't refuse. If I refused, I didn't expect to discover my prized racehorse's severed head in my bed during the middle of the night. Instead, I'd probably find my own head on the commission's chopping block.

I theorized that his disclosure of a range was a challenge: How serious was I in pursuing this deal to closure? Was I more interested in returning to arbitration? Would I have the fortitude to raise the price to more than six hundred million dollars, or would I leave Gordon with wasted time and trouble with his partners, investors, and bankers?

The other part of Gordon's conditions to the deal was an as-is, where-is sale, which meant Gordon wanted to limit any representation or warranties beyond the purchase. In other words, after he sold the plant, he didn't want to be obligated for anything that may go wrong with it. Gordon's desire for an entity sale meant he thought he could simply sell the shares in his company, not unlike a sale of stock on the market. He saw an asset sale as more costly and time-consuming.

It was obvious to me that Gordon and I were at an inflexion point. I could stand firm at six hundred million dollars and ignore the signals Gordon had given me. If Gordon rejected it, GRU customers would be stuck with the multi-billion-dollar obligations for the remaining twenty-seven years. Quite a conundrum.

As I contemplated my next move, I considered that in January of the previous year, Cape Wind had its power contracts with National Grid and Northeast Utilities terminated for its failure to secure financing by December 31, 2014. Despite Cape Wind's argument against the termination, the controversy spilt over into Cape Wind's other business dealings. Their leases with Quonset Development Corporation for a port facility, Falmouth harbor Marina for a headquarters, and New Bedford Marine Commerce for staging and construction were terminated. In the spring, the Independent System Operator (ISO)/ New England suspended Cape Wind from participating in the wholesale power market in New England. Gordon's hopes and dreams were blowing out to sea, along with significant cash.

I was reminded of Jeff Bezos, the founder and CEO of Amazon, who said, "When you can make a decision with analysis, you should do so. But it turns out in life that your most important decisions are always made with instinct, intuition, taste, heart." *What, I should argue with a Billionaire?*

My basic instinct was that GRU, and its customers could no longer absorb the impacts of the onerous PPA. We were bleeding millions of dollars each month. On the other hand, Gordon had no reason to budge from his mid 7's request (mid 700 hundred million dollars). I knew the best move would be to hook him with a 750-million-dollar price and dissuade him from so nonsense as an as-is purchase, an equity purchase, and a host of other deal-killers. I envisioned saving the utility and its customers one billion dollars.

After carefully weighing my options, I responded to Gordon that I was confident we could execute the transaction at a price of 750 million dollars under a specific set of conditions. Gordon's phone line fell silent. I had gotten his attention. I could almost hear him thinking.

I sensed he was surprised at my bold action. He had to know that he was not dealing with someone who would continue to insult him with meager 400-million-dollar offers. I also knew that I had hit upon the right price to get the deal done. Gordon was keenly aware that price GRU would still save over eight hundred million dollars in future obligations under the PPA. Gordon had to know the deal could be done. The stage was set for the battle over exactly what the specific set of conditions were to be.

Gordon reacted as I thought he would. He told me a 750-million-dollar purchase price would make me "the billion-dollar man." Gordon knew the value of the deal to the city. I chuckled as I came to understand how he had set sales records selling cable television subscriptions. However, Gordon's hype for the deal made me feel uncomfortable, as though I was being coerced into buying an ill-fitting suit from a salesperson. I pictured this guy stealthily pulling on the suit's fabric to make it appear to be the perfect fit. I sensed he would try to flatter me into a 750-million-dollar price under *his own* specific set of conditions.

I waited as Gordon took me through his script. He reiterated to me that he had spoken to his board about our conversations. He said that they were impressed with my use of GRU's inherently lower cost of capital (cheaper municipal tax-exempt bond debt). They recognized that the purchase could generate hundreds of millions of dollars of savings for GRU. *Ah, there are those eight hundred million dollars I spoke about saving.* Gordon finished his script by saying that while the board was prepared to sell the facility to GRU, they remained happy to continue operating the facility. He added that there were foreign investors who were interested in the plant, in particular Japan.

I calmly and gently told Gordon that, while I appreciated his candor, we had to agree, in principle, on the price of 750 million dollars pending the development of a written document, usually referred to as a memorandum of understanding (MOU). The development of the MOU was critical because it outlined the details of the deal, those specific set of conditions I had attached to the 750-million-dollar offer.

They included conditions such as the exact parties involved, what's being sold, the price, how due diligence is to be conducted, and other key elements of the deal. They had real economic value that would either add or subtract from the purchase price.

One of the most essential elements of the MOU had to be an interest-rate out-clause. The interest-rate out clause would be a modification of the concept I employed with my clause in the Authority's Concession with the City of Allentown. In this case, if interest rates rose beyond a level, making the financing of the deal too costly, GRU needed to retain the ability to void the deal. This clause would be harsher than the Concession clause-it gave GRU an opt-out if rates rose too high.

I knew other issues that would be important to Gordon included confidentiality of records and the finalization of the arbitration claims. As for GRU, we would have to protect the community against the possibility that GRU couldn't close the deal. We would have to set an exclusivity period, during which time GRU had sole rights to complete the transaction.

I told Gordon that I wanted Winston and Strawn to draft the MOU and retain the working copy. Gordon agreed that his law firm, Chadbourne and Park, would draft an asset purchase agreement. I agreed, knowing that the MOU, while non-binding on either party, would dictate the direction of the final agreement. I also told Gordon that the MOU would have to be vetted in public before the utility advisory board and the commission. Gordon agreed to proceed with the stern warning, "Don't waste my time."

As planned, Winston and Strawn completed the initial draft MOU on February 16th, when it was shared with Gordon's team. Internally, my team revised the MOU while Gordon's team did the same. By February 25th, GRU had an MOU not yet accepted by GREC, which memorialized my understanding of the deal. The process of reaching the terms and conditions of a deal had begun.

Behind the scenes, the *Gainesville Sun* had a standing public records request with GRU for anything related to GREC. Of course, GRU created those public records through its exchange of drafts between the two parties and in compliance with the Florida Sunshine Law, e-mailed copies to them.

Like children on Christmas day, I imagined *Gainesville Sun* staff rushing to open their presents to see what gifts the general manager had given them. The staff opened the gifts in time to print the headline "GRU sends $750 M offer to GREC." Aware of the magnitude of this announcement, I reached out to Andrew Caplan to express my perspective. In the article, I was quoted as saying, "This is an exit strategy for GREC and an entrance strategy for GRU."

By the time the MOU had been finalized, Goldman had revised their analysis to further estimate the savings on a 750-million-dollar purchase price. I informed the *Gainesville Sun*, "If GREC accepts the proposed offer, it could save the city between $600 and $700 million under the current power purchase agreement. With plans to have one of the two Deerhaven plants go offline, savings could reach about $1 billion."

On March 1st, with GREC still off-line, I presented the MOU to the commission, honoring my promise to make this a transparent, public process. I also discussed my white paper entitled "Blueprint to a Buyout," which I had previously shared with the commission and the public via e-mail. The blueprint was my perspective on how the idea of the Biomass Buyout had begun, how we reached the current understanding, the concept behind the MOU, the next steps, and the economics of the deal. It was an unprecedented move on my part.

The MOU was yet unsigned and still under review by Gordon. We were negotiating in public and performing math in real-time. The immediacy of it all placed GRU in a very unenviable position. Ever the opportunist, Gordon, after absorbing the contents of the draft MOU, called me. Jim Gordon was not a happy man. He felt blindsided by the

184

conditions we had placed on GREC and wanted to "Cronkite me" out of it. According to Gordon, I needed to "Look at it from his perspective."

I remembered Sonny Kovatch repeating his talking points over and over until he thought I'd succumb to his will. It had been a primer for Gordon. The path forward would be complicated, but somehow, I knew I could get this deal done. I envisioned the final scene in *Gone with the Wind* when after being rejected by Rhett Butler, Scarlett O'Hara muses, "Tomorrow will be another day."

Overall, it was not a bad opening night for the Biomass play. How long this play would continue to run would be in the hands of the critics along with my temperamental leading man, Jim Gordon. Gordon would need to find his singing voice because I was about to revamp the play into a musical.

Ω

No One Is Gonna Pave Over This Paradise

The consensus in the community was that our arrival at a 750-million-dollar purchase price was the end of the negotiations, unaware of the battle to come over various key conditions and terms of the MOU. The best analogy I can employ is an offer for residential real estate with a home inspection contingency and a financing clause. Until the home is inspected and the buyer is satisfied with the condition of the home, nothing is settled. If the buyer can't secure satisfactory financing, there isn't even a deal. That's where we were with the GREC deal, or transaction, as Gordon would call it.

The reality was that, as of March 1st, GRU and GREC had yet to agree on an MOU which would answer the following eight important fundamental questions;

1) Would it be a sale of GREC's assets or an entity sale?
2) What interest-rate contingency would GRU be allowed, and could it be used to void the agreement?
3) How long would GRU have the exclusive right to buy?
4) Would GREC indemnify GRU against public records lawsuits?
5) Would each party retain all its rights reserved under the PPA?
6) What state law would govern New York or Florida?

7) On what date would the acceptance of the MOU expire?
8) How would the arbitration be settled?

On our March 1ˢᵗ call, Gordon made it abundantly clear how much the draft MOU disappointed him. It was far below his expectations. Immediately, he questioned the inclusion of an asset sale in the document. Gordon admonished me for not remembering that he preferred an entity sale. In his words, an entity sale was important to transact upon because of permit transfer risk," along with all the representations and warranties. Gordon wanted as few impediments to the ultimate closing as possible. I was sensing how the original negotiators on the GREC PPA must have felt.

Pounding down the items on his list, Gordon said that he would not accept interest-rate risk on GREC's behalf. GRU would have to accept the interest rate at which they could borrow. In an accusatory manner, Gordon told me that if I had been worried about the interest rate market, I should have acted quicker. He scolded me, saying, "GRU's financing isn't my problem."

Next, Gordon took aim at the exclusivity period—that period in which both parties could only negotiate with each other. Gordon sliced the ten-month period we had placed in the MOU down to three months, not fully understanding that the exclusivity period included the time for financing and closing, which would be determined in a final asset purchase agreement.

In an over-the-top move, Gordon proposed the exclusivity period ought to be secured with a five percent non-refundable deposit by GRU. He told me that GRU would have to put thirty-seven million dollars in escrow, subject to forfeiture, if the transaction didn't go to closing. I was silent as he spoke.

On the issue of public records indemnification, Gordon wanted limited legal exposure. Gordon suggested GRU and GREC split the un-adjudicated amounts under arbitration while letting the process of summary judgement proceed.

In one last demand, Gordon told me that he had only agreed to the 750-million-dollar price tag for a "clean and simple deal." He said he saw no semblance of this clean and simple deal he thought he had bargained for. I grit my teeth as I begin to understand Gordon's modus operandi—agree to the broader concept and backfill with his demands. I couldn't complain because I had used the same strategy. We were playing a game of chicken on the non-sales price terms and conditions of the deal.

Gordon was letting me know that he would battle on every one of those eight key terms and conditions of the MOU. I told Gordon I heard him. However, what he was demanding might not be possible. In fact, I knew that most of his demands were DOA, dead on arrival. We ended the call.

When Gordon and I reconvened on the 3rd of March, he started off as a different man, as though nothing had happened. He casually talked about his day's experiences and how it must be nice to be in Gainesville, given that it was 14 degrees in Boston. We chatted about all the warm weather activities in Gainesville, such as the art walks and festivals. Gordon even mentioned that his son's girlfriend was a jewelry designer in the south end of Boston. I told him about Melinda's work in designing all sorts of beaded jewelry as well. I listened, waiting for the real reason for our call to reveal itself. *Wait for it, just wait for it.*

Gordon calmly interjected, "If we are serious and I think you are, we need to be frank about what works and what doesn't. We need to understand the impediments." I agreed but replied with a simple comment that I drafted the MOU to protect the citizens of Gainesville, as well as deliver him, meaning Gordon, a fair return. With that short exchange, Gordon was off with his continued list of demands.

I heard the message dancing in my head, "Patience, young grasshopper," from the 1970's television show *Kung Fu* starring David Carradine as Caine, the young student of the old master Po. I thought about the young Caine finally being able to leave his schooling the day he was able to reach out and snatch the pebble from Po. *Could I snatch the pebble from Gordon? Could I beat the master?*

In case I wasn't paying attention on the March 1st call, Gordon demanded that an entity sale needed to happen because neither one of us could expose ourselves to the risk of not being able to transfer the permits. There would be no acceptance of interest-rate risk and GREC would work to move as expeditiously as possible to mitigate the possibility of a rising interest-rate market. When I attempted to speak, Gordon repeatedly responded with a terse defense, "I am just not going to do it. It's got to be a simple deal."

After allowing Gordon the opportunity to recite his comprehensive list once more, I replied, "You won't get this deal from anyone else." Gordon's voice exposed his frustration. I could sense his growing irritation when he accused me, "Unfortunately, you've come out of the box. I'm trying to be helpful, but you are not going to box in the board." For emphasis, Gordon repeated these phrases multiple times.

Gordon ended his retort by saying, "Look at it from my standpoint." With that phrase, he had taken a step too far. All I could picture were the original GREC PPA negotiations where GRU had acquiesced to all of Gordon's demands turning a simple, clean deal upside down. It angered me. I shot back at him, telling him that the ship had sailed. It was time to consider GRU's viewpoint.

I told Gordon that he had originally wanted one billion dollars to buy out the GREC PPA. I set the mark at 575 million dollars. After discussions, we landed on 750 million dollars. I exclaimed, "It's called a negotiation." I wasn't willing to walk those negotiations back. It was time for him to see GRU's need for the eight terms and conditions that would make the deal happen. Gordon fell silent. We were at an impasse. We ended the call.

That weekend, our old friends from Pennsylvania, Brian, and Suzanne Miller, passed through town and we showed them around town. Yes, the Brian Miller from the "Dog Died" joke during my days at Panther. Over the years, through our shared experiences, Brian and I have become friends. Throughout the years, Brian had invited me to play at Latrobe Country Club's Member-Guest Tournament, the home of golfing legend Arnold Palmer.

***

One year, playing as a two-member team, Brian and I stood tied for the tournament lead with another team at the end of thirty-six holes. To decide the ultimate winner, we would have to continue to play in a sudden-death playoff. As we got ready to tee off, everyone who had been participating in the tournament, along with their family and friends, walked over to the first tee to watch the playoffs. Arnold Palmer was there front and center.

With weak knees, I walked up to the tee as I muttered to myself, please don't miss the ball when I swing. Thankfully, I kept my eyes on the ball and drove it just off the fairway. It was playable. Great, I didn't embarrass myself.

For my second shot, I struck the ball squarely enough for it to nearly reach the green. From where I stood, I could see the ball in the low grass at the foot of the hill below the green. Again, the ball was playable.

As I reached the ball location, I decided I had two choices; I could either pitch the ball up the hill onto the green or put the ball up the hill. Lying fifty feet from the hole, I decided to putt the ball, thinking that was the safe choice. I stood over the ball and took aim. I slowly drew back the putter and with a perfect stroke, I hit the ball crisply as it started gliding up the hill.

As the ball approached the top of the hill, it slowed down and came to a stop just off the edge of the green but still on the gentle incline of the hill. Great, I thought, as I started to walk up the hill, ready to putt the ball for a possible par. As I strolled up the hill, the ball started to roll ever so slowly backwards. I stopped in my tracks as I saw the ball returning to me, speeding up with each revolution. The crowd surrounding the green let out a collective gasp. I stood helplessly as the ball rolled past my feet to the bottom of the hill.

As embarrassing as that shot was, it was multiplied by the number of times I continued to try to make the shot. I tried repeatedly, for a total of four more times, each time with the same result—the ball rolling back down the hill to lie at my feet once more. By the time I finished the playoff hole, I ended up with eight strokes, four over par.

In that moment, I had become Roy McAvoy, a former golf prodigy played by Kevin Costner in the movie Tin Cup. In the movie's famous scene, during a US Open, McAvoy tries to make a spectacular shot for the lead. He hits a wood off the fairway, landing the ball on the green, but with a "little gust from the gods," have it roll back down the hill into a water hazard. Undaunted, McAvoy continued to hit the shot over and over again until he got the ball in the hole in sixteen strokes.

Later, McAvoy's clinical sports psychologist tells him, "Five years from now, nobody will remember who won or lost, but they're gonna remember your 12th hole." That was it. As embarrassing as that moment had been, I learned great lessons from it; don't allow your fear of failure to stop you from trying; don't over-think the moment, and you don't know what you have until you've lost it.

***

The rekindling of memories with our old friends, the Millers, made me realize that I missed my old friends. I thought, sometimes you can't get everything you want. I fumbled with that thought around the kitchen table with Melinda when she said, oh, you mean just like Joni Mitchell's song, "Big Yellow Taxi," when she sings that you don't know what you got 'til it's gone. Of course, that was it. My new musical play had found its inspiration.

Feeling inspired, the first thing on Sunday morning, I drove into my office and penned an e-mail to Gordon in which I informed him, "I can't help but reflect on why GREC hasn't executed what my team and I believe is a fair and equitable memorandum of understanding from GRU. Our analysis shows the 750 million dollars is within the high end of the net present value of your future cash flow from the plant. On our part, it provides appropriate savings to our customers and enough funds to drive our 21st century utility model. From where I come from, it's a win-win-win."

I leaned into Gordon a little further, "Speaking of where I come from, my wife and I were surprised this Saturday by an unexpected visit by a couple of old friends from Pittsburgh... When Melinda and I got back home, we both expressed a sense of rekindling old spirits and realizing that sometimes you don't know what you got 'til it's gone. That's a powerful message."

I finished my e-mail to Gordon with a closing wrapped around Joni Mitchell's lyric: 'Don't it always seem to go, that you don't know what you got 'til it's gone.' In that spirit, let me help you understand the realization of the value of the MOU I sent to you on February 17th and revised this past Friday. GRU revises the purchase price downward to seven hundred and twenty-five million dollars and if not accepted by this Friday, March 10th, the purchase price will be revised further downward to seven hundred million dollars."

By Tuesday, the *Gainesville Sun* quoted my Joni Mitchell reference, which had also received airtime on *WUFT* and *Channel 20* news. The public loved it as they sensed my pushback against out-of-towner Gordon. In this town, where I jokingly say that hippies come to retire, I had an upswing in support from the simple mention of the 60's folk singing icon Joni Mitchell. Folks were happy that I wasn't going to let Gordon pave over this swamp paradise.

It wasn't long before Gordon responded to my Paradise e-mail. On March 9th, Gordon delivered a simple, curt, and business-like message, "Attached please find an MOU executed by GREC in terms that have been authorized by its board."

The e-mail continued, "I'm confident that this MOU would result in a mutually beneficial transaction that would save GRU's taxpayers hundreds of millions of dollars." Gordon had taken matters into his own hands, executing the MOU and sending it to me, making it a public record.

Uncharacteristically, Gordon had responded in writing, making it a public record.

Gordon was also being a bit of a bully, presenting me with a signed copy of an MOU he knew I wouldn't or couldn't accept. I felt as though I had struck a nerve in Gordon. I liked that. I felt as though I could snatch the pebble away from the master now.

On Friday, March 10th, I introduced the next song in my musical. As a child of the sixties, I wrote to Gordon, "I sense you were projecting your inner Jim Croce when he sang his popular song from the 70s called, "You don't mess around with Jim." You don't pull on Superman's cape. You don't spit into the wind. You don't pull the mask off the old Lone Ranger. And you don't mess around with Jim."

With that harmonious setup, I went down the list of issues with which I could not agree. I informed Gordon that GRU would not be transacted as an entity purchase because it wouldn't allow us to use tax-exempt financing for the transaction. I also wrote that although I appreciated that he understood the value of the 750-million-dollar offer, GRU would still be reducing their offer to 725 million dollars. Remember that offer was on the clock and would fall further to seven hundred million dollars the next day. Quoting the Jim Croce song lyric, "Last week he took all my money, and it may sound funny, but I've come to get my money back." I ended the e-mail by attaching a new MOU with a 700-million-dollar price and altered conditions. The last line read, "Yeah, Big Jim got his hat. Find out where it's at, and it's not hustin' people strange to you."

I was having fun through the process, but make no mistake about it, I was delivering deadly-serious negotiating points. I had to convince Gordon that I wouldn't do the deal without those eight provisions. I was levering the price down to get them. Through it all, I knew Gordon wanted no less than 750 million dollars. I had to convince him that accepting the provisions would get him to that amount. He also had to see me as someone who could get the deal done.

Gordon took the weekend to consider my new MOU. On Monday, March 13th, he responded by e-mail in a manner aimed at trying to embarrass me. He had taken my unconventional behavior badly, or so it appeared. Knowing that these e-mails were public records, Gordon admonished me. "Your last two e-mails to me and the ultimatums contained in those e-mails have caused the GREC Board of Directors to question whether there is a serious interest for GRU to enter into and close a sale for the GREC Facility."

Once again, in true Gordon fashion, he would portray himself as the wounded party. He wrote: "You approached me with GRU's interest in purchasing the facility. You requested I approach my Board for the required parameters of a deal. I fulfilled your request and communicated back to you an acceptable price range and outline of terms. We had discussions leading up to the first MOU you sent us on February 21. You inserted a number of terms in that MOU and further revisions of the MOU that did not mesh with our initial discussions and deal parameters."

I found it interesting that Gordon changed the term transaction to deal. Others may find the change too small a distinction to matter; however, I thought otherwise. I sensed I was making an impact with the master. In this case, Gordon had delivered his words and phrases to make it appear I was the aggressive dealmaker while he was simply doing his best trying to get our deal done. I begrudgingly admired how to articulate Gordon was in his ability to couch a narrative.

As how I had hoped, Gordon ended his e-mail with a blockbuster. Seven of them, to be exact. Just when I thought he would zig, he went on to zag. In his e-mail, Gordon completely acquiesced to; 1) make the transaction an entity sale; 2) some substantial level of interest-rate protection; 3) four months of exclusivity;4) our public records indemnity language; 5) reserve all our rights under the PPA, meaning if

194

something occurred at the plant, prior to closing; GRU would have remedies; 6) give up legal home-field advantage by allowing the agreement to be governed by the laws of Florida, not New York; and 7) a reasonable date for the acceptance of the MOU.

I loved that Gordon's acquiescence to my terms came after my musical medley of Joni Mitchell and Jim Croce, as well as his insistence that I might not be serious. I had employed a non-traditional negotiating style to my advantage. I hooked Gordon with the right price and has received what I needed in the key terms and conditions of the MOU to make the deal work. *Be patient young grasshopper.* I also felt great that I had stood up for the people of Gainesville.

On Tuesday, March 14th, I doubled down on my non-traditional negotiating style when I wrote an e-mail to Gordon. "Although I have a flare for expression and can be disarmingly playful at times, it cannot be denied that I am serious in my pursuit of a mutually beneficial transaction between GREC and GRU." Gordon and I were on the precipice of reaching a historic MOU. I noted that we were down to not one, but two items left to be negotiated, the purchase price and the interest-rate protection clause. I took the time to connect the price to which GRU would agree to the ability to mitigate the interest rate risk on the money we would borrow. I quantified the importance of the remaining key condition that needed to be settled with a price of thirty-five million dollars (the difference between a 750-million-dollar purchase price and a 715-million-dollar one). Thus, I extended an offer of 715 million dollars, with a sixty-five basis-point spread as a contingency.

The sixty-five basis-point spread was the equivalent of placing an offer on a piece of real estate in a 3% interest rate market with a contingency allowing you to walk away if the interest rates go to 3.65%. It was a small window of risk for GRU, and a much larger window for GREC, given that the market could shift, and Gordon would have spent months negotiating a transaction, performing legal work, racking up

195

bills, and potentially be left with nothing but the same position he already had in the GREC PPA.

I had become addicted to my blossoming musical. I ended the e-mail with lyrics from Kenny Roger's song, The Gambler. The lyrics spoke to me. "You've got to know when to hold 'em. Know when to fold 'em. Know when to walk away. And know when to run. You never count your money when you're sittin' at the table. There'll be time enough for counting when the dealing's done." There was something about these lyrics that captured the tone and nuances of our dealings. I loved using them, probably as much as Gordon hated reading them.

Later that night, three commission seats were up for grabs. By the end of the night, Harvey Ward narrowly won Todd Chase's old seat in a three-person race, while David Arreola beat incumbent Craig Carter, and Helen Warren retained her seat. In the midst of my negotiations with Gordon, the commission that had hired me had dramatically changed. There was no commissioner on the dais who had formerly voted to hire me. The commission was now comprised of Lauren Poe as mayor, Harvey Ward, Harvey Budd, Helen Warren, David Arreola, Charles Goston, and Adrain Hayes-Santos. I was negotiating without a safety net now. *"How bad could it get?"* I wondered.

The next day, Gordon sent an e-mail informing me that his Board would accommodate GRU's interest-rate clause by allowing GRU the ability to terminate the contract with a fifty basis-point increase to thirty-year US Treasury Rates. Gordon's concession was an important development for GRU because it capped the interest rate we'd have to incur to close the deal. The 50 basis-point margin equated to a move from 3% to 3.5% and it would give GRU great stability in the future cost of the transaction and the ability to negotiate a better one if the trigger were pulled. I increased the purchase price to the 750-million-dollar price tag based on Gordon's interest-rate concession. There was just one remaining issue surrounding the exact logistics of settling the arbitration. We were getting so close.

The community was becoming increasingly engaged in the "goings on" with my negotiations. Joining in on the musical chicanery, Ray Washington sent me an e-mail with his newly constructed lyrics to "Don't Mess around with Jim:"

Boston's got its hustlers.
Florida's got its sun.
Joe Lewis got old Jim Gordon.
He's a deal making son of a gun.

Yeah, he smooth and slick as a man can come.
But that man know how to trade a boss.
And when his lawyers start to file their motions.
You know they all call old Jim boss, just because.
…And they.

You don't tug on Superman's cape.
You don't spit into the wind.
You don't pull the mask off the old Lone Ranger.
And you don't mess round with Jim.

Well outta East Pennsylvania came a skinny cat.
He say I'm lookin' for a man named Jim.
I am a deal making fool.
My name Eddie B. Cool.
But back home they call me slim.

Yeah I'm looking for the king of biomass.
He drinking high priced foreign booze.
For years now he taken all our money.
And it may sound funny.
But I got an offer old Jim can't refuse.

And everybody say boy don't you know.
You don't tug on Superman's cape.
You don't spit into the wind.
You don't pull the mask off the old Lone Ranger.
And you don't mess round with Jim.

Well a hush fell over Gainesville town.
Jimmy come bopping in off the street.
And when the cutting were done.
The only part that wasn't bloody.
Were the soles of old Jim's feet.

Yeah he was cut in bout a hundred places.
And he was shot in a couple more.
And you better believe.
They sung a different kind of story.
When old Jim hit the floor.
....Now they say.

You don't tug on Superman's cape.
You don't spit into the wind.
You don't pull the mask off the old Lone Ranger.
And you don't mess around with Slim.

Yeah, big Jim got his hat.
Find out where it's at.
And it's not hustlin' people strange to you.
Even if you got lawyers you gonna pay to sue.

Despite the success of my negotiations, Nathan Crabbe was still taking swipes at me with editorial criticism: "GRU General Manager Ed Bielarski and some city commissioners, for failing to initially be open about an offer to buy the biomass power plant." It appeared the aptly named Crabbe was upset at not having a seat at the table during the actual negotiations.

During a subsequent commission meeting, I jokingly referred to my late-night telephone calls with Gordon as my "Jake from State Farm" moment. In the light-hearted commercial, a husband in his bathrobe is caught by his wife as he talks in the early morning hours—3 AM, with a representative from the insurance company named Jake. Suspicious, the gentleman's wife asks, "Jake from State Farm, huh? What's he wearing?" Jake is then shown in his small work cubicle looking bewildered and slowly responding, "khakis?" Commissioner Chase couldn't stop chuckling.

During public comment, a lady moved up to the lectern and promptly reprimanded me for abusing my wife with these late-night impromptu phone calls to Gordon. She implied I was acting in a nefarious manner, jeopardizing the city, and disrespecting my wife. I responded that I was trying to make light of serious circumstances, but rest assured that I was acting prudently and respecting my wife.

I relayed the event to Gordon in one of our more casual conversations. I asked him what he might have said if I asked him what he was wearing. Without missing a beat, long-time New Englander Gordon softly said, "My Tom Brady jersey." We both burst out laughing at his quick wit. It was one of my first sightings of Gordon's lighter side of being. I liked it.

Over the next week, Gordon and I exchanged a series of e-mails that inched us closer to a final MOU. However, there remained critical differences surrounding the arbitration settlement. Around 2 o'clock on another beautiful March 15th afternoon, I sent Gordon another e-mail in which I laid out my understanding of the remaining points. I attached a revised MOU for his approval. I ended the communication with the words, "I look forward to your response, particularly since I'm out of song lyrics (although Bridge over Trouble Water comes to mind...)."

Gordon responded to my e-mail more quickly than usual. Within four hours, he had marked up the latest version of the MOU and forwarded it to me with the comment, "We cannot agree to any additional credit. If there is no closing, all parties will retain all rights and claims under the PPA." Most importantly, Gordon conditioned the deal on: "provided that GRU not withhold additional payments." Keeping GREC offline and withholding payments based on strict enforcement of the GREC PPA had worked. Those actions were like body blows in a boxing match. They wear your opponent down.

Within two hours of Gordon's reply, I responded. Mimicking phrases he had used in our earlier conversations, I told Gordon, "I don't think you fully appreciate my viewpoint here." It was time to push even harder. I continued, "The idea that I would give away a right in the PPA. Specifically, the right to withhold payments from GREC invoices prior to closing will ensure a political firestorm and rightfully so. I expect both GREC and GRU to conduct themselves in accordance with the rights they bargained for under the PPA until the closing." I informed Gordon that during discovery, "We identified 103 events of lockout-tag-outs of complex components, which when tagged out cannot be operated and thus leave the plant unable to deliver Dependable Capacity. We were comfortable, need be, to take this issue through the remainder of the arbitration. In fact, the whole issue of Available Energy includes the facility's early layup of the boiler, delayed start-ups, and a host of operational issues." I purposely used the phrases Gordon had used on me, such as when he said when we first met that he was happy to continue operating in accordance with the PPA.

I softened my approach by writing, "But I don't want to go there. I think the most critical issue for both GRU and GREC is to close on this mutually beneficial transaction." I continued using Gordon's words and thoughts. I remembered Gordon's *Commonwealth Magazine* interview when he said it wasn't about Koch or Gordon winning. I ostensibly told him this wasn't about winning.

I ended my e-mail with an emphatic statement, "Take the deal. It may be your best deal ever and you've had a boatload." I hit send and I waited.

That wait would take me into the next day, just after noon, when Gordon offered, "My Board is beginning to wonder if you feel, in that, you are not sure if you want to transact a fair and durable deal, or if you want to maintain and exercise undue leverage that is destined to ultimately unravel your acquisition of the GREC facility. It is imperative that if both of us are going to commit the considerable time and resources required for this transaction that it be in a constructive climate."

It was a predictable response. Once again, Gordon was portraying himself and GREC as the aggrieved parties. Of course, now I knew that it meant that I had made a valid point. That's why Gordon was attacking me and my credibility. I sent Gordon a short e-mail in which I told him that I needed to speak with the city attorney about the current impasse.

On another Saturday morning, March 18, at the office, I crafted another musical e-mail, this time invoking the soulful sounds of Otis Redding singing, 'On the Dock of the Bay.' I wrote, "I've read your correspondence once again and aside from my deeply held belief that my e-mails were exponentially more entertaining than yours, I was struck by how far you and I have come and how close GRU and GREC are to agreeing on an MOU. Of course, GRU and GREC's relationship is more complicated than most and with that complexity comes the need to address potential hurdles and ensure a proper understanding." I told Gordon, "If it were any other business relationship, I believe we would be done and working towards a definitive contract... If not, as Otis sings, 'Look like nothing's gonna change. Everything still remains the same.'"

I ended my e-mail with a heartfelt appeal to Gordon, "It is exactly at this point of every deal that I have ever done that both parties have to take a deep breath and consider the options available and how they can complete the deal with the promise it can close. Some folks wilt and agree to anything,

201

which in my experience, doesn't bode well for the development of a definitive agreement. Some folks will draw a line in the sand and never cross it, which, again, in my experience, sets both parties on the wrong path. Then there are some folks who understand the economic, political, and social justice of the deal. I think you are one of those guys. Prove me right and make me believe Otis was wrong when he sang, 'Now I'm gonna sit at the dock of the bay, watching the tide roll away. Ooo-wee, sitting in the dock of the bay wastin' time.'"

I was surprised when on the same day, Gordon called me—not a public e-mail, but a private phone call. He explained to me that of all the song lyrics I had shared, this one connected him with memories of another time in his life when he was a camp counsellor in Maine. He told me, simply, he would consider my point.

As with most of our kumbaya moments, this one didn't last long. There continued to be more misunderstandings surrounding the exact end of the arbitration and what the settlement dollars would be.

On March 20th, Gordon and I had another tense discussion, over the phone, as to how to settle the arbitration. Gordon thought we should pause the arbitration as we proceeded to close. He said, "We cannot leave an MOU that leaves the arbitration going and give you a settlement." I remember Gordon repeatedly demanding, "Look, look, Ed, Ed." When Gordon ended a sentence by saying my name twice, I knew I had him frustrated.

I told Gordon that he was changing the dynamics of what happened over the last weekend. Frustrated, Gordon muttered, "I don't know what to tell you." Growing angrier, Gordon now demanded that we pause the legal work to make the deal work. He was also upset about these documents passing through the night between us. "It turns a lot of things on its ear," he said. I surmised that Gordon was trying to create leverage as we moved closer to finalizing the MOU. He was working the deal on the courthouse steps. I knew because I would have done the same thing.

After my call, I sat down with City Attorney Nicole Shalley and Chief Financial Officer Justin Locke. We put in a last-ditch effort with GREC's counsel to clarify the issues as expressed by Gordon. A final MOU was drafted under acceptable conditions for GRU. We demanded that we retain the over seven million dollars already being withheld under our disputes and retain other claims under arbitration if the transaction were to fail to close. It was imperative to get Gordon to agree.

Later in the evening on March 20th, I wrote Gordon an e-mail invoking the images of my dad and I watching movies together when I was a young boy. Aside from John Wayne, my dad loved Paul Newman, the most as an actor. Invoking his childhood nickname, I wrote to Gordon, "In his Oscar-winning performance in *Cool Hand Luke*, Newman was told by a prison guard tired of his misdeeds against authority, 'What we have here is a failure to communicate.' After receiving what I thought would be the final MOU, I really understand the power of that line."

I continued with my plea. "After reading your revisions to the MOU today, I'd ask you to look at your words as they apply to you, and as you do put on an old Michael Jackson tune, 'The Man in the Mirror.' As you sit in your easy chair, think about these words: 'I'm starting with the man in the mirror. I'm asking him to change his ways. And no message could be any clearer. If you want to make the world a better place, take a look at yourself, and then make that change.'"

I finished with the closing comments, "I have asked the City Attorney to revise the MOU so that it incorporates the aforementioned changes. We are remarkably close to an agreement. However, if you continue to make last-minute changes to the otherwise agreed-upon provisions of documents and, in the same breath, dare question my commitment, we will be done. I am only comfortable in a mutually beneficial transaction, which ultimately can be transacted. Keep listening to the lyrics, 'I'm gonna make a change, for once in my life. It's gonna feel really good. Gonna make a difference. Gonna make it right.'"

Without any fanfare, early on the morning of March 22, 2017, Gordon delivered a signed MOU directly to me, this time with the conditions we had agreed upon. Upon receipt, I sent him a brief note in which I congratulated him with the caveat that the GRU legal team had to perform one last perfunctory review. I left Gordon with the lyrics from Neil Diamond's classic and later anthem of his hometown Boston Red Sox's Sweet Caroline, "Where it began, I can't begin to know, but I know it's growing strong. Was it in the spring and spring became the summer? Who'd have believed you'd come along." I told him, "Let's shout so good, so good, so good."

The next steps would include going before the UAB and the city commission to gain approval for the MOU so that we could proceed with an asset purchase agreement. I was proud of being able to secure all eight of the important components of the MOU, all for the original price of 750 million dollars, including the financing out clause, lucrative settlement of the arbitration, the exclusivity of the contract, public records indemnification, and reservation of rights under the PPA—all issues that I knew were so important to the people of Gainesville.

Ω

No MOU For You

With the ink not yet dry on the MOU, on Thursday, March 23rd, the *Gainesville Sun* posted a headline that read, "GRU, GREC agree to buyout." The article optimistically opined: "Although the MOU is non-binding, its execution is a pivotal step in the process of the city buying out the biomass plant and multi-billion-dollar contract." In it, I was quoted as saying, "The MOU was reached because it's good for both parties. Although sometimes contentious, it's ultimately about saving customers money and GREC receiving a fair return." The article was a fair job of reporting, and I saw it as a good start to the process.

That good start became a false start when, within twenty-four hours, during a scheduled joint city commission and UAB meeting, both governmental bodies felt compelled to hold off on any recommendation or approval of the MOU. They were obviously swayed by the outpouring of citizens who had attended the meeting. As the citizens spoke at the lectern, I couldn't help but wander back to the Authority's Concession work when over one hundred citizens showed up at city hall to protest the Concession. I had learned how powerful public opinion could be then, and I was seeing it in action tonight.

A local community activist, Paula Stahmer, stood at the lectern and exclaimed the new deal would be déjà vu if passed, comparing it to the original GREC PPA. Of course, nothing could be further from the truth. The original GREC PPA indebted the utility to approximately 2.2 billion dollars, while this deal would wipe it out and gain ownership of the plant for 750 million dollars. *Ugh!*

Days passed before the Alachua County Board of Commissioners met to weigh in. During the evening meeting, County Commissioner, Ken Cornell, spoke about continuing in arbitration before making a significant purchase. I was surprised when Cornell pontificated, "If fraud was committed and you find out, that changes the entire negotiation completely. You need to negotiate with strength, not weakness." Seemingly, he forgot, ignored, or didn't understand the work performed to date. I was taking advantage of the options left on the table for GRU. Finally, I cringed when he said we were negotiating from weakness. This wouldn't be the last time I was accused of that.

Thankfully, *Gainesville Sun* reporter Andrew Caplan was quick to respond when he correctly wrote, "But lawyers and courts have consistently ruled that the contract is binding, with no easy escape for the city."

In response to the deferral of any governing decisions, I sat down with GRU Communication's Director, Dave Warm, and developed a frequently asked questions, or FAQs section to GRU's website, in which we offered answers to community concerns about the transaction. We reached out to the *Gainesville Sun, WUFT, TV 20* news, and the *UF Alligator* with further information and an editorial or two. The *Gainesville Sun* ran a Sunday spread on April 2nd entitled, "Biomass Basics, a guide to GRU/GREC." It was accompanied by my editorial, "The Case for Buying the biomass plant."

In the editorial, I attempted to answer the question on everyone's minds, "Why buy GREC?" Simply put, based on the latest Goldman-supported analysis, if GRU did nothing, the utility would have had to absorb over two billion dollars in PPA obligations over the remaining twenty-seven years. On the other hand, buying and dismantling the plant would save approximately seven hundred million dollars, while buying and running the plant would save just over eight hundred million dollars. It wasn't exactly Gordon's "billion-dollar man," but I was getting close.

My staff and I transformed our *Why Buy GREC* question into a brand using it at public forums such as one held at Gainesville Police Department's Hall of Heroes on April 3rd. Leading up to a utility advisory meeting on April 5th, I thought GRU had gained momentum and positive messaging since the March 24th impasse.

Despite the momentum, at the April 5th UAB meeting, the transaction was met with more skepticism by the board members. Four hours of discussion led to a decision to recommend the city commission sign a separate MOU lowering the price to 675 million dollars while mandating all the savings go to GRU customers.

UAB Chairman Darin Cook was the unifying force around recommending against the MOU I had signed with Gordon. Cook was able to convince four other UAB members to vote for a lower price, with member Annie Orlando in total dissent largely because she didn't want *any* deal to buy out GREC. Orlando had been one of the applicants rushing to get first in line under Hanrahan's Solar FIT while never being selected. She opposed buying the biomass plant simply on principle.

To be fair, Cook also had a dog in the hunt. In the past, he had participated in private meetings with elected officials warning them of the potentially dire consequences of the GREC PPA. He had been rudely ignored. It was obvious Cook was not going to allow that again.

As much as I understood the UAB pushback, I found it fascinating that the members gave me so little credit for my negotiation of the MOU. They offered extraordinarily little recognition that I had hammered out an interest-rate out-clause, along with multiple protections worth well over the 75-million-dollar haircut they were proposing.

I came to realize the UAB members had a shallow understanding of the municipal bond market. Whereas Locke and I had previously shepherded billions of dollars of tax-exempt bond transactions, no one within the UAB had done one. Both of us had years of experience with firms such as Goldman Sachs and other prominent investment houses. The bottom line: the UAB members didn't know what they didn't know.

Surprisingly, the next evening, the commission approved the UAB recommendation by a slim vote of 4 to 3. I was stunned to witness Commissioner Budd explain, "Once you sign an MOU, you have a period of time to do due diligence. And that's the most important part of this deal, between now and when the contract is negotiated." Budd was close but still off base.

Due diligence would start upon the execution of some form of binding asset purchase agreement, not the MOU. I will grant Budd this: he was a great and accomplished businessperson. He was Gainesville's CPA to the stars preparing their tax returns and financial reporting throughout the years. He had also started radio and television media ventures. He was a gifted entrepreneur. His star didn't shine as brightly on the political stage this evening.

On the bright side, Hayes-Santos, Warren, along with Poe respected the position of the UAB but were concerned that it would be difficult to reduce the already negotiated price of 750 million dollars. In hindsight, it's amazing—that night, I had the support of the two people who would try to oust me later. *Note to self, stay out of Gainesville politics.*

I took to the lectern to inform the commission that, based on my experience, the elements of these deals are connected issue by issue, point by point. Unilaterally reducing the purchase price by seventy-five million dollars after months of bilateral negotiation would pull at the fabric of the transaction. Gordon had been immovable on the six hundred million dollar offer for months. I told the commission to face the facts that he wouldn't just acquiesce to the new 675-million-dollar offer.

Commissioner Warren understood my logic perfectly, "We would like a lower price. My concern with that is, is that going to kill the deal or delay the deal? And that's again where I feel we are playing chicken with no seatbelts." I giggled at her comment about playing chicken with no seatbelts, no less.

Once the vote was taken, I received a call from Gordon, who told me that the deal was a dead end of discussion. He didn't bother to warn me about wasting his time. He knew that I knew.

One week passed and I had heard nothing further from Gordon. The second week passed with Gordon maintaining his radio silence. I understood at that time certain we'd all have to decide on lifting the pause in the arbitration, which would effectively eliminate both sides' ability to close the transaction. I kept the commission informed, awaiting the next steps.

While I was fighting for a truly durable deal to use Gordon's term, the *Gainesville Sun* reported that "a new state (Florida) House bill that could take control of GRU away from the City Commission passed its third and final committee Thursday. The Government Accountability Committee approved the legislation (HB 759) sponsored by Representative Chuck Clemons, R-Newberry, with a 15 to 8 vote." While the bill had a long way to go, its final approval would dramatically change the relationship between the utility and the city commission. For now, it was smoldering fire waiting for oxygen to give it strength.

On April 20th, the commission and the UAB reconvened to re-consider the events surrounding the MOU, given the lack of any formal response from Gordon. The UAB again elected to stick with its initial recommendation of an offer of 675 million dollars with a 4 to 1 affirmative vote. I was not surprised by their actions.

The UAB, as a body, had lost sight that GRU was bleeding over five million dollars a month. We were also looking down at the barrel of a gun in full-blown arbitration hearings, legal bills, and depositions as they debated. Every basis-point change in the final interest rate would cost GRU approximately one and one-half million dollars.

If it took six more months to corner Gordon at the lower price, GRU would have lost almost forty million dollars under the GREC PPA. If interest rates moved thirty basis points higher, that would cost GRU another thirty-five million dollars. Any savings from a lower price would have been absorbed in these additional costs on the possibility Gordon would even agree.

Thankfully, the next night, the commission voted 5 to 2 to move forward with the original 750-million-dollar offer. As Commissioner Craig Carter so succinctly said, "Mr. Gordon would have to be an idiot, an absolute idiot, to take anything less than 750 (million dollars)." Ironically, the only two dissenting votes came from Commissioners Harvey Budd and Charles Goston.

During the meeting, Goston expressed the sentiment that he would not let his legacy be defined by a biomass deal. I responded, as the *Gainesville Sun* reported sternly to Goston, "We are spending less of their money (customer's money), and that's why I'm so passionate about this. I believe exactly like you do. I believe in all that you're talking about because I don't want that to happen to our citizen rates. I know that people from your district hurt the most and this is why I want to do this. It's important to everyone."

In agreeing to return to the higher price (750 million dollars versus 675 million dollars), Poe said it best, "It is likely the interest rates, highly likely will go up again. We have no guarantee the price will come down. In the meantime, we're going to be spending a million dollars a week."

On Friday, April 21st, Gordon sent me an executed copy of the MOU with a note that read, "We look forward to working with you on GRU's acquisition of the Gainesville Renewable Energy Center."

My reply was brief, "This is a transformational event for the city, and we're really excited about the cost reductions we'll see in the future." We hammered out an acceptable MOU.

Although I had further work to do, I took the time to reflect on my accomplishment. In less than two years from my appearance on the Gainesville stage, I had fought, battled, and negotiated to reach an agreement with a renowned businessperson to buy out a PPA that was crushing the city. I had negotiated that price through a complex negotiation with little or no leverage. Whatever leverage I garnered was crafted out of non-traditional negotiating styles, bold actions, and guts. I had gotten a respected businessperson to discount the value of his project by over 250 million dollars, and I anticipated saving the utility and its customers over seven hundred million dollars, at a minimum. This had been an elegant, choreographed play that morphed into a musical. The audience loved it. The critics be damned.

Ω

GRU Plays A Weak Hand, Strong

April of 2017 saw springtime arrive in Gainesville. Daytime temperatures started to rise into the mid-eighties and humidity filled the air. City elections had just concluded, and a calm settled over the town. It was the perfect setting for the next phase of the Biomass Buyout. Unleashed by the execution of the MOU, Winston and Strawn had started working on the framework of the Asset Purchase Agreement (APA) with consideration of the covenants and conditions that would populate the legally binding contract. I had a great deal of faith in reaching an acceptable final product.

The APA process began on April 24th, with a joint call between Lisa Cottle and Jonathon Birenbaum with Winston and Strawn and GREC's attorney Keith Martin with Chadbourne and Park. In a matter of hours, we hammered out an initial contract framework including the following sections, 1) definitions, 2) purchase price, 3) list of assets, 4) liabilities, 5) scope of representations and warranties, 6) indemnification provisions, 7) funding mechanisms and 8) diligence, prior to execution of the agreement. The meeting was a great start to the process. I was optimistic.

The first draft of the APA was exchanged on May 10th and, as had been promised, was posted on GRU's *whybuygrec.com* website. The *Gainesville Sun* aptly acknowledged the event with a headline, "1st draft of GREC contract delivered." I am still amazed at how transparent we were in sharing a bounty of information with the public. Each draft of the APA was posted in real-time as they bounced from law firm to law firm. The public at large could play along at home with the attorneys.

While the lawyers racked up the hours, I worked double duty. By day, I managed the utility. By night, I spoke at public events informing the public about the benefits of the transaction. One of the more noteworthy events was a public forum on the UF campus where UAB chairperson Darin Cook, City Commissioner Harvey Budd, and I would debate the importance of purchasing the GREC plant and terminating the PPA.

In advance of the UF forum, Cook laid down his thoughts on the buyout issue with and an editorial he penned for the *Gainesville Sun*. Using the incendiary phrase, "GREC played a weak hand strong," to describe my so-called failed negotiations with Gordon, the editorial was like a sucker punch. I never had the upper hand in negotiations.

Cook acknowledged that he had picked up that expression during high-stakes poker matches he had participated in across the country. He had done quite well. Cook was a statistician by trade and employed a healthy confidence in his skills of probability determination. However, from my perspective, employing poker strategies during a municipal utility's contract negotiations was simply out of touch with our mission.

Cook wrote, "In arbitration, we (GRU) asserted a material breach of the contract because they didn't have an outage. If we win on this point, we get out of the contract." Nothing could have been further from the truth—a truth backed up by our attorneys Winston and Strawn.

Cook also used outdated information about the proposed buyout itself. He cited numbers from the original Goldman Sachs report as evidence that GRU was overpaying on the deal. Cook's words infuriated me because, once again, behind the scenes, I had made it clear to him that the original report was intended to be a negotiating tool built with conservative assumptions that would drive a lower price. It was a valuation skewed towards GRU. Cook shouldn't have used it to prove that GRU was making a bad deal. Worse yet, he ended his flow of misinformation with a personal attack, "All we needed was resolve and the strong stick of continued arbitration for that resolve to bear fruit." *I'd give him resolve!*

The June 13th public forum had all the signs of another GRU deal-bashing, misinformation session. *Gainesville Sun* editor, Nathan Crabbe, began the event by giving me the first crack at the audience in attendance. I informed the people in Pugh Hall's Mackaye Auditorium, "It (the deal) unleashes us from the shackles that we're now under for having to absorb the 70 to 75 million dollars a year." Both Budd and Cook vociferously disagreed.

For them, arbitration was the preferred path instead of the $750 million buyout. Cook focused on the possibility of GREC's e-mails that had not yet been released as potential evidence of wrongdoing. "There's probably something in there they don't want to be seen. I'd love to see those e-mails, but they haven't been provided," Cook proclaimed. I was surprised as Budd joined in, saying there must be "smoke and fire" surrounding the deal.

In an odd twist, Budd took personal aim at Gordon, "We have an unwilling seller, who's a bit of a creep, in my opinion."

Not missing a beat, Cook followed by saying, "Yes, I think he's a creep, but I also think he's a very smart man."

I understood the frustration of both Budd and Cook. They had seen and felt the damage the excessive costs the PPA had on the utility. While I felt bad for them, making the negotiations personal and responding with inappropriate attacks in this forum, or any other for that matter, didn't help anyone. Tactically, it wasn't smart to jeopardize my relationship with the man with whom I'd still have to finish negotiating an APA. It was an ill-advised strategy. Again, I could hear Gordon's voice saying, "Don't waste my time."

The *Gainesville Sun* reported on this performance with an editorial on June 18th, in which they proclaimed, "Buying plant still looks like best bet."

They wrote: "GRU GM Ed Bielarski reiterated a case there that has been repeated in recent months, including on these pages: Buying the plant freed our community from the shackles of the contract, allowing electric rates to be lowered and expanding options for the future. The Sun has supported negotiating a contract at the $750 million price, and nothing said at the panel discussion changed that position."

On June 16th, my team and I conducted an extensive review of the second draft of the APA—which included GREC's revisions. We identified six deal-killers, meaning six revisions that would not allow GRU to proceed. Gordon's team wanted; 1) a new concept of excused breach of contract; 2) a new definition of fraud; 3) a new concept of an additional purchase price; 4) a lower escrow of 7.5 million plus a title policy for the difference (11.2 million dollars); 5) removal of no defects language; and 6) an update to the seller (GREC) representations and warranties more beneficial to the seller. The City Attorney Nicole Shalley openly responded to Gordon, "You don't look like you want to get a deal done."

I smiled to myself, hearing Shalley tell Gordon, "Don't waste our time."

Later, Shalley and I talked about how to better facilitate the negotiation process moving forward. We could continue to meet in marathon sessions over the phone, or we could get everyone in a room to hammer it out. I was reminded of what my CIO, Walt Banks, would say when he was confronted with conflict, "Let's get all the liars in a room." Taking that advice, we decided to have all parties gather in one room to reach a resolution on the remaining issues. That room would be a thousand miles away at Winston and Strawn's Met-Life Building offices above Grand Central Station in New York City. The time was set for the last week in June.

As I readied to go to New York, I thought back to how Gordon had envisioned a simple as-is, where-is purchase with little representations and warranties, usually called reps and warranties. I imagined the legal structure to which GRU was holding GREC must have been a large pill for Gordon to swallow. In fact, Gordon was being asked to swallow a handful of pills, the largest of which must have been losing his original vision to force GRU into placing a deposit in escrow. Instead of receiving thirty-seven million dollars in escrow from GRU in the event we couldn't complete the deal, now, GREC was being required to escrow up to nineteen million dollars in escrow monies, or 2.5% of the purchase price. *I love it when turnabout is fair play.*

The sale of the biomass plant to an entity such as GRU was a whole new process for Gordon. His background has been spent on privately financed purchases and sales. Privately secured financing didn't typically require an interest-rate out clause. Under a municipally financed deal, there were more legal nuances surrounding indemnification provisions, environmental claim limitations, fraud limitations, and a host of other reps and warranties. I sensed Gordon was rapidly losing control of the deal in more than one way.

On an early July day, basking in sunshine and mild temperatures, Tom Brown, Nicole Shalley, and I strode up Park Avenue towards our destination. We were Gainesville's three musketeers now. We were optimistic about arriving at a deal in the Big Apple. As we strolled along the avenue, we caught the first glimpse of our meeting site. Sitting like a monument atop historic Grand Central Station, the Met-Life Building was an impressive sight for this opportune day. Its grandeur fit the moment. I smiled with the expectation that the negotiations would go well. First, we had to plough through Grand Central Station's labyrinth of hallways, corridors, and elevators.

After maneuvering through the helter-skelter of the commuter's hell, we piled into the elevator to the top. As we climbed, I could feel the activity of the city below us melt away. The negotiations, the turmoil, and the worries were being left behind as we zoomed higher. We were entering a different world now. I liked the feeling.

Reality hit a time or two when I wondered how the *Gainesville Sun* would report upon three representatives from the City of Gainesville meeting with Gordon and his team of experts trying to mitigate the impact of an over 2-billion-dollar contract as they drank fresh Starbucks coffee, sparkling water, and breakfast from a fresh market in town. *Stop it and enjoy the moment.*

There was modern styling throughout the offices, with clean, sleek elements for every accessory. It made me think of Melinda. She had earned her Interior Design Degree from the University of Maryland and loved architecture, design, and art. I snapped a few photos to send her. It was nice to think of her in that way at that moment. It was as though we were sharing the experience. Birenbaum laughed as he whispered, "tourist."

As the meeting time approached, we mingled in the conference room. GRU's team moved to one side of the table while GREC's team aligned on the other. Gordon and I sat staring across the table from each other, looking eye to eye. It was the first time we had met in person since our July 1st meeting of the previous year. This was no comedians in cars getting coffee moments. This meeting was more like a Swamp Yankee going to war with a real Yankee. Gordon looked angrier than I remember. There was more grey hair around his temples as well. As we sat down to attempt to negotiate the deal-killing provisions and conditions, I saw a different Gordon.

Sitting by Gordon's side was Madison Grose, Managing Director and Co-General Counsel for Starwood, the largest of GREC's partners. Grose had participated in the previous month's conference calls, but this was the first time I had ever met him in person. He was a well-respected businessperson with a history of making significant deals. Through his mannerisms and words, Grose exuded a powerful sense of confidence.

The meeting began with Birenbaum setting the stage, carefully charting out the positions of both sides, followed by

217

a respectful exchange of thoughts and ideas. It was perfect in its tone. Thankfully, during Birenbaum's process, both Gordon and I kept quiet. That silence was inexorably broken when the topic of escrow dollars and reps and warranties came up. Gordon recoiled and grew feisty, almost itching for a fight. *This was the Gordon I knew.*

As Gordon leapt into attack mode, I stood toe-to-toe with him, not giving up an inch. And then it happened. At the peak of Gordon's attack, Grose slowly moved his hand over to Gordon's arm, not yet out of my view but beneath table level. Ever so gently, Grose touched Gordon's arm. Gordon paused as his eyes drifted downward for a moment. It reminded me of my wife's purposeful touch when I grew a little too verbose during a dinner party. Gordon immediately relaxed and stopped talking while Grose seamlessly took over speaking about the topic.

I knew that I was now negotiating, not so much with Gordon, but with Grose. In a way, I felt sorry for Gordon, whose personality and style I had come to appreciate. He was tough, professional, focused, and in many ways fair. I didn't know Grose's negotiating style nor his personality. I hoped that this wasn't a last-minute double-cross.

Over the remainder of the morning session, we discussed the six deal-killers. In the end, Grose agreed that GREC would forego any new definition of fraud. As Birenbaum stated, "Fraud is fraud. There is no need to narrow its definition with a new defined term." Grose also gave in on the concept of an excused breach, as well as additional purchase price concept. He also agreed to allow for a variation on a no-material defects representation, along with our desired level of other reps and warranties. Best of all, Grose acquiesced on the escrowing of 18.75 million dollars from the purchase price to backstop the reps and warranties. New York was becoming the perfect venue.

Throughout the session, Gordon was composed and quiet. Grose was leading the negotiation. When Grose had finished, he asked what I thought. I responded that my team would have to adjourn to another room to discuss what we heard. Grose nodded in the affirmative. Gordon looked at me as if to say, what else do you fucking want?

It wasn't until later did I become aware that Gordon's Cape Wind deal was dead at the time. Five months hence, Gordon would dramatically tell a reporter, "Think of me as the mortally wounded soldier who stays behind and holds that line so that my comrades can-."

He couldn't finish his sentence. He didn't have to. As reporter Katharine Seelye wrote, "He sees himself as a trailblazer who drew deep criticism but established legal precedents that set a course for those that followed." Why shouldn't he? Seelye further tells us, "But after sixteen years—and $100 million of his own money—that dream is, well, gone with the wind. Mr. Gordon has pulled the plug, stymied by endless litigation and a series of financial and political setbacks that undermined Cape Wind's viability."

Once our team had assembled in the separate breakout room, Birenbaum couldn't contain himself. He smiled broadly, exclaiming, "We got the deal!" Shalley and Brown concurred. For a moment, I wondered if we could push the envelope further. The new dynamic made me want more. When I told the team what I was thinking, they told me I was crazy. Of course, they were right. I had gotten the price, conditions, and the timing that made the deal work. Pushing for more would have simply diminished my credibility. Credibility, I needed to complete the deal.

We all freshened our drinks and had snacks while Gordon and his team waited. I liked making the GREC people wait a little longer. Up to this moment, the Biomass Buyout negotiations were done while GREC had the upper hand—the strong hand. I was relishing the moment. After all, a baseball player doesn't fly around the bases after hitting a home run. No, he trots so he can savor the moment.

I took a deep breath before entering the main conference room again. We were armed with a consensus to accept GREC's offer to escrow 18.75 million dollars along with the others. After sitting down, I looked at Gordon and told everyone that the road was tough. Quite frankly, I wasn't as pleased with how things had gone today. Nicole and Tom looked up from their paperwork to stare at me. Birenbaum peered at me with an expression of "What the fuck?" I told the GREC team I would not be afraid of pulling the plug on the deal. I saw in Gordon's eyes that he thought we were going to decline their latest offer. I paused and said, "But not today. We're going to agree to the terms we've just hammered out." Without saying a word, Gordon leaned out of his seat to firmly shake my hand.

The more than year-long battle would end the contentious arbitration and free the GREC plant to operate as we needed. At the same time, we were looking to lock down a minimum savings of over seven hundred million dollars. Hopefully, we could operate the plant in the manner we wanted, increasing those savings to the one billion dollars Gordon had baited me with. We congratulated each other for the fine work before leaving to board our flights out of town. I felt relief and accomplishment, equally aware that the fight was not over.

It took another month and a half until the lawyers on both sides could gain consensus to accurately incorporate all the decisions and concessions into the bevvy of documents required to get to our bond issuance and closing. On August 10th, Gordon and I executed the final APA setting the stage for approval from the city commission. We were getting closer to purchasing the GREC plant and terminating the PPA.

The *Gainesville Sun* headline recognized the achievement with the headline, "GRU, GREC agree on a contract, need city approval." The contract had grown from a 42-page draft into a 134-page executed contract. In the article, Gordon offered his thoughts, "The closing of this transaction will provide significant cost savings and benefits for the community. We've put our disagreements behind us and putting the facility in the hands of GRU will allow the city to receive significant cost savings and other benefits." I appreciated Gordon's comments, as well as his comments that negotiations consisted of give and take and vetting for both GRU and GREC. I pointed out, "This is probably the most transparent contractual process in GRU history." There had been six draft contracts shared in the light of the Sunshine Law.

On Thursday, August 16th, the UAB and commission met in a joint session to discuss the possible acceptance of the executed APA. While the UAB didn't have the power to approve the APA, they had the obligation to recommend it or not. After four hours of debate, no decision was made by the commission or the UAB on the APA. The primary reason for the impasse as expressed by the UAB, was that they hadn't been afforded the time to review the APA. I laughed as I thought about all the drafts I had sent out to the public, including the UAB. I thought the UAB was taking whatever opportunity they could nix the deal. Once again, Gainesville politics was taking the air out of the room as it suffocated reason.

The UAB and commission waited to schedule meetings until the last week in August to reconsider the APA. Annoyed, Ward addressed the deferral of the decisions by saying, "We've been working on this since December. It's not as if this is brand new to us and we have to figure it out this week."

Jonathon Birenbaum stood in attendance saying, in a matter-of-fact manner, "I don't think there's a scary part from a legal aspect."

Despite months of growing increasingly emotionally worn-out from the intellectual processing of the deal, public battles, and coping with my dad's ill health, I continued the education and information-sharing with another editorial on August 18th which compared the original GREC PPA executed in 2009 to the APA we had crafted.

I emphasized that the original GREC PPA was heavily redacted, and all its drafts were kept from public view. All our drafts and executed MOUs and APAs were available for the public to see.

The original GREC PPA was not vetted by rating agencies nor investment bankers, while the APA was vetted by both groups.

While the original GREC PPA never allowed an evaluation of the plant, the APA allowed our selected independent engineers to evaluate the plant to determine whether it was capable of long-term service.

The original GREC PPA did not result in GRU ever owning the plant, versus under the APA, GRU would own the plant.

Most importantly, based on our final analysis, GRU would save over one billion dollars for the utility. If approved, I would, indeed, become the "one-billion-dollar man." It was showtime.

I was pleasantly surprised that during its August 22nd meeting, the UAB voted 4 to 2 in favor of moving forward. Expectedly, the decision came with a lengthy airing of grievances. As Chair Cook wrote in an editorial following the meeting, he still thought "the price was too high." He also aggressively stated that "the commission lost its resolve." Despite Cook's objections along with his long-held belief that he could have negotiated a better price on better terms, he realized he had to "set aside his negative passions and make his decision based on what was best for the ratepayers."

Two days later, on August 24th, the city commission approved the APA by a 5 to 2 vote, subject to the delivery and approval of an engineer's report, litigation information, permits, and surveys at its September 7th meeting. I responded with, "This is a big vote. There's no doubt about it. It still makes it nonbinding until the guy up there in the center (Mayor Poe) signs it." Poe just stared at me as though to ask me to give it a rest.

Two commissioners, Budd and Goston, spoke out against the APA. Goston called the APA a "get out of jail free card," while Budd said, "It really comes down to the amount. It was the $70 million (the annual payments) that drove us and now it's the 750 that's driving us now. It's not 675. It should be 475 or 450 or some absolute lower number."

The journey reached its next-to-last milestone on September 7th, when the commission approved the APA by a 5 to 2 vote, allowing Mayor Poe to sign the agreement by September 14th. Exhausted but happy, I concluded that "close to twenty contracts and agreements have gone back and forth between GRU and GREC over the last six months, all in the public view. The Biomass Buyout is the most transparent deal in GRU history." I told the *Gainesville Sun*, "GRU has addressed virtually every one of the concerns that the citizens have presented to us moving forward at various meetings." All that was left to do was secure the financing and close the deal.

On a beautiful Friday morning, October 20th, Justin Locke and his finance team travelled up to New York to work with the Goldman underwriters facilitating the bond pricing auction for the financing. They left a communication link up for me to follow the process on a live hookup with the Goldman trading floor. You see, by that time, Melinda had received her pancreatic cancer diagnosis and was days away from surgery. I was not about to leave her.

Wanting to share in the potentially historic moment, Melinda and David drove to work with me to watch the auction in real-time. As badly as Melinda was feeling, she persevered throughout the morning. She was pale and skinny, the effects of losing a dozen pounds in a noticeably brief time. Her tumor had left her with no appetite and unable to eat for weeks. Once again, my worlds were colliding.

Thankfully, investors had a healthy financial appetite as we watched them gobble up each of the bond series. Soon, those bond buckets overflowed with orders. When the auction was over, almost eight times as many buyers bid than what we needed to purchase our debt. The excess demand, called an oversubscription, allowed us an opportunity to negotiate with buyers and set lower interest rates.

Bond Buyer's headline exclaimed, "Investors snapped up Gainesville biomass plant bond deal!" The oversubscription was a market validation of the strength of the Biomass Buyout and everything that my team and I had set out to accomplish. That oversubscription also increased the projected savings on the deal alone to over 770 million dollars versus our projected 698 million dollars.

Just about three weeks later, on November 7th, we executed the city's largest bond issuance ever and took ownership of the biomass plant as we terminated its onerous PPA.

While the funds were being transferred and a celebration was being set up outside the plant's gates, I was taking Melinda home after her release from her thirteen-day stay at the hospital. After escorting Melinda as she wobbled into our bedroom, I gently tucked her into bed. Almost asleep before I could talk, I told her that I'd only be gone for an hour. She kissed me and said, "Just go celebrate with everyone. I'll be fine."

In anticipation of the events, I had renamed the former GREC plant Deerhaven Renewable, or DHR. I wanted to signify to everyone that the Biomass Buyout was truly a fresh start. As I drove to the former GREC plant, I reflected on a journey of a lifetime. The benefits of the Biomass Buyout were without local precedence. GRU plant personnel were able to modify DHR, making it feasible to operate as low as 30 megawatts. With that flexibility, GRU was able to avoid the frequent dispatching of GRU's own generating assets.

DHR's operating cost reduction fell right to the utility's bottom line. Total operating expenses fell from 290 million dollars in fiscal year 2017 to just over 240 million dollars in fiscal year 2018.

GRU Operating Expenses

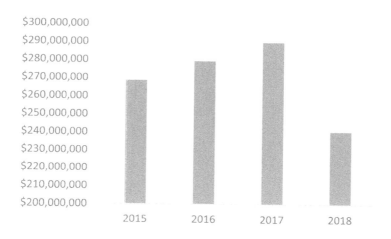

The Biomass Buyout allowed us to reduce overall electric rates between 8 to 10%, driving its rates to the lowest level the utility had experienced in a decade.

GRU Bills per 1,000 kWh

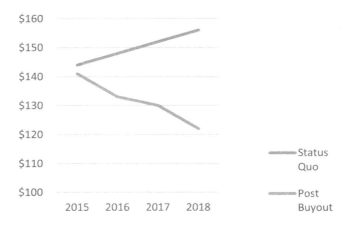

GRU's long-term debt was reduced by almost three hundred million dollars from its peak of over two billion dollars in 2015.

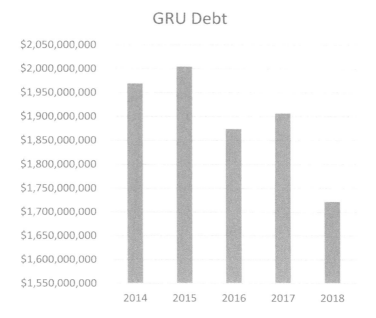

GRU Debt

$2,050,000,000				
$2,000,000,000				
$1,950,000,000				
$1,900,000,000				
$1,850,000,000				
$1,800,000,000				
$1,750,000,000				
$1,700,000,000				
$1,650,000,000				
$1,600,000,000				
$1,550,000,000				
2014	2015	2016	2017	2018

The Biomass Buyout resulted in GRU annual obligations plummeting to thirty-eight million dollars over thirty years to own the power plant, as compared to paying seventy-four million dollars a year to lease it and never own it. Just as amazing, the thirty-eight million dollars a year was lower than the original binding proposal offered by Nacogdoches Power! My team and I had righted a terrible wrong.

Nominated by Goldman Sachs as the Deal of the Year in 2017, the financial community extolled the virtues of the Biomass Buyout. I received calls from other utilities stuck with above-market PPAs asking me how I got the utility out from one of the worst PPAs in the country.

When I arrived at the plant, I was greeted by a gathering of well-wishers, including Commissioners Ward and Warren. My CIO, Walt Banks, coaxed me onto the back of his vintage Corvette convertible, and he took me on a victory lap. Waving like a dignitary atop the rear of the car, I couldn't have been more pleased. My worlds were no longer colliding. I was at peace.

Little did I know that thirty days later, the luster of my grand accomplishment would wear through Gainesville's political fabric. No longer a dignitary aboard a vintage Corvette, I'd be yesterday's news for the city's power brokers, as I'd be fighting for my career in front of people who had yet to build one.

Ω

Keep GRU Local

The day following the commission's sneak attack on December 7, 2017, the *Gainesville Sun* reported, "The commission lacked the votes to fire Bielarski, so now everyone is in the uncomfortable position of trying to work things out." I knew better. The three musketeers weren't going to give up. I returned to work, not a changed man, simply a wiser one. I realized that my battle with Gordon had been the warm-up to the war with a short-sighted, agenda-driven commission. Just like America after Pearl Harbor, I planned my counter-offensive. It would begin with a speech during an evening meeting with the UAB.

Before getting to regular business, Chair Cook looked towards me to offer the opportunity to express my perspective on the events of the previous evening. Once again, I had my opportunity at the lectern. I started with the following words, "The one thing I hate more than a poor loser is a poor winner." Taking a deep pause, I looked down at my notes and continued, "Although I had enough support at the city commission last evening to forego any vote on releasing me from my general manager role, I take the brush with disaster very seriously."

In a sterner manner, I proclaimed, "I never wanted to be a hired gun who came into town to solve the biomass contract and leave town for another conquest. I came into town because I knew I could solve the biomass contract and I could return GRU to the luster it once had. I have said I want GRU to be the Harvard of municipal utilities. I want folks to want to work for GRU. I want folks to look at GRU as a leader in the community and the state. I think we are beginning to see that as a possibility." The years of the commission abusing GRU resources had cast workers in a bad light amongst the public. Workers repeatedly told me they were afraid to wear hats and shirts with company logos in public. Customers would complain and curse at them for the high rates. Today, people needed to hear my voice spelling out a more hopeful future.

I unapologetically stated, "Terminating me would have left a terrific void at the helm of GRU. I know that sounds a little self-serving, but leadership is a tricky thing. Leaders must be able to risk their own security for the greater good of their employees. Leaders must be able to ask tough questions. Leaders must confront problems they see. I believe that GRU's success over the past year is based on not only my leadership but the executive team's work as well. It's about how you respond from adversity, not how much adversity you have."

For anyone listening, I was signaling to those commissioners that wanted to fire me. I won't back down. I couldn't. I was certain the three musketeers of city politics, Hayes-Santos, Ward, and Poe, would not stop longing for a less principled, more malleable general manager who'd instinctually acquiesce to their political agendas, such as the one-city approach to government—"All for one-city and one-city for all." *Sorry, Alexander Dumas.*

I could sense the cultural shift during meetings at city hall—less pushback, less questioning, and a whole lot more supportive head nodding had become the traits demanded of charter officers. Little did the commission understand or seem to care that this newly desired behavior was the very genesis of the challenges I had spent the past two years resolving. The city needed a Wartime Consigliere, even if only to protect the commission from themselves.

***

While I was removing obstacles to GRU's success from the inside, State Representative, soon-to-be State Senator Keith Perry, was working to improve GRU from the outside. He was on a crusade to replace GRU's governance by the Gainesville City Commission with an independent board. I first became aware of the strength of the senator's convictions while attending social and charitable events where the senator made his appearances. I took the time to talk to Perry as we sat over dinner or found ourselves standing in the dessert line. During those conversations, Perry expressed his deep displeasure with the way the commission governed the utility.

Perry was a distinguished-looking southern gentleman with close-cropped white hair and a similarly colored goatee, not unlike Colonel Sanders, after three months at a health retreat and a makeover. Perry had money, looks and, by all outward appearances, was a deeply religious man. Perry was a force to be reckoned with.

At the top of the senator's to-do list was ending the commission's use of the utility as its piggy bank. Whether it was separate money for pet projects, like Depot Park, or just the excessively high cash transfer which the commission demanded of GRU, Perry wanted it to end. I told the senator those plans were high on my list as well. Now that I didn't have a Biomass Buyout to consume my efforts, I planned to act as swiftly as I could. Perry was surprised and pleased.

GRU's annual payment to the city's general fund called a general fund transfer (GFT), wasn't an uncommon practice among municipally owned utilities. What was uncommon was the size of the GFT—the current thirty-eight million dollars a year was more than what the utility earned each year. Worse yet, such poor practice had become a long-time practice of the city—between 2003 and 2018, GRU had remitted forty-eight million dollars more to the city's general fund than what it had earned. The GFT was mother's milk to those at city hall.

Perry's mission to put an end to the commission's poor governance had earned him a dedicated public following, who rightfully argued that GRU's electric rates could be lowered if the commission stopped demanding such an elevated level of GFT. Some in Perry's contingent suggested that GRU ought not to be delivering a GFT payment at all. Others suggested that GRU's operations ought to be sold outright. Most of these arguments came from almost 40% of GRU's customers who lived outside of the city limits. I understood their arguments.

Non-city residential utility customers were funding a GFT that supported city programs and services they didn't need or partake of. Unlike city customers of GRU, they had no vote to elect a commission that would be their voice in the GFT decisions. Perry's supporters argued the dilemma as an example of taxation without representation.

Adding to the dilemma, GRU customers living outside of city limits were charged electric and water surcharges of 10% and 25%, respectively. Those surcharges filtered towards GRU's bottom line—the bottom line that funded the GFT.

Perry's solution, while serving in the Florida House, was to sponsor a series of GRU Governance Bills which would have placed the establishment of an independent board to govern GRU to a public vote, a referendum vote. *Who could argue with the concept of letting the voters decide?* His bills failed to gain final passage in 2014, 2015, and 2016. However, in 2016, Perry got the bill as far as the desk of Governor Rick Scott.

While Governor Scott vetoed the bill, he offered a reason that spread a glimmer of hope for a way forward. The reason: the governor didn't approve of paying a salary to appointed board members. He feared it would set a bad precedent for all other government boards.

In 2017, Perry was elected to the Florida Senate, passing the torch of the referendum initiative to newly elected representative Chuck Clemons. Just like Perry, Clemons doggedly pursued the cause. In his first legislative process, Clemons pushed a bill through the state capital that landed on the Governor's desk. This time, momentum was building that this would be the year for the bill's passage.

Clemons' bill, once again, granted the commission authority to appoint members to an independent board that would govern the utility. That new board would also have full authority to set rates, approve operating and capital budgets, hire or fire the general manager, and one more added responsibility—reduce the GFT by up to 3% each year. Most importantly, hearing the Governor's past objections to compensating board members, the ghostwriters of the bill removed any compensation for board members.

As much as I appreciated the aspirations behind the bill, I couldn't wrap my head around its core principle that granted the commission responsibility to appoint an independent board. How would that positively alter the current situation? While the commissioners would no longer govern the utility, they would decide on the appointees who, in turn, would govern the utility. The bill had no checks and balances to stop commissioners from seating unqualified people on the board or those that would ignore their fiduciary responsibilities. To better understand the folly of a commission-appointed board, I told him to look no further than the evolution of the Utility Advisory Board (UAB) the commission had created.

***

The original set of UAB members appointed by the commission in 2016 had moved on from their voluntary roles soon after the Biomass Buyout. The UAB grew over multiple iterations to be led by new chair Wendell Porter, a UF professor, supported by vice chair Wes Wheeler, an attorney and community solar advocate. Other members included solar businessperson and entrepreneur Barry Jacobson, community activist and Habitat for Humanity neighborhood coordinator Carla Miles, production manager Tim Rockwell, a journeyman electrician and advocate of community weatherization projects Jason Fults, and a former Florida Energy Department employee and PhD Fletcher Crowe.

This new group of activists would eviscerate the old UAB model under which Cook had balanced environmental stewardship with fiscal responsibility. The new UAB model was a retro-chic style model I called a revival of Gainesville Green. Not the well-known local cannabis, dubbed

"Gainesville Green" during the drug-infused 1970s, this Gainesville Green was an equally well-known, green-energy movement embraced by the local community in the early 2000s. I feared this environmental Gainesville Green was as addictive as any counter-culture drug.

The UAB got hooked on the new and improved Gainesville Green while completing its work on an Energy Policy to guide the commission. During each meeting or workshop, UAB members would take turns testing staff's commitment to increasing the utility's renewable power generation portfolio. Sometimes by adding commercial solar panels. Other times by promoting rooftop solar and battery-charging stations. The hell with financial viability or sustainability. The group's consensus was to reduce the utility's dependence on fossil fuels. They needed their fix.

It was as though I had stepped into Mr. Peabody's Wayback machine. It was obvious to me that the UAB was trying to seize upon a window of opportunity, not unlike the Hanrahan-led era of biomass and Solar FITs. I couldn't help but think, with all that happened, they saw me as a wounded and weakened general manager, almost certainly fearful about losing my job. Little did they know how wrong they were.

The plan hinged on the UAB's ability to infiltrate the utility with the local zeitgeist through the Integrated Resource Plan (IRP) and other generation planning portals. It was the UAB's version of a Trojan horse. Not the Greek's Trojan horse, but today's Trojan horse virus.

That retro path forward was on full display at the early UAB meeting. After GRU staff delivered a long presentation of the IRP process, Vice Chair Wheeler outright accused GRU staff of being obstructionists. He suggested that we were failing to truly embrace the future renewable needs of the utility.

Later that evening, irritated with Wheeler's allegations, I responded in an e-mail to the entire UAB, in which I pointed out the following, "First, GRU staff and I embrace the goal of reaching 100% renewable by 2045 very seriously. However, on occasions, when members of the UAB confront us with the idea that staff and I are obstructionists, not committed to the 100% mandate, not being creative enough to develop solutions you are looking for, or not taking your suggestions seriously enough I must admit that I have been disappointed and shown frustration."

I proceeded to explain, "In support of the Commission's 100% mandate, I have viewed the gap in GRU's future generating capacity as an opportunity to enable potential renewable resources to remove coal as a fuel for our generating assets. Unfortunately, as shown in the IRP just presented to you, all current options need to include quick-start combustion gas technology. Given the regulatory rules on reliability and participation in a statewide grid, GRU has little choice under current conditions. We can't speculate or gamble on reliability of the system."

I explained that my Energy Supply staff has managed the largest renewable generation portfolio (by percentage) in the state and their work has been recognized by experts in the field of renewable power generation. They operate and maintain one of the country's largest and most sophisticated biomass plants. I said, "They are the personification of due diligence in the process."

I ended the rebuke, requesting the UAB re-direct its focus towards the GFT and its impact on the financial strength of the utility, "From my perspective, the UAB has an obligation to advise the Commission that requiring GRU to remit more in GFT than what it earns is going to cause irreparable harm to the utility and endanger the city's ability to be able to depend upon it. I recently noted to a city commissioner, during the discussion concerning Commissioner Johnson's agenda item about the economic outlook for the utility, that almost forty-eight million dollars have been remitted from GRU to the City between 2003 and 2018, ABOVE what it has earned. I noted that this practice is not sustainable."

I didn't have to wait long for the backlash when the following week, UAB workshop Chair Porter and Vice-chair Wheeler took the offensive. They each shared position papers about how they saw GRU developing its next IRP in 2022. They saw themselves as subject matter experts. Both Porter and Wheeler articulated extremely bold proposals for how the utility should mitigate the need to build any additional generation assets.

Porter identified three future planning goals; 1) GRU must adopt strong energy efficiency programs; 2) GRU must sell more electricity; and 3) GRU must implement a plan of action to control the system load profile. The plan was to use less power, sell more, and, when all else failed, control what amount of power people could use. Yikes!

I was disappointed to hear Porter veer so far outside of a rational utility model. For example, on energy efficiency, Porter requested that GRU address having "All attics/roofs should be insulated to the applicable DOE levels where possible." He went further, "All lights should be converted to LED versions as soon as possible." He ended with, "All new ACs and heat pumps should be above the minimum SEER 13." There was no mention of who should pay for it, or how. These proposals were pure social re-engineering through the utility.

Porter went on to propose converting all Rapid Transit System (RTS) buses, City and County fleets to electric vehicles in five years. He wanted GRU to "encourage and plan for electric vehicle transportation" under the concept that every 10 per cent of local vehicles that are changed to electric increase electric sales by 3 per cent. No matter that, at last count, the number of electric vehicles in Alachua County was less than four hundred out of over 150,000 residents.

Porter's rhetoric grew even more fantastic when he proposed converting 34,000 natural gas customers to electric water heaters and heat pumps. I took a deep breath. I had estimated the cost to convert 34,000 natural gas customers over to electric appliances to run more than 164 million dollars. Not calculated was the impact on the utility's access to natural gas to fuel our power plants from the loss of those customers.

It was obvious that GRU would have to increase its rates to its customers to absorb those additional costs. It didn't matter, Porter was blinded to the costs by his belief that natural gas was a prime source of methane causing climate change. The utility simply had to stop importing it and burning it.

For his grand finale, Porter proposed adding the University of Florida (UF) campus to GRU's territory as though that was an easy and viable option. Just work to gain them as a customer. His demand hinted that he didn't comprehend anything I had told the UAB about GRU and its relationship with the university. The notion that GRU could simply negotiate or demand UF accept electric service from GRU had already been vetted with the city attorney's office. They had informed us that GRU turned its electric territory's rights over to Duke Energy more than 50 years ago. For GRU to serve UF's central campus complex, it would have to buy the rights from Duke.

In discussions I had held with the President of Duke Energy's Florida division, the idea of buying Duke's rights to serve UF had gone nowhere. During a particular meeting, the Duke President told me no less than four times in response to my offers to sit down and discuss a potential purchase of Duke's UF territory. Even if we had talked, GRU couldn't afford the acquisition based on our estimates of the value of the university territory, estimated at hundreds of millions of dollars.

After his logic frolic, Porter proposed the most totalitarian of options, "Pool pumps, electric cars, electric hot water heaters and duty-cycled HVAC systems all represent loads that can be managed in time. With Advanced Metering Infrastructure (AMI) and a time-of-use incentive, many of these loads can be moved from a random basis to occur in a controlled manner during a time of day when an abundance of solar energy is attempting to move into the local grid. Simply put, a utility with a constant 240-megawatt load is much easier to manage than one that varies from 130 megawatts to 420 megawatts." Oh, brother, big brother.

At the end of his last proposal, I fully understood Porter's fixation on theoretical concepts rather than economic, operational, or overall system capabilities. He simply didn't live in the utility world, or almost any businessman's world, for that matter.

Vice-chair Wheeler, as usual, was more personal, not personable, with his comments. Wheeler started by offering GRU and its staff a "compliment sandwich"—a metaphoric sandwich consisting of two small compliments surrounding the bad meat in the middle. Wheeler offered the top piece of bread by saying, "I commend the GM and his staff and appreciate all the hard work and dedication they have contributed towards making UAB (meaning GRU) a truly outstanding municipal utility."

After pausing, he plated the second slice of bread, "And for the traditional staff-driven focus on regulatory compliance that guided past efforts and past plans."

Next up would be the rancid piece of meat, "We may have always done it that way, but now is the time for bolder and more comprehensive action."

Oblivious to the details of electric power regulation, Wheeler was asking GRU to defy the authority of the Federal Energy Regulatory Commission (FERC), which regulates the transmission and wholesale

237

sale of power and natural gas in interstate commerce, as well as the North American Electric Reliability Corporation (NERC) which enforces and monitors the bulk power system. Bewildered with his arrogance, I wrote, "GRU staff will continue to follow the path of regulatory compliance in matters related to providing electric, gas, telecommunications, water, and wastewater utilities. If that approach appears to be less bold, I will agree."

Wheeler continued his theatrical performance as he dramatically demanded, "Our community exists in a world that is literally on fire. As a utility that is owned by the people it serves, we must broaden our scope and lift our gaze beyond the limited counting of cost per kilowatt hour burned." I was surprised Wheeler didn't request a hallelujah at the end of his comment.

Rather than say Amen, I responded, "While I appreciate the rhetoric, the world is, literally, not on fire. Yes, there are fires, like in California, where the inability of the utility to remove underbrush, along with failure to upgrade transformers and other equipment, has resulted in some sad consequences."

I couldn't help but return to my negotiations with all my former adversaries. I almost giggled as I thought about my childhood watching Batman fight villains like the Penguin, the Riddler, and the Joker—each one with a distinctive personality. Here, Porter was a new villain, the professor, mired in the theoretical, unable to see the forest for the trees.

My mind turned towards Wheeler. Of course, he was Anger, the emotional character in the movie Inside Out. *Lewis Black's Anger voice described the character of Anger as, "He has to stay on top of everything, and the only way he knows how to get their attention, keep it, and make sure they get things done is by getting angry. He is comfortable with getting angry. He is comfortable with his anger. It makes him happy. But when pushed too far, the top of his head bursts into flames." Maybe that's why Wheeler thought the planet was on fire. It was his own head exploding with anger.*

Rather than hail GRU staff as the subject matter experts they were, Wheeler parroted talking points from solar advocates with little understanding of their basis. My patience was lost when he mentioned that "when the subject (more solar power) comes up at meetings, Board members are continually assailed with a parade of horrible; solar is intermittent, its load fluctuates too much, battery storage is too expensive, it takes up too much land we have to discount it's generating capacity because it's not reliable, etc., etc."

In response, I wrote, "This nit-picky item, as Member Wheeler calls it, may be the most important. It is apparent that certain members of the UAB do not trust GRU staff to present the empirical evidence without skewing it to our favor, in spite of effort upon an effort to educate the UAB. These are not horribles. They are conditions under which GRU must operate to provide safe and reliable power."

The UAB's solar and renewable zealots had pushed the relatively obscure board far afield of their roles and mission. Under this new regime, the UAB was no longer useful in assisting the city commission nor in working with GRU management and staff. They were misinforming the commission and keeping staff from completing the important work of the utility.

The only redeeming quality was the UAB was still only an advisory board. God help us if they had the authority granted by the Clemons bill and its referendum.

***

In private, I told Perry and Clemons that these newly appointed members' opinions would inevitably mirror the opinions of the commissioners that appointed them. I pointedly asked Perry, "How, exactly, is that an improvement for you?"

Despite what I considered to be the bill's fatal flaw, supporters of the new bill were convinced they had hit upon a winning formula. Proponents like Jim Konish would step to the lectern during commission meetings to tell the sitting commissioners, "Your time is up." Their confidence was justified when at the end of the 2017 legislative session, Clemons fulfilled Perry's desire through gaining state legislature approval of the bill. Once again, the bill was placed on Governor Scott's desk.

This time, the Governor signed the bill, which would place it as a referendum on the city ballot for the November 2018 election. Perry and Clemons supporters relished their victory that would bring the fate of the utility to the voters of Gainesville. This was to be the new cause celebre for Gainesville to debate.

As had been the case with most GRU issues, the public narrative surrounding the benefits of the proposed new governance structure were only partially true. For example, the rallying cry of the pro-referendum folks was GRU's bills would fall if the community voted for an independent board. Anti-referendum folks said rates would rise.

The reality was that GRU's higher electric rates were primarily driven by the higher costs of operating five power plants that were passing thirty-nine years of age, and the missed opportunity of replacing them with more efficient natural gas plants, opting instead on GREC PPA and Solar FIT contracts. In addition, GRU was being forced to pay a GFT more than what it could afford.

I recognized that for an issue as important as GRU governance, it would be incredibly important for the community to get the facts versus the rhetoric. Very quickly after the bill's passage, working with David Warm, we developed a public outreach strategy which included informational press releases, Facebook posts, and other social media presence. We entitled the campaign, *Did You Know?* In it, GRU delivered truth-telling with statements supported by graphs and facts, such as, "GRU's residential electric rates fell between 8 to 10% after the PPA buyout."

I remained hesitant to immerse myself fully into the fray, knowing how intense the effort would be. Despite the hurdle, I was spurred on when my more social media-conscious commissioners asked me why GRU was so slow in responding to our critics on *Facebook*. There were those commissioners who strongly suggested that the new campaign was counterproductive, poorly designed, and, worse yet, that my communications director needed to step up his game or find another job. *Yikes!*

240

While commissioners can't make hiring or firing decisions for non-charter employees, they can exert pressure on any charter that has their intended effect. I knew I had to take decisive action.

A brief time later, in the summer of 2018, Senator Perry inundated the community with campaign mailers with the headline, "Over 94,000 GRU Customers Can't Afford Their Bills and GRU Keeps Raising Rates." On the front side of the mailer, the quote was asterisked with my name next to the asterisk, as though it was my direct quote. I was furious. I never said anything of the kind. As I said, I had not been unsympathetic to Perry or his supporters. Now, he had crossed the line. I felt like Popeye after he had been beaten up by Brutus and somehow, was able to pump the can of spinach into his tummy. Perry was about to feel my wrath.

Thankfully, the *Gainesville Sun* responded with a fact-checking column, which would foreshadow later events. Reporter Andrew Caplan wrote, "But that's not what Bielarski, who is actually the utility's general manager, wrote in the commentary. Bielarski actually wrote, 'During the last fiscal year, GRU further assisted struggling customers by making more than 94,000 payment arrangements and creating more than 12,000 instalment plans.'"

"Those 94,000 payment arrangements come from 18,426 customers who needed payment arrangements or extensions for various reasons. The number of customers affected is about five times smaller than Perry's mailer states." *Excellent job, Andrew, but this isn't over yet.* I still needed to set the record straight.

I authored an e-mail to the commission, "I am furious that Keith Perry's campaign has made it look as though I had said something I had not. My point was that GRU works with its customer base in numerous ways in order to assist them in paying their bills. The senator's abuse of the facts is not only discredit to GRU, but every GRU customer who goes to work each day and doesn't have the time to delve into the details of GRU's progress in driving down their electric bill."

The incident gave me the clarity of purpose I desperately needed. It brought me to the full realization that I couldn't allow employees like David Warm and his staff to be thrown into the viper pit of city politics. I couldn't involve my employees in the maelstrom. My mind raced back to my initial Gainesville interview with Morgan Watkins, to whom I had mentioned that I was best staying out of the social media arena. The world had changed. I felt as though I no longer had a choice but to join the battle.

As I informed Warm of my plans, I noticed an autographed photo of a previous generation's comedian, Don Rickles, on his bookshelf. Warm's first journalistic interview was with the creator of the term "You hockey puck." According to his own analysis, it was also his worst. I couldn't get it out of my head that the key to Rickles' success was his blatant shifting of social standards. Rickles said what others were scared to say, not unlike Redd Fox, Lenny Bruce, and George Carlin. I looked at Warm and told him, "No, this is too important. I can't stay on the sidelines here." I wanted to jokingly call Warm a hockey puck but showed an amazing level of discipline. I would need that level of discipline and more in the months ahead.

So began my journey as one of the only general managers of a municipal utility to engage in daily Facebook posts with his customers. You won't find the accomplishment in the *Guinness Book of World Records*, but you should. In August 2018, I started an historic dialogue, in which I exposed myself to public criticism and scrutiny with the following post: "As GRU's General Manager, I created this page to establish a platform that encourages open conversations and to bring facts to any misinformation that some may have. However, profanity, threats of violence, spam or any other inappropriate language/images are prohibited and will be removed from this page. I look forward to opening a dialogue with you on what GRU has done and will continue to do for this community."

That statement was followed by a plethora of *Did You Know* posts, such as: "The reality is that GRU is not imposing a tax on any customer. Within our competitive rate structure GRU earns a profit which is turned over to the city. Similar to Duke Energy making a profit on its utility service and returning monies to its corporate offices in North Carolina."

I further challenged readers with comments such as: "I find it fascinating that there are many very conservative/fiscally minded people who would almost always side with the ability of a business to turn a profit and use it for whatever the company's mission, are suddenly opposed to GRU returning its profit to the city." These posts were directed towards those referendum supporters that didn't understand the right of the city to receive a return on its investment. While we could argue about the level of the GFT, we couldn't argue that the city didn't deserve any level of a GFT. That logic would become the basis of later battles with the city manager and commissioners themselves.

I took the opportunity in October 2018 to explain the then-current rise in 30-year US Treasury bonds, whose rates drove the pricing on the GREC PPA Biomass Buyout financing, "The 30-year US Treasury rate is over 3.35%, or 20% higher now than when GRU financed the biomass buyout. If, as a few folks suggested, GRU would have waited to buyout the PPA until later, after more negotiation, the cost of the buyout would have gone up by approximately $75 million (based on 50 basis points @ $1.5 million a basis point) with no promise of a lower price." I enjoyed sharing the movement in the bond market and its validation of our quick and prudent decisions on the Biomass Buyout. As I mentioned before, my team and I had worked with our advisors enough to see this opportunity coming.

My daily interactions through the *Facebook* portal also helped to calm my mind as Melinda fought through her battles with chemotherapy treatments that left her weary and exhausted. As hopeful as we were, we also understood the reality that 50% of all patients who had undergone curative pancreatic resection surgery had a recurrence of the cancer within 8 months. 8 months! The weight of those probabilities would have pulled me underwater, if not for having this grander purpose. My job was to save the utility, while Melinda's job was saving herself as she visualized the treatments killing off every cancer cell in her body. *Every blessed one.*

My expanded role was primarily driven to reach the public with real facts, not baseless claims, or urban myths. Like always, I had my distractors. I was challenged every day on *Facebook,* in the newspapers, and during commission meetings. How dare you challenge a popular senator. You are just a lapdog for a commission that wanted to fire me. I was accused of being psychologically wounded by my experiences on December 7th and now was succumbing to commission pressure. I still marvel that some of these people believed that I could join the three musketeers in their one-city escapades. *What would it take for people to understand the principled battle I was fighting?*

On a brighter note, I encountered people greeting me in public to thank me for taking the heat and answering questions. The encounters confirmed that it wasn't so important to be liked. Rather, it was important to be respected for simply telling the truth. *Note to self: truth-telling is a contact sport, not embraced by the timid.*

I extended my reach to share lighter moments during my social media blitzkrieg, such as telling people that: "The Russian Intelligence Agency GRU has NOTHING TO DO with Gainesville's GRU. I do have a call into Putin to ask him to change the name, however. I think he'll respond with a simple, 'Well, we had it first.'"

I went to that dark place because, if you were to Google GRU, you'd most likely bring up articles about Felonius Gru, the main protagonist from the *Despicable Me* movie, or Russian Intelligence Agency. *If GRU didn't have enough hurdles.*

I also shared personal moments, such as finding my departed mother's notes in my father's attic, while we were getting the house ready to sell. She had written, "Maybe someday, Edward you will be putting away, perhaps in an attic, maybe you'll find an old box in a corner covered with layers of dust, the letters that marked its contents are faded. You'll open it to find an old train or an old toy. Then, my son you'll have a bittersweet feeling of that magic season, childhood, you loved it and left it because you live in that season but once. Love mom." My strong, sweet, magnificent mother had been taken away from my dad and I all too soon, when she passed away from lung cancer at 66 years of age. *Rest in peace Mom.*

One of more favorite posts included the revelation that GREC's sister plant in Nacogdoches, Texas would be sold in a transaction worth 450 million dollars. Austin Energy CEO, Jackie Sargent, told the *Austin Statesman*, "The deal…wiped out some of the financial hit of the remainder of a 20-year, $2.3 billion contract set to run through 2032." She went on to say that the utility expected to save 275 million. When people heard about the lower price, they crowed that, see, Bielarski had been snookered. Nothing could have been further from the truth.

I informed followers that "the Austin Energy buyout covers 13 years of remaining life on the PPA while GRU's covered the remaining 26 years. According to GRU's additional 950 million dollars in future obligations under the GREC PPA, the Austin Buyout would equate to an over 900-million-dollar purchase price for GRU's biomass facility."

"That sale shows that the GREC plant (along with its PPA) could have garnered over 900 million in revenue based on Austin offer. That's over 150 million dollars more than what we paid."

For all that Melinda and I had gone through, 2018 became a cathartic year for us both. Our trials, tribulations, as well as life and death decisions were laid bare. In my very public position, we managed to hang onto each other, needing each other's love and support. As a result, I became an open book on social media. I shared the thoughts behind utility decisions, addressed public concerns, and shared my life with my followers.

The referendum finally went before the voters on November 6, 2018, one day short of the one-year anniversary of the Biomass Buyout. The vote against the referendum was strong with 60% of Gainesville residents voting no. The *Gainesville Sun* headline proclaimed, "Voters shut down GRU referendum." Perry and Clemons' plans to take the governance of the utility away from the city commission had been defeated by Gainesville voters. I thought, of course, was it really in doubt?

Ironically, the people most aggravated by GRU's governance structure were GRU customers living outside the city boundaries—people who never got a chance to vote in the election.

During a late-night victory celebration, Mayor Poe was quoted by the *Gainesville Sun* as saying, "A lot of people worked very hard on this for more than four years. It's been a major distraction and it's been a major anchor around our staff and our elected officials for many, many years. We're turning the page."

While the Mayor and commission would turn the page on the referendum, they couldn't ignore the GFT and their reluctance to address the structural financial deficiencies of the utility, even after the game-savings Biomass Buyout. I wasn't going to allow them to ignore the issues or me!

Ω

GRU At A Crossroads

Mayor Poe was someone who chose his words wisely. His comments after witnessing the referendum vote go down to defeat weren't as much celebratory as they were purposeful. It was his call to action. I had a hunch Poe was telling his fellow musketeers that they were now free to escalate their primary pursuit—that golden-oldie, "All for one-city, One-city for all." Originally unveiled at my December 7th trial, I'll never forget Hayes-Santos declaring the city needed to have "one clear vision across departments, all departments." He saw disagreements between GRU and the rest of city government as impediments towards fulfilling his vision for the city. That's not conjecture. He said it.

The three musketeers appeared to care little about the different customer bases the city and GRU served. Instead, they sounded more interested in picking winners in those inter-charter squabbles. Even more nefarious, the one-city approach presented an opportunity for the commission to quell debate over needed budget, rate, and GFT decisions.

Particularly troubling to me was the siren call of a one-city approach luring other commissioners closer to the rocks along the shoreline. A one-city approach had to sound imminently reasonable to those in the community—voters in particular. A solid brand success, any perceived opposition to the one-city concept was tantamount to dissing motherhood, apple pie, and backyard picnics. What general manager of the utility could ever say, "No, I don't think I'd like to function as a coordinated, collaborative team"?

By the end of 2018, one-city government had evolved along a subterranean path, parallel with the referendum, into the sacrosanct principle of a New American City. It simply was the way the three musketeers told the charter officers to function. My GRU team and I were routinely shamed whenever we spoke of the city and GRU as if they were separate entities (despite the fact that they were). "GRU is the city," we were told, as if we had committed a sin against nature. I envisioned it wouldn't be long before our recital of the Pledge of Allegiance would be changed to, "I pledge allegiance to the United States of America and the one-city of Gainesville."

While the one-city approach was a public relations success, it was not the prescribed approach under the City of Gainesville's guiding document, it's charter. That pesky charter dictated that both the city manager and the general manager were equal but distinct officers appointed by the commission, hence the term charter officer. As a charter officer, the general manager of the utility had the powers and duties to be "responsible for and have *exclusive* management jurisdiction and control over operating and financial affairs of the Utility System…" The general manager had an exclusive, not shared management. The one-city approach and the charter were in conflict.

The charter was drawn up in this manner because previous commissions understood the business environment under which GRU was required to operate. GRU needed to respond to regulatory and operational requirements in different ways than other city functions. GRU operated in a competitive environment while needing to preserve its real contribution to the City of Gainesville—remitting over thirty-eight million dollars a year in a GFT payment.

While I remained intent on running GRU as a business, the three musketeers pressured the utility to engage in other business ventures and extensions of typical government services. Hayes-Santos led the way in gathering support for GRU providing city-wide broadband internet service. Poe and Ward were using their influence to have GRU subsidize economic development, while the entire commission was energized behind a blast from the past—further renewable clean-energy projects.

While these initiatives were worthwhile and a well-intentioned direction for a city, there seemed to be little or no recognition that these ventures were riskier, costlier, and could diminish GRU's ability to sustain its GFT payment to the city. Therein was the catch—the one-city approach was a departure from the vigilance I had spent my years establishing at the utility. I discovered that leading the utility as a business put me inherently at odds with the one-city approach.

The rift in our thinking was evidenced when I delivered GRU's five-year strategic vision to the commission. Meeting in the utility's multi-purpose room, I spoke, "GRU envisions a well-run business optimizing all aspects of the organization for the benefit of its customers and the community at large. Ward and Hayes-Santos were unmistakably upset. They fidgeted and grimaced throughout my presentation. Unable to take anymore anti-one-city nonsense, they interrupted me to teach me the folly of thinking about GRU as a business. "No," I was told by Ward, "GRU is not only a part of the city, but also the city." Hayes-Santos said, "The utility is simply a city service."

Unbelievable as it sounds, the three commissioners were unable to acknowledge that the over four hundred million dollars a year revenue-creation machine was a business. I was speechless. I knew this misguided one-city approach was fast becoming a paralyzing influence on the utility.

It's fair to say, Hayes-Santos envisioned broadband and internet services as an individual right. He thought access to the internet was akin to a right to healthcare. It was apparent that Hayes-Santos was not going to let any charter officer, especially me, stand in his way of doing what was right. With each day, he grew more vigilant, persistent, and unwavering in his pursuit of community broadband.

Hayes-Santos built his soapbox on the real work GRU had done over the past two decades when it introduced a new level of broadband infrastructure to the city. Through its separate entity, GRUCom, GRU designed, constructed, and operated an extensive fiber network throughout Gainesville. On one level, the network consisted of a robust transmission trunk that supported top-tier retail providers such as Cox and AT&T, who provided retail service to the community. To a lesser degree, GRUCom operated a business-to-business network through its GatorNet brand, through which it only provided service to apartments or other multi-unit complexes.

The business-to-business model limited GRUCom's build-out into single family housing neighborhoods. GRUCom was not A Field of Dreams, "build it and they will come" type of for-profit organization. That riskier business model was left for Cox and AT&T. GRUCom's low-risk "munici-business" model didn't accept the risk of Hayes-Santos' retail city-wide broadband internet model which required building into neighborhoods and competing against Cox and AT&T.

The governing document of Gainesville, its Charter, prescribed that no charter officer, including the general manager of the utility, reports to any single commissioner. Despite that technicality, I struggled to convince Hayes-Santos that I couldn't fulfill his desire to unilaterally transform GRU so it would operate like Cox or AT&T. In response to my hesitation, he said, "Well we can't keep doing the same thing and expect a different result." I answered, while that might have been true, it doesn't mean GRUCom ought to enter a more competitive market where a failure would burden its customers with millions of dollars of debt.

Unfortunately, Hayes-Santos had risen to a lead role among the musketeers, and his new devotees commonly ignored my advice along with my other GRU subject-matter experts. We delivered analysis after analysis that identified significant cost (over one hundred million dollars) and risk (lawsuits by retail providers) to GRU in entering the competitive retail internet market. In response to not getting the answer they wanted, in May of 2017, the commission created a new committee—the Broadband Subcommittee (or what I dubbed the BS committee) to uncover alternative paths. Frankly, it was created to give them the answer they wanted.

As anticipated, on March 27, 2018, the new Broadband Subcommittee authorized GRU to issue an Invitation to Negotiate (ITN) soliciting potential vendors to conduct a Community Broadband Study. That study would focus on the feasibility of providing lower prices, increased internet speeds for customers, and full access across the community. Secondarily, the goals were to provide the lowest-priced gigabit internet in the United States and universal free service for all residents served. The loftiness and apparent mutually exclusive nature of the goals still amazes me as I write them here on paper.

The last piece of the historic, unfolding, unfunded, mandated movement occurred on October 18, 2018, when the city commission adopted a resolution establishing the soaring goal of providing net-zero carbon emissions in the generation of the city's energy by the year 2045. Less than one year after I negotiated the termination of the GREC PPA, the commission wanted to jump back in the green at any cost in Hanrahan world. *Had they learned nothing?*

These three major strategic initiatives, a one-city government, broadband internet, and the push for yet more net-zero carbon power, were at the heart of the next transformation of the utility. A transformation I called the Trifecta. I recognized it was a hearty, unifying message to the community, strong on emotion while remarkably short on critical thought.

The relentless pressure of the commission's aspirations made charter officers simply actors in Kabuki Theater performances—the term used by pundits to deride political gamesmanship. Whether Kabuki Theater or Broadway Theatre, it was now clear that the one-city concept would be weaponized against me and any other charter who failed to follow its Trifecta mantra.

Despite the Trifecta's allure, executing the Trifecta was simply not feasible considering where the utility stood. High debt and high rates all driven by the GREC debacle had broken the GRU goose that laid the golden eggs for the commission. Unfortunately, reality didn't seem to faze the musketeers from their new misadventures.

It was becoming increasingly clear that I had limited options to stop the commissions' trajectory, other than being a lone voice against it, on any occasion I could. I had to show them, at best, these initiatives were nice-to-have, not must-have strategies. My strategy to mitigate the commission strategy would put me squarely in the line of fire.

As battle lines formed, city residents were home addressing the more pressing issues in their own lives. They didn't have time or the inclination to pay attention to the inner workings of a municipality and its utility. That was my job. Before employing my strategy, an unexpected high-level departure changed those plans.

A virtual lightning bolt struck my frenemy Anthony Lyons, when on December 7, 2018, one year to the day after my trial, he found himself in front of the governing body fighting for his job. New Commissioners Gail Johnson, and Gigi Simmons teamed up with second-term Commissioner Helen Warren because they were "tired of hearing about forced resignations, bypassed hiring policies and low morale on past and current employees" under Lyons' leadership.

Doing his best imitation of Rip Van Winkle, Poe expressed concern that the issues being discussed strayed into "dangerous territory," such as management responsibilities without "concrete accusations or evidence." Ole' Rip Van Poe saw nothing wrong with conducting a virtual trial surrounding my job one year earlier. He had no problem with the venue then, nor did he mention any dangerous territory. *Zzzz.*

Obviously tired of walking his own one-city, political tightrope, Lyons offered his resignation on December 11th and the commission accepted that resignation.

The resignation, in advance of the rising tide of votes to terminate him, was a shockingly unceremonious departure for the man who had proclaimed the need for a "New American City" just over two years before. *Gainesville Sun* reporter, Ron Cunningham, came to Lyons' support when he wrote: "Anthony Lyons was never going to be an ordinary traveler. And if the city manager's abrupt resignation arrived with the speed of an express package, it's because Lyons was deemed guilty of showing altogether too much initiative. Lyons was backed into a corner. His critics on the city commission left him the option of resigning or enduring a trial in which his competence, motivations and integrity would be fair game for anyone who cared to take a cheap shot." Cunningham ended with a response to Lyon's self-proclaimed 'Gainesville Question—How can we be more competitive?" "With the revolutionary-in-chief gone, The Gainesville Question looms larger than ever and unanswered still in the dawn of 2019."

The most ironic of the multiple ironies was Cunningham labelling any commission meeting concerning Lyons's continued employment as a trial, while offering nary a peep on my trial where my competence, motivation, and integrity were called into question. It reminded me of Hayes-Santos' grievances against me while ignoring a formal investigative report against Lyons.

My thoughts about Lyons had softened since the day of my trial. While Lyons and I had our differences, after working with him for over two years, I came to realize we had a lot in common—good things. We were both change agents challenging the status quo thinking of city government. We were both rather undiplomatic, data-driven, and built to make Gainesville a better place to live. Unfortunately, the commission had pitted us against each other in the battle over one-city government, the size of the GFT and other shared services. I knew Lyons would do well in his future endeavors.

As a result of the unexpected departure of Cunningham's revolutionary-in-chief, I sensed an opportunity to explore my own revolution. I have long believed that even the best strategy will fail if the right opportunity isn't chosen. I thought about Stanton's earlier use and misuse of topical white papers. Stanton's failure could be my success, as I imagined I could better articulate a more focused message and control the narrative by issuing topical white papers. An interim city manager would be in place and the city commissioners would be circling the wagons on the philosophical divide within their ranks. This would be my best opportunity to craft and secure internal solutions for GRU, just as I negotiated and executed upon external ones with the Biomass Buyout.

On February 7, 2019, I launched an offensive when I crafted my first white paper, *GRU at a Crossroads*, in which I presented a plan to mitigate the embedded structural financial deficits brought about by the commission's governing decisions. It was an objective step-by-step approach with potential solutions. I returned to my flair for song lyrics when I wrote: "I decided to take this approach while listening intently during the commission meeting concerning the general fund transfer (GFT) in GRU's multi-purpose room this January. It struck me that most, if not all, of the commissioners, were not even in office when the core of GRU's financial issues began. As I am apt to do, I heard the soft refrain of the lyrics from an old Billy Joel song in my head: 'We didn't start the fire, it was always burning, since the world's been turning. We didn't start the fire, no we didn't light it, but we tried to fight it."

I launched my white paper over public e-mail servers which made it available on-line public reading. I intended the white paper to be the cornerstone of discussions of GRU finances, particularly the GFT. *GRU at a Crossroads* was my philosophy of how the utility had to operate in the future. It was an historical accounting of how GRU changed over the period of the last decade, the consequences of that change, and, most importantly, what must be done now.

My primary message was simple. While GRU had spent more than a decade navigating the uncharted waters of early adoption of new climate change-driven power plants technology such as its Solar Feed-in-Tariffs, net metering solar customers, and a biomass plant, the commission continued to expect and demand an unhealthy-sized GFT from the utility to fund city services.

I pulled the issues surrounding the GFT out from behind closed doors. The community needed to be made aware of the mess the commission was creating. In 2020, the GFT was slated to increase 1.5 per cent over its 38.3-million-dollar level—a substantial portion of which were above GRU's earnings. From 2019 until 2026, my staff estimated a 6-to-12-million-dollar annual shortfall in the utility's ability to fund the GFT from current earnings. We were looking at a 60-million-dollar shortfall for the full seven years if there were no unexpected events. Part of that deficit was the increased debt service payments resulting from the Hanrahan-era 2012 debt restructurings. The other part of the deficit was the continuing burden of the decades-old burdens placed upon GRU and the inability of the city commission to keep up with the required utility rate increases. GRU was at an inflexion point, and important decisions still needed to be made.

I had been dissuaded from discussing the GFT in public. It was the sacred cow of the City of Gainesville's finances, only to be decided upon in private. If you were to ask any customer of GRU whether they were aware that GRU paid over thirty-eight million dollars a year to the city's general fund, I'd assure you that you'd receive a puzzled look. They wouldn't know such nuances of the city's finances. Hell, I'm not sure how many city employees understood them? Commissioners weren't talking about it. If I were to change the status quo, I knew it was time to bring the GFT into the sunshine. The public needed to understand its role in the utility's finances.

Every city manager I had worked with demanded the highest level of GFT payments possible. *Of course, they did.* The GFT provided almost one-third of the city's general fund budget. Without it, and without higher property taxes, the city would be sorely tested to fund the current level of police and fire department budgets, as well as social programs such as homeless shelter facilities at Grace Marketplace, living wages for all city workers, and apprenticeship programs. The bottom line was the city manager would have to cover the loss of the GFT with either higher property taxes or lower spending. Mentioning budget costs was akin to cursing in public.

Unfortunately, at thirty-eight million dollars, the size of GRU's GFT payment was vastly outstripping GRU's ability to fund it. Worse yet, in previous years, GRU used its cash reserves, not current earnings, to fully fund the payments. In the fiscal year 2017 and 2018, the funding shortfall was 11.7 million dollars and 3.9 million dollars, respectively, totaling 15.6 million dollars. To replenish its reserves, GRU had been forced to fund a higher percentage of its capital improvements with debt, along with requiring annual increases in its utility rates. It was a vicious circle, and it was an unsustainable practice.

The size of the GFT and borrowing to pay it were the concerns that a post-Biomass Buyout commission needed to address, not the imposition of a Trifecta of commission wishes which would add more debt to GRU's already massive debt burden.

Shortly after issuing *GRU at a Crossroads,* I had a productive discussion with Nathan Crabbe and Doug Ray. Supportive of my strategy, the editorial duo penned an editorial entitled, *GRU is at a Crossroads.* "Ed Bielarski makes the case that GRU is at a crossroads in a white paper issued earlier this month. The GRU general manager is partially right—only it's the City of Gainesville as a whole that is at a crossroads. With the city-owned utility experiencing rising costs and debt at a time when its reserves and revenues have declined, hard decisions have to be made to shore up GRU's finances that affect the overall city budget." The editorial finished with a sentence I could not have delivered better myself, "Whatever the commissioners do, they must not kick problems down the road—and put the city and GRU at another crossroads in a few years."

On February 15, 2019, I followed up with the second in my series of white papers with *GRU by the Numbers,* in which I analyzed each recommendation within my first Crossroads paper. I established a "Shortfall Scorecard" which showed the projected cash shortfalls from 2019 through 2025 and the impacts of my seven mitigation strategies, including 1) debt restructuring, which pushed debt payments towards future years; 2) right-sizing of GRU facilities, including potential sales of administration offices; 3) limits on all out-of-town travel; 4) charging customers for delivery of paper bills; 5) on-boarding of contract labor versus new employees; 6) real customer service level reductions; and 7) reductions in the GFT level.

I worked closely with Lyons' interim replacement, Deborah Bowie, who had tentatively agreed to consider sharing in the pain of the cash shortfalls by accepting a 6-million-dollar reduction in the GFT. We were moving towards the resolution GRU so desperately needed. It appeared that all the stars were aligned for a historical reduction of the GFT and a meaningful stabilization of GRU's finances.

Instead, the commission took the path of least resistance. They simply froze the GFT at the 38.3-million-dollar level for 2020. Their actions only accounted for approximately $500,000 of our projected 12-million-dollar shortfall or just 4%. The commission left 96% of the financial burden to fall upon GRU. It was a futile gesture, but above all, it was reckless. It was also a slap in the face to all GRU employees and its customers.

Disgusted with the commission's failure to do the right thing, I sat alone in my office one evening, pondering my next steps. I reflected on my life in this small southern town. The Biomass Buyout had been a negotiation between two savvy businessmen, while my current interactions with the commission facing a fiscal crossroads was more complex. How could any single person convince amateurish politicians that GRU was at a historic crossroads? I wondered if I would soon be finding myself on a similar path.

Ω

GM At His Crossroads

Despite the commission's egregious disregard for GRU's tenuous finances, my efforts were making me a visible, vocal leader not just of the utility but of the city. I explored issues that had been swept under the rug for years. While I sensed my effectiveness in engaging the community with genuine issues was threatening to the three musketeers, I couldn't back down. Their one-city approach to government was creating a Dickensian tale of two cities.

In June of 2019, I was pleased to see that it wasn't me on trial, but the one-city approach, when the long-awaited Community Broadband Study was completed by an outside consultant, CCG Consulting, and presented to the commission. The study detailed the possibility of fulfilling the dreams of the commissioners, but not without a hefty price tag. In particular, the report read: "There are scenarios where the city could provide low-priced broadband while operating a fiber-business that would be self-sustaining and profitable and that wouldn't need any subsidies from GRU or the city. However, creating such a business is no slam-dunk." *Ya think?*

"In the analysis, the estimated cost for building a fiber network within Gainesville city limits is $113 million in bond financing. That figure could rise to $213 million if the service extends to neighboring municipalities." You read it correctly— 213 million dollars! The shocking news didn't stop there. If the commission intended to pursue the expansion of the internet network, the report stated, "We would expect them (AT&T

and Cox) to vigorously attempt to delay or derail any plans to launch a retail fiber business." According to the report, existing law creates a series of hoops for a city to jump through. The bottom line was incumbent carriers, such as Cox and ATT, could fight the city in court for years.

The *Gainesville Sun* chimed in with a strongly stated editorial with the headline, "Internet plan comes with huge risks." In the first sentence, they left no doubt about their opinion by writing, "Gainesville city commissioners should put the brakes on the idea of providing cheap internet service through GRU." The newspaper followed with, "Given the troubled financial history of the biomass plant, city commissioners should be hesitant to make another major investment with huge risks. The study found there are 'considerable hurdles to overcome" in providing home internet service, including legal hoops, a likely voter referendum and attempts by competitors to derail the effort."

I was pleased that after years of collaborating with the editors of the newspaper, it seemed that Doug Ray and Nathan Crabbe were starting to believe what I said. So, when the smoke had cleared, it was not the study that Ward, Hayes-Santos, and Poe had envisioned. It wasn't the media response that they expected as well.

Under the weight of this new evidence, Hayes-Santos came out swinging wildly, I would add. In speaking to a WUFT reporter, he aggressively accused GRUCom competitors of "making money hand over fist, so they don't want to lose the cash cow of Gainesville. That's kind of one of the things that is expected."

I shook my head as I thought about the old expression of the pot calling the kettle black. If anyone knew about not wanting to lose a cash cow, it was Hayes-Santos. He refused to back down in the face of the facts. The *WUFT* article concluded by writing, "Hayes-Santos said he hopes the commission would vote to proceed within the next year."

Despite Hayes-Santos' petulance, the Broadband Subcommittee paused their rush to move forward. The other members, Ward and Arreola in particular, recognized the magnitude of the political hurdle in the road ahead of the initiative. As a result, informally, the community broadband scheme was placed on the back burner. I savored my partial victory in the broadband skirmish, particularly since it slowed down the one-city train. However, I suspected it was not forgotten.

It was time to endure Gainesville's "silly season" –the time in the run-up to elections when everyone comes out of the political woodwork to influence the outcome. My white papers, Facebook posts, and analysis proved to be ample fodder for people wanting to accuse me of all types of misdeeds.

In one such instance, a candidate in the mayoral race, Jenn Powell, opined at a League of Women Voters forum, "the city should go line-by-line in the budget to find savings," after which she took direct aim at me. She exclaimed that she didn't trust me, due to my lucrative salary, to understand issues facing the poorest people in the city or ensure money wasn't spent frivolously. *Oh boy.*

This type of political theater ensured Poe was never truly in danger of losing re-election. While he was wrong on issues surrounding GRU, he was seen as a well-versed public servant who was well-liked by the community. As a result, Poe cruised to a win while becoming only the second mayor to win re-election in Gainesville history (the first being Pegeen Hanrahan).

The dark horse issue of 2019's silly season was a referendum question as to whether a Charter Review Commission (CRC) should be established. The proposed CRC would be convened once a decade, eighteen months before the general election, for the purpose of reviewing and potentially proposing changes to the City's guiding document, its Charter. Those proposed changes would proceed to the commission, where it would require a super majority veto to keep the proposed changes from proceeding to the general election as referendum ballots. The voters saw the referendum as relatively innocuous, so it passed by a slim majority. I would soon find out that the CRC was anything but an innocuous entity.

In late May, city hall was packed with people seeking appointments to the new CRC. I watched as one-by-one the commission appointed members to the CRC—former assistant manager and Hanrahan devotee Walter Barry, long-time GRU critic Richard Blount, former commissioner and Hanrahan mentor Susan Bottcher, and others. There were a number of Hanrahan-era people being appointed to a board that could place a motion in front of the city commission to change the Charter. I felt my first pang of impending danger. It was heightened when Hayes-Santos' political sidekick, Bryan Eastman, was appointed as an alternate.

Eastman had run Hayes-Santos' campaign and was extremely active in the public broadband internet movement. He was on record saying that he believed publicly-owned internet was the solution to the digital divide—the gap between those with and without reliable technology and the internet. He would become the administrator for the Facebook group *Connected Gainesville*, which advocated for accessible and high—speed internet for the community. In a shot at GRU, he said, "It's internet-owned and operated by the people that use it. The same way our utilities are owned by people who are actually using it." *There's the weaponization of that phrase again.* GRU isn't owned by the people it serves. If it were customers outside the city would be voting the three musketeers out of office!

While I recognized that the CRC that had been appointed might have a bone to pick with me, I hadn't expected such overwhelming political bias on display. In the end, the commission appointed thirteen members to the CRC, many of which were considering dramatic changes to the Charter.

On the steps of city hall, during a break in a later commission meeting, I casually talked with Jorge Campos, a CRC appointee whose full-time job was serving as an officer in the Gainesville Police Department (GPD). I found out that Campos thought there were too many charter officers. "It made it hard to get things done," he opined.

I moved back, stunned, looked into his eyes and asked, "Who would you remove, Jorge?" Campos looked down at his feet and muttered that he thought that there ought to be one voice for the city. I howled, "Not you too, Jorge!" He responded quite seriously that I had fought with the city managers too often and it kept things from getting done.

Campos had been infected with the one-city bug. I wondered who else was carrying the germ. Whatever the case, we needed to develop an antidote in a New York minute before everyone was walking around like zombies extolling the virtues of one-city as the finances of GRU collapsed around them.

The importance of this encounter epitomized the unsubstantiated bias CRC members could carry into the process. I heard rumors that other CRC members might agree with Campos—a charter change to remove the general manager of the utility as a charter officer. *OMG, could you all just let me do my job?*

Over the remainder of the year, the CRC met monthly to develop the recommendations they would bring before the commission. By the spring of 2020, the CRC had finalized its recommendations—the primary one being one that would eliminate the general manager of utilities as a charter position. *Here we go again.*

***

Whatever matters I was coping with, my year was still markedly better than City Auditor Carlos Holt. At the end of his audit of an exceedingly popular charitable organization, the Reichert House Youth Academy, Holt reported the "thirty-one-year-old program had a lack of standard business processes, lack of transparency, poorly documented purchases, and a lack of oversight, among other issues."

The Reichert House program had been overseen by the City of Gainesville's beloved Chief of Police, Tony Jones, as well as others within the Gainesville Police Department (GPD). The Reichert House program successfully assisted hundreds of predominantly Black at-risk youths into adulthood. While Holt made it clear that his report was not meant to take away from the positive aspects of the program, it would soon become apparent that it ruffled a few feathers. As Ray Washington wrote in an editorial, "It should not be surprising that plain-spoken City Auditor Carlos Holt has become a target of attacks by commissioners bracing for public outrage when the magnitude of coming property tax hikes, fire assessment fee hikes and electric rate hikes becomes widely understood." It grew even more personal.

Interim City Manager Deborah Bowie said Holt's report was flawed and told the City Commission that Holt had a conflict of interest due to fourteen police visits to his home since 2015. In response, Holt didn't get angry, he tried to get even. Holt hired an attorney who promptly filed a claim with the city requesting hundreds of thousands of dollars in restitution for how he had been treated.

The environment spiraled downward when on May 16th, the commission debated the possibility of terminating Holt's employment. Much like the situation I had faced on my December 7th trial, the commission didn't have the votes to terminate Holt. Still, there were three commissioners who voiced strong displeasure over Holt's submission of a claim. The strongest opinion came from Hayes-Santos, who said, "This is highly unethical the way he's doing this. He'd trying to get more money out of us." I roared aloud as I thought about Hayes-Santos using GRU as the commission's piggybank.

With no viable pathway towards resolution of the continuing controversy, on June 6th, the commission voted 5 to 2 in favor of terminating Holt, effective immediately.

Commissioners Gail Johnson and Gigi Simmons voted in dissent. Ward best expressed the majority of feelings when he said, "That letter looked a lot like—to me—that—Mr. Holt doesn't want to be here anymore." I couldn't blame Holt.

Holt and I had been warriors in the day-to-day battles against the three musketeers. I knew all too well how the constant risk of termination could wear even the best man down. Holt was a former Marine serving the country in Iraq and Afghanistan. I was going past four years with GRU at this point. I pondered whether Holt's treatment was foreshadowing my upcoming engagement with the CRC.

***

By the fall of 2019, GRU's combative budget process, along with my issuance of two white papers, the termination of the city auditor, the commission's non-decision on the GFT, and the potential charter amendment to remove the general manager of the utility gained the attention of both State Senator Keith Perry and State Representative Chuck Clemons.

On October 24, 2019, Perry and Clemons requested that the Joint Legislative Auditing Committee (JLAC) direct the State Auditor General to conduct a "comprehensive and in-depth audit of the operational practices and managerial oversight of the City of Gainesville." They noted that their constituents "were concerned with GRU's lack of financial transparency and stability."

I found Perry/Clemons' request for GRU's inclusion in the audit misinformed. The request offered no added information on GRU. The request was more about the commission, the city and GRU's guilt by association. It was supported with citizen claims, sprinkled, like confectionary sugar, with inaccuracies from an army of anti-GRU activists. I began to think of my daily routine as a game of "Whack-a-Mole."

The State Legislature rubber-stamped the request, approving the performance of an audit. During my perpetual battles with the commission to reduce the GFT to an amount

265

the utility could afford to pay, I would now be under further scrutiny of a politically driven audit from the Auditor General's office. I outlined my concerns in an editorial to set the record straight. In my editorial, "Audit is based on merit less claims," I wrote, "The lawmaker's latest low blow marks a turning point in their decade-long rift with the city of Gainesville, including GRU. In the past, their arguments have focused largely on policies implemented by the elected officials overseeing GRU. The arguments were never about whether the employees of GRU were doing inadequate or even fraudulent work. But this time, it's different."

It was different because; "This is a personal attack on the managers, supervisors, employees of GRU and my chief financial officer, finance and accounting director, community and government relations officer and the many folks who perform their excellent decisions. For all their past rhetoric about how Senator Perry and Representative Clemons have no issue with GRU employees, they have even less issue with making these same employees the subject of an unnecessary audit and effectively attacking their professional judgment and endangering their careers. The majority of this is based on letters from seven concerned citizens whose stories were not corroborated or authenticated. In fact, neither Senator Perry nor Representative Clemons have ever attempted to talk to my staff or me about any of these issues, the unfortunate result of which is an audit based on meritless claims."

I ended my editorial strongly, "I am further concerned that this new round of posturing by Senator Perry and Representative Clemons will only perpetrate the mythology of GRU as a bad actor and, this time, even drag our employees into the viper pit of Gainesville politics." I had grown weary of outside interference in the utility business from all political factions.

The language of my editorial was strong enough to illicit a call from Perry himself, who tried to tell me that he was only responding to his constituents. I jumped at the opportunity to tell the senator that I, too, was one of his constituents, and a phone call to me at any time would gladly be accepted if it could clear up any of his confusion. Not surprisingly, the senator had failed to call me at the time. It was unfortunate because, on multiple levels, I appreciated Perry's business savvy and discipline. We shouldn't have been such adversaries.

These events were on my mind as I sat in the GRU multipurpose room on April 23, 2020, awaiting the CRC's decision on whether they would approve a recommendation which would remove the general manager as a charter officer. I was less nervous than I had been two- and- one-half years before. It was becoming an all-too-familiar event for me. I had grown accustomed to having a job that was always in jeopardy. Whatever the reason, my mind drifted back to the origins of how the CRC arrived at this juncture.

***

The recommendation to remove the general manager as a charter officer had grown legs at a CRC meeting on September 16, 2019, when they had a conversation with George Forbes, a former city manager for Jacksonville Beach and Clermont. During the meeting, Forbes pointed out, "One of the things you're going to find, if you are going to make this change, you have to have a very good reason for why you want to do this, so the public will understand so they will support it." The CRC Chairwoman, MaryAnn Hildreth, responded that "We have too many charter officers, basically."

Late in the year, as the recommendation became more inevitable, I asked to speak to the CRC about its consequences. I took a few days to build my case into a six-page document which I forwarded to each CRC member ahead of time. On the day of the meeting, I took the elevator down from my third-floor offices. As I arrived in the room, I didn't warrant a glance from the thirteen members in attendance. I sat down on a folding chair along the windows, awaiting my call. As Hildreth discussed the recommendation, I winced as she bungled the implications. I made my notes.

At the appropriate time, Hildreth stopped the member discussions and asked if "Mr. Bielarski was in attendance and does he want to

267

speak." I raised my hand and blurted out, "I'm here, chair. Yes, I'd like to address the committee." I moved to the lectern at the front of the room, where I looked out over the U-shaped configuration of the member seating.

I began by telling them that the actual language of the amendments and my removal as a charter officer meant that amendment would serve to terminate the general manager's contract since the position would be removed. In the city, you can't hire or retain an employee for which there is no position. It's that simple.

Beyond that, preserving the GM in a charter role was important in maintaining the utility's independence. An independent GM better served the complexities of the utility. It also allowed direct community access to the officer, who wouldn't be hidden behind a city manager. Even more importantly, it was necessary for an equal city manager and general manager to balance the GFT negotiations.

I invoked Georges Forbes' comments from the September meeting, in which he said, "There's going to be some tension over the rated tension to the general fund. No matter what you do or what governance you go to, that's going to exist." As a result, if the CRC made their recommendation, there would no longer be a dynamic tension between the roles of a general manager and a city manager, particularly regarding the GFT.

As I spoke, I was stunned to witness Hayes-Santos wander through the door and take a seat behind the CRC members. I immediately wondered why he was there. There was an unspoken protocol for the CRC members to meet by themselves, not to be influenced by the commission. Seeing him in attendance brought me back to my trial, where he was my accuser once again. I could see others in the room were shaken as well.

Once more, I glared at Hayes-Santos as I finished. I told the group that they should return to whether there was a very good reason to remove the general manager. I said, "I think the answer is clear. There is not a very good reason."

I saw Hayes-Santos's attendance as just another power play. After I finished speaking, Hayes-Santos moved to the lectern. He proceeded to address the group and urged them to continue their consideration of the amendment. I shook my head as he told the CRC members it was important to stop the "two-headed monster" of General Government and GRU managers arguing while things were not getting done. Wow, now I was part of a two-headed monster as compared to the pleasantry of one-city.

After the meeting concluded, I stumbled upon Hayes-Santos outside the elevator leading to my office. He quietly told me, once more, that this was something he had thought about for a long time. It wasn't personal. I quickly answered, "This is bullshit, this is bullshit," as I stormed off.

***

As I mentally re-engaged in the meeting, it was obvious that certain members of the CRC were gaining traction with the arguments I had made in the *Gainesville Sun* entitled, "Proposal would cut GRU general manager," where I wrote, "My growing concern is a public narrative suggesting that the proposed amendment merely reassigns the general manager of utilities, which is misleading to our customers. Proposed amendment No. 191054 eliminates the general manager of GRU position from the charter and transfers authority over GRU to the city manager. This is not my interpretation; it is a fact."

The editorial touched on the sensibilities of influential Gainesville people such as former GRU GM and, at a different time, Gainesville City Manager, Karen Johnson, as well as other CRC members. Johnson was so inclined to set the record straight that she drafted a compelling e-mail to the CRC and commission in which she wrote, "The City Commission needs to hear the voice of both the City Manager and General Manager as equals. There is a dynamic tension between the roles of the CM and GM and as our elected representatives, you need to be the ones to sort out and balance those priorities. This is simply too important to our community to be delegated to an unelected City Manager." It was soothing to hear such wisdom.

Just like the commission's vote to approve me in 2015, Hildreth quickly put the recommendation up for a vote. By a 6 to 4 vote of CRC members in attendance, the proposed amendment *failed* to *remove* the general manager as a charter office, meaning it would not move forward to the city commission. Once again, I had beaten the odds and avoided the fate of termination.

I saw my work life extend beyond that of both Lyons and Holt. GRU was still at a crossroads, but at least I'd be around to lead the effort to influence the right decisions for GRU customers and Gainesville residents on the net-zero carbon emission goal, a sustainable GFT, and city-wide broadband all wrapped in the one-city bow.

As I walked out of the building, I marveled that the December 7, 2017 commission meeting was a trial, while April 23rd had simply been an attempted coup.

Ω

The Great GFT Grab

By the end of 2019, the commission on-boarded a new city manager, Lee Feldman. Unlike Lyons and interim replacement Bowie, this wasn't Feldman's first rodeo. He was a veteran city manager who had earned his stripes in southern Florida municipalities, such as Palm Bay, North Miami, and Fort Lauderdale. A simple Google search produced a series of ominous red flags surrounding Feldman's tenure as Fort Lauderdale's city manager between 2011 and 2018. Those red flags included a series of newspaper articles detailing sewer infrastructure failures immediately after Feldman's tenure.

Inarguably, from 2019 through 2020, Fort Lauderdale's sewer system experienced historic overflows as more than two hundred million gallons of raw sewage spilled out into the streets and properties across the community. In an article by *WLRN 91.3 FM* written one year after the sewage spills, the media source wrote, "City officials place most of the blame for the delayed repairs on the city's former administration. During his tenure, City Manager Lee Feldman used $120 million from utility funds to balance the general budget over six years. That practice was stopped in 2020 after Feldman was fired in late 2018."

Another article from the *Florida Bulldog*, a watchdog group, reiterated the harm caused by Feldman's budgetary tactics. The article spelled out the failures, "For many years, city administrators used a budgeting method called return on investment (ROI). Instead of tapping a dedicated utility budget to fund sewer projects, they shifted the money to a general budget to support police and fire departments and other services. Between 2012 and 2107, Feldman used ROI to move about $90.4 million earmarked for water and sewer projects to the general budget, the *South Florida Sun Sentinel* reported in August 2017. Before the current city administrator phased out ROI budgeting and ended it completely this year, the total had climbed to an estimated $120 million. So, at the moment the money was required for some crucial sewer repairs, it wasn't immediately available. ROI is legal, but the DEP rejected it, at least the way it was used in Fort Lauderdale." It seemed that Feldman already adhered to the Hanrahan-era philosophy—if the general government can't afford it, oh well, the utility surely can.

The more I read, the worse it sounded. The *Florida Bulldog's* article continued laying blame at Feldman's doorstep. "While there is no villain in this saga, the state blames a budgeting technique that siphoned funds away from sewer projects to other services at times when money was desperately needed for sewer projects. And the most zealous practitioner of this-now abandoned technique was former City Manager Lee Feldman, who was fired in October 2018. 'I blame a lot of people,' said Stan Eichelbaum, spokesperson for the Fort Lauderdale Association for Good Government. 'I blame Feldman for the diversion of the money and for ignoring the public safety issues."

Of course, working in the public sector has made me quite skeptical about these blanket accusations while engaging in the blame game. I learned a long time ago. There are multiple sides to every story. However, in Feldman's case, there seemed to be little question that he had used utility funds to balance the city's budget at the expense of utility infrastructure repairs. In the current environment where a reduction in the GFT was urgently needed, I feared that Feldman would be my new obstacle.

As a test of how the new city manager would cope with our GFT issue, I set up a meeting on December 16, 2019, to meet Feldman, along with members of his staff, in my conference room. As the room filled in, I took a seat alongside my Finance Director, Mark Benton. I trusted Benton, who had served as the Director of Finance for the city, or should I say general government, for over twenty years before moving over to the utility. He was a respected, objective, and prudent public servant. I knew his objective presence could be useful at this opening meeting.

The presentation was crafted on the long-held understanding of how the GFT formula should work—one that I still had reservations over. The GFT formula should emulate what an investor-owned utility would pay the city if GRU was an investor-owned utility. The three elements, 1) estimated property taxes, 2) franchise fees, and 3) a return on investment for this fictitious utility, added up to the new data point for a GFT. Not one for exchanging pleasantries, Benton placed the bottom-line dollar amount in front of Feldman— thirty-three million dollars, down from the 38.3 million dollars in the city's budget. I told Feldman that I placed the condition upon the formula that the number couldn't exceed what GRU was able to pay, which in our case was twenty-seven million dollars.

Feldman's collegial attitude dissolved as he sat through the presentation, looking bored and unengaged. When Benton ended the presentation, he looked at Feldman to ask if he had any questions. Feldman mumbled, "I'd like a formula that gives us 38.3 million dollars." Benton and I looked at each other and just shook our heads. Feldman laughed sheepishly. After all, I had been through, I wanted to take a swing at him.

Composing myself, I told Feldman that he might want to get serious about the matter. GRU's ability to fund the GFT was diminishing every day. Even at the 33-million-dollar level, GRU couldn't readily afford it. It was the start of the concept.

Feldman was unmoved. It was obvious to me that we were about to enter the mosh pit of what I call the Great GFT Grab.

Speaking of not waiting until it was too late before engaging in the next battle, Melinda and I shared down time at the beach. She had reached a milestone in her life—she survived three years beyond her pancreatic cancer surgery, and we were blessed to be able to celebrate her upcoming 65th birthday. During that weekend at the beach, at a local restaurant, a live band played the Beatle's classic song, *"When I'm 64."* Melinda looked at me with those beautiful blue eyes and exclaimed, "Oh, my god. I've listened to that song forever, and now, I'm here. I'm sixty-four." We laughed and hugged as we enjoyed the night.

We arrived back in land-locked Gainesville on July 9, 2020, just in time for me to deliver the final 2021 budget presentation—the most transparent of any budget presentation that I have ever given. I called the current 38.3-million-dollar GFT unsustainable. I told the commission that "cash from operations had fallen below established levels, requiring the utility to use reserves to pay the GFT payments." I warned them that immediate actions were necessary to avoid 1) negative rate stabilization cash within the next year; 2) further debt downgrading by rating agencies; 3) higher interest rates; 4) erosion of investor, bondholder, and rating agency trust; 5) immediate need to reduce GFT to the level of GRU profitability; and 6) reduction of essential services, safety, and reliability. It was meant as a wake-up call.

The commission slept right through the alarm, not even bothering to hit the snooze button. At the end of the budget process, the commission once again froze the level of the GFT at the 38.3-million-dollar level. I was furious that eighteen months removed from my *GRU at a Crossroads* whitepaper, and the commission still could not pull the trigger on reducing the GFT. The Gainesville City Commission would get my vote as the year's most inept board of directors.

In yet another purely political act of deflection, the commission self-righteously admonished the city manager and I for failing to deliver an appropriate GFT solution. Rather than act themselves, they voted to engage a consultant to develop a formula for the GFT calculation for future years. *I'd give them a formula at no charge—don't demand more than what GRU earns.*

Allowing my blood to simmer below its boiling point, I allowed myself to see the use of a consultant as the opportunity we needed. In the fall of 2020, GRU entered a contract with a consulting firm called nFront, whose goal was to "develop alternative General Fund Transfer mechanisms based on a formula that balances General Government's need for certainty of funding, with GRU's ability to sustainably fund the GFT over an extended period of time." In other words, construct a formula that balances the interests of the city and GRU.

On January 25, 2021, at the height of the COVID outbreak, nFront was ready to share its findings. I was excited to sit down and participate in nFront's ZOOM teleconference call. As one by one, people popped in from cyberspace, I was hopeful of seeing a useful, objective evaluation of the GFT. Within the first fifteen minutes of the call, my exuberance crumbled, appalled at the level of inconsistency and inaccuracy in nFront's presentation. It was like watching the Broadway performance of *Cats*—I just wanted to leave the theater.

Inexplicably, nFront had "developed parameters for each option to result in the targeted GFT on average ($38.3 million) under the Base case projections over the Study Period." In other words, they built their model based on matching our current level of GFT. That damn 38.3 million dollars. It was as though they were carrying Feldman's water.

Furthermore, nFront defined the city's "Certainty of Funding" to mean "Stable or increasing GFT over Study Period." On the other hand, GRU's "Ability to Fund" was defined as a minimal reduction in cash reserves over the Study

Period." nFront set artificial parameters and definitions based on GRU's reserves falling and the GFT stable to increasing. They weren't the agreed-upon assumptions.

Worst yet, nFront observed that Option #2 was the most balanced option because it *failed* to provide GG with their certainty of funding and equally *failed* to account for GRU's ability to fund. You read it right. Option #2 was chosen because it failed both parties equally.

My thoughts floated between speechless, angry, and embarrassed for nFront. When nFront concluded the presentation by recommending the new formula, which would reduce the GFT from 38.3 million to a still costly thirty-six million dollars, I was thrown into my Wartime Consigliere mode.

Wasting no time, I fired off an e-mail to nFront's project team expressing my displeasure with their work product. I informed them they had savings from a debt refinancing that the commission had already assigned to pay the GFT, which "effectively overrides the expressed will of the City Commission of Gainesville." I wrote that their selection of an option that failed to provide GG's certainty of funding or GRU's ability to pay was like saying, "the ending to Romeo and Joliet was a happy one because neither lover got what they wanted." nFront seemed to be missing the forests for the trees.

I was equally upset because, in the process of nFront's due diligence, I submitted data to them that showed that GRU was the only utility among the top five municipal utilities in Florida that transferred more than their financial statement earnings to its city brethren, by far.

In GRU's case, over the past four years, its GFT was 122% to 236% of its earnings. On the other hand, JEA, Orlando Utility Commission, Tallahassee, and Lakeland transferred 33% to 78% of its earnings to the city it served. nFront simply ignored that data (see following graph).

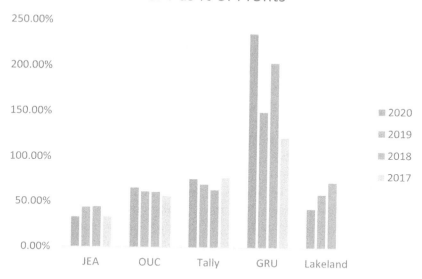

GFT as % of Profits

In response to my letter, nFront's CEO, John Painter, issued a tepid-sounding e-mail. As part of a 7-page response, Painter wrote that he was "very comfortable we have not breached our obligations with the city and GRU." Despite its length, his unresponsive e-mail was everything that I had come to hate about corporate America. Painter was telling me, "I hear you but trust me, there's nothing to see here. Just move along."

While Painter's response was insulting, I was more upset about missing a golden opportunity to provide the commission with the proper rational for a much lower GFT. I had positioned the commission to be ready to accept the numbers. Instead, Painter and his nFront colleagues had stolen that chance from me and my team. They wasted my time, as Gordon would say. I would not go away without a fight. I would need to steal the opportunity back.

I weaponized my computer keyboard to pound out an e-mail to Painter. This was familiar territory for me. As I typed, I absorbed my view of the city. I was reminded of my first thoughts of this town. I realized that my mission was greater than the utility. It was about this town itself. Without a viable, self-sustaining utility, the city would suffer unbearably. I found new energy in that thought.

"While I appreciate your review of the work of nFront's project team, as well as your commitment to stand ready to work diligently with GRU and the City, forgive me if those words ring hollow," I wrote, as I was just getting started. "As with any dispute of this nature, it is important for the aggrieved party's concerns to be addressed, not denied." That's a lesson I learned working with Melinda. Having endured the burden of a husband ready to fight for his passions at a moment's notice, sometimes unyielding in his pursuit of justice, Melinda taught this old dog to take time to listen long enough to affirm her feelings. It was time to demand that Painter affirm my feelings.

I envisioned Alistair Cooke in his chair while introducing *Masterpiece Theater* when I cynically wrote, "Your letter was written in a structured, albeit legal way to deny any validity to our well-founded claims, with the added comfort of a well-heeled gentleman smoking his pipe in his study. I could almost hear the fire crackling in the background, as you stated on the first page of your letter; 'I am very comfortable we have indeed fulfilled our obligation to assess and develop alternative mechanisms that in our professional judgment reasonably balance the above-competing objectives."

Painter was more like Dan Aykroyd in his series of *Saturday Night Live* skits playing critic Leonard Pinth-Garnell. In each of his ten skits, he would talk about bad performances from the performing arts, such as cinema, ballet, and theater. The nFront performance was beyond bad theater. It was bad business.

278

"Just in case I didn't absorb the level of your comfort the first time you wrote it, you finish the paragraph with another expression of your comfort; 'Therefore, I am very comfortable we have not breached our obligations to the city and GRU.' To be clear, I am expressing to you that I have little time for nFront dismissing our claim or hearing about the level of comfort you have. I need nFront to recognize GRU's perspective that they have failed to fulfill their obligations under the contract and are in breach. As Count Adhemar so dramatically said in the pop classic, *A Knight's Tale*: You have been weighed, you have been measured, and you have been found wanting."

I always wanted to use that line on someone who deserved it. I had found my opportunity with Painter. I wasn't finished.

I followed my scathing e-mail with another one that questioned nFront's philosophy in balancing GRU's ability to pay with GG's certainty of funding. Put simply: "GRU's ability to pay grants GG certainty. GG's certainty is actually diminished when GRU is required to fund more than what it earns. Only when GRU's ability to pay is determined can GG's certainty of funding be ascertained." It was clear to me that nFront had simply wanted to split the baby, like King Solomon on a consulting gig.

"I'll close with another great quote from *A Knight's Tale*. When asked if he would withdraw from the competition, King William said, 'It's not in me to withdraw.' Nor shall I, Mr. Painter."

Shockingly, Painter absorbed my abuse and responded in an e-mail on February 4th, in which he acquiesced to include another option under the parameters I had set forth. This new option, Option #10, reduced the GFT in FY 2022 to 27.7 million dollars versus the thirty-six million dollars under Option #2.

What Painter didn't say, nor did I think he cared to say, was Option #10 fulfilled the commission mandate that we don't use debt restructuring savings for anything other than reserves, technology enhancements, and debt defeasance. I didn't care because I had secured an option I needed. There was still an avenue to reducing the GFT.

While my staff and I were battling nFront's misguided findings, Rasnick, Benson, and I delivered a report to the commissioners on an individual basis called "The State of the Utility." This report was a clarion call to the commission in which I outlined the utility's must-haves and a list of decisions the commission would need to make. For starters, I told the commissioners that GRU must not pay more in the GFT than it earns. A debt defeasance plan must also be developed, and our next steps in power generation must be balanced with ability to fund it.

I also told the commissions that they needed to decide whether to; 1) continue as a power generator; 2) pursue a net-zero or 100% renewable plan so quickly; 3) layoff/reduce workforce; 4) deliver the same level of utility services; 5) consider a cycle of constant financial restructurings to meet current debt service requirement; 6) risk downgrades from rating agencies and higher borrowing costs and limited capital market demand.

The meetings must have felt like a gut punch to the commissioners. A few admitted as much. They had never been confronted with a general manager who never, never gave up. I would not, nor could not, let the issues at hand be swept under the rug. Decisions had to be made for the utility to flourish and maintain its role as the economic engine of the city. I left the meetings hopeful that we had been heard.

A month later, on April 8, 2021, the commission met to decide upon the final disposition of the FY 2022 GFT during an afternoon General Policy Meeting. nFront was on the call along with both Feldman and I along with our respective staff. After hearing all three presentations (GRU, GG, and nFront), the commission deliberated as one by one they spoke from the dais.

While several commissioners spoke at length about accepting the opportunity to drop the GFT to twenty-seven million dollars, when the final vote was taken, the commission voted 4 to 3 for Option#2—a small reduction to thirty-six million dollars. The commission had done it again. Faced with making the right decision for the utility, in the face of overwhelming facts and reason, the commission had taken the wrong path again. Three years in a row. I had warned them that dominoes would begin to fall...

It didn't take long before the commission found karma could be a bitch. On May 3rd, as we had warned, one of the three bond rating agencies, S&P Global Ratings, lowered its long-term rating on GRU's combined utility revenue debt two notches to 'A' from 'AA-.' I notified the commission in a two-page e-mail: "This two-notch downgrade is the first of its kind for GRU and is the fifth bond rating downgrade since 2010. Unlike other utility downgrades, this action was not driven by a specific event, which is what you normally see with a two-notch downgrade. Instead, this downgrade is the result of decisions that adversely impact GRU and create financial inflexibility. Specifically described by S&P: 1) 'two power supply decisions made more than a decade ago—a solar FIT paid to behind-the-meter generators and a power purchase agreement (PPA) for a biomass plant'; 2) 'significant transfers to support the city's general fund transfer'; 3) 'an uncertain approach to achieving a stated goal of 100% of energy from renewables by 2045, there is a risk that this goal could become an unfunded mandate, which could have further implications for GRU's credit worthiness.'"

In case people didn't understand the magnitude of the two-notch downgrade, I wrote: "Although a downgrade to 'A' sounds fairly innocuous, it is five notches away from the loss of investment grade status and four notches away from the highest investment grade status of 'AAA+.' An 'A' rating is not like an 'A' on your children's report card. It's more like a 'B-' or a 'C.' GRU will incur additional costs with its liquidity facilities and letters of credit. Interest costs will increase on both existing and future debt issuances."

I was tired of walking the tightrope with commissioners who pandered to the worst among us. They were elected to make the gut-wrenching decisions, not offer glittering generalities in the face of hardship and strife. Damn them. I needed to use this downgrade as an opportunity to snap them out of their malaise.

I wrote, "I requested that the commission significantly reduce the GFT in 2020, 2021, and 2022. Unfortunately, in 2020 and 2021, the GFT was simply frozen, not reduced, and GRU continued to remit payments in excess of what it earned. In 2022, the commission reduced the GFT by $2 million, not the $11 million GRU had recommended in accordance with the conditions set forth in the 2019 debt restructuring. S&P addressed this action directly by writing, 'Although the city modestly reduced the amount to be transferred in 2022, this nevertheless represents a substantial burden on the utility, and in our view, partially contributes to GRU's high rates." It was all there. S&P had given a particularly unvarnished, direct, and unflattering appraisal of the commission's actions.

"Just this February, GRU finance staff met with commissioners individually to discuss the future state of the utility if the commission chose to 1) forego a sizeable reduction in the GFT while 2) undertaking the 100% renewable goal with the current state of technologies. In this presentation, 'State of the Utility,' the commissioners were shown the financial impacts. The results of which are that GRU does not have the financial condition to continue to pay more than it earns in the GFT, nor could GRU or this community financially support the 100% renewable goal at the present time, under the state of current technologies. That is why I have consistently battled with the UAB concerning their approach to energy policy that has little or no regard for the financial health of the utility."

Admittingly, in a self-serving manner, I concluded, "This two-notch downgrade by S&P is a signal from knowledgeable industry experts that GRU is now beyond the crossroads. GRU will be forced to navigate the ship against stronger headwinds of higher utility rates, higher leverage, high GFT, and financial inflexibility."

With the downgrade, there was no doubt what brought us to this tenuous state of the utility. Warned of GRU's inability to fund the GFT because of low growth, high fixed costs, and the burdens of two ill-advised contracts, the commission needed to act in 2019, 2020, and 2021. Failure to act in 2021 was the commission's third strike.

Of course, my bold, unscripted response to the commission's incompetence did not go unnoticed. *WCJB* television immediately reported on the unwelcome news with the headline "GRU debt rating lowered by S&P, General Manager writes critical letter to Gainesville City Commission." They wrote, "Alarm bells are ringing at Gainesville Regional Utilities (GRU) after they were dealt a historic downgrade by S&P Global Ratings." I knew that this was going to get ugly quickly.

During a May 6th commission meeting, in response to the two-notch bond rating downgrade, Ward asked for "the possibility of bringing in an outside management consultant to review GRU management practices." He indicated that I had signed off on the review during an earlier afternoon meeting with him.

As I listened, I grew ever more furious over the commissioner's comment. I had not signed off on that idea. That's not what happened at all. Earlier in the day, Ward had met me in my office to tell me that he was going to bring up the concept of bringing in a consultant to review *city-wide* practices for added efficiencies. I told him that I had no problem with looking across the city. *We were one-city, weren't we?* I had not agreed to have GRU placed under a microscope under the umbrella of a rating downgrade witch hunt.

Ward didn't stop there. He followed that inaccuracy with an observation that "We also have a lot of departments that look a lot like duplication, not with the intent of firing people, absolutely not, but with the intent of running a more, not only efficient operation but one operation, the City of Gainesville, not general government over here and GRU over there because that's not what the charter says."

I couldn't believe what I was hearing. Ward had met with me earlier in the day to alert me to the fact that he'd be calling for a review of ALL city operations, not just GRU. He had been outright deceitful. Other charter officers called me and said that it didn't sound like me to agree to that request. I told them, "You're right. It doesn't and I didn't."

It was obvious to me that Ward was using the two-notch downgrade to sully my reputation and that of my staff. He was indeed driven by larger political forces. There were rumblings that he was eyeing a run for mayor. What better way to launch a run than by dredging up more GRU animus?

Later that evening, I reflected on why I had been so incensed by Ward's comments. It was easy. He was making another play for the three musketeer's one-trick pony—a one-city concept. Since 2017, the public discussion of the need for the city to operate as one-city was piggy-backed on placing blame on me. First, it was the public discussion of my termination on December 7th. It was followed by the potential charter amendment to remove the general manager of the utility as a charter officer. Now it was the need to review GRU management practices on the heels of a two-notch downgrade which I had been warning about for years. Of course, I'd be incensed. Who wouldn't be?

The next night, I regained my composure long enough to pen an e-mail to the commission addressing Ward's comments, "At last evening's city commission meeting, the 'possibility of bringing in an outside management consultant to renew GRU management practices' was referred to the Policy Research Group. It was stated that this action was in light of the S&P downgrade. Although the request was somewhat vague and subject to further refinement by the research group, it appears to be a search for yet some undiscovered efficiencies and potential 'leaning' of the utility."

"As part of the City of Gainesville, One-City, I was somewhat surprised to hear that the utility was singled out for such scrutiny. Although I had, indeed, had a conversation with the commissioner making the motion, I apparently misunderstood that it wasn't a review of all city operations but rather, simply GRU management. When I arrived in the office this morning, the staff was universally disappointed after watching a commissioner propose a review of GRU management, as that was perceived as a direct insult to their integrity, professionalism, and subject matter expertise. I don't think that was what was intended, but as we are learning from the current culture survey, words spoken from the dais can have unintended consequences for the folks that serve the city."

Hitting the send button, I shot my e-mail through cyberspace to the commissioners. Once again, I was in a battle over the soul of the utility. In my almost six years with GRU, I had reshaped, reorganized, and renewed the utility to better serve our customers. However, like a never-ending storm, the commission had refused to adhere to any semblance of fiscal accountability.

The animus was on full display one week later during the special commission meeting where Ward and Hayes-Santos took verbal shots at me as CFO Claudia Rasnick began her presentation. Both Ward and Hayes-Santos interrupted her by taking issue with her use of the term profit. Ward indignantly stated, "It's less a question than just a—I want to point out that a word, words matter, and a word that we have not consistently used that I'm noticing we are using consistently throughout this presentation, and I've noticed the last month, or so is the word profit." Ward marched on, "I don't like where that's headed. I really don't like the use of that word. I want to put that right out there up front. I see where we're going with this, and I don't think that's probably your word, but I—I'm concerned about that and wanted to put it out there early."

The facts were that my staff and I had been using the term profit since 2018 to describe GRU's bottom line necessary to remit the GFT. Imagine any business's board of directors complaining about their CEO using the word profit. I snickered as I wondered how I could harness the power to piss off Harvey Ward even more.

Hayes-Santos piled on to Ward's comments with the statement, "I agree with Commissioner Ward. I—That's a new thing that's popped up, and I think it's being used for—not the greatest reason, and I think it's not the normal nomenclature used in municipal utilities." Unsatisfied with his first bite, Ward took a second bite at the apple by saying, "There are a lot of things we could call this. Many things that a general fund transfer could be called. I believe we've chosen the word profit to be adversarial, to be honest. I don't know who chose it, certainly wasn't the commission."

Later when I relayed the night's events to Melinda, she suggested I use a different acronym for the term GFT. She suggested GIFT representing general internal fund transfers. Oh, yes, my snarky trait was not limited to consanguinity. It was now passed on through affinity.

Throughout the presentation, Rasnick continued to professionally deliver the facts. After finishing, the commissioners discussed their thoughts on how to address GRU's budget and rate requests. Ward, once again, used his time to tell the public that charter officers don't always hear that GRU and GG are not separate organizations. They are one city. He really did.

Hayes-Santos used his time to recommend that GG pursue city-wide broadband instead of GRU. He also supported Ward's call to end duplicative services and suggested that future conversations with bond rating agencies should have the mayor in attendance.

After being recognized by the mayor, I used my time to deconstruct Ward's narrative. As I had done in the past, I couldn't allow lies to be spread. The falsehoods had to be disputed directly with facts.

"Everyone should know that I spent 30 years in private industry. So, when I look at revenue and I subtract expense, that's a profit. I apologize if its usage caused consternation. I wasn't trying to go against its standard use. So, again I'm sorry. The other thing that's really, really important to understand here is that this GFT reduction, and the mayor mentioned it and, I think, another commissioner, talked about doing it for one year. What are we going to do for the next year? Frankly, that's the point. We're in a structural financial deficiency right now that requires a formula that matches our ability to pay. So, the GFT is not a one-time issue. We need it to be formulaic and the trend, quite frankly, is not our friend. There's been a fundamental shift in the utility."

I didn't want the commission to think one action would fix the problem. The solution I was requesting demanded political courage, not demonizing the GM.

Finally, I had no choice but to explicitly set the record straight on the one-city government. "The charter does not say we are one city. It says that we are... I'm responsible, in accordance with the charter, for the efficient administration of the utility system. I'm responsible for—fully responsible for that as well as the city manager who is responsible for the general government system. That's not to say that we don't work very closely, and we try to coordinate and collaborate, but you can wrap around the axle thinking about it as one city when you have people that have specific responsibilities and prepare their own budgets. We don't comingle our budgets, et cetera, and we have different types of operations."

Ward and Hayes Santos remained silent. It didn't take a high emotional quotient to recognize Gainesville's Bonnie and Clyde of politics were not happy. It had never been standard protocol to dress down commissioners in public meetings.

Tonight, it was necessary. They should have been glad that I tempered my response. When it was over, I brooded over the fact that fighting to save the utility was a shit-ton of hard work.

Ω

Get Your Love At Work

While the world was spending 2020 and 2021 battling the COVID-19 pandemic, I was battling a minority of the commission, whether it be the three musketeers or just Bonnie and Clyde. One slip-up on my part and I was in danger of losing support from one of the other four. I absolutely had to count noses lest I lose my job.

I fondly remembered how in addition to the success of the Biomass Buyout, I had originally restructured the executive team and, in doing so, changed the leadership dynamic of the utility. The employees of the utility saw that I was unafraid of speaking truth to power. They recognized that I, along with my executive team, would stand up for them. I battled for a reversal of the 1590 plan in the face of placing my own career in jeopardy. I fought against the blatant political gamesmanship of the one-city approach. In my final act, I needed to bring it all home. I wanted to accomplish what others had failed to complete—a stabilization of the utility's financial health and an end to the size and bickering over the GFT.

In one last ditch effort, I worked with the City Commission to agree to reduce the GFT to the 26-million-dollar level. While they agreed to the goal, they decided to do it over six years at two million dollars a year (two million dollars the first year, four million dollars the second and so on). The installment basis of the reduction left us thirty million dollars short of the goal my finance team and I had wanted. However, I couldn't ignore saving forty-two million dollars between 2022 and 2027.

After working with the City Attorney on the language of the resolution, on July 19, 2021, by a vote of 6 ayes and 1 nay, I took the best I could get when the commission approved a series of two million dollars a year reduction in the GFT every year over the next six years, leaving the GFT at 26 million a year in 2027. I was pleased but not satisfied.

***

On a late summer Saturday afternoon in Gainesville, I spent time in my office considering my future with the utility. I remember it well because it was the day marking the twentieth anniversary of the 911 terrorist bombing of the World Trade Center. My emotions matched the solemnity of the day. The Fortress of Solitude that I had envisioned had become my Fortress of Despair. The reason—three days previously, around noon on an otherwise quiet Wednesday, September 8th, Mayor Poe called me with a request for my resignation.

Poe wasted no time expressing his disappointment with me. In particular, he no longer saw a path forward with me as the general manager. Before I could feel the devastation or even ask why, Poe said that he felt that the commission had caused him to fire me. Poe seemed to think I had committed illegal, termination-worthy offenses.

When I asked what they might have been, Poe declined to say. Instead, he said, "You can always poll the commissioners, but listen, I have always been honest with you, Ed. I don't believe you are the right fit for the organization anymore. I know you can find a new job and do an outstanding job somewhere else."

Whereas December 7, 2017, was a trial and April 23, 2020, had been a coup, Poe's ultimatum felt like a carefully orchestrated hit job. Hadn't he called me a Wartime Consigliere? It might be time for the re-emergence of my alter-ego.

While our conversation was calm and professional, we understood the ramifications to the city and each of us personally. As he expressed in multiple ways that he no longer had confidence in me, I was reminded of how Gordon kept to his script when he had spoken to me during the Biomass Buyout.

Poe quietly said, "You're not a match that made sense anymore." He admonished me for being defensive and not building better relationships with the advisory boards like the UAB, but couldn't elaborate on any details. When I tried to tell him that the UAB and CCAC were not willing to work with GRU and denigrated my staff as biased and obstructionist, the mayor simply told me that he was not comfortable with where we were anymore. Poe suggested, "The cleanest way forward has to come from you. You know that you need to resign. I want you to go out in a dignified transition." *Dignified for whom?*

Aside from informing me that I couldn't work with the UAB or CCAC as efficiently as he'd like, Poe wasn't specific about what had brought about his lack of confidence. Rather, he spoke to me from a 30,000-foot level. Like a bomber pilot flying at a high altitude, Poe dropped his payload on me when he said that I ought to consider resigning. I was shocked. Despite our differences, we had always gotten beyond them with reason and maturity. *What had gone wrong?*

At that point, the mayor said the most curious of things. He said with a chuckle that I had once told him that sometimes you have to blow things up and put them back together better. A kind of local build-back better program. That's what needs to happen in the city. I was surprised by his comment.

While it was true that I had told Poe about that type of chaos theory, I hadn't applied it to people. People were different. I applied chaos theory to policy, strategy, and direction. However, I saw that the mayor needed to hit the restart button. In fact, he called it the *great* reset. *Great for whom?*

For all the years Poe had known me, I thought he ought to have known that I didn't give a hoot about the dignity he was promoting. I cared about integrity, honesty, and doing the right thing. To me, that was dignity. My mind drifted as Poe talked about these administrative needs to give notice and set a termination date two months hence. I could not stop thinking while he talked. *I need to air my thoughts and feelings. That's what I had earned.*

Calmly but with a righteous tone, I told Poe that I could not resign. I would not resign. I had entered an employment contract of my own accord, and I would live by that agreement. I told Poe that I would welcome a public airing of grievances in a sort of *Seinfeld* Festivus moment. That was simply how the system worked. Besides, I told him, "I have done nothing wrong."

Poe responded by saying, "Sure, just let me know. I'll be free most of the day." *Free most of the day?* The mayor expected that I would reconsider and call him and repent before the day was out? Obviously, the mayor had done his own "counting of noses" and assured himself that he had enough votes from the other commissioners to fire me. Without knowing it, the mayor was stoking a fire inside of me. My Fortress of Solitude was melting.

I thought about what was really behind Poe's change of heart and why he thought he had the votes of other commissioners. I wasn't at a loss for ideas.

***

By the end of July, Poe had asked the charter officers to meet and bring forth protocol surrounding a potential vaccine mandate. It was during a time when the Delta Variant had begun to hospitalize more and more Floridians, and the commission wanted to take action to prevent more people from getting gravely ill. After conducting a deep dive into our workplace morale, managers warned me of a hard-core group of individuals that would simply not agree to being vaccinated. I was told that the situation had the potential of shutting down our water plant and our power plants. It was quite serious.

Ahead of an August 5th scheduled commission discussion on the mandate, I sent an e-mail to the commission in which I outlined the possible impacts of a mandate to GRU operations. "As the GM of the Utility, I feel the need to offer my understanding of the situation from the utility's perspective. Over the following pages, I will offer my thoughts from the utility's operational, management, and organizational perspective. Take it for what it is. It is not a substitute for City Attorney Shalley's legal opinion, nor is it meant to be."

I continued to ask the commission four key questions surrounding their upcoming vote: " 1) Is it appropriate and fair to terminate employees, who have admirably served the utility under the worst of safety conditions, when they decide to forego a vaccine they deem unnecessary; 2) Is the city ready to replace hundreds of skilled workers, and if so, will that safety risk be greater or less than simply requiring masking and social distancing; 3) Should the City of Gainesville require an employee to receive a not-fully approved FDA vaccine, in spite of their belief of their long-term health implications; 4) How do you bridge the credibility gap within the Black community and others that this government mandate isn't another connection to a more disturbing past."

"Let me close by saying I am simply trying to fully vet the concerns I've heard from employees and the possible unintended consequences of possible commission action. Thank you for considering my thoughts. I trust you will do the right thing for the community and city employees."

As a public record, GRU and other city employees had access to my e-mail. My words swept through the city ranks. They used it as a rallying cry to sway the upcoming commission's vote on the mandate. My well-articulated words of caution and risk assessment were now symbols of their growing no-mandate movement.

On August 5th, before the commission meeting, hundreds of employees showed up in front of city hall and protested a vaccine mandate. In the chambers of city hall, union representatives from the Communication Workers of America (CWA), firefighters and police unions all opposed the mandate. When the topic of the vaccine mandate was introduced, each commissioner made their feelings known. Gail Johnson, Desmon Duncan-Walker, and Harvey Ward were obviously against a mandate, while Hayes-Santos, Arreola, and Mayor Poe were for the mandate. Just before the vote was to be taken, newly elected commissioner, Reina Saco, seemed to be the swing vote.

As an immigrant to this country, Saco had experiences that compelled her to admonish the employees who were against the mandated vaccines. During her allotted time, she spoke in an ever-increasing sense of disgust

293

when she said, "I can only imagine how many of my relatives wouldn't be at risk if they could comfortably sit in air conditioning at a CVS and get a free shot. The fact that there are people who in this country have the privilege, the absolute privilege, of walking, like 500 feet in any direction in this town- just about- and getting a free vaccine that could save them from dying- and there are people rejecting it- I would love for my aunt to not die and leave my cousins orphaned. I would love that. Their country doesn't have that. But I learned a long time ago that people in this country take a lot of privilege for granted."

As Saco delivered such powerful words, opponents looked mystified. Was she a supporter of the mandate, or wasn't she? Her earlier words had given people the impression that the vaccine mandate would be approved. Now her last words before citizen comment were, "That said, I don't think it's my job to force you to get a vaccine." Employees were stunned. It looked as though the vaccine mandate was not going to be approved.

It was unfortunate that during citizen comments, an entourage of people espoused falsehoods about the efficacy surrounding the vaccine. The comments took an even more regrettable detour when an employee got up and said he was sorry about Commissioner Saco's family members dying while ending the sentence by saying, "Or whatever." You could see how Saco grew visibly distraught after hearing, "Or whatever."

What Saco didn't know at the time was that the speaker was an incredibly nervous individual who, in public settings, would use the term "whatever" the same way as others would say um. It was a verbal tic. It wasn't meant as a sign of disrespect.

When the public comments were over, and right before the commission vote, Saco asked to be recognized by the mayor one more time. Saco began her response, "I have a philosophy that when I meet someone-everyone-starts at 100% for me and we're going to give you the benefit of the doubt that you're a good—or whatever is not an appropriate response to people getting sick and dying. Just saying it doesn't help your case. I'm sorry about your situation, or whatever is dismissive and sick. I can't even. That is not how you win an opinion for your side, just objectively dismissing that people died. If an employee kills me from COVID, please make sure to put, or whatever, on my tombstone because, apparently, that's the mentality around here."

By now, Saco had raised her voice noticeably as she spoke to the audience. She continued, "I—I am disgusted to represent a lot of people right now that are that selfish, that are that entitled, that are that willfully misinformed." She finished, "Do you know how you lost that vote? With a lot of dumb comments. I'm completely for the mandate right now. So, if you counted the votes, and you want to do it, I'm with you (speaking to the other commissioners)."

When Saco finished, so had the hope for the rejection of the vaccine mandate. The mayor promptly called for a vote. All eight conditions of a vaccine mandate were passed. The charters were instructed to develop a plan to implement vaccinations as soon as possible.

In the final result, and in an ironic twist, the City of Gainesville's vaccine mandate was approved through a single commissioner's misunderstanding of someone's personal verbal tic, not because of their strength of conviction. Not surprisingly, Saco's actions were seen as mean-spirited and vengeful by city employees. It set the tone for more confrontations and nasty meetings.

There were certain commissioners that saw my words as the inspiration for employee pushback. They told me about their concerns. In particular, Hayes-Santos told me that I shouldn't be giving credence to anti-vax talking points.

My response was simple: the commission needs to pay attention to the impending loss of key employees that may place critical services in danger. It doesn't matter what employees believe. If they are willing to leave because of it, we must recognize that possibility. We needed to develop a well-thought-out plan that minimized the need to terminate employees. Like so many of my suggestions to the commission, that reasoning fell upon deaf ears.

***

On August 30th, as the chair of the Climate Change Action Committee (CCAC), Megan Walker, spoke before the Joint Water and Climate Policy Board, my staff alerted me that she was making disparaging remarks about the utility and my staff.

"We've had a lack of participation from GRU on CCAC. So, our liaison (GRU's employee) has attended one or two of the meetings he was assigned. But, more recently, CCAC reached out to GRU on some

information requests. The gist of these requests was how GRU is thinking about emission reductions in the context of Net Zero 2045 and what options you have considered in working towards that goal. And, I believe, Mr. Bielarski's response to those requests are included in your packet, and I very much hope you all have a chance to read it. The bottom line is that the tone of the response was extremely unprofessional and disrespectful. It was condescending. It was dismissive, and it was fairly hostile to collaboration. So, the bottom line seems to be that GRU is not planning, not seriously planning for Net Zero 2045, and they don't want to discuss it with us either." Wow!

Effectively, Chair Walker was telling the committee (comprised of two city and two county commissioners) that GRU had no plan, only a host of horribles (as UAB Chair Wheeler called it). Of course, nothing was further from the truth. As my Energy Supply Officer, Dino De Leo, had told me, "We can't invent a new technology and put it in an IRP." De Leo was right. It would be lazy, ill-advised, and dishonest. However, Walker didn't stop there.

Walker proceeded to say, "Instead, the members of the CCAC, who are volunteers, many of whom have expertise in various climate-related areas, we were pretty explicitly compared to Mr. Bielarski's children on a family road trip and were told to—I'm not going to sugarcoat it—were told to sit down, shut up, and enjoy the ride, basically. And that was incredibly disappointing and incredibly frustrating for all of us."

Of course, my analogy of the road trip was meant to demonstrate that no matter how much any one of us wants to get to Net Zero in 2045, we need patience because we aren't there yet, at least technologically. What's worse is that we have been at this crossroads before. At the former crossroads, we chose a biomass PPA and a solar FIT that we are still paying for today. What was even more frustrating to my staff and I were that I had discussed this very issue with the city commission before the budget hearings. The commission is aware of our limitations and what it would cost to try to make large incremental steps once again.

Despite this knowledge, in response to Chair Walker, Mayor Poe said, "I want to offer my profound apologies for both the specific response you got from GRU leadership, as well as the lack of participation." Ward also apologized on my behalf, saying, "I apologize for any City of Gainesville staff not being courteous and willing to work with you."

Poe and Ward didn't bother to mention that I had alerted the entire commission of my response to the CCAC a month previously. There was no criticism of me until this very day in response to Walker's complaint. It was with that knowledge that I walked, maybe ran, over to the County Commission chambers to first set the record straight. Second, I had to clear my staff of any misdeeds.

When I arrived at the chambers, I was clearly on a mission. I was only allowed three minutes to speak during citizen comments, so I was focused. However, Chair Marihelen Wheeler, not to be confused with UAB chair Wes Wheeler, repeatedly interrupted me during my remarks. I said, "Most of our meetings are done under the umbrella that GRU hasn't done enough, yet we are the, as a percent, if the Archer solar deal had gone through in the manner it was contracted, GRU would have the highest density of solar in its portfolio than any other utility in the state of Florida. We have the highest number of renewables. And I will tell you, I have meetings chock throughout the rest of the day and pulling my staff off to answer questions that have been answered 10, 11, 12 times, under the idea that we're not doing enough is incredibly frustrating. It's counterproductive, and, frankly, people don't want to hear the truth about what is being said right now."

My emotions got the best of me when I said, "GRU can't put more than 50 megawatts of solar onto its system without jeopardizing the reliability of the system." Pounding my fist into the lectern, I exclaimed, "Point blank, that's it." Both Commissioner Wheeler and Prizzia's heads jumped up. I'd pay for that action.

I went on to say, "So, I think it's important that you have these citizen groups that need to understand what GRU has done for the community. And the tone of the letter? That letter included remarks from—I forgot the person's name—that said, why aren't we doing more with Solar PPAs? Why aren't we doing more? The county commissioner is the one that struck down the Solar PPA (Origis deal)." I pointed at Prizzia as I finished, "I think you were one of the votes. Why aren't you doing more?" That ended my performance. Unfortunately, I had made the cardinal sin of calling out the county commission.

***

After receiving the resignation ultimatum, Melinda and I talked throughout the evening and the next day. While we discussed our options, one thing was clear—both of us would fight for my job and our place in the city. If I was a Wartime Consigliere, Melinda would be my Wonder Woman. I went to work on September 9th to draft a compelling response to the mayor's resignation request. The letter was my personal "Hell no, I won't go" statement.

That statement began. "I have thought about yesterday's conversation a great deal, and I wholeheartedly stand by my decision to stay on as general manager of GRU and to fight for my job, if necessary. I am not concerned with the perceived loss of dignity that may come with the Commission calling for my resignation if it comes to that. My sole concern is and always has been managing the utility to the best of my ability. And, frankly, my management is as important now as it was when I was hired to find a solution to the biomass PPA." When I finished the letter, I e-mailed it to the mayor around noon on the 9th.

Because my e-mail to the mayor was a public record, the local media soon discovered it on the city website. That night, a local conservative blog, The Alachua Chronicle, *had posted a story entitled, "GRU General Manager's job in jeopardy." WCJB television noticed the story and ran a story for their 11 o'clock news broadcast. Although both media sources quoted extensively from my letter to the mayor, there was no mention of any upcoming vote. People across the community heard the news and started contacting me about when the impending vote would occur. I told them, as far as I knew, the mayor hadn't committed to when the item would be heard by the full commission. I added that I suspected it would be soon.*

Adding to the intrigue surrounding my potential resignation was the unexpected announcement of the resignation of two other charter officers, City Attorney Nicole Shalley and City Clerk Omichele Gainey. These resignations were unexpected to the public but not to me. Employee morale around city hall had been falling like a rock throughout the pandemic and after the vaccine mandate. Charter officers may have gotten shots to increase their immunity to COVID-19 but not to commission shenanigans.

298

Shalley was even willing to take an almost $70,000 pay cut to become the County Attorney at smaller Levy County, while Gainey simply was willing to leave with a severance package. The events should have been red flags to the commission, particularly the mayor. Instead, the Mayor doubled down in what I can only say was an attempt to sweep the city clear of its charter officers and put the leadership team back together in another image. This was the great reset the mayor had in mind.

***

That was the political environment as I came into my office this 9-11 Saturday to reflect on my next moves. I knew that I was in as tight a bind as I had ever been. I felt my enemies proliferating like crabgrass around me. I drafted a letter to the entire commission expressing my desire to remain with the utility. I ended the letter with, "I continue to want to serve as the GM of the utility I love, in a community both Melinda and I love."

Just when I thought it couldn't get worse, I received a text from Omichele Gainey, the City of Gainesville's City Clerk. She wrote, "As a heads-up, the mayor asked me to add the subject of your contract termination to Monday's budget meeting." It ended with a sad emoji. When I asked her when the item was planned, she wrote: "The meeting starts at 6… probably last on the agenda." Because of the way the city system works that meant the electronic agenda would not be modified until Monday morning. No one in the city would be aware of the exact time the city commission would be discussing my termination.

I knew the mayor thought he had the votes to terminate me. He had also slipped the vote into agenda for a Special Budget Meeting set to run from 6 PM until 8:30 PM. The last item would be a vote on whether to terminate my employment contract. *Who would show up to speak on my behalf? How would the community find out?*

As I ended my day, the *Gainesville Sun* reported, for the first time, that "Gainesville Mayor calls on head of city's utility company to step down." In the article, they wrote, "Bielarski agitated some commissioners recently with comments that they viewed as critical of the city commission's COVID vaccine mandate for city employees. But the mayor said his decision involved much more than just one issue. 'I don't want to get into the nitty-gritty details, but I will confirm that I had a conversation with Ed Bielarski. I just expressed to him I no longer thought he was the right fit for the organization, and we wanted to head in another direction." I suspected that the commission was simply tired of me informing them about the consequences of their actions. Every time they decided, I had a response. I could hear them saying, "Why couldn't he just be quiet and carry out our policies?

The next day, Feldman texted me to ask, "Have you decided what you are doing?" I responded, "I'm 90% thinking of staying and fighting." Feldman quickly responded, "I think it is a mistake. Go out with your head held high. If they terminate you, you get 20 weeks and your PTO. Resign and you get a date and a few shekels under the Anthony Lyons' model." Ominously he wrote, "Plus, hard to fight it if it comes up on Monday." That was all the incentive I needed to turn my 90% cause into a 100% cause.

I would not resign under a deal in which I effectively quit while still garnering a 20-week severance package. That was simply wrong. I also wouldn't let the mayor slide an agenda item into a Special Budget meeting and get away with it. It wasn't transparent. It wasn't ethical. It was against everything I had fought against in my tenure and in my life. I might lose, but I was ready to lose with dignity. With that, the stage was set for my second "trial" on charges of being a Wartime Consigliere.

Shockingly, as a prelude to my second trial, Feldman resigned. I shook my head when I read that he had taken the deal he had told me to consider! When the agenda for the evening's meeting was completed, the mayor had placed Feldman's resignation and contract amendment on the agenda. *Holy cow, the city was in free fall.*

The stage was set for my exit. I was quickly becoming the last of the Wartime Consiglieres.

***

On September 13th, I arrived at city hall in a much different state of mind than my previous trial. I didn't aim my car; I simply drove it to city hall. I casually walked into the chambers, knowing that I truly had little to no chance of getting four votes to retain me. Oh, I'd fight, but I was going up against significant odds.

People in my office had wished me well. Others had reached out to me, telling me to fight. I received hugs and good luck wishes. I had no illusions. It would require a miracle for me to garner four votes of support for my continued employment. I took my seat on the dais at about twenty minutes to 6 o'clock to make myself comfortable. The commission would have to churn through nine separate budget, rate, and tax ordinances before they would discuss my termination.

Friends, co-workers, and people I didn't even know started to filter into the city hall chamber and the downstairs overflow room. People like Ray Jordan and Darrin Briscoe, both long-time GRU employees who were loyal, dedicated, and fierce. I walked over to them to tell them they'd be there for hours. My item wouldn't be brought up until close to midnight. "No problem, boss," Jordon told me. "I will stay here as long as it takes."

Ray had shared a Harry Truman quote with me earlier in the week when he repeated, "I didn't give 'em hell. I just told them the truth and they thought they were in hell."

As the night progressed, more people showed up at the commission chamber. My executive team and members of my former executive team arrived. M Smith, who served as my Chief Change Officer, came in, and I walked off the dais to greet her. Smith had been there for me in 2017 at my first trial. She had left the GRU executive team to go on to greener

301

pastures at the University of Florida. Smith was one of those special human beings. She had that blend of intellect, spirit, and compassion that made her a force of nature. Her arrival tonight was emotional for me. We hugged like long-lost siblings. She fed my soul with a belief that, just maybe, I would be able to stay at the utility I loved.

Tonight was shaping up to be a different night than my previous trial. People were assembling like celebrities for a prize fight. *Don't let it be a first-round knock-out.* Most importantly, my own Wonder Woman was in the house. Whereas, on December 7, 2017, she couldn't be with me, tonight, my strength, my essence, was dressed up and ready for action. She was no longer frail, sickly, or scared. Almost four years after her pancreatic cancer surgery, her latest scan showed no recurrence of any pancreatic cancer. Tonight, as emotional as it was, she insisted on being there for me. Also, she wanted to thank anyone who supported me.

That's when I felt a hint of my dad's presence. I felt it in the mighty men and women of GRU. Those heroes came to work throughout the pandemic while others sheltered in place. Modern-day warriors who brought the essentials of life to our customers. Unsung heroes who climbed poles, descended into sewers, and comforted distraught customers. They were the folks I wanted on my side.

I sat on the dais for five hours as the commission discussed elements of the budget, rate, and property taxes, along with a grudging acceptance of Feldman's resignation and amended contract. I had plenty of time to consider my upcoming speech. I wrote from the heart, including the men and women of GRU in it. Reminiscing about that December 7th night, once more, I was not going to "go gentle into that goodnight." Then it was time.

As I watched history repeat itself, there was Hayes-Santos, once again, being the prime antagonist, making the motion to terminate my contract. *How ironic was this night turning out to be?* Ward seconded the motion. Poe set the stage by discussing, ever so briefly, the circumstance surrounding his decision to ask for my resignation. Finally, Poe looked my way and asked if I'd like to address the commission.

I walked to the lectern and pulled my speech out of my breast pocket. With all the strength I had to control my feelings, I began, "It's been said that the reason for my possible termination is, 'I am no longer fit for the organization.' However, I respect my governing board's right to decide that I also stand before you tonight to challenge that belief. It is within that very attitude to resist the urge to resign and challenge what you believe that shows why I continue to be the right person for the job and the right fit for the organization. Having an executive who is willing to challenge his governing board, his employees, and himself is the very essence of what we should be doing as stewards of the public's resources and trust."

I watched Poe as he stared intensely back at me. "It is what I do every day in managing the utility. I poke and I prod. I question and I coach. Above all, I'm always engaged in ensuring that every one of my employees has a voice, a sounding board, and an opportunity to disagree with me. I invite it. It is a process that builds respect and trust. Frankly, it is how I have been successful in building a formidable team at GRU and other organizations where I've worked."

I heard people around me encouraging me. Someone whispered to take my time. I offered an olive branch to the commission when I said, "I am not here tonight in an attempt to rebuke, deny, or discredit any of your perceptions. They belong to you. I am here to add to them. You see, I am proud of GRU, what it represents, and the people that are loyal to it. I love the folks that risk their lives, sweat and toil, stress and strategize and provide service and relief. GRU is more than a job to me. GRU is part of my life."

As I finished, I could see commissioners looking at their cell phones. Either they were not interested, or people were contacting them. I hoped for the latter. I reached out to my supporters by saying, "I am appreciative of the many people throughout the community who have shown their support for me. I am particularly pleased to hear from folks with whom I have not always seen eye-to-eye. Their support is really heartwarming because it demonstrates that I am someone who may raise passions during the debate but can ultimately resolve differences."

I really felt the intensity of the moment when I told the commission that I kept a plaque on the wall of my office containing a quote from Supreme Court Justice Earl Warren that said: "Everything I did in my life that was worthwhile, I caught hell for." With tears in my eyes and a lump in my throat, I implored, "With that, mayor and commissioners, I ask that you allow me to remain as the GM of the utility that I love." I had given it my best shot. I was proud that I had not acquiesced to pressure.

Upon returning to my seat at the dais, Poe opened citizen comment. No commissioner, other than Johnson and Commissioner Duncan-Walker, made eye contact with me. As soon as I sat down in my seat awaiting public comments, my sons, David and Jonathon, texted me. My cell phone started to light up. My whole family soon joined in. Soon, my other friends joined in. Like a cyber-lifeline, they kept encouraging me that everything would be okay.

I smiled as I remembered that spring day in 2015 when the family watched the live stream of the commission meeting when I was selected as the next general manager. This night, I marveled at the symmetry of the moment. I hoped that the events didn't form bookends for my career with GRU.

Ironically, the first person to speak was my oft-time frenemy, Nathan Skop, who said, "The mayor and city commission are merely players in a comedy whose ending has already been written, but by all means, continue with the performance. Mayor Poe, I was at the county meeting where GRU employees and Mr. Bielarski were unjustly attacked by the CCAC chair, whatever they call her. I was at the meeting.

You apologized to them profusely. Commissioner Ward apologized profusely. Didn't defend your general manager or GRU employees and then bailed on the meeting."

A twenty-seven-year city employee, Joe Wolf, moved to the lectern to say, "Ed has made this utility safer and fiscally stronger. That's very, very important. Any resignation does a disservice to the citizens of this community, your neighbors, and my neighbors, and this utility. Ed has got integrity. He has got honesty. He has got transparency and passion. Those qualities provide trust for our employees, pride, and you can't ask for better leadership." Joe finished by saying, "He cares about the utility. He cares about this community, and I'm proud to have him as my general manager."

One by one, people followed me to the lectern to speak on my behalf. Others called in and were placed in the cue to speak over the broadcast sound system. Another GRU employee, Pam Dalziel, spoke next, telling the commission, "Ed has been a good leader, and his employees look up to him."

A community leader and one-time *Facebook* sparring partner during my "Keep GRU Local" days, Shanae Jackson stepped forward. What I find to be so ironic is the one thing that the poor leadership on this commission did do was put Ed Bielarski and Nathan Skop on the same side." I couldn't help but smile as another frenemy came to support me. She continued, "The reason you can't lay out a laundry list is because Ed is the same person he was a year ago, two years ago, and three years ago. Things have changed?" Shanae just laughed.

Another GRU employee, Darris Friend, called in to say, "I can't believe that we're here tonight terminating a charter officer that has led the utility with excellence, but we are accepting the resignation of a charter officer who should be terminated. You want a puppet who will follow your command for net zero 2045 and try to preserve the revenue for the utility which funds the general fund transfer. You are terminating a person with documented success for many years."

Scott Holowosko, another long-time GRU employee, moved to the lectern to say, "In overcoming the situation of the biomass contract, shows how a leader cannot only meet challenges but build a strong team to face challenges. He's always encouraged the staff of the utility to challenge the status quo and new endeavors by offering different points of view. We challenge ourselves to always look for the best options in moving forward. Being challenged is not a threat but is an invitation for continuous improvement." I was so proud to hear that my vision had been so well absorbed and articulated back to the commission. Scott ended by saying, "I support Mr. Bielarski, professionally and personally, and implore each of you to continue to recognize him as a valuable member of GRU's leadership and vote to retain him."

People extolled my virtues in ways that I could only imagine. They told stories of how they had been inspired by my leadership. The accolades kept coming and coming. It was as though a higher spirit had struck people. A spirit of love and loyalty, respect and admiration filled the room.

Don Wilkes, a union leader representing the CWA, was next up to support me. I was amazed that the leader of GRU's collective bargaining unit stated, "We feel that Mr. Bielarski is the right fit and should continue being the general manager of the utility." *Wow, a union was endorsing management.*

Future mayoral candidate, July Thomas, called in and exclaimed, "You are the ones that should be resigning tonight, not Ed." Yvonne followed with, "At what point do you hold yourselves accountable to the same standard you hold others to? Ed isn't responsible for your costs. If you want to change direction or rest, it should start from the top down. If you need another person to resign, it should start with the mayor, not GRU's GM."

Laura Voitle, another GRU employee, was next up. She stated, "At the end of the day, we provide safe, reliable, competitively priced utility service in an environmentally responsible manner to enhance the quality of life in our community. Although Ed came to the utility in 2015 saying get your love at home, I believe that today, what you don't realize is we are family; this is home. I'm here to show him some love." It was more than I could take. I put my head in my hands and tears started to flow as I felt the emotional impact of such admiration and love. Laura would not stop. She said, "Our utility manager, our leader, quite frankly, was given a pile of poo to clean up, and accepted that pile of poo, and turned our utility into something fruitful for our community, despite negativity from others. He came in and cleaned up the biomass plant disaster, exceeding expectations that were set for him. This year alone, he oversaw the conversion of DH2, the retrofit of the Kelly Plant, and the overhaul of the water treatment plant, a reduction to the GFT, just to name a few of his accomplishments. He held the utility together, despite the commission. He hasn't backed down from supporting us, and that's why I'm here tonight because I'm not backing down from supporting him. I'm here to ask you, as a longtime citizen of Gainesville and current GRU employee, please keep Ed Bielarski as GRU's General Manager." Oh, my lord. I was such a lucky man. This wasn't the night that I had dreaded. It was a wonderful night that I will never forget.

The idea of a wonderful night flowed into thoughts about those heartwarming moments in one of my all-time cinematic favorites—*It's a Wonderful Life*. I felt like the erstwhile George Bailey, played by Jimmy Stewart, when the town came to his aid when he thought all had been lost.

At the height of George's despair, he tried taking his own life. After being saved by his guardian angel, Clarence, George admits that he wished that he had never been born. Clarence takes George on a spiritual journey of self-discovery and shows George what a wonderful life he has truly led. Returning to his mortal existence, George wanders back to home and his loving family, where he is met by neighbor after neighbor who shows up to help him with his troubles. They recognize what a treasure George has been and support him with money to replace the funds his absent-minded uncle had misplaced. Tonight, I was George Bailey, being recognized by my friends, family, and co-workers in and around Gainesville. *A wonderful life, indeed.*

My heart now knew that my guardian angel was spending the evening by my side. I could feel my dad's love all around me, as I remembered us watching *It's a Wonderful Life* every Christmas. We'd both shed a tear and act like we hadn't. I couldn't believe how at the moment, my world had turned from despair to a celebration of my life. It was truly divine. My job was still in jeopardy, but I didn't care. My life's work was being affirmed before my very eyes. *What man would ever be given that sort of send-off?*

The night also took me back to my early days when I had told GRU employees that they ought to get their love at home. The catchphrase was meant to remind people that their self-worth wasn't built on what they had done at work. How ironic, I thought, that I was getting my love tonight for what I had done for my employees, as well as the community. I felt as though I was part of a larger family. My hands trembled with the realization.

When I thought the comments couldn't be topped, they were. Dr. Denslow, the brilliant economics professor from the University of Florida, whom I had tussled with during the Biomass Buyout, slowly walked up to the lectern. A skilled speaker, Dr. Denslow, started by saying, "I joined the UAB some time ago. One of the pleasures was getting to meet the head of the generation. Another was the head of T&D and gas. Great people. Wastewater and Water was Tony Cunningham. The Chief Operating Officer, Tom Brown. They're all still here. They've been here for the six years that Ed's been here. Not every top official has stayed on. We have some new people, Claudia Rasnick and Cheryl McBride. But it's a great team, and it's been a real pleasure to get to know them. Probably, I should not try any levity tonight, but, nonetheless, it's an amazing manager who's able to hire seven top people, all who have better personalities than he does." The great professor made me laugh.

Dr. Denslow continued, "With a team like that, who needs him? Would you say that about a baseball or basketball team? Fire the manager? Who needs the manager? You need the manager to keep them working together. It's a very open organization where people say what they want; they work together well. I think it would be a shame to break that up."

The city's interim director of equity and inclusion, Sylvia Warren, was next up on the phone. "I respect the way Ed stands for what he believes is the right thing to do. He's passionate about his employees, as well as the areas of responsibility, as he should be. He is candid in his stance on various topics. I watched Ed put himself at risk in the line of fire. And that, to me, is admirable. I support Mr. Bielarski, and I believe he has served the city well. I believe it will be a great loss for the city if we lose Ed." Sylvia ended by saying, "Ed, we're here to support you. You're in our thoughts and prayers. Thank you."

Former commissioner Helen Warren, Maureen Leslie, Darrin Briscoe, realtor Darlene Pifalo, GRU safety director Doug Beck, Don Fields, and Sharon Bernie all spoke on my behalf before giving way to the Yvette Carter, the soul of GRU's culture, as the Chief Inclusion and Government Relations Officer.

Carter recounted, "I have enjoyed working for Ed since 2015, and I believe you hear this united front from employees because not only does he fight for us, he does challenge us, but he supports us and empowers us, and I think I speak for the majority of the employees when I say that we know that Ed has the utility's best interest at heart. I think I was even going to talk about Ed getting his love at home, and what he said tonight was impassioned and brought tears to my eyes about the utility that he loves. I believe that. He has shown us that, and I believe that after hearing all of us, you will vote to retain him as general manager, or at least, that's my prayer. Go with

God, know that we love you, and, so, I know you get your love at home, but your employees support and love you, too."

By this time, my children were texting me to tell me that they had never experienced such a public outpouring of support for someone. How could so many people call from midnight to one in the morning during the work night?

My one-time Chief Change Officer, M Smith, strode to the lectern. She looked over towards me and smiled that "I got this" type of smile. "I'm here in support of Ed," she confidently stated. After a pause, she continued, "I am here in support of GRU. I am always GRU strong. I've benefited from his leadership firsthand." Smith looked at the mayor and purposely said, " I am wholly unconvinced by your statement, mayor, that he is not the right fit and the list that Commissioner Ward ran down to demonstrate it briefly." When the mayor told Smith that her time was up, she looked at him with a nasty kind of stare. She turned and looked at me to softly say, "He is a beautiful fit.

I was amazed by the folks with whom I disagreed, showing up or calling in to speak on my behalf. Alachua County NAACP Chairperson Evelyn Foxx, environmental activist Nancy Deren, and others acknowledged my leadership. I was overwhelmed, humbled, and honored. My GRU family and the Gainesville community had shown up for a late modification to an unusual Monday night budget meeting to save me, just as I had come to town to save them from the GREC PPA.

There was one more caller, Armando Grundy-Gomes, the first person that spoke to me when, on December 7, 2017, I entered city hall chambers. His words, "This is just wrong," synthesized the moment. Completing the cycle of the two trials, Grundy-Gomes began his comments, "I definitely want to talk about Mr. Bielarski. Let's go talk about the date. That date, December 7, 2017, for Edward Bielarski. Hayes-Santos motioned to terminate the man's contract when the man's wife was in stage 4 cancer getting chemotherapy, and I don't think Mr. Bielarski will forget that day. He came in looking disheveled, looking like he was having a rough day, maybe to some of you, that doesn't matter. Maybe you don't care. That will never happen to me. Maybe you don't value family. Maybe you do. Maybe you don't seek understanding. But this isn't about his not being a good fit. This is because he's not stroking egos."

Grundy-Gomes was pulling my past into the present. He was bringing my worlds together. He boldly stated, "So, Mr. Bielarski has a rough disposition. This is about personality conflicts because Harvey (Ward) doesn't like him, and Adrian (Hayes-Santos) doesn't like him. What, Ed refused to take the secret sauce? Instead, he does what the general government doesn't. He gives opportunities to women. He gives opportunities to minorities." And with that, the speakers were done. The floor was returned to the mayor. All eyes were upon him.

Without offering a comment, the mayor recognized Commissioner Ward. Ward spoke the obvious, "GRU workers, you have put me in a position to play. Let's make a deal with Ed." I looked over at Ward and our eyes squarely met. I realized that this was my shot. This was the moment. Ward continued, "Really, it's the workers. You all are turning out and speaking for Ed has put me in a different position. I appreciate that." *No turning back now, Harvey.*

Ward looked out into the audience as he advanced his idea, "So, I want to see if we can make something happen here. This is not going to make a lot of folks happy." I saw the heads of Poe and Hayes-Santos slump a little. "The love you have shown Ed Bielarski is a good reason for me to work on this here," Ward maneuvered. Ward turned to look at me when he said, "Ed, I need a few things to change my mind. First, I need you to name a Chief Climate Officer and a team that can work with the Climate Change Action Committee, the citizen's committee, and the UAB and brings back, by the end of January, to this commission, a plan for how we're going to get this 100% goal. I know it's really, really hard. I know it is not an easy thing to do."

A huge smile grew under my masked face. Ward was giving me an offer I couldn't refuse. I couldn't believe it—it was another *Godfather* reference! In return, I was going to give him a sleeve off my vest. My staff and I have already built the 100% renewable goal. It was part of the 2019 Integrated Resource Plan. It was done. Would it change? Absolutely. The number would probably grow larger. For now, it was a three-billion-dollar price tag.

Ward followed his first request with another, "I need you to find duplicative services together with the general government. I need this to happen, and I need it to happen by the time we hit next year's budget. We are the City of Gainesville." Okay, I got it. Ward hadn't forgotten his one-city mantra. It would be a fight for another day.

Lastly, Ward looked at me rather intently. He said, "And here's the big one. This is the hardest one for you. We've talked about it for years. You can't go to the County Commission Building and talk on a public matter and fuss at the county commission. You can't. Call somebody and tell them to hold you back. I appreciate the passion. Everything you said to Commissioner Wheeler and Prizzia was correct. But you can't go bang on someone else's table and represent us. You can't do that. If you feel like you can meet these three things, and you can commit to it, you'll have my support." The ball was squarely in my court.

I stared back at Ward and mentioned that my staff had already begun to take the actions that he had suggested. I didn't want to accept his offer too quickly. I told him that, yes, I could be too passionate sometimes, and I agreed that I should hit the pause button at other times. Finally, I stated, "Absolutely, I can commit to that."

Just like Gordon accepting my offer in New York, Ward responded quickly, "Then I can commit to keeping you on."

With that exchange, the three musketeers' political will had been broken, at least for this night.

Given an opportunity by the mayor, Commissioner Johnson wanted everyone to recognize the moment when she said, "Ed, I'm kinda floored. I knew there was a lot of deep love for you out there. But the way your employees showed up for you tonight is really heartwarming, and I think it speaks to—I always knew this about you—you're not a manager, you're a leader. It's clear. You and I have had our thing. We've worked through them. I have always appreciated that you're authentic. So, even when you're passionate, what I appreciate about anybody is their authenticity because that means I can trust you. You are who you say you are. You represent yourself that way at all times. So, I appreciate you, Ed. That's really all I have to say. This has been one of the best hours of my tenure. I could feel the love." *So, could I, Commissioner Johnson, so could I.*

Hayes-Santos ended the commissioner's comments when he quietly informed the mayor, "I withdraw the motion." With that, my second trial was over. My supporters remained to feel the love as the lights got systematically turned off in the chamber.

As Melinda and I sauntered out to the parking lot at around 2 in the morning, I told her about the promise I made to myself on that December 7th night—"I would not go gentle into that good night." She hugged me and said, "Neither will I."

Ω

It's Not A Threat...

By all outward appearances, my role as the general manager of the utility was finally secure. When I was running errands about town, folks would shake my hand and congratulate me on my late-night victory. "What a wonderful night," they would say. "You must be so happy." I was, but in my heart, I knew that the three musketeers plus D'Artaganan were madder than a swarm of bees whose hive had been invaded by a family of bears.

Unexpectedly, the musketeers were about to have more than the general manager to worry about.

Soon after the September 13th debacle, the Gainesville Professional Firefighters delivered a vote of no-confidence in Mayor Poe. In a scathing letter, Nick Gonzalez, the President of IAFF Local 2157, wrote, "The mayor has bred a dysfunctional culture within our city's government, which peaked in the last six months." Gonzalez went on to ask for the mayor's resignation. Poe remained silent on the request.

Commissioner Saco was caught on surveillance video "extending her middle finger" in the direction of city workers during their anti-vaccine mandate rally. Even in this college town, flipping employees the bird is not a valued expression of free speech. Like Poe, Saco remained silent.

The editorial board at the *Gainesville Sun* took note of the rapid devolution of the city's governing board. "Monday marked a low point for Gainesville's city government during a period that has had plenty of them." The editorial board wrote,

"Gainesville is better than this," while asking all involved to step up. In a few months, four of the sitting commissioners would be stepping out—Hayes-Santos, Arreola, Ward, and Poe were all term-limited.

As fall turned into winter, the commission grew increasingly insulated from public opinion. The four commissioners had really failed to make much of a mark during their tenure—aside from forcing GRU's bond rating downgrades, taking more in a GFT than what GRU earned, and trying to fire me twice and eliminate my job once. In their silence, I worked diligently on Ward's deal. Just before Christmas, I delivered an unprecedented $3.6 billion dollar plan of how GRU would get to Net Zero by 2045. While it wasn't what the commission wanted to hear, it was an objectively developed, professional plan forward. All told, to accomplish the goal, GRU's debt would swell to over 6.5 billion dollars, up from the current 1.6 billion dollars. I told the *Gainesville Sun*, "If the utility does incur the $6.5 billion in debt outlined in the estimates, it would significantly and materially increase customer rates."

Like clockwork, Poe shot back, "I think the first thing to acknowledge is the cost of addressing climate change is dwarfed by the cost of not addressing climate change. And that is borne out by every credible scientific study that exists." He followed that blast by saying, "Those debt numbers are based on our 2018 integrated resource plan." What Poe missed was the updated report would show even higher numbers. Once again, facts were the enemy, as was I.

On January 25, 2022, I e-mailed the commission and UAB that I had completed my part of the bargain Ward had struck with me on September 13th, including the path to hire a chief climate officer and establish a liaison role to act on my behalf at the various citizen advisory committees. I ended the memo, "I believe this is significant progress for the utility and the community." Soon after receiving my e-mail, Ward called me to tell me that he was still concerned with other elements of my performance, such as 1) the bid for a natural gas plant on the UF campus, 2) failing to get the new 50-megawatt commercial solar deal to break ground, and 3) not following up on the expansion of electric transmission interconnections with FPL.

I told Ward that I had read similar complaints from Poe and other commissioners in the previous night's *Gainesville Sun*. I told him that Hayes-Santo's comment that he "was disappointed with how we rated because of the proposal we put forth" was just misguided. No bidder put forth a proposal. It was a list of qualifications. Given what is happening with city finances, it was no wonder GRU received such a low score. There were no less than a dozen adverse reports about city finances in the news. From headlines that read "Florida Auditor General finds city employees didn't know how to write financial statements" to "Auditor General withdraws criticism of GRU's accounting but maintains concerns about debt." The current fiscal crisis had made the bid even more problematic. I reminded him that he was the one that told me that he didn't think GRU would even be considered.

I explained further that it was the county commission that voted down the Origis solar PPA by 4 to 3 votes, not me. I sarcastically told Ward to talk with his friends across the street at the county commission. I had executed a great deal for the community that the county commission killed.

Finally, the potential FPL agreement would have added over twelve million dollars in cost every year to the utility when we could least afford it. Particularly when GRU can't even pay the GFT. Ward was unimpressed with my answers and told me that he needed to think about things. He'll get back to me later.

As my own spider senses tingled, I suspected that a third bite at the apple was coming for another bite out of me. Concerned about the distractions in an industrial setting, I reached out to my loyal employees and sent out a mass e-mail. "Unless informed otherwise, I will continue to carry on my duties as best I can while serving you as the general manager

316

of GRU. Thanks, and again, please be careful as you live, work, and play."

On January 27, 2022, I arrived at a general policy review meeting in which I intended to deliver my thoughts on consolidating GRU and city support services. That opportunity never came, as Poe waived the rules and moved the commissioner's comments up to the beginning of the meeting. Immediately, Poe recognized Ward as having the floor.

Slowly and methodically, Ward laid out his "thought process." He began by acknowledging that I had "successfully and creatively saved our city 900 hundred million dollars and changed the Deerhaven Renewable plant from a rarely used curiosity into one of our least expensive, most productive energy producers." *Oh boy, here it comes,* I thought. "That was in 2017, and it remains a very big deal. It was an audacious and audaciously successful effort," Ward complimented me.

That's when Ward dropped the bomb. He said, "Sadly, since then, we have missed—big—on three other large ventures." While Ward was "thrilled" about the Origis solar deal, he said, "We had not done the proper due diligence with the community surrounding the installation." I sat dumbfounded as I recalled my discussions with him and the commissioners about how GRU had done everything right while the county commission had done everything wrong.

After mentioning my failure to secure the FPL expansion of GRU's interconnection, I just shook my head. We were fast approaching a *Twilight Zone* episode. Undeterred, Ward cited my failure not to communicate GRU's inability to secure the bid with UF. "Are you kidding me?" I screamed in my head. "UF wants nothing to do with this ship of fools."

In what I can only imagine Ward thought of as a storybook ending, he said, "It is completely acceptable to swing big, and I encourage it. But if we swing big and miss, we can't pretend we were never up to bat and quietly move on to the next game." I put my head in my hand as I listened to Ward close his comments, "Now is the time to build an operation where both sides of the house are working in the same direction, rather than competing for resources… I move that we terminate Mr. Bielarski's contract immediately."

Saco almost leapt out of her seat with a hearty, "I second." With that, I could easily count the noses in the room. The three musketeers had their D'Artagnan in Reina Saco. At least she didn't flip me the bird.

I understood it all. Ward's last reference was, once again, a call for a one-city government insulated against reality. Let's just get along. I felt sick to my stomach. I could barely listen as Commissioner Desmon Duncan-Walker, Hayes-Santos, and Arreola spoke. Poe got the last word when he said, "This is a decision I wish we had made several months ago, so we could already have been moving in that direction."

In the blink of an eye, the few people in the chamber got their chance to speak. Poe followed by asking the maker of the motion to fire me without cause and to add the appointment of my Water/Wastewater Director, Tony Cunningham, as the GM. Before taking the vote on the motion, the call-taker informed Poe that calls were still coming in to speak to my potential termination. Poe responded with a short, "We've already taken public comment."

Prior to the final vote, Poe allowed me one more opportunity to speak. I was angry, but I was purposeful.

I said, "I think I will leave the utility in a better place than when I first came here… The last time I was in this position… hearing all the love I got from my folks was, really, in a lot of ways, the end of the story." I stopped to gain my composure.

I continued, "There didn't need to be anymore. I had accomplished what I wanted to do. I turned the utility around… I feel their love… It's why I fight every day."

Looking directly at each of my three musketeers plus one, I said, "There's one thing that gets in the way of that (one city). It's the city charter. We do communicate… we don't do each other's jobs… One thing I got from Commissioner Ward was to swing big. I'll swing big; I'll run for mayor." I slammed my book on the lectern in my last act of defiance as General Manager.

As I exited City Hall one last time, Ward left the meeting in progress and barreled out of the chamber doors. Holding the city hall entrance door open with one arm and pointing his finger at me with the other, he exclaimed, "I don't appreciate the threat." Slowly, I walked over to Ward as he held the door agape.

I peered into his eyes and calmly said, "Oh, it's not a threat, commissioner. It's a promise."

Ward replied, "Bring it on."

Ω

Stop The Malarkey

For the first time since my arrival, Ward and his fellow musketeers had imposed their ultimate will upon me. They had purged me from their rotten system—or so they thought. When I told the commission I would run for mayor, I meant it - at least until I drove home and got Melinda's okay. You see, even a Wartime Consigliere has a boss.

Upon entering our house, I slinked into the room where my wife sat quietly, working on her projects. She looked up at me long enough to see my face and say, "What happened?" Immediately, I said, "Well, they finally got their way." Melinda moved away from her work, stood up and gave me a big hug.

After we hugged, I pulled her back from me, looked into her face and said, "I told them I was going to run for mayor."

She laughed and went to sit down again. Stopping before she laid her butt in the chair, she said, "Oh, you're serious?"

I shook my head yes.

"Well," Melinda hesitantly said, "You wouldn't have been the man I married if you didn't finish this and run for mayor. Give those bastards hell." I laughed and asked if I had her vote. She said, "We'll see. Depends on what you promise me. Dinner out would be a good start." We both laughed.

And so, it began—my entry into the blood sport of Gainesville politics, the arena I swore I'd refrain from entering. Two days later, on January 29' 2022, I made it official when I filed my papers to run for mayor of Gainesville. Days later, my nemesis, Commissioner Ward, filed his paperwork to run as well. It was the classic matchup, or so that's what the papers wrote.

I chatted with Melanie Pena, a reporter for the *UF Alligator* and told her, "In that moment, I realized that I had an impact on people's lives." In pointing out this was my first foray into politics, I confessed, "I'm not a politician. I'm just a leader."

Over the next seven months, I reprised my historic role as the *Facebook* general manager, complete with a new set of DID YOU KNOW data. While I called upon people to contribute to my campaign during the day, I sat in front of my laptop screen at night, pounding out all the damning information I had shown the commission during my tenure.

The information included, but was not limited to, handwritten calculations from GRU's financial statements that showed evidence that the utility was simply the city's piggybank; letters to the UAB that showed Hanrahan's Solar Feed-in-Tariff had cost the utility almost $50 million; charts that showed the City had dramatically abused GRU by taking up to 230% of its profits in some years; budget analysis that showed GRU's expenses had grown less than1/2 of 1% during my last two years, while the city's budget has grown by over 9% per year. My followers grew as folks seemed to gobble up the "old" information now reformatted in the form of a weekly DID YOU KNOW series.

I joked with Melinda; little did Ward know that he had unleashed the beast when he made the motion to terminate my contract. I was a man on a mission only limited by the hours in a day.

By the end of my first month of campaigning, I produced my first campaign slogan: Stop Malarkey, vote for Bielarski. It really got a laugh and the desired attention. Early in the campaign, I thought name recognition was important. I also knew people had a challenging time pronouncing my name. Now I have offered them help with Joe Biden's use of the retro term.

In response, my other old nemesis Wes Wheeler—the UAB chair who thought the world was on fire—authored an editorial in the *Gainesville Sun* entitled, "Ed Bielarski was taking Gainesville Regional Utilities down the wrong path." It was a companion piece to another social media blast sent out to staunch democrat voters in the community he called, "Stop the Malarkey, Mister Bielarski." I must admit, that was a cute retort.

What wasn't cute was what he went on to write. "Let's cut to the chase, Ed was the wrong person for the job, and it was past time for him to go," Wheeler opined. Showing his true colors, he wrote, "The City Commissioners, particularly Harvey Ward, are to be commended for making the tough decisions needed to lead us forward." *And I thought we were such good friends.*

True to form, Wheeler once again built a compliment sandwich by offering a morsel of meat in between his scorn; "I'll credit Ed for re-negotiating an unfavorable contract," and completing it with, "But since that singular accomplishment, he has sought to impede and delay any further environmental progress." *Impede further environmental progress? Was Wheeler joking?*

***

On May 13, 2020, I presented a 50-megawatt power purchase agreement (PPA) I had executed with Origis Energy, a Miami-based company, to Wheeler's UAB. Wheeler was three. The deal was the result of a public bidding process that began a year earlier on May 5, 2019, when GRU asked for proposals to construct and deliver energy from a turn-key Solar Photovoltaic (PV) facility with a total rated electrical capacity of 40 to 50 megawatts with a term up to 20 years. Unlike the GREC PPA, we were granted the potential to buy out the facility. Most importantly, we'd only pay for the actual energy delivered, or as I jokingly called it, the Hanrahan clause.

The PPA included battery storage that would be maintained for consistent delivery of power, so-called intermittency. Most importantly, we got a rate lower than GRU's average cost of generation. It was a slam dunk.

Soon after the Wheeler-led UAB recommended the PPA, the commission granted its approval. It was GRU's first commercial-grade solar farm, with a capacity was 50 megawatts, almost tripling the current level of solar through the Solar FIT and Net metered rooftop solar customers.

***

Not sure how Wheeler missed the deal, but he also ignored the crafty way in which my team and I had facilitated the conversion of GRU's coal plant to operate on natural gas. He was oblivious to our upgrade to the Kelly plant, which lowered the overall heat rate and thus reduced carbon emissions.

Of course, Wheeler was gaslighting the community by disregarding most every positive development I had undertaken. That was okay, I didn't turn a blind eye to his hit piece.

I responded with my own editorial in the *Gainesville Sun* entitled, "I was fired for speaking truth to power." Not as catchy but effective, nonetheless. I shot back hard against Wheeler's allegations. "While I am no longer the general manager of Gainesville Regional Utilities, I still retain a solid understanding of all the facts surrounding the utility. In the face of voices perpetuating false narratives surrounding my dismissal, it's time to set the record straight." I laughed as I recalled former City Manager Anthony Lyons telling me if I had a rap name, it would have been For the Record. I concurred.

In the editorial, I excoriated Wheeler and his non-factual allegations, "The inconvenient truth that the UAB and the City Commission are afraid to tell the community is this: The cost of attaining the 100% renewable goal will come at the cost of over $3 billion and will include another biomass plant for reliability. My unpardonable sin was that I questioned that path. I spoke truth to power, just like I had in my unending pursuit of pushing the commission to reduce the greater than

100% dividend they take from GRU, called a general fund transfer, to lower utility rates. And you know, I'd do it again."

During the campaign, I walked almost every neighborhood knocking on doors and delivering my message. Up through the August 23rd election, I knocked on over 13,000 doors, went through three pairs of shoes as I walked over four hundred miles. I sent out three separate sets of mailers and let my hair grow 70's era long, even sporting a ponytail, prompting local radio drive-time guy *Bob Rose Show on Sky Radio 97.3* to nickname me Ponytail Ed.

I even settled on a less cavalier slogan; It's time to make City Hall make sense again. My three main points were to stop using GRU as a piggy bank for City Commission pet projects, pursue renewable energy that's affordable, and end the war on single-family homes. I had arrived as a real candidate. I still wondered if the voters would accept the old general manager as the new mayor.

In the midst of my mayoral run, natural gas prices spiked and families across GRU's service territory were seeing summertime bills skyrocket. While higher usage and higher natural gas prices were the primary reason, the secondary causes were the inefficiency of GRU's aging power generation fleet and the continued subsidization of city expenses through the excessive GFT. My campaign saw a boost in popularity. That is until…

The matriarch of the Alachua County Democratic Party rose up once more and took to social media. "Are you aware that biomass is the lowest cost generation that GRU has in its fleet?" she wrote on a *Facebook* post. "The spike in bills is due to natural gas. GRU under Mr. Bielarski manipulated the rate stabilization fund so it is now collecting way more than it should be, which pushes prices way up."

I was speechless.

If anyone was manipulating anything, it was Hanrahan who was spreading falsehoods about my legitimate and prudent use of the Rate Stabilization Fund, as well as my leadership to sway the election.

It got worse.

With momentum clearly building on my side, the Alachua County Democratic Executive Committee decided to send a dirty trick's mailer out less than one week prior to the election. The front of the mailer had me photoshopped between Donald J. Trump and Florida Governor DeSantis and read, "REPUBLICAN BACKED ED BIELARSKI DOESN'T STAND WITH GAINESVILLE."

Worse yet, the back of the mailer made false allegations such as 1) raising GRU bills and putting them $757 million more in debt; 2) damaging our environment by advocating for dumping toxic coal ash; 3) putting resident's lives at risk by fighting the city's COVID vaccine push and spread right-wing misinformation; 4) standing with Republicans by donating to Trump Republicans. Of course, none of the allegations were true. All the while, my primary mayoral opponent, Harvey Ward, remained silent.

The county's public affairs director, Mark Sexton, posted snarky comments and memes about my work as the general manager. "Bielarski says that after collecting $300k+ per year and giving advice, he has nothing to do with GRU woes. Please."

Queen Pegeen continued with her attempts discredit me by writing on *Facebook* that "the net present value of the contract (Biomass Buyout of GREC PPA) he signed was something north of 95% of the old contract's value plus the cost of operating it ourselves. And now we have all the risks and responsibilities." I couldn't believe it, Hanrahan was using fake news to influence a public that still trusted her. The Biomass Buyout price wasn't anywhere near 95% of the old contract's $2.2 billion value. It was approximately 50%. I was pissed. Showing no shame, she finished by writing, "We won't know for another 20 years if it was the smartest option or not."

Note to self: I should have read my prior note to self in which I recommended staying out of city politics.

I was running as an Independent, a self-described purple candidate. In a city comprised of nearly 60% Democrat voters, it was important for me to be seen as Democrat leaning, or at least not overly conservative. While I worked overtime dispelling the lies in the mailer, lies in social media, and lies elsewhere, I worried this last-ditch effort casting me as a Trump Republican made my election unlikely.

The biggest hurdle to clear in winning the August 23rd election outright was needing to gain one more vote than 50%, which was made even more unlikely because nine candidates had entered the race. The best I could hope for was to finish in the first or second position and head to a runoff in November. However, the way the loyal Alachua County Democrats were going after me, I wasn't so sure I'd last until then.

Election day coinciding with Melinda's half birthday (the date six months between her yearly birthdays) was about the only good news I had going for me. As the polls closed at 7:00, Melinda and I got ready to go to the Watch Party to view the returns at Ballyhoo Grill and Restaurant. As we mingled with friends and family, the results started posting on the Alachua County Supervisor of Elections website. One by one, folks told me that I was hanging strong in second place, ahead of former City Commissioner David Arreola and, decades ago, former Mayor Gary Gordon.

When the votes were finally counted, Harvey Ward carried 27.94% of the vote. I came in second with 26.43%. David Arreola and Gary Gordon came in with 15.38% and 14.44%, respectively. I had gotten what I needed. I was in the runoff election for Mayor of Gainesville. I told my followers on *Facebook*, "It's looking like Harvey and I are heading to a run-off—November 8th. Looks like I gotta get some walking shoes. LOL."

Ward offered strong sentiments when talking to the *Gainesville Sun*. He said, "We're confident going into November." I followed with, "The next step in my life's journey begins."

The same *Gainesville Sun* played up the battle between the guy that got fired against the guy that fired him to the point it rehashed the events of the January 27th meeting in which I was terminated. Actually, more specifically, Ward's comment, "Bring it on." I hoped that storyline wouldn't play out as though my candidacy was my revenge tour. I had heard rumors that my opponent's camp had already suggested it to whoever would listen.

The next two and a half months went by in a blur. Throughout the debates and my public appearances, I stuck to my message of fiscal responsibility and turning the utility away from the brink. For the first time in Gainesville's mayoral history, two media sources sponsored televised debates— *WUFT and WCJB Channel 20*. I believe the *WUFT* debate on October 26th, just over a week before the election, was the defining moment of the whole campaign.

WUFT's headline after the debate said it all, "Gainesville mayoral candidates Harvey Ward and Ed Bielarski spar in an acrimonious debate." It was true. The college news source wrote: "He (Bielarski) seemed to use every question as an opportunity to hammer Ward for the city's budgetary dependence on GRU's GFT, which currently totals $34 million. He likened the city's ballooning budget to a kind of extortion upon city-owned utility company and city's residents."

To describe Ward's bewildering hand motions, *WUFT* wrote: "Ward, a native of Gainesville and current Gainesville city commissioner, made dramatic hand gestures of disagreement and called for a fact-check whenever Bielarski made an accusation."

In response to a moderator's question about the city budget, I said, "Reign in spending." Looking at Ward, I exclaimed, "The city budget has gone from $107 million to $154 million in the time Mr. Ward has been in office. GRU is sending a transfer larger than what they make to the city government. They make $20 million a year on average and over the past four years, they have submitted $38 million. That can't be sustainable."

Even after all that I had been through in trying to enlighten the commission, Ward responded by saying, "I'm hoping there will be a fact check because some of the figures are just inaccurate, which is shocking since Bielarski is an accountant." I couldn't believe that Ward would question the very numbers my finance team and I had presented to him for years. His strategy was apparent. He would continue to gaslight me and the community for the remainder of the campaign. He had done it during his time on the commission. Why not go with your strengths?

I ended the debate with the following remarks, "City Hall has become a place where Commissioner Ward can look at people who come up for public comment and shame them. Some of them have been arrested (for speaking longer than the 3-minute limit). You do not know me, Commissioner Ward. We have to make our community a civil place to be. I am standing up for those people who have been kicked out of City Hall." Looking at the audience, I exclaimed, "Have we had enough of Harvey Ward?"

Apparently, the community had not had enough of Harvey Ward. As the final election results came in on the night of November 8th, Ward won a commanding victory garnering 57.6% of the vote to my 42.4%. WUFT must have been waiting to print its headline, "Ed Bielarski cannot muster enough power as Harvey Ward elected the new mayor of Gainesville." They followed it with the comment: "The lights have gone out on Ed Bielarski's run for Gainesville mayor." Cute. Almost 48% of the voting public cast their ballots— almost triple the average turnout for a Gainesville City election. I couldn't quibble. I had lost the battle.

In the afterglow of Ward's election, the community of Ward's supporters thought they had vanquished people of my ilk from the city. As they waited for the next generation of musketeers, little did they know that two powerful legislators, Keith Perry and Chuck Clemons, had paid close attention to my campaign and the arguments I set forth. My DID YOU KNOWS were about to become fodder for yet another attempt to separate the city from its GRU piggybank.

Ω

A Utility governed by the people it serves

Within a few weeks of my election defeat, I celebrated my 66th birthday. I took the time to reminisce about a career that had begun when I was hired by the old Martin Marietta Corporation in 1979. During my almost 45-year career, I had worked for all types of bosses, supervisors, and boards. None of them could top the dysfunctionality of the Gainesville City Commission. I knew that I had to publish the book I had been working on – a tell-all of an abysmal contract and short-sighted vision of an unprofessional board.

On January 5, 2023, Harvey Ward launched into his first day as mayor on the spirit of his overwhelming victory – a virtual political mandate to continue the pursuit of a one-city nirvana. Leading a cadre of devote progressives, Reina Saco, Casey Willits, and Bryan Eastman, the stage was set for a veritable fearsome foursome of unbridled social activism and disciplinary amnesia. Around noon, Ward and his fresh band of musketeers were sworn in on the lawn of the historic Thomas Center.

Proud as a new papa, Ward stood before the celebrants as they waited for his words to flow. He didn't disappoint as he waxed lyrical. "Our strength lies in the diversity of our personal stories, of our backgrounds, and our upbringings, of our various paths to the dais and of the constituencies we represent. Each of us wants the very best for each of our neighbors. That does not mean we should expect our journey together to be a smooth one."

While Ward was basking in the glory of the city's political royalty, I imagined the whole network of shadow government elites high-fiving each other as they anticipated the joyous return to Hanrahan-era politics. I wanted no part of that celebration. I was more concerned with writing my book. I had known Ward too long and too well to believe he wouldn't help me with just the right ending.

Later the same day, while presiding over his first commission meeting as mayor, Ward showed the community how he would govern. Immediately, he tried to change an agenda item – an intended discussion over the recruitment plan for charter officers. Jumping in before city staff could speak to the topic, Ward said, "Prior to starting this, I wanted to put an idea out there." *Boy, did this sound familiar coming from Ward.* Rather than expend "about $250,000," Ward asked, "If there is a will and an interest for someone to make a motion that we remove the interim and make permanent any of these (four interim charter officers)… So is there any appetite for bringing on any of our charters permanently as a motion right now?" It seemed Ward was ready, willing, and able to use his mayoral position as his personal bully pulpit. *No surprise there.*

I watched and listened as Ward obliterated the whole idea of conducting competitive searches for charter officers. While none of the interim charter officers had been vetted through a third party or tested through an interview process, Ward didn't care. He liked the charter officers he had acquired through Poe's great reset. Not a Wartime Consigliere to be seen anywhere. For a moment, I thought I was watching Monte Hall in *Let's Make a Deal.*

Commissioner Saco said she would " welcome conversations on keeping the others permanently…but there is one that I think should go without too much argument, that Mr. Cunningham be kept as permanent General Manager of GRU, given his skill set…" I shook my head as I listened to Saco try to scrap the city's time-honored hiring process and pick her own winner and loser. What made her comments more appalling was who she was fighting for. Cunningham had no power generation, transmission, or distribution experience, a substantial 60% of GRU's business. He had never led a similar sized organization. In a competitive search, he wouldn't have made the final cut to be interviewed. However, he did play well in the sandbox with a commission intent on a one-city direction. Thankfully, her motion would die for the lack a seconding motion from anyone on the dais.

Speaking of dying, during an earlier November 22, 2022, commission meeting, Saco was so upset with long-time city hall activist, Jo Beaty, that she was captured on a live microphone telling the erstwhile citizen, "You're supposed to be dead already. You're a waste of air." *Wow, I had underestimated Saco's ability to help me with an ending to my book.*

Two weeks hence, at the January 19th commission meeting, the mayor returned to the same matter – deciding whether to hire the interim charter officers as permanent employees without a competitive search. No recruitment firm. No expansion of the candidate pool. No equity toolbox, as they referred to it. With very little discussion, at least in the Sunshine, by a vote of 6 to 1, the new commission abruptly changed its thoughts from the previous meeting and agreed to allow the mayor to negotiate contracts for the four interim charter officers. *Hmmm.*

Without following the formal process used for all of the city's over 2,000 employees, Ward explained his vote. "I don't think it's going to surprise anyone that I support this motion…I have not seen a group of charter officers work together as well as this group."

As Ward was nearing his one-month anniversary, there were rumblings that the State's Joint Legislative Auditing Committee (JLAC) was nearing its checkup with the city on outstanding audit items – a veritable checkup from the neck up. Prior to the checkup, during a commission meeting, almost in a fit of temper, Ward made it clear that he was not concerned about cutting GRU rates but for the "folks in crisis."

"Doing that through a 'let's cut the rates' approach is something that is not beneficial, in my opinion, to anybody in the community and really doesn't help as much as it sounds it ought to help." In other words, Ward was no longer interested in the annoying concept of "fair and equal" treatment of GRU's customers, as prescribed by the Florida Public Service Commission. *Wow!*

I was amazed at how out of touch Ward had become. The city could no longer operate on a business-as-usual basis—still blissfully unaware that the city was in crisis. He was wholly unqualified to be leading a now 500 hundred million a year in revenue utility as its chairman of the board. People in Tallahassee saw it as well.

On February 23, 2023, JLAC held its scheduled audit checkup during a public meeting two hours away in Tallahassee. Surrounded by a contingent of Gainesville residents and city staff, Ward stood helplessly as Derek Noonan, the Audit Manager for the Florida Auditor General's office, delivered a scathing report on the crumbling state of affairs within the city—high GRU debt (caused by poor city governance), burdensome GFT payments, lack of accounting internal controls at the city, and the inability of city staff to generate financial statements. *Hmm, sounds familiar.*

Noonan's words prompted State Representative Mike Caruso, a CPA himself, to declare, "These are major, major items that the audit has revealed." However, he lamented, "Mr. Noonan, I think the audit doesn't go far enough… if we could have sound effects in here with lightning, fire, and thunder, I think that would more appropriately show the magnitude of what this audit has touched light on."

Caruso was a man after my own heart. *Thank God,* I thought. *People other than Perry and Clemons got it.*

"The audit inadequately addresses the fact that GRU is not sustainable… with $1.7 billion in debt, GRU technically may be in default for breach of the anti-subsidizing clause (use of

GFT and other interdepartmental payments)… the city is using the GRU as its own piggybank, without consideration of its own fiscal responsibility… without consideration of the hardship it places on GRU customers… I don't think the magnitude of all this has been addressed."

Caruso finished by dramatically saying, "We have a GRU that is on the verge of failing and a city that will tumble after it."

Get me some popcorn, this is gonna be good.

Ward moved to the lectern, as a much more demure fellow outside of Gainesville's little blue island of liberal, progressive political support. Looking as though he had been triggered by Caruso's remarks, he told the representatives that the commission has voted to reduce the GFT by two million a year. Why "the current GFT is lower than it's been in a decade," proclaimed Ward, looking as though he had delivered something quite extraordinary. No one on the Tallahassee dais applauded Ward for his efforts. They knew better.

Senator Perry took the opportunity to ask Ward if the city was ready to incur the billions of dollars necessary to reach its stated goal of NetZero by 2045. He quizzed Ward, "Is that misinformation?" Surely Ward would stand up to Perry and admit the obvious – yes. Ward retreated by saying, "I am not ready to sign off, nor do I have any plan of signing off, on a billion dollars of new debt." I almost chocked on my popcorn as my former mayoral opponent publicly admitted that the Net Zero goal was a toothless, virtue-signaling, piece of paper that appeased the environmentalists and hammered certain general managers.

Perry proceeded to ask GRU GM Conningham how the modest GFT reductions would reduce GRU's debt. Cunningham hemmed and hawed until alternating chair of JLAC, Jason Pizzo, asked whether the measures kept up with interest payments. The vastly qualified GM, according to Saco, said, "I don't know."

Caruso, like Goston five years previously, was on a rhetorical roll. He wasn't having any of Cunningham's obtuse answers. Trying to elicit some sort of informed response from Cunningham, he asked him how much of the new GFT reductions would pay down debt. The new general manager said, "Some of it will." I thought I was watching Vinnie Barbarino in *Welcome Back Kotter* when he'd tell Kotter, "What?" followed by "Where?"

Undaunted, Caruso replied, "Some is a dollar…So we don't know how much of the $42 million over six years' time is gonna go to $1.7 billion of debt. And if all of it went, have we really touched the debt?…I'll bet you in six years, we're over $2.5 billion in debt."

Cunningham didn't respond. He apparently didn't know.

Perry took the opportunity to ask about the modification of the Origis solar contract that increased GRU's liability to 75 megawatts, up from 50 megawatts, and increased the price by almost 25%. Perry pointedly said, "What is the justification for entering into a contract that the general public can't know about, or you won't let them know about?"

Ward responded that "signing the contract gives us reliable, predictable purchasing of power…" Of course, under federal electric generation standards, solar power is not considered reliable power – information GRU had informed the mayor of on numerous public and private meetings. *Jeez.*

The JLAC's coup de grace was when Perry asked about the cost of solar. Cunningham, with a straight face, said, "That's a trade secret." *Game, set, match.*

Whereas my September 13, 2021, meeting had been *My Wonderful Life* moment, February 23, 2023, was the affirmation of my life as a Wartime Consigliere. I had fought the commission for seven years and never, never gave up. Even after being fired, I threw my hat in the ring to continue fighting for the city. Prior to the meeting, Clemons and Caruso had reached out to me to make sure they had understood the numbers correctly. My recounting of the extent of GRU's financial quagmire left them speechless, until now. Now, I had my own three musketeers in Tallahassee using my words, my numbers, and my thoughts to carry it home for me. I was thrilled.

Just when I didn't think it could get better, Caruso told Ward, "I'm telling you, go back and make those bold moves, or we will take action. What action? We will write letters to the governor, ask him to remove you from office and put people in that will take the bold actions to save GRU, to save the utility, to ultimately save the city." *Boom, baby!*

While JLAC was pressuring the commission to take bold action, State Representative Clemons was traveling uncharted territory of his own. On March 9, 2023, Clemons filed a proposed local bill that would allow Governor DeSantis to appoint a new governing board for GRU. It could serve as a Disney-style takeover of GRU.

The same day, during a general policy meeting at city hall, Commissioner Bryan Eastman brought up Clemons' bill under member comments. He said, "Putting the partisanship aside, putting politics of this aside, I want to make sure we have a working city government, one where, when someone needs a police officer, an officer is there, one where, when they turn on the lights, their lights are on. GRU and the City of Gainesville have grown together for 110 years… I don't know how we provide core services when half the city, under GRU, is overseen by a board not accountable to the city, whether it's a Democrat or a Republican appointing them."

I smirked when I heard Eastman speak. He had been Hayes-Santos campaign manager before running for a commission seat himself. He was an avowed democrat activist. During my campaign for mayor, he was one of the political operatives that combed through the internet to find "dirt" on me. One such item was a conservative editorial my dad had authored. I am a junior, while my dad was a senior. The articles were written by senior Bielarski, not me. It didn't matter. The truth became the first casualty of the campaign as the false information was distributed among Gainesville's democrat elite in an attempt to destroy my credibility as a purple, independent candidate.

Today, Eastman seemed just as comfortable conflating Clemons' Bill with GRU being unable to deliver electricity and water services to its customers. Heaven forbid, the residents might also lose police and utility services. What shall we do? Balderdash. What Eastman needed to do was vote for budget reductions at the suites at city hall and leave the folks working in the streets of the city.

Near the end of the meeting, Commissioner Cynthia Chestnut got to the heart of the issue when she said, "The one critical point… is that GRU is owned by the people (conveniently leaving out the people it served part)." Looking at the City Attorney, Daniel Nee, she asked, "Can the Legislature take a core service that is owned by the people without a referendum?"

Nee replied, "Yes, the Legislature has a tremendous amount of power over the municipalities. We aren't counties. We aren't constructs of the constitution: we are creations of the Legislature… aside from ensuring that the debt owed by the municipality is protected and that its creditors are protected, the Legislature has wide latitude in the ways in which it can create and destroy and change a municipality."

Yikes!

On March 17, 2023, the Alachua County Legislative Delegation held a public meeting in Tallahassee to discuss and vote on Clemons' Bill. Clemons read a statement in which he said, "The Legislature has the authority and retains the authority to represent the best interests of the citizens by deciding local issues by Special Act if we have to, and we would be derelict if we didn't exercise our constitutional and statutory authority to correct, or help to correct, decades-long problems

337

when they get worse by being ignored." *The calvary has arrived, my friend.*

Once again, Caruso attended the meeting, this time telling Ward, "The idea that you would take one dollar more than the profits of GRU, one dollar, is wrong... Let's get it down to zero excess over the profits of the GRU. That I haven't heard from you yet." I was waiting for Ward to admonish Caruso for talking about profits like he had at our budget meeting from years ago. I marveled at how little courage Ward had in standing up to the Florida Legislators.

When asked about the size of future GFT payments, Ward said that the GFT would be "probably south of $10 million." Coming from a man that had fought me tooth and nail to get a reduction to $27 million, I was dumbstruck by Ward's acquiescence. He didn't stop there. He was really into all-out self-preservation mode now. "It's currently $34 million. Those are the kind of bold moves that I am interested in... I'm willing to entertain zero." Ward was simply a bully. This time a bully that had been punched in the nose. Confronted with an opponent he couldn't fire, coerce, or lobby against, Ward was simply a lifeless blob.

When the meeting ended with the delegation voting 4 to 1 in favor of passing the Bill, I could see that Gainesville was indeed a city in danger of losing control – control of the utility and possibly the city.

On April 14, 2023, the commission held a general policy meeting to discuss the unexpected turn of events. In the face of the concerted actions of the Florida Legislature, it appeared the commission's will power was wilting fast. Rather than wilting, the commission's willpower disappeared as they staged a full-scale retreat. They voted unanimously to adopt a new formula for the GFT, along with a promise to cut GRU debt and require substantial cuts to the city's budget. I smiled as I recognized the scope and magnitude of the changes. While I wasn't the general manager when it finally happened, my years of battle and publicizing the issues had brought it into the light of day.

Renaming the GFT the GSC, or Government Services Contribution, the commission dropped the GSC to $15.3 million, an astronomical $19 million reduction. The city would reduce its expenses by that same $19 million so as to not place the additional burden on property owners. Along with that, the commission agreed to drive GRU's debt capitalization rate from 87% to 70% over ten years, or a $315 million reduction—the equivalent of the debt I had saved the city in the Biomass Buyout. Ward noted, "This is bold. This is a big deal. This is going to be hard to figure out; this is not the last meeting that is going to be painful."

Knowing the commission as I did, I seriously questioned if it was a smoke screen to take Perry, Clemons, and Caruso off their trail.

I also couldn't help but wonder what might have been, what could have been if the commission had listened to my pleas over the past five years. The pain wouldn't have been so severe, so dramatic. It would have just been a course correction. Now, it was a culture shift with hundreds of employee's jobs on the line and a Bill barreling towards the Governor's desks before the end of June.

I recalled the words of City Attorney Nee when he spoke about the power of the Florida Legislature, "The Legislature has wide latitude in the ways in which it can create and destroy and change a municipality." I realized that the commission was scared to death that Governor DeSantis would appoint the independent board for GRU and force the city to modify its charter to facilitate any and all changes necessary. If the commission refused, DeSantis could remove the commissioners from office as well. Gainesville Regional Utilities and the City of Gainesville could end up on the governor's resume as he stumped through Iowa. Better to comply then be tossed out on their asses.

339

On April 27, Clemons' Bill (now House Bill 1645) was brought before the Florida House for its next rite of passage. Addressing the membership, Clemons calmly presented his reasoning for why the Bill should be passed. In no particular order, he said that the Bill maintained local control because all five members must live in GRU's territory. The new board wouldn't draw salaries. The Bill restricted the GFT to what GRU earned. Finally, the decisions made by the board would not be based on social or political objectives.

Representative Hinson stood up to voice her displeasure with the Bill. I couldn't forget that Hinson was seated on the city commission from 2012 until 2015. She had advocated for the embarrassing low offer made to Jim Gordon to buy out the GREC PPA. She never seemed to grasp the concept that the GREC PPA is what drove the value of the buyout, not the value of the plant. Today, Hinson displayed her inability to read the room when she asked Clemons what compelling interest the state has in GRU. I smiled as I recalled discussing this very question with Clemons. He was loaded for bear.

Clemons began, "Over the past ten years, Representative Hinson, the governing board has withdrawn $100 million more than the utility's net profits," Clemons began. "In the last four years, the government of Gainesville has withdrawn $68 million more than the utility has earned in the net profit level. So, the compelling reason is this: the decisions coming out of Gainesville...are not in the financial well-being of the Gainesville Regional Utility." Clemons' comments were like a dagger to the heart of any argument against the Bill.

Hinson proceeded to ask for five amendments to the Bill. Each time, the amendment failed on a voice vote. While multiple House members praised Hinson for her resolve in the fight against the Bill, it was clear that her understanding of the Bill was lacking in context and content. She simply didn't want the city to lose control of the utility. The overall sentiment was not in her favor. Looking more and more like House Bill 1645 would be swept in on the shoulders of the Republican majority, the mood of the body was captured by comments by two House members.

Representative Bobby Payne declared, "This is about your city commission breaking your community because of the acts of draining and siphoning money off of the utility." *Wow!*

Representative Stan McClain, from nearby Marion County opined, "GRU has been the laughingstock of counties surrounding Alachua for a long time...The citizens of Gainesville have been begging for relief as long as I can remember...It is time."

Frankly, I was amazed at the speed of the legislature's assault on the commission. I had grown accustomed to the sluggish process at city hall. Now, state legislators were simply fed up. When the House speaker called for the vote, I watched HB 1645 sail through on an 81 to 33 vote. *Holy cow.*

On May 4, Clemons" Bill was introduced in the Florida Senate along with 23 local bills, in a process called the rocket docket. It's called the rocket docket because it had been the senate's tradition to vote on all the local bills in one block. Hence, multiple bills are voted on and shot through like a rocket to the governor. No individual debate on specific bills. By a 39 to 0 vote, HB 1645 passed along with 22 other local bills. With that action, the Gainesville City Commission's continuing role as the governing board of GRU was squarely in the hands of Governor Ron DeSantis, as HB 1645 would go to his desk for signature.

Over the years, I sat through commission meetings where DeSantis had been regularly mocked. Once, I was stunned when then-Commissioner Arreola accused the Governor of having "a mental disease." I guess it was okay to accuse someone you hate of having issues you wouldn't allow anyone else to accuse someone of. Of course it didn't stop at the commission level. When I ran for mayor, Gainesville's progressive voters would regularly compare DeSantis to Hitler, and other totalitarian dictators.

I couldn't imagine the Florida Governor vetoing Clemons' Bill. In fact, I could see him being quite pleased to remove the city's governance of the beleaguered utility. The only question in my mind was how long would he make the inhabitants of our little Blue Island squirm?

As the community speculated over if and when DeSantis would sign the bill, the war of words raged on social media and throughout the community. It was silly season once more.

Commissioner Bryan Eastman took up the fight by taking to social media in a series of posts under the mantle, "Correcting the Misinformation on GRU." He unapologetically called the Clemons' Bill and the reported facts, "a cynical misinformation campaign." He reiterated the same tired arguments about the GFT being "one of the lowest in Florida" (actually one of the highest as a percentage of available net income). Worst of all, he stated, "We don't take more from the utility than what it earns and that is easily proven." Not surprisingly, Eastman never tried to prove it. Of course, he couldn't.

When I confronted the young commissioner on *Facebook*, he wrote back, "Its 2023 and we still have not spent 68 million more than we earned, that number exists only in your head." He proceeded to call my analysis an "invented metric." Coming from an elected commission, his words were stunning…if delivered outside of Gainesville.

On May 17, the commission held a budget workshop in which they got their first look at partial city budgets. The preliminary budget reflected an over $10 million of increase – split largely between Police and Fire Department budgets. That meant that in order to reach the $19 million budget reduction, the city would have to cut $29 million from some unnamed city programs, services, or employment.

On May 26th, at the following city budget workshop, the city's Acting Director of the Office of Management and

Budget, Steve Varvel, stated, " I'm here to tell you that we will just not be able to produce a budget that provides a level of service that the city deserves at 5.5 (millage rate). So we are hoping that we can get at least some thoughts on developing that budget at a 6.5 millage rate, which will still result in going back to the departmental budgets and looking for an additional $3 million of savings." As I had predicted, the commission was not serious about cutting the size of its kingdom. They would rather increase city property taxes by almost 20%. Their earlier vote on cutting the city budget had simply been a last-ditch effort to curry favor with my three musketeers.

This time, none of the commission's rhetoric mattered. They had been exposed for who they were. The city was on a path to lose control of their cherished utility - GRU. With a stroke of DeSantis' pen, the utility would no longer be a piggybank for commissioner's special projects, burdened with unfunded mandates and unattainable goals. I was no longer the lone Wartime Consigliere. In spite of our differences, I had been joined by State Senator Keith Perry, Representative Clemons and Caruso who served as GRU's champions shepherding the bill to the governor's desk.

Rather quietly at 4:56 PM on June 28, 2023, while taking a break from his presidential campaign, Governor DeSantis signed the Clemons' Bill into law. My work as Gainesville's Wartime Consigliere was done.

After almost two decades of historic turmoil, the utility that had been ceremonially described as "a utility owned by the people it served", would now rightfully be hailed as the "utility governed by the people it served." A new governing board would be appointed by a governor who represents all of GRU's customers, not just customers living in the city. While my worlds were no longer colliding, past and present commissioners' worlds sure as hell were. For them, June 28th became the date that will live in the city's infamy, serving all

343

that followed to forever remember the names Hanrahan, Poe, and Ward as the ones who led the city to lose control...

.

Endnotes

Chapter 1—Trial for a Wartime Consigliere:

Dialogue culled from the December 7, 2017, City Commission meeting: December 7, 2017, Gainesville City Commission meeting from the public records of the City of Gainesville. The commissioner comment section of the meeting was transcribed by GRU General Manager's executive assistant, Robin Baxley.

Pied Piper analogy: "Pied Piper of Hamelin," *Wikipedia*, Wikimedia Foundation, accessed July 16, 2021, http://en.wikipedia.org/wiki/Pied_Piper_of_Hamelin.

The exorbitant cost under the GREC Power Purchase Agreement (PPA): GRU Finance Staff, Power Point Presentation entitled, "City of Gainesville, Florida, Utilities System Revenue Bonds, 2017 Series A," Posted on October 11, 2017, to City of Gainesville portal, 12.

High-level investigative report left unmentioned by Commissioner Hayes-Santos: Reported by Andrew Caplan, "Report: City policy not followed in search," *The Gainesville Sun*, October 11, 2017.

Internal struggles between Anthony Lyons and Edward Bielarski: Reported by Andrew Caplan, "Gainesville officials quarrel over raises for city workers," *The Gainesville Sun*, November 25, 2017.

The elephant in the room—The Report of the Joint Investigation against City Manager Anthony Lyons: Torey Holt and Carlos Holt, "Internal Investigation-Case 2017-004 A, October 11, 2017.

CFO Justin Locke's resignation: Reported by Andrew Caplan, "High-ranking GRU official resigns over pay," *The Gainesville Sun*, December 4, 2017.

Poe only thought Bielarski met job expectations: Reported by Andrew Caplan, "City Commission debates firing GRU general manager," *The Gainesville Sun*, December 7, 2017.

Poe's performance review of Bielarski: Completed by Lauren Poe, "Charter Officer Performance Review—Ed Bielarski," Gainesville, December 6, 2016.

Bielarski response to Poe's performance review: E-mail from Ed Bielarski to Lauren Poe, "Re: Performance Review," December 7, 2016.

Reasons for Lyons' return to Gainesville: Undocumented but gathered in conversations between Edward Bielarski and Anthony Lyons.

The haunting lyrics to the song heard at Jacksonville train station: *My Old Man* by "Zac Brown Band," *The Lyrics Library*, accessed July 16, 2021, http://google.com.

The eulogy written for Ed Bielarski Sr. while Melinda was in surgery: Eulogy and obituary for Edward Joseph Bielarski, Sr, written by Edward Bielarski Jr.

Timeframe of events throughout the summer of 2017: Documented through Edward Bielarski receipts, personal notes, and interviews with wife.

***The Godfather* and the Wartime Consigliere:** In blockbuster movie, *The Godfather*, the concept of a Wartime Consigliere was introduced into our pop culture lexicon during an iconic scene, when Michael Corleone told his crime-family attorney, Tom Hagen that he had reluctantly decided to remove him as the mob's attorney. Confused, Hagan responded with the question, "Mike, why am I out?" Michael Corleone delivers the fateful line to Hagen, "You're not a Wartime Consigliere, Tom. Things may get rough with the move we're trying."

"*The Godfather*", *Stackexchange*, accessed July 16, 2021, http://movies.stackexchange.com/questions/69933/why-did-michael-fire-tom-hagen-as-consigliere.

Today's meaning of a Wartime Consigliere: The *Godfather's* popularity lifted the Wartime Consigliere's narrow definition from its crime-family origins into a more friendly business term. According to the Urban Dictionary a Wartime Consigliere became to be known as: "A senior advisor with cunning and ruthlessness needed to defeat a n enemy during times of open conflict, unconstrained by the caution and deliberation called for during regular business order. "Wartime Consigliere," Urban Dictionary, accessed March 21, 2021, http://urbandictionary.com.

The "this is business not personal" quote from Sonny Corleone: "*The Godfather*," *Techcrunch*, accessed July 16, 2021, http://techcrunch.com/2011/02/19/this-is-business-not-personal/

The "leave the gun, take the cannoli" scene: "*The Godfather*" *The Seventies*, accessed July 16, 2021, http://theseventies.berkeley.edu/godfather/2018/06/07/leave-the-gun-take-the-cannoli-the-hgitman-as-family-man/

The words of Dylan Thomas: Dylan Thomas, *The Poems of Dylan Thomas*, New York, New Directions, 1952.

Chapter 2—A Sunshine State of Mind:

Buddy Bielarski's racing feats: *Misschicken*, accessed December 16, 2021, http://www.misschicken.com/91-Buddy Bielarski-Super Mod-JIS-1968.htm.

Buddy Bielarski's racing history and accomplishments: *AL.com*, accessed December 16, 2021, http://AL.com.

Legend of Jan Bielarski: As told to Edward Bielarski by Phillip and Jakob Bielarski in a series of interviews.

Rudolph Belarski's professional career as master pulp fiction artist, John P. Gunnison, Belarski, *Pulp Art Masters*, Silver Spring, Maryland, Adventure House, unknown, Introduction.

Edward Bielarski's early career: Public resume submitted for general manager job.

Recollections of Jim Gordon's early years spending time at the West End Camp in Maine: Wendy Williams and Robert Whitcomb, *Cape Wind: Money, Celebrity, Class, Politics, and the Battle for our Energy Future*, New York, Public Affairs, 2007, Prologue, 54-55.

Size of Gainesville Regional Utilities: Fitch Ratings, "Gainesville Regional Utilities, Florida, Utilities System Revenue Bonds, New Issue Report," 2.

History of Gainesville Regional Utilities: Communication Department's published timeline.

Partial lyrics of song, *Living here in Allentown,* as written and sung by Billy Joel: "Living here in Allentown," *A to Z Lyrics,* accessed December 16, 2021, http://azlyrics.com/lyrics/billyjoel/allentown.html.

Timeline of Bielarski and wife's visit to Gainesville: E-mail from Scott Fry to Edward Bielarski, "MFP LLC—Finalist Interview Info," Denver, March 1, 2014.

Conversations held at the Meet and Greet: E-mail from Ray Washington to Edward Bielarski, "Re: letter to commissioners," Gainesville, April 29, 2015.

Final six candidates left standing: The City of Gainesville's public record entitled "General Manager-Utilities Executive Search Plan."

Approval of the employment contract for General Manager Edward Bielarski along with controversial Facebook posts: Reported by Morgan Watkins, "City Commission approves contract with new GRU chief," *The Gainesville Sun*, May 21, 2015.

General Manager Edward Bielarski's reaction to selection: Reported by Morgan Watkins, "Bielarski ready to come to Gainesville as GRU's General Manager," *The Gainesville Sun*, May 22, 2015.

Chapter 3—The Contract doesn't pass the sniff test:

Discussion/interview notes conducted by Navigant: *GRU Utilities Attorney Shayla McNeill, Commissioner Randy Wells, Commissioner Lauren Poe, Commissioner Helen Warren, Commissioner Craig Carter, Commissioner Yvonne Hinson-Rawls, Commissioner Todd Chase, Mayor Ed Braddy, City Attorney Nicole Shalley, City Litigation Attorney Elizabeth Waratuke, Interim General Manager Kathy Viehe, GRU Purchasing Manager Joann Dorval, GRU Assistant GM John Stanton, GRU Electric System Planning Director Richard Bachmeier, Citizen Group members Jim Konish, Jo Beatty, and Paula Stahmer, GRU Finance Director Mark Benton, GRU Interim CFO David Richardson, IT Manager David Darius, IT Designer Leo Whitman, Ray Washington, GRU Supervising Engineer Rob Klemons, El Paso Electric VP Andy Ramirez, Mycoff Fry and Associates General Manager Scott Fry, GRU Lead Analyst Todd Kamhoot, Former Mayor Craig Lowe, GRU Rates Manager Diane Wilson, and Former GRU GM Robert Hunzinger*

Jim Gordon's acquired fortitude: Wendy Williams and Robert Whitcomb, *Cape Wind: Money, Celebrity, Class, Politics, and the Battle for our Energy Future*, New York, Public Affairs, 2007, Prologue.

Skop's critical vote: The Florida Public Service Commission Docket No. 090451-EM, Order No. PSC-10-0409-FOF-EM, issued June 28, 2010. Key analysis is offered by Chairwoman Nancy Argenziano, Member Lisa Polak Edgar, Member Nathan A. Skop, Member David E. Klement, and Member Ben A. "Steve" Stevens III that would later foreshadow the financial distress of the GREC PPA.

Sonia Sotomayor's Supreme Court confirmation hearings in which she discusses her childhood legal hero: Reported by Cynthia Dizikes, "Klobuchar, Sotomayor discuss illegal searches, Perry Mason and mothers," *The Minnesota Post*, July 15, 2009.

Ray Washington's reference to Edward Bielarski Jr. as the character Godot: "Waiting for Godot," *Wikipedia*,

Wikimedia Foundation, accessed December 16, 2021, http://en.wikipedia.org/wiki/Waiting_for_Godot.

The independent review of the failures and costs of the GREC PPA: In-depth analysis of GREC PPA, Navigant Consulting (PI) LLC, *Independent Investigative Review of The Gainesville Regional Utilities (GRU)*, San Antonio, Navigant, April 15, 2015.

"As long as they're not Tennessee fans—Georgia, for that matter:" Pegeen Hanrahan quote as memorialized from the transcript of a May 7, 2009, City of Gainesville City Commission meeting where was approved. The agenda item was entitled "Evaluation of Bio-mass Generation Facility Proposals." The transcriber was Lisa D. Freeze, RPR, CFR, Notary Public who worked for Accurate Stenotype Reporters, Inc, Pages 6, line 6.

"It's a 30-year contract:" Ed Regan quote as memorialized from the transcript of a May 7, 2009, City of Gainesville City Commission meeting where was approved. The agenda item was entitled "Evaluation of Bio-mass Generation Facility Proposals." The transcriber was Lisa D. Freeze, RPR, CFR, Notary Public who worked for Accurate Stenotype Reporters, Inc, Pages 12, line 1.

"A little bit about the company:" Ed Regan quote as memorialized from the transcript of a May 7, 2009, City of Gainesville City Commission meeting where was approved. The agenda item was entitled "Evaluation of Bio-mass Generation Facility Proposals." The transcriber was Lisa D. Freeze, RPR, CFR, Notary Public who worked for Accurate Stenotype Reporters, Inc, Pages 12, line 6.

"Tyr Energy:" Ed Regan quote as memorialized from the transcript of a May 7, 2009, City of Gainesville City Commission meeting where was approved. The agenda item was entitled "Evaluation of Bio-mass Generation Facility Proposals." The transcriber was Lisa D. Freeze, RPR, CFR, Notary Public who worked for Accurate Stenotype Reporters, Inc, Pages 12, line 18.

"American Renewables:" Ed Regan quote as memorialized from the transcript of a May 7, 2009, City of Gainesville City Commission meeting where was approved. The agenda item was entitled "Evaluation of Bio-mass Generation Facility Proposals." The transcriber was Lisa D. Freeze, RPR, CFR, Notary Public who worked for Accurate Stenotype Reporters, Inc, Pages 13, line 1.

"We can't do it for that:" Ed Regan quote as memorialized from the transcript of a May 7, 2009, City of Gainesville City Commission meeting where was approved. The agenda item was entitled "Evaluation of Bio-mass Generation Facility Proposals." The transcriber was Lisa D. Freeze, RPR, CFR, Notary Public who worked for Accurate Stenotype Reporters, Inc, Pages 18, line 22.

The Euro-to-dollar ratio: Ed Regan quote as memorialized from the transcript of a May 7, 2009, City of Gainesville City Commission meeting where was approved. The agenda item was entitled "Evaluation of Bio-mass Generation Facility Proposals." The transcriber was Lisa D. Freeze, RPR, CFR, Notary Public who worked for Accurate Stenotype Reporters, Inc, Pages 22, line 11.

"Share the risk through the index period:" Ed Regan quote as memorialized from the transcript of a May 7, 2009, City of Gainesville City Commission meeting where was approved. The agenda item was entitled "Evaluation of Bio-mass Generation Facility Proposals." The transcriber was Lisa D. Freeze, RPR, CFR, Notary Public who worked for Accurate Stenotype Reporters, Inc, Pages 22, line 11.

Ability to negotiate with next highest proposer: *City of Gainesville,* City Commission Meeting Minutes, May 12, 2008.

"We all agreed to go for 100% of the output:" Ed Regan quote as memorialized from the transcript of a May 7, 2009, City of Gainesville City Commission meeting where was approved. The agenda item was entitled "Evaluation of Bio-mass Generation Facility Proposals." The transcriber was Lisa

D. Freeze, RPR, CFR, Notary Public who worked for Accurate Stenotype Reporters, Inc, Pages 39, line 6.

Nacogdoches could have sold 50 MW of power to another utility: Nacogdoches Power, LLC, "Revised Confidential Proposal for Renewable Energy Generation in response to GRU's RFP 2001-135, Biomass Fueled Generation Facility, Aprill 11, 2008, 7 of 80.

"We now have three companies that are lined up for this:" Ed Regan quote as memorialized from the transcript of a May 7, 2009, City of Gainesville City Commission meeting where was approved. The agenda item was entitled "Evaluation of Bio-mass Generation Facility Proposals." The transcriber was Lisa D. Freeze, RPR, CFR, Notary Public who worked for Accurate Stenotype Reporters, Inc, Pages 39, line 17.

"We only pay for the energy they give us:" Ed Regan quote as memorialized from the transcript of a May 7, 2009, City of Gainesville City Commission meeting where was approved. The agenda item was entitled "Evaluation of Bio-mass Generation Facility Proposals." The transcriber was Lisa D. Freeze, RPR, CFR, Notary Public who worked for Accurate Stenotype Reporters, Inc. Pages 25, line 15.

The actual cost of the GREC PPA: Power Purchase Agreement for the Supply of Dependable Capacity, Energy, and Environmental Attributes from a Biomass-fired Power Production Facility by and between Gainesville Renewable Energy Center (GREC) and The City of Gainesville, Florida d/b/a Gainesville Regional Utilities. This document is modified from the original May 9, 2009, agreement to include the Equitable Adjustment and the Final Construction Cost Adjuster.

"Sitting here wishing you guys had negotiated the contract between the County and Shands": Pegeen Hanrahan quote as memorialized from the transcript of a May 7, 2009, City of Gainesville City Commission meeting where was approved. The agenda item was entitled "Evaluation of

Bio-mass Generation Facility Proposals." The transcriber was Lisa D. Freeze, RPR, CFR, Notary Public who worked for Accurate Stenotype Reporters, Inc, Pages 34, line 21.

"It (the plant) will not need to have sulfur controls or any other advanced scrubbers (known as SCR's): Ed Regan quote as memorialized from the transcript of a May 7, 2009, City of Gainesville City Commission meeting where was approved. The agenda item was entitled "Evaluation of Bio-mass Generation Facility Proposals." The transcriber was Lisa D. Freeze, RPR, CFR, Notary Public who worked for Accurate Stenotype Reporters, Inc, Pages 11, line 8.

How the use of scrubbers came to be: In-depth analysis of GREC PPA, Navigant Consulting (PI) LLC, *Independent Investigative Review of The Gainesville Regional Utilities (GRU)*, San Antonio, Navigant, April 15, 2015, 94-105.

First time the use of scrubbers is brought up: Memo from Josh Levine and Len Fagan to Bob Hunzinger, Ed Regan, and John Stanton, "Re: Changes in Regulatory Environment," November 15, 2010.

Agreement from Regan that the move from SNCR to SCR was a change in law: Memo from Josh Levine and Len Fagan to Bob Hunzinger, Ed Regan, and John Stanton, "Re: Changes in Regulatory Environment," November 15, 2010.

Details of Stanton's approach that GRU needed to play hardball: E-mail from John Stanton to Ed Regan, "Re: PDF of Initial Brief in SC10-1512," November 5, 2010.

$105 million cost of scrubbers: In-depth analysis of GREC PPA, Navigant Consulting (PI) LLC, *Independent Investigative Review of The Gainesville Regional Utilities (GRU)*, San Antonio, Navigant, April 15, 2015, 94.

Jennifer Hunt signs Equitable Adjustment: In-depth analysis of GREC PPA, Navigant Consulting (PI) LLC, *Independent Investigative Review of The Gainesville Regional Utilities (GRU)*, San Antonio, Navigant, April 15, 2015, 102.

GREC no longer claiming confidential treatment of the GREC PPA: Letter from John LaVia II with Young Van Assenderp PA to Raymond O. Manasco, Jr, "Re: Gainesville Renewable Energy Center—PPA," Tallahassee, March 30, 2011.

E-line announcement of Equitable Adjustment: In-depth analysis of GREC PPA, Navigant Consulting (PI) LLC, *Independent Investigative Review of The Gainesville Regional Utilities (GRU)*, San Antonio, Navigant, April 15, 2015, 102.

Navigant's conclusions about the Equitable Adjustment: In-depth analysis of GREC PPA, Navigant Consulting (PI) LLC, *Independent Investigative Review of The Gainesville Regional Utilities (GRU)*, San Antonio, Navigant, April 15, 2015, 102-103.

Biomass plant as a shovel-ready job: "Shovel-ready," *Wikipedia*, Wikimedia Foundation, accessed December 17, 2021, http://en.wikipedia.org/wiki/Shovel_ready.

Chapter 4—Pay no attention to the woman behind the curtain:

Discussion/interview notes conducted by Navigant: *GRU Utilities Attorney Shayla McNeill, Commissioner Randy Wells, Commissioner Lauren Poe, Commissioner Helen Warren, Commissioner Craig Carter, Commissioner Yvonne Hinson-Rawls, Commissioner Todd Chase, Mayor Ed Braddy, City Attorney Nicole Shalley, City Litigation Attorney Elizabeth Waratuke, Interim General Manager Kathy Viehe, GRU Purchasing Manager Joann Dorval, GRU Assistant GM John Stanton, GRU Electric System Planning Director Richard Bachmeier, Citizen Group members Jim Konish, Jo Beatty, and Paula Stahmer, GRU Finance Director Mark Benton, GRU Interim CFO David Richardson, IT Manager David Darius, IT Designer Leo Whitman, Ray Washington, GRU Supervising Engineer Rob Klemons, El Paso Electric VP Andy Ramirez, Mycoff Fry and Associates General Manager Scott Fry, GRU Lead Analyst Todd Kamhoot, Former Mayor Craig Lowe, GRU Rates Manager Diane Wilson, and Former GRU GM Robert Hunzinger*

"Vegetarian, bike-riding environmentalist:" *Wikipedia*, Wikimedia Foundation, accessed March 8, 2021, http://en.wikipedia.org/wiki/Pegeen_Hanrahan.

Costs of the Depot Park project and EOC: Edward Bielarski, White Paper—*GRU at a Crossroads: How we got here and what path to take*, Gainesville, February 7, 2019.

GM's remarks at Depot Park opening: Edward Bielarski personal note cards from Depot Park speech.

Hanrahan's "We're so super lucky that you rode in on your white horse" message: From Pegeen Hanrahan to Edward Bielarski on Facebook's Messenger.

GRU's Solar Feed-in-Tariff: From Pegeen Hanrahan's Berlin, Germany presentation.

Excessive costs of Solar FIT contracts: E-mail from Edward Bielarski to Chairman Wes Wheeler and rest of Utility Advisory, "Untitled," Gainesville, February 11, 2021

Quotes and insight on Solar FIT: Sara Peach, *Yale Climate Connections*, "Biomass plant seen as culprit in solar program suspension."

Rachel Meeks as "Rowdy Dangerfield": *Gainesville Roller Rebels,* accessed March 8, 2021, http://gainesvillerollerrebals.com/people/rowdy_dangerfield-411/.

Reverse Robinhood: "Reverse Robinhood," *Urban Dictionary,* accessed December 16, 2021, http://urbandictionary.com.

Understanding Off-Balance Sheet Financing: *Investopedia,* accessed December 17, 2021, http:/Investopedia.com/articles/investing/071513/understanding_offbalance-sheet-financing.asap.

Hanrahan's statements under oath declaring, 1) the credit agencies were concerned with GRU's reliance on fossil fuels, 2) the GREC PPA would not be classified as debt, and 3) the excess power was very marketable: The

Florida Public Service Commission Docket No. 090451-EM, Order No. PSC-10-0409-FOF-EM, issued June 28, 2010.

Pegeen Hanrahan claims that GRU only pays for the energy produced by GREC: "Pegeen Hanrahan: Biomass was and still is a good deal for Gainesville," *The Gainesville Sun*, March 16, 2011.

Hanrahan's "Whether they ran the plant or not" message: From Pegeen Hanrahan to Edward Bielarski on Facebook's Messenger.

Hanrahan is no Churchill: "Winston Churchill's Never Give in Speech," *UWaterloo,* accessed December 17, 2021, http://www.eng.uwaterloo.ca/~jcslee/poetry/Churchill_never_givein.html.

Hanrahan's "Over the long course of time" quote: Sara Peach, *Yale Climate Connections*, "Biomass plant seen as culprit in solar program suspension."

Hanrahan and her comparison to the omnipotent Wizard of Oz: "Pay no attention to the man behind the curtain," Forbes, accessed December 17, 2021, http:/forbes.com/forbestchcouncil/2017/11/08/pay-no-attention-to-the-man-behind-the-curtain-technology-vs-transparancy/.

Hanrahan's "as long as you go around bad mouthing" message: From Pegeen Hanrahan to Edward Bielarski on Facebook's Messenger.

Chapter 5—GRU wasn't my first rodeo:

History and impacts of the Public Utility Regulatory Policy Act (PURPA): David E. Dismukes, PhD, *The Urgency of PURPA Reform to assure Ratepayer Protection*, LSU Center for Energy Studies, August 7, 2019, 2—3.

Gordon and his business enterprises: Wendy Williams and Robert Whitcomb, *Cape Wind: Money, Celebrity, Class, Politics, and the Battle for our Energy Future*, New York, Public Affairs, 2007, 55-57, 64.

Energy Management Inc: "Energy Management Inc," *Wikipedia*, Wikimedia Foundation, accessed March 10, 2021, http://en.wikipedia.org/wiki/Energy_Management_Inc.

The Rich Man, Poor Man reference to compare Bielarski and Gordon: "Rich Man Poor Man (Miniseries)," Wikipedia, Wikimedia Foundation, accessed December 14, 2021, http://en.wikipedia.org/wiki/Rich_Man_Poor_Man_(minise ries).

Centralia Mine Fire: Reported by Leon Bogdan, "Searing chasm was landowners bootleg mine," *Press-Enterprise*, April 15, 1988.

Amil Bielarski's life and times through obituary: "Amil Bielarski," *Legacy.com*, accessed October 2, 2021, http://www.legacy.com/us/obituaries/newsitem/name/amil -bielarski-obituary?pid=87965282.

Bootleg mining: "Bootleg mining, *Wikipedia*, Wikimedia Foundation, accessed October 18, 2021, http://en.wikipedia.org/wiki/Bootleg_mining.

Centralia condemned to destruction: Harry M. Bobonich, PhD, *Big Mine Run: Our home at Woodlands Heights*, Indiana, Author House, 2005, 366.

Enormity of the buildings at Lakeside Ballroom in Barnesville: Reported by John Usalis, "Owner hopes to soon establish Lakeside Ballroom in Ryan Twp," *The Standard Speaker*, February 14, 2020.

Entertainment history of Lakeside Ballroom in Barnesville: Reported by Donald Serfass, "Looking back 133 years," *The Times News*, January 11, 2013.

Jim Gordon—man behind the Cape Wind project: Reported by James Burnett, "Top of Mind: Jim Gordon," *Boston Magazine*, June 25, 2009.

Life and times of Sonny Kovatch: Obituary written by Ron Gower, "Sonny' Kovatch, 85, founder of KME, dies," *The Times News*, January 31, 2011.

Financial crisis facing independent power plant: Reported by Ross Kerber, "Independent Electric Producers are losing the power struggle," *The Wall Street Journal*, August 7, 1996.

Life and times of Chuck Parente: Obituary written by Bob Kalinowski, "Business Chuck Parente remembered as a visionary," *Citizens Voice*, November 9, 2016.

Panther Creek Partner's finances and operations: Offering Memorandum produced by Banc of America Securities, *Carbon County Industrial Development Authority Resource Recovery Revenue Refunding Bonds*, June 21, 2000.

Life and times of William Dimeling: Reported by Joseph DiStefano, "An investment Joyride," *The Philadelphia Inquirer*, April 13, 2003.

Jim Gordon plans after selling natural gas plants: Wendy Williams and Robert Whitcomb, *Cape Wind: Money, Celebrity, Class, Politics, and the Battle for our Energy Future*, New York, Public Affairs, 2007, 68-69.

The Non-Utility Generators (NUGs) fight against EPA over-reach: Reported by the Hazleton Standard Speaker Staff, "Argall hits EPA proposal," *Hazleton Standard Speaker*, March 23, 2000.

Coal Ash debate: Reported by Donald Serfass, "Argall asks governor to intervene," *The Times News*, March 23, 2000.

David Argall's EPA fight: "News Release—Argall urges Feds, Ride to support effort to declare coal-waste ash non-hazardous," Commonwealth of Pennsylvania-Joint Legislative Air and water Pollution Control and Conservation Committee," Harrisburg, March 21, 2000.

Community groundswell against Pennsylvania Department of Environmental Protection's permitting of New York Harbor sludge: Reported by Michael Rubinkam, "Environmentalist back plan for PA Mine," *Associated Press*, March 2003.

Dante Picciano and Love Canal: Reported by Joanne Omang, "Stirrings of Life Return to Love Canal," *The Washington Post*, November 9, 1981.

Power industry's rebuttal against Dante's Army: Editorial written by Edward Bielarski, "Letters from our readers: Picciano- white knight or someone with agenda?" *The Times News*, June 30, 2003.

Kennedy Gordon debate: Wendy Williams and Robert Whitcomb, *Cape Wind: Money, Celebrity, Class, Politics, and the Battle for our Energy Future*, New York, Public Affairs, 2007, 118-120.

Chapter 6—The Great Allentown Water Fight:

History of Hess's Department Stores: Frank A. Whelan and Kurt D. Zwikl, *Hess Department Store*, Charleston, Arcadia Publishing, 2008, 7-9.

History of Max Hess's mansion in Allentown: Reported by Staff writer, "8 reasons why the Hess's mansion fits the lifestyle of the rich and famous," *Capital Gazette*, January 5, 2016.

History of Hess Department stores—part 2: "Hess's," *Wikipedia*, Wikimedia Foundation, accessed December 20, 2021, http://en.wikipedia.org/wiki/Hess%27s.

Growth in Lehigh Valley under Aurel Arndt's tenure: Reported by Tom Shortell, "Lehigh Valley water official calls it a career after 41 years," *The Morning Call*, December 27, 2015.

Lehigh County Authority's finances and operation: "Offering Memorandum," produced by Goldman Sachs and Company, *Lehigh County Authority Water and Sewer Revenue Bonds*, July 31, 2013.

Official request for qualification for Water and Sewer Concession: Allentown City Staff, *Allentown Water and Sewer System: Request for Qualifications for Water and Sewer Concession*, July 19, 2012.

Mayor Pawlowski's case to lease Allentown's water and sewer system: Reported by Gregg Bortz, "Allentown city council hears case for proposed lease of water and sewer system," *The Express-Times*, January 3, 2019.

Life and times of Allentown's Mayor: "Ed Pawlowski," *Wikipedia*, Wikimedia Foundation, accessed March 8, 2021, http://en.wikipedia.org/wiki/Ed_Pawlowski.

Lehigh County Commission's failure to vote on lease concession: Reported by Samantha Marcus, "No decision on Lehigh County Authority extension," *The Morning Call*, February 27, 2013.

Early indications that upfront payment can go beyond $200 million: E-mail from Edward Bielarski to Aurel Arndt describing value of Allentown's water and sewer system, "Untitled," Gainesville, March 20, 2013.

$1.5 billion in free cash flow: E-mail from Edward Bielarski to Brad Landon describing value of Allentown's water and sewer system, "Untitled," Allentown, March 23, 2013.

Proposed lease concession bid proposal: Goldman Sachs' staff, "Allentown System Concession Financing Considerations," Goldman Sachs, New York, March 26, 2013.

Lehigh County Authority's decision to bid on lease concession: Reported by Samantha Marcus, "Lehigh County Authority to bid on Allentown water, sewer lease," *The Morning Call*, March 26, 2013.

Upfront bid of $220 million: E-mail from Edward Bielarski to staff referencing the KKR model, "Untitled, Allentown, March 30, 2013.

Disclosure of bid to board members: E-mail from Edward Bielarski to Norma Cusick answering questions posed by board members, "Untitled," Allentown, March 31, 2013.

First-round bids results: E-mail from Brad Landon to Richard Bohner, based on Scott Shearer's thoughts, "Untitled," Allentown, April 3, 2013.

Congratulatory remarks: E-mail from Mike Jarmin to Edward Bielarski, "Re: News as it happens," Harrisburg, April 3, 2013.

Congratulatory remarks: E-mail from Richard Bohner to Edward Bielarski, "Untitled," Allentown, April 3, 2013.

E-mail acknowledgement of Edward Bielarski's accomplishment in securing Lease concession: E-mail from Liesel Adams to Edward Bielarski, "Couple Thoughts,' Allentown, April 5, 2013.

Allentown's public reaction to lease concession: Reported by Emily Opilo, "Allentown City Council approves water/sewer lease," *The Morning Call*, April 26, 2013.

Last-minute dispute between Allentown and Lehigh County Authority: E-mail from Asa Hughes to Edward Bielarski, "Re: 7_25—Interest Rate Protocol and Closing Date Extension Side Letter," Allentown, July 26, 2013.

Confirmation of Bielarski's actions by Lehigh County Authority's Chairman of the Board: E-mail from Tom Muller to Edward Bielarski, "Re: 7_25—Interest Rate Protocol and Closing Date Extension Side Letter," Allentown, July 27, 2013.

Official turnover of city assets: Reported by Brian Pederson, "LCA officially takes reins of Allentown water today, puts caps on rate hikes," *Lehigh Valley Business*, August 8, 2013.

Impact of interest-rate protection: Reported by Samantha Marcus, "Allentown water-sewer lease commands $9 million less than expected," *The Morning Call*, August 6, 2013.

Deal of the Year announcement: Bond Buyer staff, "The Bond Buyer announces finalists for 12th annual deal of the year awards," *Bond Buyer*, November 8, 2013.

Details of the lease concession impacts: Jeff Hughes and Carol Rosenfeld, *Allentown Water and Wastewater Utility*

Concession, UNC Environmental Finance Center, October 2016, 3.

Details of lease concession impacts: Dilworth and Paxson staff, "Press Release—Allentown financings with Bond Buyer Northeast Deal of the Year," Philadelphia, November 4, 2013.

National gala honoring the lease concession: Reported by Stacy Wescoe, "Allentown bond transaction to be honored at national gala," *Lehigh Valley Business*, November 7, 2013.

Consequences of the lease concession: Reported by John Tierney, "The city that turned its water into cash," *The Atlantic*, September 22, 2014.

Koch thinks Cape Wind will be visual pollution: Reported by Katharine Seelye, "Koch Brothers wages 12-year fight over wind farm," *The New York Times*, October 22, 2013. 1.

"I'm not working on a plantation:" Reported by Bruce Mohl, "Jim Gordon: Am I a true believer? Absolutely," *Commonwealth Magazine*, April 9, 2013. 15.

Chapter 7—A Swamp Yankee:

Swamp Yankee reference: "Swamp Yankee," *Wikipedia*, Wikimedia Foundation, accessed December 20, 2021, http://en.wikipedia.org/wiki/Swamp_Yankee.

Stories of previous GRU general managers: GRU's Communications staff, GRU *History Manuscript*, Gainesville Regional Utilities, 45 -47.

First GM staff meeting: Recorded by Edward Bielarski, *Diary of Edward Bielarski, Volume 1: June 22, 2015, through August 4, 2015*, June 22, 2015, Bielarski Personal library.

Talking Points for Carlos Holt memo sent from David Richardson to Carlos Holt, written on May 4, 2015, warning Holt of consequences of failure to make GREC PPA payments, delivered subsequently to General Manager: Recorded by Edward Bielarski, *Diary of Edward*

Bielarski, Volume 1: June 22, 2015, through August 4, 2015, June 25, 2015, Bielarski Personal library.

John Stanton as Joe Friday: Recorded by Edward Bielarski, *Diary of Edward Bielarski, Volume 1: June 22, 2015, through August 4, 2015*, June 25, 2015, Bielarski Personal library.

Follow-up memo reiterating the potential consequences of ceasing payments to GREC: Memo from David Richardson to Edward Bielarski, "Potential Consequences of Ceasing Payments to GREC," June 29, 2015.

$24 million competitiveness gap: Recorded by Edward Bielarski, *Diary of Edward Bielarski, Volume 1: June 22, 2015, through August 4, 2015*, June 26, 2015, Bielarski Personal library.

Handwritten note from John Stanton stating "Ed, I drafted these portions of the GREC PPA:" Copy from John Stanton to Edward Bielarski, "Untitled," July 1, 2015.

Full "I want to compliment John on that" quote: Ed Regan quote as memorialized from the transcript of a May 7, 2009, City of Gainesville City Commission meeting where was approved. The agenda item was entitled "Evaluation of Bio-mass Generation Facility Proposals." The transcriber was Lisa D. Freeze, RPR, CFR, Notary Public who worked for Accurate Stenotype Reporters, Inc. Pages 34, line 8-18.

Richardson didn't have qualifications for CFO position as expressed by City HR director: Recorded by Edward Bielarski, *Diary of Edward Bielarski, Volume 1: June 22, 2015, through August 4, 2015*, July 1, 2015, Bielarski Personal library.

Note about phone call with Jim Gordon, in which *Comedians in Cars getting Coffee* was mentioned: Recorded by Edward Bielarski, *Diary of Edward Bielarski, Volume 1: June 22, 2015, through August 4, 2015*, July 1, 2015, Bielarski Personal library.

GM's first city commission meeting and introduction to Keith Perry and Goston's comment about folks needing a checkup from the neck up: Recorded by Edward

Bielarski, *Diary of Edward Bielarski, Volume 1: June 22, 2015, through August 4, 2015*, July 2, 2015, Bielarski Personal library.

Full "Keep GREC at full load" quote and reference: "Affidavit of John Stanton," City of Gainesville, May 31, 2016. 4.

Full "Run and break plant" quote and reference: "Affidavit of John Stanton," City of Gainesville, May 31, 2016. 4.

Stanton commented that he was criticized by members of City Commission and general public rightly or wrongly: "Affidavit of John Stanton," City of Gainesville, May 31, 2016. 1.

$2 million could be saved by dispatching GREC: Memo from John Stanton to Edward Bielarski, "Impact of GREC Dispatch on System Production Cost," July 10, 2015..

Stanton's memorialization of a discussion he had with City Commissioner about breaking GREC: Memo from John Stanton to City Commissioner Todd Chase, "Re: Our discussion of April 2, 2015, on the topic of 'Breaking GREC,'" Undated.

30-day anniversary at GRU—Top 10 Initiatives: Recorded by Edward Bielarski, *Diary of Edward Bielarski, Volume 1: June 22, 2015, through August 4, 2015*, July 23, 2015, Bielarski Personal library.

Full "The contract doesn't pass the smell (sniff) test" quote and context: "Affidavit of John Stanton," City of Gainesville, May 31, 2016. 5.

GRU's new leadership team appointments: Staff, "GRU shakes up executive team," *Business Report of North Central Florida*, October 5, 2015.

Stanton's communication with City Commissioners with possible opportunity to reduce GREC fixed cost: Letter from John Stanton to Ed Bielarski, Mayor, City Commission, and Carlos Holt, "Possible Opportunity to Reduce GREC Fixed Cost," Gainesville, August 6, 2015.

August 7, 2015, meeting in which John Stanton was asked to resign: "Notes from 11:30 AM meeting on Friday,

August 7, 2015, between John Stanton, Lewis Walton, Kathy Viehe, and Edward Bielarski," Gainesville, August 7, 2015.

Kathy Viehe's notes on Stanton's August 7, 2015, meeting: "Kathy Viehe Notes of Meeting between John Stanton and Ed Bielarski: Friday, August 7," Gainesville, August 7, 2015.

Lewis Walton's notes on Stanton's August 7, 2015, meeting: "Summary of Ed Bielarski meeting with John Stanton- Kathy Viehe in attendance as well," Gainesville, August 7, 2015.

Chapter 8—An Act of God:

GREC's limited number of shutdowns events: Recorded by Edward Bielarski, *Diary of Edward Bielarski, Volume 1: June 22, 2015, through August 4, 2015*, July 21, 2015, Bielarski Personal library.

First GM meeting with Winston and Strawn concerning representation in PPA agreement matters: Recorded by Edward Bielarski, *Diary of Edward Bielarski, Volume 1: June 22, 2015, through August 4, 2015*, July 24, 2015, Bielarski Personal library.

Contentious GM meeting with Albert Morales: Recorded by Edward Bielarski, *Diary of Edward Bielarski, Volume 2: August 5, 2015, through October 10, 2015*, August 5, 2015, Bielarski Personal library.

Morales believed I was creating a public ruckus: Memo to File by Albert Morales, "Re: Meeting with Ed Bielarski on 8.5.15," Gainesville, August 17, 2015.

Instructions that were given upon GREC's request to come back on-line: Details from John Stanton's logbook recovered during discovery during Arbitration, Gainesville, August 7—8.

Costs of GREC dispatch: Memo from John Stanton to Edward Bielarski, "Subject: Impact of GREC Dispatch on System Production Cost," Gainesville, July 19, 2015.

Conversation between Jim Gordon and Edward Bielarski immediately after the act of God: Recorded by Edward Bielarski, *Diary of Edward Bielarski, Volume 2: August 5, 2015, through October 10, 2015*, August 10, 2015, Bielarski Personal library.

Public support for GM's actions on August 7: Reported by Nathan Crabbe, "Editorial: Making the best out of biomass," *The Gainesville Sun*, September 1, 2015.

Public Support—part 2: Reported by Morgan Watkins, "Manager praised for call to not buy power," *The Gainesville Sun*, August 8, 2015.

Public Support—part 3: Reported by Morgan Watkins, "Power play puts biomass plant on pause," *The Gainesville Sun*, August 13, 2015.

Playing hardball on GREC's return to generation: Reported by April Warren, "GRU in no hurry to buy power from biomass plant," *The Gainesville Sun*, August 28, 2015.

Utility Advisory Board (UAB) is formed: Reported by April Warren, "City gives initial thumbs up to," *The Gainesville Sun*, November 5, 2015.

Citizen protests former Mayor Hanrahan: Reported by Hunter Williamson, "Gainesville residents protest biomass plant," *The Florida Alligator*, August 31, 2016

Anthony Lyons introduced as the new city manager: E-mail from Helen Harris to City of Gainesville employees, "Subject: Hello from Interim City Manager," Gainesville, November 12, 2015.

GREC's Demand for Arbitration: Memo from Ed Bielarski to Mayor Ed Braddy and City Commission, "Subject: GREC's Demand for Arbitration," Gainesville, December 23, 2015.

Idea of a biomass buyout is disclosed: Reported by Hunter Williamson, "City discusses buying biomass plant," *The Florida Alligator*, January 8, 2016.

Disputed funds of $223,000 are returned to GREC: Reported by April Warren, "GRU agrees to pay back $223 K, discusses purchase of biomass plant," *The Gainesville Sun*, December 28, 2015.

Chapter 9—Know thy enemy:

Gainesville's version of Comedians in Cars Getting Coffee: "Comedians in Cars Getting Coffee," *Wikipedia*, Wikimedia Foundation, accessed December 29, 2021, http://en.wikipedia.org/wiki/Comedians_in_Cars_Getting_Coffee.

Gordon's demeanor and style fit the part of a formidable businessperson: Williams and Robert Whitcomb, *Cape Wind: Money, Celebrity, Class, Politics, and the Battle for our Energy Future*, New York, Public Affairs, 2007, 8-9.

Insight into Edward Bielarski: Reported by Chris Eversole, "Get to know: New GRU GM Edward Bielarski," Business in the Heart of Florida, August 1, 2015.

GM's request for renegotiation of GREC PPA: Staff reporter, "GRU's GM asks for biomass renegotiations," *WCJB*, August 4, 2015.

Thumbnail sketch of Gordon by people who knew him: Reported by Stephanie Ebbert, "Wind + Energy- Executive has both, as he tries to sell his wind farm," *Boston Globe*, November 15, 2004.

Recollections about Jim Gordon's life when he was known as Toughie and Cool Hand Luke: Wendy Williams and Robert Whitcomb, *Cape Wind: Money, Celebrity, Class, Politics, and the Battle for our Energy Future*, New York, Public Affairs, 2007, 54.

Epiphany in 1970's long gas lines: Reported by Bruce Mohl, "Jim Gordon: Am I a true believer? Absolutely," *Commonwealth Magazine*, April 9, 2003.

Gordon's success in cable television industry: Reported by Stephanie Ebbert, "Wind + Energy- Executive has both, as he tries to sell his wind farm," *Boston Globe*, November 15, 2004.

EMI was pioneer in natural gas and renewable plants: Reported by Bruce Mohl, "Jim Gordon: Am I a true believer? Absolutely," *Commonwealth Magazine*, April 9, 2003.

Foes of Cape Wind: Reported by Doug Struck, "The dogged, dauntless determination of Jim Gordon," The Daily Climate, October 13, 2014.

Full "Three of our natural gas-fired power plants killed three coal plants" quote with context: Reported by Bruce Mohl, "Jim Gordon: Am I a true believer? Absolutely," *Commonwealth Magazine*, April 9, 2003.

The test of a first-rate intelligence: *"F. Scott Fitzgerald: Quotes,"* " PBS.org," accessed October 2, 2021, http://www.pbs.org/wnet/americanmasters/f-scott-fitzgerald-essay-the-crack-up/1028/.

Gordon's early days establishing himself in energy industry: Reported by Stephanie Ebbert, "Wind + Energy- Executive has both, as he tries to sell his wind farm," *Boston Globe*, November 15, 2004.

Nacogdoches power project in Austin, Texas: Staff, "Nacogdoches Wood-Fired Power Project," *Power Technology*, April 10, 2013.

Full "Koch says you are a developer in love with his project" quote and context: Reported by Bruce Mohl, "Jim Gordon: Am I a true believer? Absolutely," *Commonwealth Magazine*, April 9, 2003.

Gordon's mother, Florence reflects on Jimmy (Gordon's brother): Reported by Stephanie Ebbert, "Wind + Energy- Executive has both, as he tries to sell his wind farm," *Boston Globe*, November 15, 2004.

Full "We've put in more than $65 million" quote and context about Gordon's investment in Cape Wind: Reported by Bruce Mohl, "Jim Gordon: Am I a true believer? Absolutely," *Commonwealth Magazine*, April 9, 2003.

Gordon influencing Walter Cronkite story: Reported by Bruce Mohl, "Jim Gordon: Am I a true believer? Absolutely," *Commonwealth Magazine*, April 9, 2003.

Quotes from Glenn Wattley and William Moonmaw, along with the financial pressures on Jim Gordon financially and emotionally: Reported by Wayne Drash, "The wind man who beat Cape Cod's elite," *CNN*, April 29, 2010.

Chapter 10—Secret agent man:

John Stanton announces future retirement on April 28, 2017: E-mail from John Stanton to Ed Bielarski, "Subject: Separation from GRU," Gainesville, October 19, 2015.

Full "John Stanton is not authorized to make changes to the four corners of the PPA," quote and context: "Petition in the Circuit Court of the Eighth Judicial Circuit in and for Alachua County, Florida," Case No: 01-2016-AP-0015, July 18, 2016, 3.

"Why buy the biomass plant:" Editorial by Edward Bielarski, "Edward Bielarski: Why buy the biomass plant," *The Gainesville Sun*, January 7, 2016.

Stanton puts a value on GREC and their damages: White paper written by John Stanton, "White paper— Questions about GREC," Gainesville, January 1, 2016.

Reference to being hoisted with his own petard: "Hoist with his own petard," *Wikipedia*, Wikimedia Foundation, accessed September 23, 2021, http://en.wikipedia.org/wiki/Hoist_with_his_own_petard.

Full context of "I have the letter from Len canceling the outage" quote: E-mail from John Stanton to Eric Walters, Dino DeLeo, and Shayla McNeill, "Re: GREC Outage Correspondence," Gainesville, February 3, 2016.

Full context of "GREC plans no Maintenance or Planned outages in 2016" quote: Memo from Leonard

Fagan to John Stanton, "Subject: Notice of Maintenance Schedule 2016," Gainesville, October 14, 2015.

Stanton's acknowledgement of outage cancellation: E-mail from John Stanton to Carolyn Wasdin, "RE: Notice of GREC 2016 Maintenance Schedule," Gainesville, October 15, 2016.

"If there is to be blame, it should be on me" with context: E-mail from John Stanton to Eric Walters, Dino DeLeo, and Shayla McNeill, "Re: GREC Outage Correspondence," Gainesville, February 3, 2016.

"This is unacceptable behavior for any employee of GRU, much less the Energy Supply Officer" with context: "Petition in the Circuit Court of the Eighth Judicial Circuit in and for Alachua County, Florida," Case No: 01-2016-AP-0015, July 18, 2016, 7.

"I offered that I felt that nothing is more operational than planning" with context: "Affidavit of John Stanton," City of Gainesville, May 31, 2016, 8.

"You continue to show me that you don't grasp the magnitude of the situation" with context: "Petition in the Circuit Court of the Eighth Judicial Circuit in and for Alachua County, Florida," Case No: 01-2016-AP-0015, July 18, 2016, 8.

"Stanton's actions clearly constituted subordination:" "Petition in the Circuit Court of the Eighth Judicial Circuit in and for Alachua County, Florida," Case No: 01-2016-AP-0015, July 18, 2016, 8.

Mayor Braddy loses mayoral race: Reporting by April Warren, "Lauren Poe unseats Ed Braddy as mayor of Gainesville," *The Gainesville Sun*, March 15, 2016.

"In the latest row…:" Reported by Mickie Anderson, "GRU, biomass plant battle gets uglier," *The Gainesville Sun*, July 30, 2016.

GREC claims were without merit: Reported by Mickie Anderson, "GRU, biomass plant battle gets uglier," *The Gainesville Sun*, July 30, 2016.

"GRU does not operate the facility" and more context: Reported by Mickie Anderson, "GRU, biomass plant battle gets uglier," *The Gainesville Sun*, July 30, 2016.

Stanton's recollections of City and GRU officials trying to break the plant: Reported by Mickie Anderson, "GRU, biomass plant battle gets uglier," *The Gainesville Sun*, July 30, 2016.

Alerting GREC that commission wants to make it hard for GREC to do business: E-mail of Albert Morales' e-mailed Note to File, "RE: Conversation with John Stanton," Boston, October 1, 2014.

Alerting GREC that GRU would dispatch the plant offline for economic reasons: Jim Gordon's e-mailed Memo to File, "GREC: Memo to the file," Boston, April 19, 2015.

Alerting GREC that things were getting crazy at GRU: Jim Gordon's e-mailed Memo to File, "GREC: Memo to the file," Boston, April 19, 2015.

Alerting GREC that Bielarski knows how to inflict damage on a NUG: Albert Morales' e-mailed Memo to File, "RE: Conversation with John Stanton," Boston, May 12, 2015.

Alerting GREC that commission is out for blood: Albert Morales' e-mailed Memo to File, "RE: Conversation with John Stanton," Boston, May 12, 2015.

Alerting GREC that Carlos Holt is full of piss and vinegar: Albert Morales' e-mailed Memo to File, "RE: Conversation with John Stanton," Boston, June 17, 2015.

Carlos Holt's background and character: Reported by April Warren, "Carlos Holt making his mark," The Gainesville Sun, October 3, 2015.

Alerting GREC that City is making GREC out to be the problem: Albert Morales' e-mailed Memo to File, "RE: Conversation with John Stanton 8/26/15," Boston, August 26, 2015.

Sharing news with GREC about an FDLE investigation into Jeff McAdams: Albert Morales' e-mailed

Memo to File, "RE: Conversation with John Stanton today," Boston, December 1, 2015.

Full "I am looking around for other interesting opportunities" quote and context: John Stanton's e-mail to Jim Gordon in which he appears to be currying favor to further his job opportunities, "Subject: Fwd," Gainesville, December 14, 2015.

Full "Today is the day" quote: E-mail from John Stanton to Jim Gordon, "Today is the day…" Gainesville, March 10, 2016.

Details of an alleged elevator conversation between John Stanton and GRU GM: E-mail from John Stanton to Jim Gordon, "Untitled," Gainesville, April 5, 2016.

"EB had fired or marginalized everyone" with context: Albert Morales' e-mailed Memo to File, "RE: Dinner with John Stanton," Boston, April 21, 2016.

Reference to the lyrics of Secret Agent Man: "Johnny Rivers," The Lyrics Library, accessed December 30, 2021, http://www.mathematik.uni-ulm.de/paul/lyrics/johnnyrivers/secret-1.html.

Stanton sharing contacts for Kathy Viehe, David Richardson, and John Stanton: E-mail from John Stanton to Jim, "Untitled" Gainesville, May 3, 2016.

Available energy hasn't been available: Memo from Edward Bielarski to Jim Gordon, "Untitled," Gainesville, October 31, 2016.

Gordon's warning that I was escalating the battle: Letter from Jim Gordon to Edward Bielarski, "Re: GRU Threat to deny GREC Available Energy Payments due under the PPA," Boston, November 9, 2016.

Thoughts culled from the timeline of events submitted by John Stanton during his disciplinary hearing: Written by John Stanton, "Timeline," Gainesville, undated.

Who is Carlos Holt? Reported by April Warren, "Carlos Holt is making his mark," *The Gainesville Sun*, October 3, 2015.

<u>**Chapter 11—All the world's a stage:**</u>

The deal first put on the table: Letter from Rich McCarty to James Robertson, "Subject: Mediation—GREC v. GRU—GRU Courier—Settlement Discussions only, pursuant to Fla. Stat. Section 90.408," Houston, December 1, 2016.

2013 low-ball offer to Gordon: Draft of GREC Right of First Offer (ROFO) Notice. October 21, 2013.

Financial template for a deal: Presentation from Goldman Sachs to GRU on the potential buyout of the GREC PPA, "Presentation to GRU: GREC Considerations," Gainesville, December 21, 2016.

Goldman model sent to Gordon: E-mail from Edward Bielarski to Jim Gordon sharing Goldman Sachs' analysis with GREC, "Subject: Goldman analysis," Gainesville, December 28, 2016.

Gordon's written affirmation of acceptable price: E-mail from Jim Gordon to Edward Bielarski in which he presents a buyout range, "Subject: Re: Response to revised MOU from GREC," Gainesville, March 15, 2017.

Details and history of the Cape Wind project: "Cape Wind" *Wikipedia*, Wikimedia Foundation, accessed January 22, 2021, http://en.wikipedia.org/wiki/Cape_Wind

I should argue with a billionaire: David Rubenstein, *How to Lead: Wisdom from the World' Greatest CEOs, Founders, and Game Changers,* New York, Simon, and Schuster, 2020, 3.

First offer to buy GREC PPA: Reported by Andrew Caplan, "GRU offers $750M to buy biomass plant from GREC," *The Gainesville Sun*, February 24, 2017.

First public viewing of the buyout path: White paper from Edward Bielarski, White Paper—*Blueprint to a Buyout*, Gainesville, March 1, 2017.

Chapter 12 –No one is gonna pave over this paradise:

Phone conversations of March 1, 2017, between Edward Bielarski and Jim Gordon: Recorded by Edward Bielarski, *Diary of Edward Bielarski, Volume 7: December 12, 2016, through March 13, 2017*, March 1, 2017, Bielarski Personal library.

Phone conversations of March 3, 2017, between Edward Bielarski and Jim Gordon: Recorded by Edward Bielarski, *Diary of Edward Bielarski, Volume 7: December 12, 2016, through March 13, 2017*, March 3, 2017, Bielarski Personal library.

References to scenes in the movie *Tin Cup:* "Tin Cup" *Wikipedia*, Wikimedia Foundation, accessed December 30, 2021, http://en.wikipedia.org/wiki/Tin_Cup.

Full "You don't know what you got 'til it's gone" song lyrics and context: E-mail from Edward Bielarski to Jim Gordon, "Big Yellow Taxi" are invoked, "MOU revision," Gainesville, March 5, 2017.

Gordon sends executed MOU to GRU: E-mail from Jim Gordon to Edward Bielarski, "Subject: Executed GREC/GRU MOU," Boston, March 9, 2017.

$750 million offer is dropped to $725 million: Reported by Andrew Caplan, "GRU reduces GREC offer by $25M," *The Gainesville Sun*, March 7, 2017.

Informed commission about major sticking points in negotiations: E-mail from Edward Bielarski to City Commission, "Subject: Resend of executed GREC/GRU MOU," Gainesville, March 10, 2017.

Gordon's compromise on 7 major items in deal: E-mail from Jim Gordon to Edward Bielarski, "Subject: Re: Responses to revised MOU from GREC," Boston, March 13, 2017.

Invoked lyrics from Kenny Roger's *The Gambler.* E-mail from Edward Bielarski to Jim Gordon, "Subject:

Response to revised MOU from GREC," Boston, March 14, 2017.

Gordon's agreement on 50 basis-point out clause: E-mail from Jim Gordon to Edward Bielarski, "Subject: Re: Response to revised MOU from GREC," Gainesville, March 15, 2017.

My name is Eddie B cool: E-mail from Ray Washington to Edward Bielarski, "Untitled," Gainesville, March 11, 2017.

Jeers for GRU's secrecy: Reported by Nathan Crabbe, "Editorial: Cheers for BRAND, jeers for GRU's secrecy," *The Gainesville Sun*, March 3, 2017.

"Uhh… Khaki's:" "What are you wearing, Jake from State Farm," *Carta*, accessed December 31, 2021, http://carta.flu.edu/gasc_creative/2014/06/15/what-are-you-wearing-jake-from-state-farm/.

Bridge over troubled water memo: E-mail from Edward Bielarski to Jim Gordon, "Subject: GRU MOU rev 6.docx," Gainesville, March 15, 2017.

Gordon agrees to allow GRU to retain full number of withholdings: E-mail from Jim Gordon to Edward Bielarski, "Subject: Response to revised MOU," Gainesville, March 15, 2017

"I don't think you fully appreciate my viewpoint here," and other quotes: E-mail from Edward Bielarski to Jim Gordon, "Subject: Re: GREC-GRU MOU rev 7.docx," Gainesville, March 15, 2017.

"Sittin' in the mornin' sun" with other quotes and context: E-mail from Edward Bielarski to Jim Gordon, "Subject: GREC—GRU MOU rev 8.docx," Gainesville, March 18, 2017.

"What we have here is a failure to communicate" with other quotes and context: E-mail from Edward Bielarski to Jim Gordon, "Subject: Response to latest revision," Gainesville, March 20, 2017.

Executed Memorandum of Understanding: "Memorandum of Understanding regarding Gainesville Renewable Energy Center Facility," Gainesville, March 22, 2017.

"So good, so good, so good:" E-mail from Edward Bielarski to Jim Gordon, "Subject: MOU," Gainesville, March 22, 2017.

Chapter 13—No MOU for YOU:

GRU, GREC agree to buyout: Reported by Andrew Caplan, "GRU, GREC agree to buyout," *The Gainesville Sun*, March 23, 2017.

"Déjà vu" with other quotes and context: Reported by Andrew Caplan, "City holds off on MOU vote," *The Gainesville Sun*, March 24, 2017.

"You need to negotiate from strength not weakness" with other quotes and context: Reported by Andrew Caplan, "Alachua Co. commissioners urge city to rethink biomass deal," *The Gainesville Sun*, March 23, 2017.

"Your guide to Gainesville's Guide to buy GREC:" Reported by Andrew Caplan, "Biomass Basics: Your guide to Gainesville's deal to buy GREC," *The Gainesville Sun*, April 2, 2017.

The case for the GREC buyout: Editorial by Edward Bielarski, "Ed Bielarski: The case for buying the biomass plant," *The Gainesville Sun*, April 2, 2017.

UAB recommends a drop in price from $750 to $675 million: Reported by Andrew Caplan, "UAB recommends changes to biomass MOU," *The Gainesville Sun*, April 6, 2017.

"We're playing chicken with no seatbelts on" with other quotes and context: Reported by Andrew Caplan, "City takes UAB advice on pact," *The Gainesville Sun*, April 6, 2017.

The referendum bill passes Florida House vote: Reported by Andrew Caplan, "GRU bill passes final House committee," *The Gainesville Sun*, April 13, 2017.

City Commission votes 5 to 2 for the MOU: Reported by Andrew Caplan, "City approves $750 mm offer for GREC," *The Gainesville Sun*, April 20, 2017.

Gordon executes the MOU: Reporting of the MOU acceptance process from Andrew Caplan, "GREC OK's City $750 biomass proposal," *The Gainesville Sun*, April 21, 2017.

Chapter 14—GRU Plays a Weak Hand Strong:

The first draft of Asset Purchase Agreement (APA) is delivered: Reported by Andrew Caplan, "1ˢᵗ draft of GREC contract delivered," *The Gainesville Sun*, May 11, 2017.

"GREC played a weak hand strong" with other quotes and context: Editorial by Darin Cook, "Darin Cook: Price is too high for biomass plant," *The Gainesville Sun*, June 8, 2017.

"Quotes from June 13ᵗʰ GREC, GRU forum:" Report by David Hoffman, "GRU-GREC panel discusses buyout, audience voices concerns," *The Florida Alligator*, June 15, 2017.

Gainesville Sun supports buyout: Editorial by Gainesville Editorial Board, "Editorial: Buying plant still looks like best bet," *The Gainesville Sun*, June 18, 2017.

List of deal-killers: Recorded by Edward Bielarski, *Diary of Edward Bielarski, Volume 7: March 20, 2017, through October 23, 2017*, June 16, 2017, Bielarski Personal library.

The pathway to the final deal: Recorded by Edward Bielarski, *Diary of Edward Bielarski, Volume 7: March 20, 2017, through October 23, 2017*, July 6, 2017, Bielarski Personal library.

Cape Wind is gone with the wind: From Katharine Seelye, "After 16 Years, Hopes for Cape Cod Wind Farm Float Away," *The New York Times*, December 19, 2017.

"We've put our disagreements behind us" with other quotes and context: Reported by Andrew Caplan, "GRU,

GREC agree on contract, need city approval," *The Gainesville Sun*, August 11, 2017.

"It's not as though this is brand new to us" with other quotes and context: Reported by Andrew Caplan, "City, UAB postpone biomass decision," *The Gainesville Sun*, August 17, 2017.

Buyout is a turning point for GRU: Editorial by Edward Bielarski, "Ed Bielarski: Biomass purchase is turning point for GRU," *The Gainesville Sun*, August 18, 2017.

Primer for why the Buyout makes sense: Reported by Andrew Caplan, "Biomass buyout takes some big steps this week," *The Gainesville Sun*, August 21, 2017.

"Commission lost its resolve" with other quotes and context: Editorial by from Darin Cook, "Darin Cook: Recommending biomass buyout was difficult decision," *The Gainesville Sun*, August 24, 2017.

The events of the August 24th City Commission meeting: Reported by Andrew Caplan, "City approves $750 million purchase of GREC contract," *The Gainesville Sun*, August 24, 2017.

The Asset Purchase Agreement (APA) is approved: Reported by Andrew Caplan, "City gives final OK for biomass plant," *The Gainesville Sun*, September 7, 2017.

Details concerning the preliminary pricing of the 2017 Series A bond financings: E-mail from Yamini Kalidini to Edward Bielarski, "Subject: FW: Gainesville Regional Utilities**Preliminary Pricing until 11 AM ET**," New York, October 24, 2017.

The Buyout is completed: Reported by Andrew Caplan, "Controversial Purchase," *The Gainesville Sun*, November 7, 2017.

The Buyout begins a new era: Editorial by Edward Bielarski, Biomass plant purchase begins new era for GRU," *The Gainesville Sun*, November 12, 2017.

Chapter 15—Keep GRU Local

New Era off to rocky start: Reported by Andrew Caplan, "Editorial: Rough start for GRU's new era," *The Gainesville Sun*, December 12, 2017.

Context surrounding the day after the failed termination attempt: Speech by Edward Bielarski, Speech to UAB, UAB Public Meeting, Gainesville, December 8, 2017.

Size of GFT problem: Edward Bielarski, *GRU's comprehensive response to AG's Audit Team*, Gainesville, undated.

Clemons Referendum Bill history and challenge: Reported by Andrew Caplan, "Control of Gainesville's utility decided in November referendum," *The Gainesville Sun*, October 18, 2018.

Clemons Referendum Bill 759: Florida Legislature, 2017 Session, History of House Bills, CS/HB759.

Makeup of UAB-post Darin Cook: Fletcher Crowe, White Paper—*Outline of Proposed UAB recommendations for the GRU 2022 IRP*, Gainesville, March 1, 2021, attachment 1.

GRU's 2019 Integrated Resource Plan: Written by Gainesville Regional Utilities and TEA, *GRU IRP Final Results*, Gainesville, July 17, 2019.

GM addressing UAB's misunderstanding about GRU's mission: E-mail from Edward Bielarski to UAB members, "Untitled," Gainesville, January 21, 2021.

UAB Chair Wendell Porter's vision for GRU: Handout from Wendell Porter to UAB and Edward Bielarski, "Written notes of comments made at 1/26/2021 UAB Meeting," Gainesville, January 26, 2021.

UAB Co-chair Wes Wheeler's vision for GRU: Handout from Wes Wheeler to UAB and Edward Bielarski, "Written notes of comments made at 1/26/2021 UAB Meeting," Gainesville, January 26, 2021.

GM's responses to Co-chair Wheeler: E-mail from Edward Bielarski, to UAB and City Commission, "GM's response to Member Wheeler's comments," Gainesville, January 28, 2021.

GM's responses to Chair Porter: E-mail from Edward Bielarski to UAB and City Commission, "GM's response to Chair Porter's comments," Gainesville, January 28, 2021.

Reference to Anger character described in the movie *Inside Out:* "Inside Out" *Wikipedia*, Wikimedia Foundation, accessed December 30, 2021, http://en.wikipedia.org/wiki/Inside_Out_(2015_film)

Mailer from Perry that misquotes GM of GRU: Mailer from Florida Republican Senatorial Campaign Committee, *What Florida Needs Are Common Sense Solutions*, Gainesville, July 2018.

Perry's mailer statement is fact checked: Reported by Andrew Caplan, "Fact check: Keith Perry's GRU mailer," *The Gainesville Sun*, August 8, 2018.

"Let's Talk," GM's opening statement on FB page: Edward Bielarski, "Let's Talk" Facebook Post, August 13, 2018.

Facebook post about GRU not imposing a tax but levying a service: Edward Bielarski, "DID YOU KNOW?" Facebook Post, October 2, 2018.

Facebook post about Perry's mailer: Edward Bielarski, "DID YOU KNOW?" Facebook Post, October 29, 2018.

Facebook post about success of Biomass Buyout financing: Edward Bielarski, "DID YOU KNOW?" Facebook Post, October 11, 2018.

Facebook posts about GRU not representing the Russian Intelligence Agency known as GRU: Edward Bielarski, "DID YOU KNOW?" Facebook Post, October 30, 2018.

Facebook posts about Bielarski's mother: Edward Bielarski, "I finished cleaning out my dad's old house..." Facebook Post, October 29, 2018.

$460 million purchase price for Nacogdoches: Reported by Phillip Jankowski, "Austin buys troubled power plant for $460 million," *The Austin Statesman*, April 18, 2019

Facebook posts about Austin Energy sale: Edward Bielarski, "The Austin Energy buyout…" Facebook Post, April 21, 2019.

Analysis of Referendum vote: Reported by Andrew Caplan, "Voters shut down GRU referendum," *The Gainesville Sun*, November 6, 2018.

Deal of the Year nomination: Gainesville Regional Utilities Press Release, "GRU Biomass Financing Nominated for Deal of the Year," Gainesville, October 2018.

Chapter 16—GRU at a Crossroads

"The general manager shall be responsible for and have exclusive management jurisdiction and control over operating and financial affairs of the Utility System:" City of Gainesville, Florida Code of Ordinances, Section 3.06— General Manager for Utilities, 9.

"GRU envisions a well-run business optimizing all aspects of the organization for the benefit of the customers and the community at large:" Gainesville Regional Utilities, Strategic Plan 2017—2022, Gainesville, May 2017.

Broadband subcommittee formation: Reported by Andrew Caplan, "Committee aims to fix city's internet woes," *The Gainesville Sun*, May 29, 2017.

Public broadband exploration: City of Gainesville, "Gainesville Regional Utilities ITN for Broadband," Gainesville, undated.

Net Zero by 2045 resolution: City of Gainesville, "Commission Resolution Number 180442," Gainesville, undated.

Use of the Kabuki Theater reference: "Kabuki," The Urban Dictionary, accessed January 5, 2022, http:/www.urbandictionary.com/define.php?term=Kabuki.

December 7, 2018, meeting in which Lyons' job was put in jeopardy: Reported by Andrew Caplan, "Commissioners 'fractured' over city leadership," *The Gainesville Sun*, December 7, 2018.

Lyons' resignation: Reported by Andrew Caplan, "Gainesville city manager submits resignation," *The Gainesville Sun*, December 11, 2018.

No ordinary traveler editorial about Lyons: Ron Cunningham, "Ron Cunningham: City manager's resignation raises questions for Gainesville," *The Gainesville Sun*, December 31, 2018.

Crossroads White Paper: Written by Edward Bielarski, White Paper—*GRU at a Crossroads: How we got here and what path to take*, Gainesville, February 7, 2019.

Commissioners must not kick the can down the road: Editorial staff, "Editorial: GRU is at a crossroads," *The Gainesville Sun*, February 17, 2019.

GRU by the Numbers: Written by Edward Bielarski, *GRU by the Numbers*, February 15, 2019.

Chapter 17—GM at his Crossroads

The broadband cost could rise to $213 million: Reported by Joseph Hastings, "CONSULTANT'S REPORT: CHEAPER, FASTER INTERNET POSSIBLE IN GAINESVILLE, BUT NOT WITHOUT SIGNIFICANT CHALLENGES," *WUFT*, June 11, 2019.

Gainesville Sun understands huge costs of broadband: Gainesville Editorial Board, "Editorial: Internet plan comes with huge risks," *The Gainesville Sun*, June 18, 2019.

Comment that Bielarski couldn't be trusted because of lucrative salary: Reported by Andrew Caplan, "Candidates debate at league of Women Voters forums," *The Gainesville Sun*, February 25, 2019.

Details on how the Charter Review Commission was set up to work: "Charter Review Commission," City of Gainesville, accessed September 22, 2021, http://www.cityofgainesville.org/ClerkoftheCommission/AdvisoryBoardsCommittees/CharterReviewCommission.aspx.

Eastman makes the case for municipal internet: Reported by Troy Myers, "Publicly owned internet proposal coming to Gainesville City Commission," *The Florida Alligator*, September 13, 2021.

First meeting of Charter Review Commission: Reported by Cameron Rivera, "Gainesville Charter Review Commission holds first hearing- Virtually," *WUFT*, April 16, 2020.

City Auditor Holt in trouble with commission: Reported by Andrew Caplan, "City votes to cut ties with auditor," *The Gainesville Sun*, May 17, 2019.

Holt's the case of shooting the messenger: Editorial by Ray Washington, "Ray Washington: Audit is case of shooting the messenger," *The Gainesville Sun*, April 26, 2019.

City terminates Holt: Reported by Andrew Caplan, "City cuts ties with auditor," *The Gainesville Sun*, June 6, 2019.

Request to audit city and GRU: Letter from Senator Keith Perry and Representative Chuck Clemons to Chairman of Joint legislative Auditing Committee, Jason Fischer, "Request for Auditor General Audit," Tallahassee, October 24, 2019.

GRU perspective on AG audit: Editorial by Edward Bielarski, "Ed Bielarski: Audit is based on meritless claims," *The Gainesville Sun*, November 21, 2019.

The argument against removing the GM as a charter officer: Presentation from Edward Bielarski to City of Gainesville's Charter Review Commission, "General manager's response to CRC proposed amendment under which the general manager of utilities would be removed as a charter officer of the city," Gainesville, undated.

The charter amendment would terminate the GM: Editorial by Edward Bielarski, "Ed Bielarski: Proposal "would cut GRU general manager," *The Gainesville Sun*, April 23, 2020.

"This is bullshit, this is bullshit:" E-mail from Edward Bielarski to himself, "Note to file," Gainesville, February 3, 2020.

Chapter 18—The Great GFT Grab

Feldman's history of delaying repairs: Reported by Jenny Staletovich, "A Year since the spills: Fort Lauderdale sewage problems a sign of infrastructure woes for other coastal cities," *WLRN*, February 25, 2021.

"I blame Feldman for the diversion of funds," and other context to his tenure in Ft. Lauderdale: Reported by Norren Marcus, "Fort Lauderdale's sewer calamity blamed on budget strategy that diverted funds meant for fixes," *Florida Bulldog*, July 2020.

Details of Mark Benton's presentation of the GFT formula: As requested by Lee Feldman, Gainesville Regional Utilities, "GFT Proposal," Gainesville, December 2019.

Details of GFT meeting: Recorded by Edward Bielarski, *Diary of Edward Bielarski, Volume 11: April 10, 2019, through February 28, 2020*, December 16, 2019, Bielarski Personal library.

Birthday wishes to Melinda Bielarski: Letter from Edward Bielarski to Melinda Bielarski, "When I'm sixty-four," Gainesville, February 23, 2019.

Details of budget workshop in GRU multipurpose room on July 9th: "Budget Workshop: Final Presentation," Gainesville, July 9, 2020.

Explanation of nFront's failure in its work: Memo from Edward Bielarski to Steven Stein, "GRU General Fund Transfer Policy Review," Gainesville, January 29, 2021.

Explanation on nFront's level of comfort in its work: Memo from John F. Painter to Edward Bielarski, "GRU General Fund Transfer Policy Review," Gainesville, January 29, 2021.

The level of general manager's discomfort: Markup by Edward Bielarski, "Markup of nFront's presentation," Gainesville, January 30, 2021.

Back and forth communication between Edward Bielarski and John F. Painter: E-mail chain between Edward Bielarski and John F. Painter, "Re: your e-mail of Jan 25," Gainesville, January 30, 2021.

Reference to Leonard Pinth-Garnell: "Leonard Pinth-Garnell in Saturday Night Live performances", *Wikipedia*, Wikimedia Foundation, accessed December 30, 2021, http://en.wikipedia.org/wiki/Recurring_Saturday_Night_Live_characters_and_sketches_introduced_1976-77.

"It is not in me to withdraw" letter: E-mail chain between Edward Bielarski and John F. Painter, "Re; your e-mail of Jan 29," Gainesville, January 31, 2021.

Option 10 emerges: E-mail from John F. Painter to Edward Bielarski, "GRU General Fund Transfer Policy Review," Gainesville, February 4, 2021.

State of the Utility bombshell: Presentation by Gainesville Regional Utilities to commission, "State of the Utility," Gainesville, February 2021.

Professional affirmation of precarious position: Authored by Jeffrey Panger, "RatingsDirect: Gainesville, Florida; CP; Combined Utility; Joint Criteria," S&P Global Ratings, May 3, 2021.

The "I told you so" e-mail: E-mail from Edward Bielarski to City of Gainesville Commission, "Ratings announcement," Gainesville, May 3, 2021.

Reporting of hostilities: WCJB staff, "GRU debt rating lowered by S&P, General Manager writes critical letter to Gainesville City Commission," *WCJB*, May 4, 2021.

Dialogue culled from May 6, 2021, commission meeting between Ward and Hayes-Santos: Partial Transcript of City of Gainesville Commission meeting, Gainesville, May 6, 2021.

Response to bringing in outside consultants to review GRU management practices: E-mail from Edward Bielarski to city commission and UAB, "Untitled," Gainesville, May 7, 2021.

Dialogue culled from May 12, 2021, commission meeting between Harvey Ward and Adrian Hayes-Santos: Partial Transcript of City of Gainesville Commission meeting, Gainesville, May 12, 2021.

Chapter 19—Get your love at home.

Phone conversation in which mayor asks GM to resign: Recorded by Edward Bielarski, *Diary of Edward Bielarski, Volume 15: August 5, 2021, through January 5, 2022*, September 8, 2021, Bielarski Personal library.

GM's thoughts on possible vaccine mandate: Memo from Edward Bielarski to City of Gainesville Commission, "Letter to CCOM.pdf," Gainesville, July 29, 2021.

Vaccine Mandate Recommendations from Charter officers of the City of Gainesville: "COVID-19 Public Health Discussion (Legistar No. 210242)—8/5/2021 City Commission Regular Meeting: Actions and Recommendations from the Charter Officers," Gainesville, August 5, 2021.

Partial dialogue of August 5, 2021, commission meeting: Transcribed by Claudia Rasnick and sent to Edward Bielarski, "Saco Comments—Transcript from meeting," Gainesville, August 9, 2021.

Details about final vaccine mandate motion on August 5, 2021, commission meeting: "Partial Transcript of City of Gainesville Commission meeting", Gainesville, August 5, 2021.

Dialogue of August 30, 2021, Joint Water and Climate Policy Board Meeting (JWCPB): Transcribed by Robin Baxley "Partial Transcript of Joint Water and Climate Policy Board (JWCPB) meeting", Gainesville, August 30, 2021.

Response to JWCPB: E-mail from Edward Bielarski to members of JWCPB, "GRU GM response to Climate Action Committee questions," Gainesville.

Letter from Edward Bielarski to Lauren Poe informing him that's he wouldn't resign: Letter from Edward Bielarski to Lauren Poe, "Follow-up to yesterday's meeting," Gainesville, September 9, 2021.

GM's job in jeopardy once more: Reported by Jennifer Cabrera, "GRU General Manager's job in jeopardy," *The Alachua Chronicle*, September 9, 2021.

Last ditch effort to inform commission of GM's value: E-mail from Edward Bielarski to City of Gainesville Commission and UAB, "Untitled," Gainesville, September 11, 2021

Heads-up about meeting: TEAMS message from Omichele Gainey to Edward Bielarski, "Untitled," TEAMS, Gainesville, 5:44 PM and 5:57 PM, September 11, 2021.

Reporting on GM's e-mail to mayor: Reported by WCJB staff, "Gainesville mayor asks GRU general manager to resign," *WCJB*, September 9, 2021.

Mayor tells the world that GM is no longer right fit for job: Reported by John Henderson, "Gainesville mayor calls on head of city's utility company to step down," *The Gainesville Sun*, September 11, 2021.

Feldman's query about GM's resigning: TEAMS message from Lee Feldman to Edward Bielarski, "Untitled," TEAMS, Gainesville, 12:15 PM, September 12, 2021.

GM's response about 90% sure he's staying: TEAMS message from Edward Bielarski to Lee Feldman, "Untitled," TEAMS, Gainesville, 12:27 PM, September 12, 2021.

Feldman says it's a mistake: TEAMS message from Lee Feldman to Edward Bielarski, "Untitled," TEAMS, Gainesville, 12:35 PM, September 12, 2021.

Feldman decides to leave: TEAMS message from Lee Feldman to City of Gainesville Commission, "Untitled," Gainesville, September 13, 2021.

City manager is fourth charter to resign: John Henderson, "City manager submits resignation letter; fourth charter to do so in four months," *The Gainesville Sun*, September 13, 2021.

Dialogue culled from September 13, 2021, commission meeting: Partial Transcript of City of Gainesville meeting, Gainesville, September 13, 2021.

List of GM's angels: Handwritten list of supporters recorded on the night of September 13, 2021, Edward Bielarski, *Diary of Edward Bielarski, Volume 15: August 5, 2021, through January 5, 2022*, September 13, 2021, Bielarski Personal library.

Bielarski speech: Recorded by Edward Bielarski, *Diary of Edward Bielarski, Volume 15: August 5, 2021, through January 5, 2022*, September 13, 2021, Bielarski Personal library.

Reference to the September 13th meeting as "It's a Wonderful Life:" "It's a Wonderful Life," *Wikipedia*, Wikimedia Foundation, accessed September 20, 2021, http://en.wikipedia.org/wiki/It%27s_a_Wonderful_Life.

Chapter 20—It's not a Threat.

Firefighters ask for mayor's resignation: "News Release," Gainesville Professional Firefighters, Inc," Gainesville, September 15, 2021.

Firefighters find video evidence that Saco flipped them off: Reported by Jennifer Cabrera, "Firefighters find video evidence that Saco flipped them off," *The Alachua Chronicle*, September 15, 2021.

Dysfunction at city hall: Reported by Editorial Board, "Stop the dysfunction at Gainesville's city government," *Gainesville Sun,* September 16, 2021.

$3.7 billion in cost to go 100% renewable: Eric Walters, "Worksheet," November 23, 2021.

GRU's Climate Action Plan: White paper written by Edward Bielarski delivered to commission In December 2021.

Net zero could add up to $6.5 billion in debt: Reported by John Henderson, "Gainesville's 'net zero' carbon emission goal could swell to $6.5 billion," *Gainesville Sun,* December 14, 2021.

Ward's deal is complete: E-mail from Edward Bielarski to commission and UAB, "Completion of City Commission's assigned goals," Gainesville, January 25, 2022.

GRU's general manager, who almost lost job in September, again on hot seat: Reported by John Henderson, "GRU's general manager, who almost lost job in September, again on hot seat," *Gainesville Sun,* January 24, 2022.

Failures with city's accounting: Reported by Aaron Adelson, "Florida Auditor General finds city employees didn't know how to write financial statements," *CBS4*, Gainesville, November 30, 2021.

AG findings: Reported by Camille Syed, "City of Gainesville has major problems per Fl Auditor General's preliminary report," *WCJB*, November 30, 2021.

Mayor's retort to mishandling finances: Reported by Taniqua Pennix, "Mayor says city didn't mishandle finances," *CBS4*, Gainesville, December 1, 2021.

GRU's 2023 budget: Reported by WCJB staff, "Gainesville City Commission meets to examine and develop GRU's 2023 budget," *WCJB*, December 1, 2021.

Defeasance program: Reported by Ruelle Fludd, "GRU staff present debt defeasance program ahead of FY2023 budget plans," *WCJB,* December 1, 2021.

Concerns over state audit: Reported by Cindy Swirko, "Preliminary state audit raises concerns over Gainesville, GRU finances," *Gainesville Sun,* December 3, 2021.

Audit absolves GRU: Reported by John Henderson, "Auditor General withdraws criticism of GRU's accounting but maintains concerns about debt," *Gainesville Sun,* December 10, 2021.

GRU bid to deliver power on UF campus: GRU Staff, "Statement of Qualifications for the Central Energy Project," Gainesville, December 16, 2021.

Denial of Origis' solar site: Reported by Jennifer Cabrera, "County Commission denies special exception for Archer solar array," *The Alachua Chronicle,* July 8, 2021.

Solar deal stalls: Reported by Seth Johnson, "Solar plan stalls with no location," *The Main Street Daily News,* Gainesville, August 6, 2021.

Letter to Ward telling him I might run for mayor: E-mail from Edward Bielarski to Harvey Ward, "Appreciate our conversation today," Gainesville, January 27, 2022.

Rumors, distractions, and actions: E-mail from Edward Bielarski to GRU employees, "Message from GM," Gainesville, January 27, 2022.

GM thoughts on support service consolidation: Edward Bielarski to commission, "Joint City Manager/General Manager Thoughts on Consolidation of Shared Services," January 27, 2022.

January 27, 2022, termination details: Reported by Jennifer Cabrera, "Bielarski fired at General Policy Committee announces he's running for mayor," *The Alachua Chronicle,* January 27, 2022.

"Oh, it's not a threat:" Reported by Andrew Caplan, "Gainesville Mayor: Ward, Bielarski top field of 9 candidates to succeed Lauren Poe," *Gainesville Sun,* August 24, 2022.

<u>**Chapter 21—Stop the Marlarkey.**</u>

Thoughts on running for mayor—Bielarski: Reported by Melanie Pena, "Two new candidates join the race for Gainesville mayor," *UF Alligator,* February 22, 2022.

Bielarski was taking GRU down the wrong path: Editorial by Wes Wheeler, "Ed Bielarski was taking Gainesville Regional Utilities down the wrong path," *Gainesville Sun,* February 16, 2022.

Solar deal was an all-around win: Editorial by Ed Bielarski, "Ed Bielarski: Solar deal is all-around win for GRU customers," *Gainesville Sun,* June 16, 2020.

Speaking truth to power: Editorial by Ed Bielarski, "I was fired for speaking truth to power," *Gainesville Sun,* February 27, 2022.

Mr. Bielarski manipulated the rate stabilization fund; Pegeen Hanrahan, *Facebook* post, August 7, 2022.

Mailer from Alachua County Democratic Party: Mailer from Alachua County Democratic Party, *Here's What Republican Backed Ed Bielarski Doesn't want you to Know,"* Gainesville, August 2022.

95% of the old contract's value; Pegeen Hanrahan, *Facebook* post, August 19, 2022.

Bielarski says he has nothing to do with GRU's woes; Mark Sexton, Facebook post, August 19, 2022.

Ward and Bielarski are in a run-off: Reported by Andrew Caplan, "Gainesville Mayor: Ward, Bielarski top field of 9 candidates to succeed Lauren Poe," *Gainesville Sun,* August 24, 2022.

August 23rd official election results: 2022 Primary and Gainesville Election-August 23, 2022-Alachua County Florida Official Results

https://www.votealachua.com/Portals/Alachua/Election SummaryReport.PDF.

Acrimonious debate: Reported by Joey Weslo,"Gainesville Mayoral Candidates Harvey Ward and Ed

Bielarski spar in acrimonious debate," *WUFT*, October 26, 2022.

Election results: Reported by Joey Weslo, "Ed Bielarski cannot muster enough power as Harvey Ward elected new mayor of Gainesville," *WUFT*, November 8, 2022.

November 8th, official election results: 2022 Primary and Gainesville Election-November 8, 2022-Alachua County Florida Official Results.

https://www.votealachua.com/Portals/Alachua/Election SummaryReport%20GE

.

Chapter 22– A Utility governed by the people it serves.

Changing of the guard: Reported by Andrew Caplan, "Changing of the Guard: Harvey Ward sworn in as mayor, 3 others join City Commission," *Gainesville Sun,* January 5, 2023.

Ward fails to secure vote on permanent jobs for all charters: Reported by Jennifer Cabrera, "Ward's bid to make interim charter officers permanent fails to gain support from new city commission," *The Alachua Chronicle*, January 9, 2023.

Commission comes back and reverse course on permanent jobs: Reported by Jennifer Cabrera, "City commission makes 4 interim charter officers permanent in abrupt motion," *The Alachua Chronicle*, January 19, 2023.

"You're supposed to be dead already" quote from Saco: Reported by Jennifer Cabrera, "You're supposed to be dead already," *The Alachua Chronicle*, November 22, 2022.

State of the City Address: Reported by Andrew Caplan, "Mayor Harvey Ward delivers 2023 State of the City address," *Gainesville Sun,* February 14, 2023.

No rate cuts for GRU customers: Reported by Jennifer Cabrera, "Mayor Ward says cutting GRU rates is 'not beneficial to anybody in the community," *The Alachua Chronicle*, February 16, 2023.

JLAC demands drastic action: Reported by Jennifer Cabrera, "Bipartisan legislative committee tells Mayor Ward to take drastic action on GRU debt or face removal from office," *The Alachua Chronicle*, February 23, 2023.

City Attorney says the State legislature can remove commissioners from office: Reported by Jennifer Cabrera, "City commissioners express concern about Clemons' proposed bill," *The Alachua Chronicle*, March 9, 2023.

Governor may appoint new board: Reported by Jennifer Cabrera, "Clemons' local bill that would put a governor appointed board over GRU moves forward," *The Alachua Chronicle*, March 17, 2023.

Bielarski tells city to face reality: Written by Ed Bielarski, "Bielarski: City must face reality," *The Alachua Chronicle*, March 18, 2023.

Bill is filed: Reported by Jennifer Cabrera, "Clemons files bill establishing governor appointed GRU," *The Alachua Chronicle*, April 10, 2023.

Commission takes steps to reduce debt: Reported by Nora O'Neill, "Gainesville City Commission approves plan to reduce GRU debt by $315 M," *Gainesville Sun*, April 14, 2023.

City cuts its budget as Bielarski had requested: Reported by Jennifer Cabrera, "Gainesville City Commission cuts transfer from GRU to City, requiring budget cuts of about $19 million," *The Alachua Chronicle*, April 14, 2023.

Clemons' GRU Bill passes in the House 81 - 33: Reported by Jennifer Cabrera, "Clemons' GRU Bill passes in the House 81 - 33," *The Alachua Chronicle*, April 27, 2023.

Clemons' GRU Bill passes in the Senate: Reported by Jennifer Cabrera, "Clemons' GRU Bill passes in the Senate," *The Alachua Chronicle*, May 4, 2023.

Few cuts promised: Reported by Jennifer Cabrera, "Few cuts promised in Gainesville Chater Officer and GPD budgets," *The Alachua Chronicle*, May 17, 2023.

Property tax increases: Reported by Jennifer Cabrera, "'Nothing I've ever voted on in a previous budget was frivolous': City Commission discusses budget proposals, considers closing Ironwood Golf Course," *The Alachua Chronicle*, May 26, 2023.

Popular city program is cut: Reported by Seth Johnson, "GNV eliminates Reichert House after 30 years," *The Main Street Daily News*, May 22, 2023.

Frequently Asked Questions (FAQs) about Clemons' Bill: Mike Murtha, "FAQs about HB 1645," Tallahassee, 2023.

Clemons' Bill is signed: Reported by Jennifer Cabrera, "DeSantis signed HB 1645 today – what happens next," *The Alachua Chronicle*, June 28, 2023.

A Glossary of Terms

Authority – The shorthand name given to the Lehigh County Authority and the winning bidder in the Concession Agreement.

ARIPPA – Acronym for the Anthracite Region's Independent Power Producers Association, a trade association for a group of non-utility power generating plants in Pennsylvania.

Available Energy payments – Under the GREC PPA, the amount GRU paid for the number of kilowatt hours the biomass plant was capable of delivering at any particular moment, as evidenced by testing or their declaration.

BACT – Acronym for the USEPA's concept of determining the Best Available Control Technology for air permits, known as Title V permits.

BAFO bid – Acronym for the procurement/bidding process known as the Best and Final Offer in which the top two bidders from the first bid compete in a final round bid to determine the winner.

Biomass plant – A power plant designed to use organic material as its feedstock. In GREC's case, the feedstock was wood waste.

BTU – Acronym for British Thermal Unit which is amount of heat needed to increase a pound of water one degree Fahrenheit. The higher the BTU, the higher the economic value of the fuel.

Capacity payments – Generally, payments made under a power purchase agreement (PPA) for the amount of energy a power plant could have delivered if requested to do so.

Cape Wind – Off-shore wind project Jim Gordon and his company attempted to develop off the coast of Cape Cod.

Change in Law – A common provision in most commercial contracts which allows for negotiations, modifications, or possible abrogation of the contract when there has been an unexpected and material change in the law making the contract difficult for the vendor to perform under.

Charter – The document granting authority to the City of Gainesville, effectively serving as the city's constitution.

Charter officers – Employers of the city, whose jobs are specifically defined with the City of Gainesville Charter and report directly to the commission.

Concession Agreement – The agreement between the Lehigh County Authority and the City of Allentown, created out of a public bidding process, in which the Authority was granted access to operate the city's water and sewer system, in exchange for an upfront payment and annual fees over the term of the agreement.

Depot Park – The land originally owned by Gainesville Gas which GRU acquired and converted into Gainesville grand central park.

Determination of Need – Florida Public Service Commission (FPSC) process to determine the need for any proposed power generation facility.

Dispatch – The act of requesting a power plant to come online, go offline, or remain in standby operations.

Economic dispatch – Dispatching a power plant on the basis of cost instead of reliability such as the case with minimum generation emergencies.

Electric Generation Customer Choice and Competition Act of 1996 – Deregulation of Pennsylvania's utilities that provided fundamental restructuring of ritual electric services.

Electric grid – The network of power generation facilities, transmission and distribution lines that allow the safe and reliable delivery of electricity to customers.

EMI - Acronym for Energy Management Inc, the company Jim Gordon founded.

EOC – Acronym for Eastside Operations Center which was constructed by GRU to replace the operations and maintenance group housed in the Power District.

Equitable Adjustment – Agreement resulting from GREC's claim that the requirement of an SCNR was a change in law under the GREC PPA.

Feed-in-tariff – The program where customers are allowed to generate electricity which can be fed back into the electric grid for a pre-establishing price, or tariff. In GRU's case, the program was known as the Solar Feed-in-tariff.

FERC – Acronym for the Federal Energy Regulatory Commission which as a United States federal agency, regulates the transmission and wholesale sale of electricity and natural gas.

FDEP – Acronym for Florida Department of Environmental Protection.

Florida Sunshine Law – Florida's Government-in-the-Sunshine law that provides the public the right of access to governmental proceedings and communications.

FPL – Parent company of Florida Power and Light.

FPSC – Acronym for Florida Public Services Commission who holds regulatory authority over investor-owned electric utilities and limited authority over municipally owned utilities.

GAAP – Acronym for General Accepted Accounting Principles which are promulgated by the Financial Accounting Standards Board (FASB).

GFT – Acronym for General Fund Transfer which was the funding GRU provided to the City of Gainesville each year.

GREC – Acronym for the Gainesville Renewable Energy Center.

GREC PPA – The PPA between GRU and GREC, approved on May 7, 2009.

GRU – Acronym for Gainesville Regional Utilities.

GRUCom – The telecommunication's arm of GRU.

Home Rule – Short phrase for Florida's Home Rule Powers Act of 1973 which grants governmental, corporate, and proprietary powers to municipalities.

LCBC – Acronym for the Lehigh County Board of Commissioners.

Lift stations – Sewage infrastructure, often referred to as wet wells, used to pump wastewater from lower to higher elevations.

MetEd – Represents Metropolitan Edison, a wholly owned subsidiary of GPU Energy, and off-taker of the power generated by the Panther Creek Energy Facility.

Millage rate – Dollars assessed per $1,000 of assessed value.

MinGen – Shorthand for minimum generation emergency which represents times in which utilities must reduce power plant generation in order to balance the native load of their territory.

MUG-a-NUG – Clandestine program used by a group of utilities in the northeast to exert pressure on NUGS.

Native load – The power demand imposed on an electric company by its customers.

Navigant Report – The investigative report generated in 2015 that identified significant and material weaknesses in the procurement, negotiation and execution of the GREC PPA.

NEA – Acronym for National Energy Act.

Nitrogen Blanket layup – During long periods when power plants remain idle, nitrogen is used to purge and blanket steam spaces to minimize oxidation.

NUGs – Acronym for non-utility generators, the new brand of power generation facilities created out of the 1976 PURPA statute.

Offline – The status of a power plant when it is not connected to the electric grid and unable to transmit power.

Online – The status of a power plant when it is connected to the electric grid and transmitting power through its connection to the electric grid.

Panther – Shorthand name given to Panther Creek Partners, the owner of Panther Creek Energy Facility and the PPA with MedEd.

Peak shaving – A process by which the peak native load of a power Grid is lowered through reducing the demand for electricity.

Potable water – Water that is safe to use as drinking water.

PPA – Acronym for power purchase agreement, which is a contract between a power generating company and another utility, user, or wholesaler of power.

PURPA – Acronym for Public Utility Regulatory Policy Act of 1976 which was the first federal legislative move away from the traditional regulated utility monopoly model.

QF – Acronym for qualifying facilities, representing a power generation plant qualified under PURPA.

SCR – Acronym for Selective Catalytic Reduction which is a power plant technology that removes NOx from the flue gas from a power plant in equipment

SNCR – Acronym for Selective Non- Catalytic Reduction which is a power plant technology that more cost effectively removes NOx from the flue gas from a power plant during operations.

Solar FIT – Acronym for Solar Feed-in-Tariff, which was program whereby GRU granted long-term PPAs to participants to install roof-top solar panels to feed power into GRU's power Grid.

Standby - The status of a power plant when it is ready to connect to the electric grid and transmit power through its connection to the electric grid.

Title V permits – Derived from Title V of the 1990 Federal Clean Air Act Amendments, Title V permits refer to the air permits required by the USEPA to allow a power plant to legally operate.

USEPA – Acronym for United States Environmental Protection Agency.

Made in United States
Orlando, FL
27 July 2023

35507551R00225